P9-DMB-378

E
SE
S
SW
W
NW
N
NE

An Uncommon History of Common Things

Volume 2

Foreword by Henry Petroski

NATIONAL GEOGRAPHIC

Washington, D.C.

CONTENTS

Foreword

Just a glance at the Contents page of this book tells you that you hold in your hands a volume full of reading pleasure spread across a broad range of topics and dozens of categories of common things. Some of the things described in these pages are so common—like sand, baseball caps, and loaves of bread—that you might not have thought much about them. But here, they are put in a cultural and historical context that can forever change how you will see and think of them in the future. Other things described are ones that you may or may not have long wondered about—backpacks, thumbtacks, tattoos—or never even heard of at all. What are, for example, artificial blood, fake caviar, and vegetarian leather?

Riffling through the pages that follow shows that the engagingly illustrated individual entries are at the same time whimsically chosen and appropriately grouped. Chapter 2, "Weird Science," introduces the secrets of such everyday amalgamations as asphalt, antifreeze, and dental fillings. "Beastly Facts" in that chapter looks at some oddities of nature: that penguins' knees are located inside their torsos, that the tongue of the chameleon is as long as its body, that the skin of the snow-white polar bear is black, and that no two tigers have identical patterns of stripes. And who will forget reading that dolphins sleep with one eye open or that hummingbirds are the only bird that can fly backward? This is thus also a book of trivia that can go a long way in making for interesting conversation, whether in a tent in the tropics or an igloo at the North Pole.

This second collection of uncommon histories of common things is every bit as engaging as the first, and *Common Things Volume 2* goes beyond that earlier book in having sidebars featuring not things but uncommon people who changed common history. Thus you will read about the unique contributions of entrepreneurial pioneers like Apple's Steve Wozniak,

Amazon's Jeff Bezos, and McDonald's Ray Kroc; of environmentalists John Muir, Rachel Carson, and Bill McKibben; of architects Michael Graves and his mass-market designs for Target stores, Buckminster Fuller and his angular geodesic domes, I. M. Pei and his elegant glass pyramid over the entrance to the Louvre, and Antoni Gaudí and his unfinished cathedral in Barcelona.

It is virtually impossible to open this book to any page and not find something new, fresh, informative, enlightening, inspiring, surprising, amazing, whimsical, humorous, or just plain interesting. In chapter 3, "Incredible Edibles," you can read the stranger-than-fiction truth about such familiar snack and fast food items as cola drinks, gummi bears, popsicles, mustard, and chicken nuggets. You name it, and chances are it is written up in this book—and the entry makes for fascinating reading. In the section quizzically titled "You Can Eat That?" we find clustered together entries on seaweed; fried grasshoppers; thousand-year-old eggs; Roquefort cheese; and the traditional Norwegian dish of lutefisk, which is prepared using lye. How's that for a five-course meal? A section in "Tried and True," chapter 9, is headed "Perfect Tools." Who can wait to read the justification for grouping under this rubric the eight diverse objects of book, hammer, paintbrush, scissors, protractor, ruler, shovel, and spatula? And what makes them perfect?

Like a dictionary or encyclopedia, this is a book that may be better read from the inside out, that is, from an entry to which the reader has been drawn by a question about some common thing that arises in some common circumstance, such as reading another book, watching a television show, or talking with family or friends. You may, for example, come across a reference to a person living in a yurt. Sure enough, you can find "yurt" in the index to this book and we read in its entry a description of the structure, something of its origins among nomadic tribes of Central Asia, and of its adaptation in the 1960s and 1970s by the American counterculture. And while reading about yurts, you may be drawn to nearby entries on prefabricated homes that can be transported and built just about anywhere, on sod homes located on the American prairie, and on cave dwellings in Turkey. Reading a book like this is an adventure in exploration and learning.

Some of the common things you can learn about in this book are commonly known places and structures that you may not have had direct experience with and may not expect to do so in the near future. Among the things in this category could be travel into deep space or to the depths of the ocean or even to far-off cities and their unique attractions. Nevertheless, you can read here about Burj Khalifa, which is located in Dubai, United Arab Emirates, and is currently the tallest building in the world, and about Shanghai Tower, the second tallest building in the world and the tallest in China.

There is also plenty in here for those who travel in place, an experience covered well in chapter 5, "That's Entertainment." Here you can reminisce or learn about the forerunners of today's familiar video technology, electronic games, and music-playing devices. You can read about *Myst,* the first interactive computer game, as well as *Pac-Man* and Wii. In the section "Music to Your Ears," you can read about the portable record players that enabled teenagers to take their 45 rpm recordings of rock-and-roll out of the basement and into the backyard. These valise-size machines and later the pocket-size transistor radio were, unlike the later Sony Walkman and Apple iPod, suitable for group rather than personal listening. They were the social media of their time. And this book, like all other books (including e-readers), can serve a similar function by being read aloud to a group around a campfire or fireplace.

However it is read, silently or aloud, straight through from this Foreword to the end, or dipped into here and there to experience the joys of chance discovery, this book will reward readers. There are few other experiences as satisfying as reading a good book, and this is definitely a good book. It may not have the extensively developed characters or elaborately complex plot of a great historical novel, but its evocative entries together convey a human drama as grand as that of any masterpiece of literature. It reveals the inventive passion of human beings to strive to make their lives and the lives of their fellows more safe, comfortable, and enjoyable through the constant improvement of the common things on which we all depend or simply just appreciate in going about our daily lives.

Knowing the uncommon histories of those common things helps us realize that underlying all the achievements are uncommonly talented, focused, and dedicated individuals who work toward a common good: the advancement of human achievement. What all of us can take away from a book like this is a heightened appreciation for how central the pursuit of invention and innovation is to the human spirit. And even the commonest of things that lifts the spirit should not go unheralded as an example of what makes us human. Nothing should be admired simply as something made, but for what it symbolizes about the relationship between human beings and the world of things, natural and man-made, that they inhabit, conserve, and improve.

—Henry Petroski

About This Book

An Uncommon History of Common Things Volume 2 explores the origins of hundreds of things we use and think about every day and the stories of how they came to be so important to our lives. From sriracha hot sauce and the space station *Mir* to disposable diapers and 3-D printers, this book is full of the fascinating history behind things big and small, old and new. Did you know that humans have been using cork for more than 5,000 years, not only for sealing wine bottles but also for making fishing nets float? Or that the first Popsicle was invented inadvertently—and by an 11-year-old boy? How do engineers create buildings that are earthquake proof? Who decided to make a museum of the abandoned sewers under Paris, France? More than 350 brief histories showcase innovations, creative solutions, and accidental inventions that have changed how we live. Some histories will break the myths surrounding common objects, while others will add little-known details to familiar origin stories. Nine chapters are organized by topic: "All Natural," "Weird Science," "Incredible Edibles," "Building Blocks," "That's Entertainment," "Gadgets and Gizmos," "Perfectly Preserved," "Danger Zone," and "Tried and True." Within each chapter, sidebars and fact boxes are filled with uncommonly known facts, stories about people who changed history, and eye-opening information about what's inside common objects and structures. These engrossing and surprising accounts will reshape how you see the world around you.

If one way be better than another, that you may be sure is nature's way.
–ARISTOTLE (384–322 B.C.)

All Natural

We tend to think that the things we humans create have to be the most effective products of all time. But since the beginning of our history, we have relied on nature's bounty for food, medicine, warmth, and light. In fact, we still do. Some of our most powerful and influential tools have come out of nature's own toolbox.

In this chapter, you will discover the history of staples you're likely to have in your kitchen: honey, olive oil, sea salt, and vanilla. You will also find some of nature's great luxuries, such as silk and pearls, worn against our skin and on our necks for thousands of years. They, like a great many other things in nature, have been all around us, though we haven't always known they were there or what to do with them. Hydrogen peroxide, present in mother's milk, wasn't officially discovered until 1818. And the element iron has an entire age named after it.

The natural world is sometimes tough, sometimes dangerous, and sometimes surprisingly fragile. This chapter presents the history of threatened organisms, such as coral, as well as examples of how the natural world can itself be threatening. Phosphorus, the element that sets a match aflame, was known to maim people before its use was perfected. Lead may have slowly poisoned Beethoven to death.

Nature has provided us with uncounted treasures, but humankind is nothing if not enterprising. We have twisted some of these treasures and refined others, inventing things that have the power to harm and to heal. In these pages, we're reminded how incredibly important the natural world has been in shaping our modern lives, from the batteries that charge our phones to the glass in our windows—reality that is equal parts mystery and revelation.

13

CHAPTER INTRODUCTION

The introduction at the beginning of every chapter gives an overview of the theme of that chapter and describes what kinds of objects are included in the entries that follow. An opening quote provides a humorous or historical take on the chapter's topic.

SECTION INTRODUCTION AND ENTRIES

Every chapter is divided into sections, each with its own introduction. For example, one section of the "All Natural" chapter focuses on underwater things. This introduction explains what you'll find in that section and why it's important. Each section has six to eight entries. A photo marks the start of each entry, followed by a quick fact and an exploration of the history of each item.

"UNCOMMONLY KNOWN" AND "WHAT'S INSIDE?"

Fascinating facts are sprinkled throughout each chapter. "Uncommonly Known" (blue boxes) features little-known facts about familiar things. In "What's Inside?" (green boxes) you'll find out what common items are made of and how they work. Discover the intriguing answers to questions you never even thought to ask.

"PEOPLE WHO CHANGED HISTORY"

Each chapter includes short biographies of people who have made landmark contributions in areas related to the chapter theme. You'll meet famous and lesser known explorers, inventors, entrepreneurs, scientists, celebrities, and even one dog!

If one way be better than another, that you may be sure is nature's way.

—ARISTOTLE (384-322 B.C.)

All Natural

We tend to think that the things we humans create have to be the most effective products of all time. But since the beginning of our history, we have relied on nature's bounty for food, medicine, warmth, and light. In fact, we still do. Some of our most powerful and influential tools have come out of nature's own toolbox.

In this chapter, you will discover the history of staples you're likely to have in your kitchen: honey, olive oil, sea salt, and vanilla. You will also find some of nature's great luxuries, such as silk and pearls, worn against our skin and on our necks for thousands of years. They, like a great many other things in nature, have been all around us, though we haven't always known they were there or what to do with them. Hydrogen peroxide, present in mother's milk, wasn't officially discovered until 1818. And the element iron has an entire age named after it.

The natural world is sometimes tough, sometimes dangerous, and sometimes surprisingly fragile. This chapter presents the history of threatened organisms, such as coral, as well as examples of how the natural world can itself be threatening. Phosphorus, the element that sets a match aflame, was known to maim people before its use was perfected. Lead may have slowly poisoned Beethoven to death.

Nature has provided us with uncounted treasures, but humankind is nothing if not enterprising. We have twisted some of these treasures and refined others, inventing things that have the power to harm and to heal. In these pages, we're reminded how incredibly important the natural world has been in shaping our modern lives, from the batteries that charge our phones to the glass in our windows—reality that is equal parts mystery and revelation.

Clean and Green

We often reach for cleaning products that boast a laundry list of ingredients we can't pronounce, forgetting that nature has long offered solutions that are just as effective for doing the laundry. We've always looked for ways to keep our lives fresh and clean. Sometimes, in the case of wood ash and pumice stone, for instance, nature's fiery processes left us with something we could make into soap and polish. Other times, an agent such as hydrogen peroxide fell on us in rainwater, even if it took a while for us to discover it was there and put it to use.

Pumice

THE WORD "PUMICE" COMES FROM THE LATIN *PUMEX*, MEANING "FOAM." THE SUBSTANCE IS SO LIGHT THAT IT CAN FLOAT ON WATER'S SURFACE.

The ancients found pumice stone endlessly useful. Glass-like pumice forms when superheated molten rock spews from a volcano and quickly cools. Even when pulverized, pumice doesn't lose its sharp edges. It was such a popular commodity that it traveled as far as volcano-less Egypt, where archaeologists have uncovered it on ancient worktables. The Egyptians found its abrasiveness useful as a polisher and exfoliant. They mixed pumice with vinegar and used it as toothpaste, despite the fact that it eventually wore away tooth enamel. Greeks and Romans used pumice to remove unwanted body hair. Its popularity continued into the 12th century, when it was featured in the Trotula, a widely read collection of books on women's health.

Pumice is low density, making it a key ingredient in concrete. Mix pumice with lime and you get pozzolana, the smooth plaster that ancient Romans used to construct the dome of the Pantheon. Today, the addition of sandpapery pumice to industrial washing machines gives jeans that coveted stonewashed look. Ground pumice is an ingredient in low-density paint, is incorporated in rubber and plastics for its antiskid properties,

UNCOMMONLY KNOWN ...

BAKING SODA AND VINEGAR Whether together or apart, baking soda and vinegar can clean and disinfect almost anything. Scrub baking powder gently over dry lips to get rid of dry skin, sprinkle it on patio furniture to keep it from becoming moldy, and use it to rejuvenate a barbecue grill. A dash of vinegar added to laundry will stop static cling. Mix baking soda and vinegar together, and they become an environmentally friendly potion strong enough to cut through whatever's clogging your bathtub drain.

and is beauticians' choice to scrub off dead skin during a pedicure. After several millennia that humans have used pumice, its possibilities remain seemingly endless.

Wood Ash

SOME HISTORIANS SUGGEST THAT THE ROMANS LEARNED ABOUT SOAP FROM THE CELTS, WHO CALLED IT *SAIPO* AND USED IT AS HAIR GEL.

As long as humans have been burning fires for warmth and worship, we have been entranced by the way wood smolders to ash. But wood ash is more than the smudgy remains of fires' past: It's a crucial ingredient in a substance that's kept us clean for millennia. One legend has it that soap got its name from the mythical Mount Sapo, where Roman worshippers made animal sacrifices. Women liked to wash their clothes nearby in the Tiber River, where animal fat and wood ash from the sacrifices mixed together to produce a sudsy substance that made clothes look (and smell) new.

Babylonians are credited with inventing soap around 2800 B.C., but their ingredients were no different. Recipes left on Babylonian clay containers detail how wood ash must be mixed with fat and water. Despite the prevalence of wood ash soap, the Greeks and Romans used it mostly for washing clothes and cleaning statues rather than themselves.

Since then, people have discovered that wood ash can do more than clean. Early American potters used it to make beautiful glazes. Today it's used for fertilizing gardens, repelling slugs, melting ice on a driveway, even deskunking a pet. It's the dead remnant of a living tree, but wood ash works wonders when it comes to making things fresh.

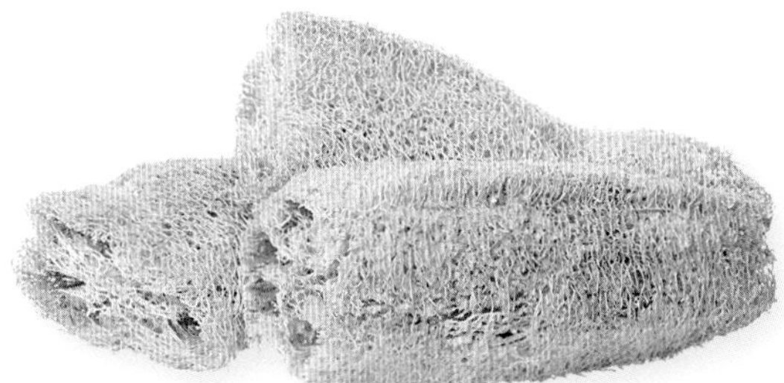

Loofah

THE LOOFAH AND ITS JUICE HAVE BEEN USED IN ASIAN COUNTRIES FOR EVERYTHING FROM RESPIRATORY AILMENTS TO SOFTENING THE SKIN.

There is a common misconception that loofah comes from the sea, but it's actually a gourd that has grown wild for thousands of years. The loofah, also known as luffa and rag gourd, has an easy-to-remove outer shell protecting a dense thicket of vascular bundles that, when cleaned and dried, form an absorbent mesh ideal for a sponge.

Loofah has been cultivated for so long that it's hard to know where it originated, but we know it flourishes in tropical climates. Settlers brought loofah to North America, where it became one of the first domesticated crops in the colonies.

Until the late 19th century, baths were still taken infrequently in the United States, and

loofah was used mostly to scrub teapots. But once doctors reported that "friction baths" drew poisons out of the skin and made it glow, American women started looking for the most effective scrubbing implement. In 1893, journalist Nell Cusack wrote that ladies' enthusiasm for it left their faces "red as lobsters."

The U.S. Navy later employed loofah to filter oil in ship engines during World War II. But the use of the humble loofah as a sponge still prevails today.

Hydrogen Peroxide

FOUND NATURALLY IN MOTHER'S MILK, HYDROGEN PEROXIDE IS A CRUCIAL INGREDIENT IN BOOSTING A NEWBORN BABY'S IMMUNE SYSTEM.

As one of the world's most common cleaning agents, this household staple wasn't actually discovered until 1818. That's when French chemist Louis-Jacques Thénard, inspired partly by Napoleon's directive to make batteries, combined barium peroxide with nitric acid and, later, hydrochloric acid. One of the first things Thénard found out was that solutions containing more than 8 percent hydrogen peroxide were corrosive and left temporary marks on the skin.

In the 1920s, scientists attempted to use it to treat patients suffering from pneumonia and cancer, with no success. It found use during World War II in submarine turbines and as a propellant in torpedoes, too, but its explosive potential required an exceedingly careful hand. Despite its harshness, peroxide was one of the ingredients that Jean Harlow, the original "blonde bombshell," used in the 1920s and 1930s to dye her hair platinum. It has also been added to toothpaste to whiten teeth. A sometimes toxic past notwithstanding, hydrogen peroxide remains a workhorse for cleaning wounds, bleaching laundry, and generally making our lives less grimy.

Borax

SOME CLAY POTS FOUND AT AN 11TH-CENTURY SITE NEAR THE GREAT WALL OF CHINA WERE COVERED IN A GREEN GLAZE MADE WITH BORAX.

Borax is also called *tincal,* a Sanskrit word for the soft, colorless mineral that's been used and traded for centuries. It was first extracted from salty lakes in places like Tibet and Kashmir, then traded

WHAT'S INSIDE?

Zesty Lemon

The seedy, brightly scented pulp of this familiar fruit contains 5 or 6 percent citric acid, making its juice extremely useful in removing grease, getting stains out of clothes, and keeping foods such as avocado and apple from browning because of oxidization. Historically sailors prized lemons' healthy dose of vitamin C to prevent scurvy. The potent fruit is also rich in calcium, iron, phosphorus, magnesium, potassium, copper, zinc, and manganese.

along the Silk Road from the ninth century A.D. Arab gold- and silversmiths used borax to separate and purify metals. Potters in tenth-century China used it to add durability and shine to their pots—just as modern potters still do today.

When borax made it to Europe in the Middle Ages, it was employed in the soldering process to clean metal pieces soon to be melted and joined. Borax was expensive, though—an exotic import. Deposits were discovered in Italy in 1776, but America had to wait another hundred years. That's when F. M. Smith—"the Borax King"—unearthed it in the salt flats of Death Valley, California, and established his Harmony Borax Works. Smith's famous 20-mule teams would haul the mineral from Furnace Creek to the railway near Mojave, a grueling 165-mile trek through one of the world's hottest places. The mules made those trips for only about six years before being supplanted by railroads, but the continued marketing of "20-Mule-Team Borax Soap" turned the journeys into symbols of the Old West.

Around 50 percent of the world's borax now comes from Southern California. The ancients may have used it for crafting metals, but its value as a natural water softener means it's most likely to be found in laundry detergent today.

Deodorant

WITH FEW OTHER OPTIONS AVAILABLE, QUEEN ELIZABETH I BANISHED EVIL SMELLS BY WEARING A POMANDER FILLED WITH AROMATICS.

The first patents for deodorant were filed in the 1860s, but body odor has always been an issue. Since the beginning of human history, we have been looking for ways to banish bad smells and usher in pleasant ones. The classic remedies were washing—often infrequent—and strong perfumes. Ancient Egyptians, Greeks, and Romans all bathed with sweet-smelling oils and scraped hair off the sweat-prone parts of their bodies. In Asia, people found that applying mineral salt crystals to their underarms helped keep bad smells at bay.

As daily washing became more common in the modern era, the rise of chemical deodorants soon followed. Aerosol versions, led by Gillette's Right Guard, became popular in the 1960s but eventually fell from favor because of health and environmental issues. Many people have since turned back to natural deodorant crystals. Both potassium alum and ammonium alum crystals are highly soluble in water. Applied under your arms, they quickly dissolve as you sweat, leaving behind a layer of salt that provides protection from odor-causing bacteria.

Creature Creations

Over the centuries, humans have used science and synthesis to create new luxuries, but nothing beats what you can find in the natural world. Evolution has given animals and insects tools and weapons, warming coats, and silken spools of filament to wrap themselves up in, the likes of which we have worked hard to replicate. For as long as creatures have been producing these wonders for us to notice, we have coveted them for decoration, protection, and ritual. Occasionally we've even worshipped the creatures—or driven them close to extinction.

Honey

HONEY WASN'T ALWAYS JUST A SWEETENER. IN MEDIEVAL EUROPE IT WAS RECOMMENDED FOR DYEING HAIR GOLD AND SOFTENING LIPS.

Honey is one of the world's oldest sweeteners, tied closely to worship, tribute, and celebration. The world's oldest honey has been found in clay vessels in the country of Georgia that date back around 5,000 years. The ancient Greeks referred to mead, or honey wine, as the drink of the gods. They made honey cakes too, as did the ancient Egyptians, and used the cakes as religious tribute. The Egyptians also employed honey in preparing bodies for embalming.

The bee and its syrupy honey have long been symbols of power and longevity. Napoleon's flag and robes featured a line of bees, and the Greek god Cupid was said to dip his arrows in honey before shooting them at unsuspecting lovers. This "liquid gold" was prized so highly it was sometimes used as payment: In the 11th century, German peasants paid their feudal lords in honey and beeswax. Honey can last as long as its history. Archaeologists who discovered honey in an Egyptian tomb reported it was still edible, suggesting that maybe the ancients weren't wrong to see it as divine.

WHAT'S INSIDE?

A Beaver Dam

Crawl inside a beaver dam, and you'll quickly understand why we call them "busy beavers." The dams can be simple huts or more imposing structures, built from tree limbs and other materials found nearby. No matter how rough or extravagant the outside is, the inside is always lined with soft bark, wood chips, and grass. It has a vent hole at the top and access tunnels to the water from a single dry room. The room is multipurpose, used for nesting, birthing, and raising young. It's so well patched with dried mud and grass that all is dark and safe inside.

Silk

SILK WAS COVETED IN THE ROMAN EMPIRE, BUT SUMPTUARY LAWS PROHIBITED MEN FROM WEARING IT, SO IT WAS CONSIDERED A FEMININE LUXURY.

Silk has a long and literally colorful history. The fabric, dyed in rich hues and as soft as water, has been a symbol of luxury and royalty for thousands of years. Silk is produced by silkworms, which feed on mulberry leaves. It takes only two or three days for a well-fed silkworm to spin about a mile of the filament that it uses to make its cocoon. The cocoons are what we unspool and turn into thread.

The story of silk begins in China, where samples have been dated to as far back as 3650 B.C. Even then, silk was considered a luxury item, reserved for the emperors and their families, and they kept its method of production a well-guarded secret for hundreds of years. That secrecy helped make it one of the world's hottest—and most expensive—trading commodities, one that drove and shaped entire economies. By 200 B.C., it was so coveted that it inspired the name of one of the ancient world's most famous trade routes: the Silk Road.

Silk didn't find its way to Europe until A.D. 550, when it's said that Byzantine emperor Justinian had monks smuggle silkworm eggs out of China in hollow cane stalks. Even as silk spread around the world, it remained off-limits for most. In Elizabethan England, where sumptuary laws meant that people wore their status on their sleeves, it was illegal for anyone but royalty to wear purple silk. To this day, silk is valued as a luxury.

Pearls

MEDIEVAL KNIGHTS WERE KNOWN TO WEAR PEARLS INTO BATTLE, AND RENAISSANCE WOMEN SEWED THEM INTO THE HEMS OF THEIR GOWNS.

The pearl is one of the world's oldest and most fascinating treasures. Natural pearls are grown inside an oyster's body when a small foreign object makes its way into the mollusk shell and the oyster, to protect itself, wraps it in layers of gleaming nacre. This "queen of gems" was probably first discovered by people foraging the seashore for food, and it didn't take long for it to become an object of value. The desire for pearls in ancient Rome reached its peak when, as historian Suetonius reports, Roman general Vitellius paid for an entire military campaign through the sale of just one of his mother's pearl earrings. And then there was Cleopatra, who won a wager with Marc Antony by putting a crushed pearl in her wine and downing it to prove her extravagance.

Ancient pearl divers would free-dive 100 feet or more and have to bring up a ton of oysters to find three or four good pearls. Today pearl

oyster cultivation, begun in the 19th century, is a thriving industry that has made pearls more affordable—though no less loved.

Ivory

GEORGE WASHINGTON'S FALSE TEETH WERE MADE PARTLY OF IVORY, NOT SO STRANGE CONSIDERING THAT IVORY ORIGINATES FROM TEETH.

Though we tend to think of ivory as coming from elephant tusks, the chemical makeup of all mammalian teeth is basically the same. But the teeth need to be large in order to carve or engrave them, which is what has drawn people to elephant tusks for centuries. Strong yet soft enough to be easily worked, ivory has been transformed into religious objects, knife and mug handles, billiard balls, jewelry, and piano keys. Ancient Greeks and Romans coveted ivory to make delicate boxes and artwork; they even used it for the whites of their statues' eyes.

But it has a dark side as well. Elephants, once abundant in Africa, have been decimated by foreigners plundering Africa's "white gold" for generations. Ivory was the primary motivator for King Leopold II of Belgium to take over the Congo in the 19th century. The Ivory Coast got its name because of its profusion of elephants; today there are almost none there. Harvesting ivory is a bloody business, one that nations and conservation groups are fighting to end. An international ban on African ivory has been in place since 1989, but poachers continue the slaughter, and the lucrative trade in ivory still thrives. In China, where much of it reportedly ends up, ivory sells for a thousand dollars a pound.

Wool

IN RENAISSANCE ITALY, THE MEDICI FAMILY MADE THEIR FORTUNE FROM WOOL. CATHERINE AND MARIE MEDICI BOTH BECAME QUEEN OF FRANCE.

It makes sense that wool—the stuff that keeps sheep, goats, and llamas warm and dry—should be one of history's most tried-and-true materials for durable human clothing. More than fur, wool's crimping and scaling make it easy to spin, give it bulk, and help it hold insulating air.

Wool has to be sheared, scoured to remove sweat and dirt, and then dyed. Before shears were invented in the Iron Age, wool was gathered by hand or with a bronze comb. For centuries it has been used as insulation and for horse rugs and saddlecloths, and it has been compressed to make felt. Felt lined the helmets of ancient Greek soldiers, and Roman legionnaires had breastplates made from wool felt. In fact wool was a staple of Roman wardrobes; cotton was considered an oddity.

By the Renaissance, wool was popular enough that it propelled economies and made family fortunes. Its influence can be seen in England's House of Lords, where, since the 14th century, the presiding officer has sat on the "woolsack," a chair stuffed with wool. Today, competing with cheaper synthetics, the storied fiber may not be in quite the same demand, but it remains a staple of the textile industry.

PEOPLE WHO CHANGED HISTORY

Rachel Carson (1907-1964)

Few other people have done more to change the way we view and treat our environment than this outspoken biologist, writer, and advocate. Born in the Industrial Age, Rachel Carson spent a landlocked childhood in Pennsylvania longing for the sea. She studied marine biology in college and went on to write best-selling books about the ocean. More than simply presenting science, they captured the public's imagination by Carson's lyrical, personal way of explaining the sea.

It was this talent that made her 1962 book, *Silent Spring,* about the potential dangers of chemicals such as DDT, a controversial hit. It sparked heated conversations around kitchen and political tables about a new idea: that maybe synthetic chemicals could come back to haunt us. Many observers credit Carson with inspiring the environmental movement that led to the banning of DDT and creation of the U.S. Environmental Protection Agency.

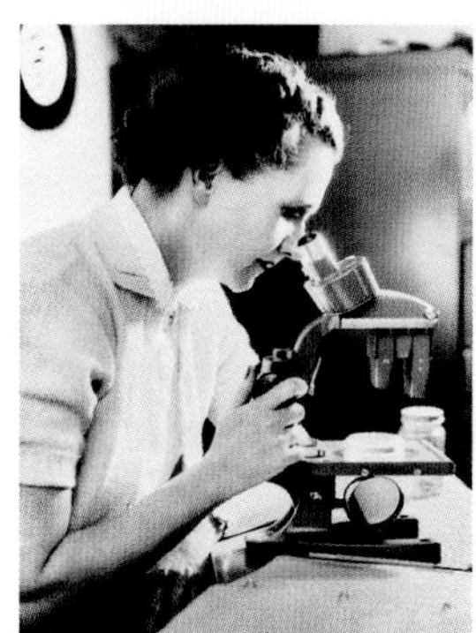

Carson at her microscope

Horn

IN ITALY DURING THE 15TH AND 16TH CENTURIES, SO-CALLED HORNERS CREATED PORTRAIT IMPRESSIONS IN THIS MALLEABLE MEDIUM.

Many animals carve out lives for themselves with their horns, using them to attack, defend, and impress. For a material designed to gouge and gore, horn is surprisingly pliable when harvested to form objects people have been making throughout history. Horn's principal component is keratin—what human nails are made of—that grows around living bone and can be worked and molded. Hollowed-out horns have been used as drinking vessels and as handy means of carrying gunpowder while keeping it dry. Horns are the bugles of old—in Jewish tradition, a musical instrument called a shofar. Horn has long been a favorite material for combs and buttons. Some historians believe that practices developed to press horn inspired some of the techniques we first used to mold plastic. Fifth-century Persians believed rhino horn could be used to detect poison in liquids, a belief that eventually made its way to the royal courts of Europe. Recent studies suggest that the idea might not be entirely far-fetched: Most poisons are heavily alkaline, which may react when in contact with keratin.

Tree-mendous

Since the beginning of time, trees and forests have sustained us: fueling our fires, providing shelter, and making the oxygen we breathe. No wonder ancient cultures often held them to be sacred. People may not have known the scientific properties that allowed trees to give us so much bounty, but that didn't stop them from finding ways to let trees shape what they ate and wore, how they bathed, and how they treated illness. Whether wood, resin, fruit, or oil, each of these forest treasures has had a profound effect on our lives, and our history, in far-reaching ways.

Shellac

SHELLAC ONCE PROTECTED SHEETS OF BRAILLE, AND IT CONTINUES TO SERVE AS AN EDIBLE COATING THAT INCREASES THE SHELF LIFE OF APPLES.

Transparent, glossy, sticky, sometimes brittle, varnish has a long history protecting wooden boats and carved artworks, clay pots, and myriad other objects we hold dear. Most varnishes originate from conifer tree resin, but shellac proves an interesting exception. How many people know that this smooth glaze comes from a bug? It's the lac bug, to be precise, which lives on trees in the forests of Thailand and India and tends to congregate in huge numbers. Female lac bugs secrete resin onto the tree bark. It's scraped off, dried into a flat sheet, then broken up into flakes or "buttons," which can be reconstituted in ethyl alcohol.

Shellac has been in use for at least 3,000 years. In ancient India and China, people turned to shellac for dyeing silk and leather. Its staining quality made it an ideal cosmetic. Leftover residue was often applied to grinding wheels to bond with abrasives. Shellac was so sticky that it worked well for setting jewels and sword hilts. It made a fine finish for buildings too: According to one Indian epic, an entire palace was constructed from lac resin.

All around the world, shellac made a name for itself sealing, staining, and providing a high-gloss varnish. In Spain and Italy of old, painters used shellac as a pigment and to protect finished works from wear and tear. In the 19th century, shellac replaced oil and wax to become one of the most widely used wood finishes. You can still find musical instruments and vintage furniture pieces that were dressed with shellac.

Some uses of shellac might surprise you. Before vinyl came along in the late 1940s, phonograph records were made of shellac. And until the 1960s, archaeologists used shellac to stabilize dinosaur bones. Among many applications today, shellac is found in fireworks, creating green and blue displays.

Cork

WINE AMPHORAE HAVE BEEN FOUND IN THE RUINED CITY OF POMPEII; THEIR CORK STOPPERS GUARDED AND PRESERVED THE CONTENTS FOR CENTURIES.

Elastic, impermeable, buoyant, even fire retardant: no wonder cork has long been the favorite stopper to protect and preserve wine. Contrary to the myth that cork comes from the sea, it in fact is the sub-bark of oak trees that flourish in the Mediterranean. The cork oak evolved to protect itself against droughts, fires, and fluctuations in temperature by making water-resistant cells that keep its insides warm and dry. Its resulting qualities are rare in nature: Though exceedingly light, it can keep out both gas and liquid.

Humans have been using cork since around 3000 B.C., when Chinese fishermen relied on its buoyancy to float their nets. It has been found in bottles of ancient Egyptian wine stowed away for the afterlife; some archaeologists have said it's still drinkable, probably because of its cork stopper. The Greeks regarded cork oak trees so highly that only priests were allowed to chop into them. Pliny the Elder memorialized the tree in his *Naturalis Historia,* explaining how it was consecrated to Jupiter, king of the gods, and its branches were used to crown victorious athletes.

Harvesting cork is considered sustainable because the tree doesn't need to be chopped down. Every nine years, it's partially stripped of its bark, which grows back in good health. In recent years the use of cork in wine bottles has been threatened by twist-tops and plastic stoppers. Some observers say this hurts woodland ecosystems that rely on the cork oak. Environmental concerns aside, many wine enthusiasts maintain that nothing compares to a good old-fashioned cork.

PEOPLE WHO CHANGED HISTORY

Chief Seattle (1780-1866)

Chief Seattle and his deeds inspired Washington State's capital city, then a nameless settlement. Chief of the native Duwamish and Suquamish tribes around Puget Sound, he became known as both a warrior and a diplomat. He built his oratorical skills as he forged cooperation among his own tribes. He wanted to work and live in peace with everyone, including the European settlers arriving in the Pacific Northwest. Chief Seattle did so much to pave the way toward cooperation between the tribes and the newcomers that the early white settlers, led by David Swinson "Doc" Maynard, named their village Seattle. Though he was a peacemaker, the chief had grave concerns about the impact of the influx of settlers on the local populace and on the environment. In 1855 he gave an inspiring speech to the governor of the Washington Territory (now Seattle), which was later transcribed and printed. It turned Chief Seattle into a folk icon. He became a prominent figure in conversations about the treatment of native people, and he promoted the idea that humans should see themselves as part of nature, not tamers of it.

Bust of Chief Seattle, sculpted in 1909

Mastic

ANCIENT ROMAN DOCTORS ADVISED THAT THOSE LOOKING TO FRESHEN THEIR BREATH OR CALM AN UPSET STOMACH SHOULD CHEW ON SWEET MASTIC.

Mastic may be a relatively new flavor in trendy restaurants, but it has long been a secret to success in Greek and Turkish cuisine. Not quite a spice or an herb, mastic is the resin from trees of the same name that grow throughout the Mediterranean, most notably on the Greek island of Chios. On the tree, mastic dries into beads called tears (the "tears of Chios") that are brittle and crystalline—until they're chewed, which makes it unsurprising that mastic became the world's first chewing gum. The word itself derives from the Greek word meaning "to gnash the teeth" and is the root of our verb "masticate."

Over the centuries the substance has had many uses, from fragrant incense to an embalming agent. Around 1566, when Chios fell under Turkish Ottoman control, mastic was so important that villages where it was produced received special privileges. Women in the sultan's harem reportedly cherished it for their beauty regimens.

Recently mastic has found use in pharmaceuticals, paint and varnish, and even dentistry as temporary fillings. But its role in Mediterranean desserts is sweetest. Mastic is found in pastries, puddings, ice cream, and cakes. It's what helps set the consistency of the traditional candy Turkish delight. And after dessert, try a glass of the Greek liqueur masticha.

UNCOMMONLY KNOWN ...

AUTUMN LEAVES The colors of fall are determined by a balancing act of temperature, moisture, and, above all, longer nights. With fewer daylight hours, leaves' veins start to close. Chlorophyll production, which makes leaves green, eventually stops, and the chlorophyll is destroyed. What's left behind are red and yellow carotenoids and anthocyanin, as well as trapped sugars that intensify the colors.

Pine Tar

PINE TAR IS TRADITIONALLY USED TO SEAL WOOD, BUT VETERINARIANS APPLIED IT IN THE PAST TO HORSES' HOOVES TO PREVENT CRACKING AND INFECTION.

If you burn pine wood in a sealed pit and hit it with high-intensity heat and pressure, you will reduce it to a tacky resin called pine tar. The resin keeps the tree safe and dry. Scandinavians have been using pine

WHAT'S INSIDE?

Bird Nests

Nest-building birds have a lot to consider: insulation, camouflage, and comfort. If you're a bowerbird, you even have to think about what color schemes might impress potential mates. Most nests start with a foundation of twigs and dead branches, dry grass and straw, held in place by mud to fill in any cracks. Moss and leaves, along with hair shed by house pets and other animals, serve as insulation. Sticky spiderwebs and caterpillar silk are effective for keeping everything together. For male bowerbirds, ribbons, mirrors, and old CDs are also deemed impressive nest-ware to woo a lady.

tar for the same purpose on wooden ships for more than six hundred years. They paint coats of tar on decks and rigging and use it to position masts and sails. And the Scandinavians are not alone. When vessels were made entirely of wood and the ocean was the international superhighway, pine tar was a global maritime staple. By the 1500s and 1600s, England's demand for the sticky substance increased due to wars and increasing trade. In the early 1700s, they encouraged the American colonies to produce it. In Virginia, tobacco was simply too profitable, but in North Carolina, where there were millions of acres of pine trees, pine tar became a crucial export by the 1770s.

These days, pine tar is used in soaps to help treat skin conditions. It has also become a point of controversy in the world of baseball. Batters are allowed to use it to get a better grip, but pitchers are not. In 2014, Yankees pitcher Michael Pineda was ejected from a game for sporting a stripe of the pine tar within easy reach on his neck. Many in baseball believe such use is cheating, while others maintain that it just keeps the ball from flying wildly out of a pitcher's sweaty hands. Either way, it's a sticky situation.

Cedar Oil

NATIVE AMERICANS USED CEDAR OIL TO HEAL WOUNDS, SOOTHE SORE MUSCLES, CURE HEADACHES AND CONSTIPATION, AND EVEN REMOVE WARTS.

If you've ever stuck your nose inside a cedar chest, you'll remember the warm, woody, comforting smell that greeted you. But the oil present in cedar does more than smell good: It disinfects, preserves, soothes, and keeps bugs at bay.

Ancient civilizations understood its power to cleanse and heal. The Sumerians considered the cedar tree to be the Tree of Life. They used its oil for medicinal purposes and ground it up with additives such as cobalt and copper to make brightly colored paints. Egyptians sometimes used cedar oil as part of their embalming process, and ancient Greeks found it worked well in warding off infection. In the Middle Ages, some people believed that burning cedar and applying its oil could rid a house of plague (though rats may not have agreed). The 17th-century English herbalist Nicholas Culpeper noted that cedar wood and oil eased everything from heart problems and shortness of breath to labor pains. Today, commercial "cedar oil" often derives from distilling the wood, leaves, and other parts of a variety of conifers besides cedar, such as juniper and cypress, but the result is similar. Cedar oil continues to shine as an insect repellent and a favorite scent in aromatherapy.

Almonds

THE ALMOND BLOSSOM INSPIRED THE SHAPE OF THE CUPS ON A MENORAH, THE ANCIENT HEBREW CANDELABRA THAT IS LIT DURING HANUKKAH.

Almonds have become an increasingly trendy health food, but people have been enjoying them for thousands of years. Although we tend to call the almond a nut, it's actually a seed. The almonds we consume are called sweet almonds, which are rich in flavor and monounsaturated fats. Bitter almonds, which are poisonous in large enough doses, are often used in essential oil. Early nomads of the Middle East discovered that wild sweet almonds made a hardy traveling snack. By the Bronze Age, domesticated almonds had spread throughout the ancient world. Religious texts mention them as a sustaining force and a giver of life. The Egyptian boy-king Tutankhamen took a handful of almonds with him to the afterlife, and Persians ground almonds with water to make refreshing almond milk. New World missionaries eventually brought almond trees to California, where most almonds come from today.

Almonds have long been a staple not just as a snack, but in such sweet treats as marzipan, macarons, and liqueur, providing a fragrant and unmistakable flavor.

UNCOMMONLY KNOWN ...

CHICLE A latex substance that can be tapped from sapodilla trees, chicle is native to Latin America. In 1869 exiled Mexican president Antonio López de Santa Anna persuaded U.S. inventor Thomas Adams to try making chicle into a rubber alternative. That didn't work, but Adams happened to notice a girl buying paraffin wax gum and realized chicle's potential. He called his candy "Chiclets," kicking off an American confectionery icon.

Olives

GREEK ATHLETES SLATHERED THEMSELVES WITH OLIVE OIL BEFORE THEIR COMPETITIONS AND WERE CROWNED VICTORIOUS WITH OLIVE BRANCHES.

Few other substances have a more sacred history than the olive and the oil it yields. For more than 6,000 years, olive oil has been used to cleanse, purify, anoint, and create divine connections. The tree itself, gnarled and squat, is hardy enough to inspire reverence:

PEOPLE WHO CHANGED HISTORY

Julia "Butterfly" Hill (1974-)

In 1997, Julia Hill chose "Butterfly" as her "forest name" and joined activists opposing a logging company that threatened to cut down California's giant redwoods. She wasn't the only person who did "tree sitting," but she was at it the longest: She lived in a thousand-year-old redwood for a record-breaking two years and eight days. The loggers baited her with helicopters, horns, and even a climber sent to force her out, but eventually they agreed to leave the tree alone. Hill's feat made her an environmentalist icon and focused public attention on the threat to ancient forests.

Julia Hill, Humboldt, California, 1998

It can thrive in both severe heat and frost, and its wood will burn even when it's wet. In Greek mythology the goddess Athena became the patron of Athens because she gave Greeks the gift of the olive tree. The fruit-bearing tree became a symbol of endurance, victory, and peace, which is why when someone tries to end a dispute, it's referred to as "extending an olive branch."

Olives are inedible straight off the tree; they must first be cured or sun dried, or processed and pressed into oil. Olive oil has been memorialized in religious texts, on the sides of Greek clay pots and Egyptian tombs, and in a host of ancient tales. In *The Odyssey,* Homer (who called olive oil "liquid gold") relates that Odysseus is transformed from a salty sailor into a near god by bathing in it. Indeed history tells us that ancient Greeks used scented oil to soften and condition the skin, a common practice today around the world.

Cellulose

THE ACCIDENTAL COMBINATION OF CELLULOSE AND NITRIC ACID RESULTED IN GUNCOTTON—FLASH PAPER—USED IN 19TH-CENTURY GUNPOWDER.

Cellulose plays a crucial role in the clothes we wear and in many household objects. Cellulose is an organic polymer—a long chain of small molecules linked together—that helps strengthen plant cell walls. Cellulose can be isolated, twisted, and stretched into a great fiber: Cotton, hemp, flax, and jute are made almost entirely of cellulose. Archaeologists found evidence of ancient spinning devices in Greece and Turkey, suggesting that people were weaving textiles as early as 5000 B.C.

The Chinese invented the papermaking process around A.D. 100, combining mulberry leaves, tree bark, and hemp waste. The mixture of cellulose and other material was pulped, washed, bleached, and then dried before being pressed into a sheet thin enough to write on. In the 19th century, cellulose developed as a stand-in for silk, and produced rayon and celluloid, the base material of photographic film until the 1930s. Today, cellulose is still spun into all sorts of everyday products: sponges, wallpaper paste, and cellophane, to name a few. We don't give cellulose a lot of thought, but our lives wouldn't be the same without it.

It's Elementary

The elements featured in this section all contain some contradiction: unstable and stabilizing, light and strong, healing and harmful. No matter their complexity or their origin, in one way or another they have all left their mark on our shared history. Some of the materials have had a profound enough impact that we've named whole time periods after them. Others have provided us our most prized—and sometimes our most deadly—innovations. These elements are all around us, in our buildings, our laptops, and the matches in the kitchen drawer.

Phosphorus

IN *THE HOUND OF THE BASKERVILLES*, HOLMES AND WATSON CONCLUDE THAT PHOSPHORUS WAS WHAT GAVE THE HOUND ITS EERIE GLOW.

Imagine a chemist stoking his fire with coal and watching in astonishment as fumes from what he was heating begin to emit a subtle glow, and drops of a shiny liquid precipitate and suddenly burst into flame. That chemist—or rather alchemist—was Hennig Brand, and that substance came to be known as phosphorus. In 1669, Brand was looking for the "philosopher's stone," the mythical material said to turn base metals into gold, when he stumbled across fiery phosphorus. In one of history's more unsavory elemental discovery stories, he came on this glowing miracle by boiling buckets of urine. Brand was so sure that the "cold fire" would lead him to the stone that he kept his process a secret for several years before money troubles forced him to put it up for sale.

Phosphorus's luminescent properties may be how it got its name. In Greek, it translates to "bringer of light." But its toxicity and combustibility have led to another name: the *devil's element*. Phosphorus can be found in two forms. White phosphorus glows in the dark and ignites when it touches the air; red phosphorus is less combustible and therefore far safer for use in household products. It has played a part in the production of detergents, fertilizer, and light-emitting diodes (LEDs), as well as its most famous application, matches.

White phosphorus has a darker history. It was first used to make matches, but its volatility had the power to kill and indeed led to accidental deaths. It also has been harnessed as a terrible weapon of war. In World War I it was used to make fiery bullets to shoot at zeppelins, and in World War II it fueled incendiary grenades. Phosphorus indeed has become a "bringer of light," both to destroy and to illuminate.

Scandium

SCANDIUM IODIDE IS USED IN MERCURY VAPOR LAMPS TO MAKE DAYLIGHT-BRIGHT LIGHTS USED IN HOLLYWOOD STUDIOS AND SPORTS STADIUMS.

Scandium, a silvery metal almost as light as aluminum but with a higher melting point, was discovered by Swedish chemist Lars F. Nilson in 1879. Ten years earlier, Dmitri Mendeleev, the Russian who was the father of the periodic table, predicted there should be an element between calcium and titanium, which he called ekaboron. Nilson proved Mendeleev right but chose to call it *scandium,* for the region of its discovery.

Nilson came upon scandium by accident while studying so-called rare-earth metals. Most such metals aren't actually rare, but scandium proved an exception: It's more plentiful on the moon than on Earth. Pure scandium is created in the cosmic furnaces of supernovas, but on our home planet, it occurs only in small quantities bound together with other elements. The first pound of pure scandium wasn't produced until 1960. One of the few scandium mines in the world is located in Russia, where the low-density metal was combined with aluminum to create an alloy for military aircraft.

Scandium is much more expensive to produce than aluminum, so it is not widely used. Nevertheless, it turns up in lightweight bike frames and lacrosse sticks. And scandium-alloy baseball bats create a springy "trampoline effect" that helps the bats propel balls more efficiently. The metal is also used in components of aerospace products.

PEOPLE WHO CHANGED HISTORY

Daniel Boone (1734–1820)

An outdoorsman, adventurer, and folk hero, Daniel Boone's exploits made him an American icon, a symbol of the American pioneering spirit. Born in Pennsylvania in 1734, Boone showed an early keenness to explore the wilderness. After moving with his family to North Carolina, young Boone hunted and trapped his way west to the frontier. He was so entranced by uncharted Kentucky that he blazed a trail to it through the Appalachian Mountains. The path came to be called the Wilderness Road and opened the way for tens of thousands who followed. Boone founded Boonesborough, Kentucky, and lived there from 1775 to 1778. He and other settlers had frequent clashes with native peoples. In one instance local tribes captured him, but in legendary Boone fashion, he escaped. Author John Filson cemented Boone's legacy in a 1784 book relating his adventures, called *The Discovery, Settlement, and Present State of Kentucky.*

Daniel Boone leads settlers through the Cumberland Gap, painted 1851–1852

Tin

WE USED TINFOIL FOR SO LONG AS OUR PRIMARY MEANS OF WRAPPING LEFTOVERS THAT SOME PEOPLE CALL ALUMINUM FOIL BY THAT NAME.

Although tin wasn't given pride of place like bronze when it came to the naming of eras, it nevertheless helped give birth to the Bronze Age, when bronze tools began showing up in the historical record around 3000 B.C. Early toolmakers discovered, perhaps accidentally, that adding tin to copper lowered melting points and made the result stronger: bronze. From Egypt to Peru's Machu Picchu, it was tin that enabled ancient people to cast shapes in closed molds, producing not only complex tools and weapons but also timeless works of art that archaeologists have discovered. The ancient Greeks traveled by sea to source tin, collecting it from mines around Spain and the British Isles and then trading it throughout the ancient world.

Tin has been alloyed with many other metals, including steel, antimony, and silver. It has even loaned its name to some of the things it helped create. Food-preserving tin-coated steel cans—"tins"—were patented in England in 1810. In Australia beer cans are still referred to as tinnies. The tin whistle is so-called because it was originally mass-produced using tin-plated steel. Tin is functional, but it can also be decorative. Artfully punched tin was once a popular way to allow air to circulate into food boxes, and it can still be found decorating many people's tables today.

UNCOMMONLY KNOWN ...

NORTHERN LIGHTS The swirling beauty of the northern lights (aurora borealis) has inspired both awe and dread. The Inuit believed they were made by giants playing football, and a Civil War-era aurora was heralded as a bad omen. Auroras are created when the sun emits gas that collides with the Earth's magnetic field, generating charged particles that light up the sky. They're usually green but can also be red, blue, or silver.

Sulfur

SCIENTISTS DISCOVERED SULFUR ON MARS IN THE 1970S, A SIGN THAT LIFE MAY HAVE ONCE SURVIVED THERE.

The Bible refers to sulfur as brimstone, long associated with fire and destruction. That association makes the yellow element memorable, but so does its smell. A rotten-egg odor is one of the first things you're likely to notice in a bubbling sulfurous hot spring. In fact sulfur is responsible, at least in part, for many distinctive smells, including those of natural gas, skunk, grapefruit, and garlic. Sulfur was a key ingredient in the world's first gunpowder, developed in China more than a thousand years ago.

Despite the fact that it's smelly and potentially destructive, sulfur has long been used for cleansing and healing. Along with carbon, sulfur was the only nonmetallic element known to the ancients. It was used as a medicine and fumigant in ancient Egypt and Greece. In Homer's *The Odyssey,* Odysseus asked for it by name: "Bring me sulfur, old nurse, that cleanses all pollution."

In the 19th century it was burned with alcohol to rid homes of infectious diseases. Sulfur was later mixed with creams to treat skin conditions such as acne and eczema, and it continues to be what keeps wine from turning to vinegar. By the mid-19th century sulfuric acid had become a lucrative commercial product, helping vulcanize rubber, bleach paper, and keep bugs off food crops.

WHAT'S INSIDE?

Fossils

Fossils are time's blueprint. They provide us with evidence of ancient life preserved in rock. But how are these blueprints made, and what are they made of? Fossils are created through a number of complex processes, but the steps in those processes are more or less the same. When an animal's remains are buried quickly and for a long time—protected by sediment, sap, or the seafloor—soft tissues ultimately decompose, and the skeleton is left behind. Water inevitably creeps in, its minerals creating crystals that cause the skeleton to harden. Even if the bones are eventually dissolved by water, minerals crystallize in the space they occupied. The result: casts that reveal stories about the history of life on Earth.

Lead

GLADIATORS STRENGTHENED THEMSELVES WITH LEAD WEIGHTS, BUT LEAD MAY HAVE WEAKENED LUSTY JULIUS CAESAR'S ABILITY TO SIRE CHILDREN.

Lead was one of the first metals to find its way into our daily lives—for better and for worse. Ancient Egyptians used it to glaze pottery, and the Babylonians used it for constructing buildings. But perhaps no one else appreciated lead more than the Romans. They used it for everything from pipes and dishes to coins, bullets, paints, and cosmetics. They even preferred lead pots for winemaking because it gave the finished product a sweet overtone. When a host of mysterious ailments began plaguing the Roman populace, some suspected lead might be to blame, but few changed their lead-loving ways. By the Middle Ages, people were adding lead acetate, or "sugar of lead," to their food to make it sweeter.

In the 15th century lead helped father one of history's great game-changing inventions: the printing press. The movable type that turned ideas into printed expression was made of lead. The heavy metal continued to have darker consequences: We now know it probably caused the ailments that plagued Ludwig van Beethoven.

By 1600, Americans were using lead in industry. Benjamin Franklin expressed concern about the widespread use of lead in the 1700s. The metal was finally regulated in the 1970s, and new laws were passed to reduce or eliminate lead-based products.

Iron

WITHOUT IRON TO MAKE STEEL, WE WOULD BE WITHOUT SKYSCRAPERS, WIRE, WATCHES, CUTLERY, WASHING MACHINES, AND POWER LINES.

We equate iron with impregnable strength, hence the Ironman comic book and movie superhero. In a more sober vein, it was Winston Churchill who called the Soviet Union's post–World War II barriers an "iron curtain." It's true that iron, one of the world's most abundant metals, makes things strong. It helps plants create chlorophyll, carries oxygen through our red blood cells, and has proven one of the most useful materials for making tools.

The Iron Age dawned around 1000 B.C. as the metal slowly replaced bronze. Iron tools and weapons, especially those needing sharp blades, were clearly superior and more durable than bronze. Ancient blacksmiths placed iron ore in a fire, producing a spongy mass, then pounded it against an anvil to compact the metal. This process yielded wrought iron ("wrought" meaning "worked"). For much of history, wrought iron was more common, because refining cast iron was grueling, time-consuming work, which made it costly.

In the 1700s, England's Abraham Darby helped make the industry more efficient when he discovered that using coke ("coal-cake") in blast furnaces instead of charcoal allowed him to produce more iron, making cast iron cheaper, more accessible, and—eventually—a driving force in the industrial revolution. In 1856 Sir Henry Bessemer discovered that a strong blast of air through molten iron would harden it. This led to the design of a converter that made steel—containing more carbon than cast iron—cheap to produce. It was industrialist Andrew Carnegie's realization that steel was the answer that allowed him to dominate the railroad industry.

Lithium

SCIENTISTS THINK LITHIUM WAS ONE OF THREE ELEMENTS, ALONG WITH DEUTERIUM AND HELIUM, CREATED IN LARGE AMOUNTS BY THE BIG BANG.

Silvery lithium, the lightest of the solid elements, keeps things running that sometimes seem to run our lives. A Brazilian chemist named José Bonifácio de Andrada e Silva discovered the mineral

UNCOMMONLY KNOWN ...

CANARIES IN COAL MINES The idea of using canaries in coal mines was hatched near the start of the 20th century by John Scott Haldane, a Scottish expert in respiration. The canaries' high sensitivity to toxic gases let miners know if the air was safe to breathe. The feathered sentinels were used until the 1980s, when technology provided other options. The phrase "canary in a coal mine" lives on as a metaphor for something that can warn of danger.

petalite in 1800, but did not recognize that it contained lithium. About 20 years later, Swedish chemist Johan August Arfwedson found great quantities of lithium in the mineral, though he was not able to isolate the metal. Arfwedson named the new substance after the Greek word for "stone": *lithos.*

When combined in alloys, lithium makes other metals stronger and lighter, which is why it's used in aircraft construction. Small amounts of lithium carbonate can strengthen ceramics and glass—crucial in the manufacture of reliable Pyrex. Lithium is unstable enough that its pure form can't be found in nature—and powerful enough that it has long been a component of thermonuclear weapons.

Its instability makes somewhat surprising the fact that it's become a vital source for medicines that calm and batteries that charge. Lithium's effect on patients with mental disorders was known in the 19th century, but Australian physician John Cade reintroduced the idea in 1949. He noticed that small doses of lithium could even out the mood swings of patients with bipolar disorder, thus making lithium the first effective treatment for the ailment.

The element's lightness was a game changer for batteries too: Lithium has proved essential in keeping our laptops, phones, cameras, and lifesaving pacemakers charged.

Nickel

FAIRLY RARE IN THE EARTH'S CRUST, NICKEL IS THE SECOND MOST ABUNDANT ELEMENT, AFTER IRON, FOUND AT THE PLANET'S CORE.

Chances are that if you dug through your purse or your car's cup holder, you'd find nickel in the form of a coin. The U.S. five-cent piece is called the nickel even though it's actually an alloy: three-fourths copper and only one-fourth nickel. But it's nickel that gives the coin its silvery shine. Nickel is mined all over the world, and it's also found in meteorites, which is how ancient peoples first got their hands on it. Archaeologists uncovered nickel beads in an Egyptian tomb dating back to about 3200 B.C. Medieval copper miners in Germany were annoyed when a dark red ore failed to yield any copper. They called it *kupfernickel,* which translates as something like "Old Nick's [the devil's] copper."

One of nickel's most helpful tricks is that it makes other metals stronger, shinier, and corrosion resistant. Before rare-earth magnets (used in cars, computers, and many other products), the strongest magnets were made of nickel alloy; they retained their magnetism even when heated red-hot. Today, some 65 percent of nickel in the Western world is used in the production of stainless steel. Nickel also goes into wire, batteries, armor-plating—and coins.

From the Deep

Human history has always been irrevocably tied to the sea. Since our earliest days, the ocean has been a source of healing remedies, a pathway to new places, and a major food supplier—not only of fish but much else, like sea salt and seaweed, that shows up on our tables. Yet the watery depths have given us far more than food. Many of the items featured in this section are among our most precious commodities, even if we don't always realize the impact they hold for us on land. From potential bone grafts to shimmering jewelry, the sea is full of treasures.

Coral

CORAL JEWELRY AND TALISMANS, PURPORTED TO CURE MADNESS AND PROTECT SHIPS FROM LIGHTNING, HAVE BEEN AROUND FOR MILLENNIA.

Coral has always been a vital part of the ocean's landscape—one that we've been taking advantage of for thousands of years. People believed coral was a plant until the 18th century, when it was proved to have animal cell membranes. Coral is actually an animal related to jellyfish and anemones. While most of its nutrients come from photosynthesis, it also eats small fish and phytoplankton. At its base is a hard limestone skeleton that forms the backbone of coral reefs. Yet coral is surprisingly fragile, and reefs can take thousands of years to grow.

Coral provides a habitat for countless creatures beneath the waves and also has a history out of the water. In ancient times, it was ground up and used to treat everything from menstrual cramps to poor circulation. In the 16th century some believed coral could prevent the Black Death.

Today, dried coral is used in bone grafts, including in cosmetic surgery. Coral is porous, and when it's grafted to bone, the body forms a bond with its tiny hollows; the encroaching bone eventually replaces the coral.

WHAT'S INSIDE?

Tide Pools

As author John Steinbeck once put it, tide pools are "ferocious with life." They exist in intertidal zones, forming along rocky shorelines where the sea washes up and out again, leaving behind the shallow pools that are their own tiny worlds. They provide gulls and other creatures—sometimes even bears—with sources of food, and they let us peer through a window into ocean life. Only the most adaptable species can survive in these wind-tossed, sun-bright microcosms, where it's every creature for itself. You'll find sea slugs, sea urchins, clams, barnacles, and more, including sea stars, which are famous for being able to regenerate limbs.

Sand

SAND IS CLASSIFIED BY GRAIN SIZE; FOR PARTICLES OF ROCK TO BE CALLED SAND, GRAINS MUST MEASURE BETWEEN 0.02 AND 2 MILLIMETERS.

What is tiny, but takes up a lot of space? What moves constantly, but doesn't really go away? Sand—ever shifting through weather, waves, and time—has become one of our most coveted natural resources. It comes from mountain ranges and volcanoes, where wind and rain eat at the rocks and carry the sediment down to streams and rivers heading toward the sea. Sand is always flowing somewhere. And much of it has been around for a very long time, which makes it convenient for studying geologic history. Conservationist and ocean lover Rachel Carson (see p. 21) once said, "In every grain of sand there is a story of the Earth."

We tend to think of sand as belonging to the seashore and the desert, but it plays an important role in our daily lives. We use sand's silicone dioxide to make glass as well as powdered foods. Sand is a primary ingredient in the production of microchips, lightweight metal alloys, paints, and cement.

Though it seems sand is everywhere, it's disappearing in parts of Asia. In the fast-developing region, industrial demand for sand has made it tempting to criminals. Smugglers steal sand from one coastal area and sell it in another. Ironically, the deserts are safe. Desert sand is considered "bad sand": Constant wind has smoothed the grains such that they don't stick together the way ocean grains do, thus making desert sand unsuitable for use in construction.

UNCOMMONLY KNOWN ...

HARVESTING CORAL IS UNREGULATED In recent years, humans have started being more careful about how much of the sea's bounty we take, but coral hasn't received that care—at least not enough to trigger serious regulation. Harvesting coral for industry, medicine, and jewelry often requires blasting or dredging, which can decimate reefs that take millennia to form. Wholesale harvesting can reduce the underwater landscape from a forest to a desert, depriving countless sea creatures of the habitat they depend on.

Jellies

JELLIES TEND TO RANGE FROM HALF AN INCH TO 16 INCHES ACROSS, BUT THE LION'S MANE JELLYFISH CAN GROW UP TO 6 FEET WIDE.

These floating, sometimes colorful, mostly transparent masses may look like aliens from another world, but they're actually some of our planet's oldest inhabitants. The term "jellies" is more appropriate than *jellyfish,* as the creatures are not fish at all. They come in two types: the more

recognizable bell-shaped tentacle-trailing jellies and comb jellies—ovoid blobs with hairlike appendages. Though jellies don't have brains exactly, they do have a nerve net that lets them sense what's going on around them. They detect when water chemistry changes, whether they're facing up or down, and how much light there is around them. They have stinging cells in their tentacles to stun prey, which they then maneuver to the opening that serves as a mouth.

In recent years, environmental changes have caused "blooms" of jellies to grow to massive numbers, despite the fact that they're scooped up for consumption in Asian cuisines. Jellies have also become a viable source of collagen, used to treat rheumatoid arthritis.

PEOPLE WHO CHANGED HISTORY

Sylvia Earle (1935-)

Crowned "Her Deepness" and named a "Hero for the Planet," Sylvia Earle is a marine biologist, National Geographic explorer-in-residence, and champion of the oceans. She came of age as a young scientist when no one thought human activity could drastically have an impact on the seas. We know better now, and Earle has been an advocate in the effort to understand and protect the ocean. The "sturgeon general" has logged more than 7,000 hours underwater—setting a record for solo diving at 1,250 feet. She founded Deep Ocean Engineering and Deep Ocean Technologies, which pioneered innovative deep-sea submersibles.

Sylvia Earle in a submersible, 2002

Seaweed

DASHI—A BASIC JAPANESE BROTH OFTEN MADE WITH SEAWEED—IS A MODERN-DAY CURE FOR HANGOVERS.

A weed, the dictionary tells us, is a valueless plant growing wild. Seaweed these days is often not wild, and it's decidedly not valueless. It's a vital part of the ocean's ecosystem. It can be as small as floating phytoplankton and as vast as thick kelp forests. Some people think of it mostly as the exotic health food that holds sushi rolls together, and perhaps that's made seaweed more visible. In reality, we've been swimming in it forever. Asian countries have long cultivated seaweed and coveted it in their cuisine, but it's been a star across the world. Ancient Romans used it to treat burns and rashes. In Ireland and Scotland monks ate "Irish moss" and gave it to the poor. Seaweed baths have been around since the Edwardian era. During the industrial revolution, scientists learned how to extract agar, alginate, and carrageenan from it, thickening agents that have found their way into myriad foods and household goods: toothpaste, ice cream, yogurt, dyes, gels, and hundreds of others.

During World War I when Germany cut off America's supply of potash, used in explosives, a derivative of California kelp came to the rescue.

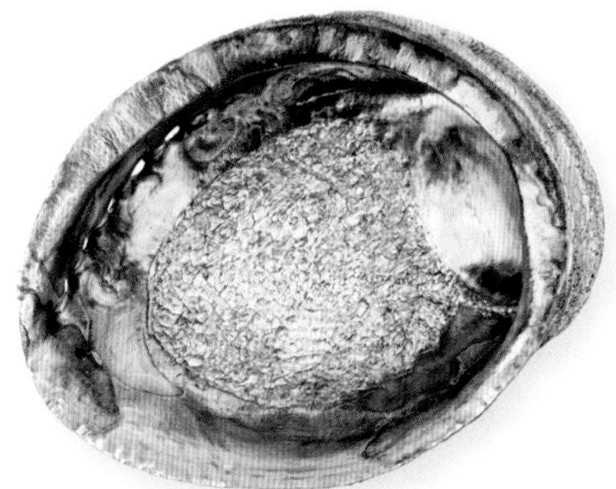

Abalone

THE LARGEST SPECIES OF ABALONE CAN GROW TO NEARLY A FOOT ACROSS. THE VALUABLE SEA SNAILS ARE THREATENED FROM OVERFISHING.

You would be forgiven for not noticing an abalone shell while you're walking along the beach. The exterior is humble, but flip it over and you'll find a treasure that's been used to make jewelry for thousands of years. The abalone is a sea snail that lives in cold coastal waters all over the world. They have flattish shells, which is why they're sometimes called "ear shells," and tend to range in size from four to ten inches wide. Their muscular foot helps them cling to rocks and boulders, making them easy to find and harvest. Sea otters love cracking them open and eating the fleshy insides. Humans too enjoy the delicacy, but it's the animal's shell that holds special value. The interior is coated with nacre (mother of pearl), whose rich colors and opalescent sheen inspired the Navajo to consider it one of their sacred stones. Commercially, it's used to make buttons and knife handles, as well as jewelry. And the creature has yet more to offer: Abalone juice has been shown to inhibit penicillin-resistant bacteria. Sadly, overfishing has decimated wild populations; today most abalone is farmed.

UNCOMMONLY KNOWN ...

UNDERSEA STALACTITES A stalactite occurs when water drips from the roof of a cave over a long period of time to form a mineral-rich icicle. But when seawater freezes in the Arctic, events can move quickly. Supercold brine sinks down through cracks in the ice and freezes on contact with the water below because the brine is denser and colder. In several hours, an ice stalactite, called a brinicle, can reach the seafloor, where luckless sea stars, anemones, and other creatures can be trapped in its icy reach.

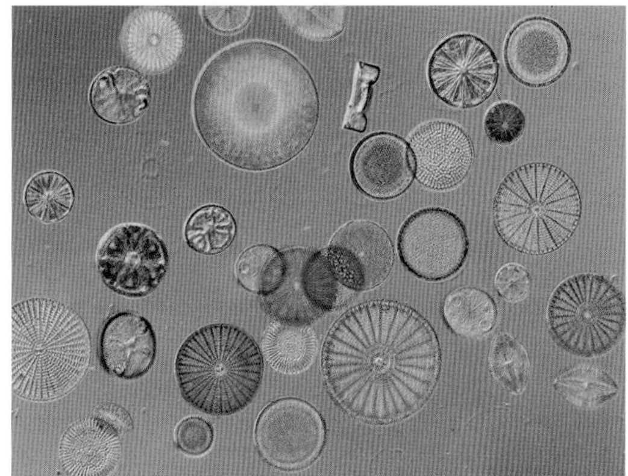

Diatoms

BECAUSE THEY HOLD THEIR SHAPE IN HIGH TEMPERATURES, THESE TINY SEA CREATURES HAVE PROVED USEFUL AS INSULATION IN FIRE DOORS.

Observed under a microscope, the minuscule phytoplankton could easily be mistaken for strings of blown-glass jewelry. In reality these algae are some of the hardiest and most successful organisms

found in nature. Diatoms emerged at the same time as the dinosaurs, easily surviving them and still thriving.

They live in both fresh and salt water. They are unicellular organisms with a hard, glasslike shell that forms in shapes that resemble everything from delicate fans to elegant buttons. They are so abundant that blooms of diatoms around the North and South Poles can be seen from space. The blooms draw the attention of mollusks, tunicates, and fish that feast on the phytoplankton.

You might not guess it, but much of the world's limestone and petroleum are made up of ancient diatoms. Over eons, they fall to the ocean floor and form thick layers of diatomaceous earth. The slow churn of the Earth's crust brings the layers to the surface, where they can tell us a great deal about climate change over geologic time.

This layering of diatoms also allows us to easily harvest them. Diatoms do a great job of trapping particles and air bubbles, making them ideal for use as both filters and fillers. They filter medicines, chemicals, and alcohol and can bolster paper, paint, and ceramics. Diatoms may look like glass, but they have strengths that glass can't muster.

WHAT'S INSIDE?

Seashells

They're often empty when we find them, but seashells begin their existence as the external skeletons produced by and vital to animals that call them home. To a mollusk, a calcium-rich shell is protective armor, a backpack, and a house all wrapped up in one. Shells protect their occupants from storms and many threats, though some predators still manage to wedge and drill their way through them. The chambered nautilus, which constructs its lovely shell from mother-of-pearl, adds internal chambers so that its home grows with it. Even after shells lose their original owners, creatures such as hermit crabs sometimes move in and claim them.

Sea Salt

SALT CURES WERE RECOMMENDED IN THE EARLY 19TH CENTURY, AND THE SICK TRAVELED TO SIMPLE SPAS AT SALT SPRINGS.

Salt is a staple in every kitchen and on every table. More than that, it's an essential ingredient for life. The components of salt, or sodium chloride, can be dangerous. Sodium ignites if it touches water, and pure chlorine is poisonous. But together they compose the stuff that helps our bodies balance water and keep our hearts beating. We literally couldn't survive without salt. But too much of this good thing can cause high blood pressure, increasing the risk of heart attack and stroke.

There is little difference between sea salt and table salt, but the latter comes from land deposits and requires much more processing before it's edible. Sea salt is produced when salt water evaporates from the ocean or a saltwater lake. Once the salt has crystallized, harvesters rake it up, and then wash and dry it before shipping it to market.

Salt historically has played a pivotal role in both religion and economics, purifying sacred rituals and guiding the rise and fall of empires. Salt was so valuable in ancient times that, at one point, it was traded for gold.

In ancient Egypt, salt was prized as a religious offering and was an important tool used in embalming. It could also be used as currency. For example, Slaves in Greece were sometimes purchased with salt, which is where the phrase "not worth his salt" comes from.

Even now, the idea of payment has a link to the ancient salt trade: Roman soldiers were given money for the purchase of salt, called *salarium argentum,* which is where the word "salary" originates. The salt in our kitchens today is the same treasure fought over for thousands of years. No wonder it's considered bad luck to spill the salt.

Jade

JADEITE IS SO HARD THAT IT HAS TO BE DRILLED TODAY. IT'S THIS HARDNESS THAT THE ANCIENTS VALUED FOR MAKING TOOLS AND WEAPONS.

Jade has been coveted in China since Neolithic times, used as jewelry, tools, and funerary treasures. The ancients believed it formed connections between the physical and spiritual world. When emperors died, *yu* ("royal stone") was placed on their tongues before burial to keep the bodies pristine and ward off bad energy. Often found around China's rivers, this "stone of heaven" has long been tied to the virtues of goodness and purity: Confucius once said that the good virtue of man is like jade.

Jade comes in two closely related forms: jadeite and nephrite. Jadeite has more color variety, and its colors are usually more intense, especially the deep green that we most associate with the gemstone. It can also be lavender, red, orange, and yellow, among other colors. Nephrite is more common, and when polished has a waxier luster.

Though the Chinese probably remain jade's biggest fans, Mesoamerican cultures and the New Zealand Maori have carved it into weapons and talismans and revered it for its reputed ability to heal. The word "jade" comes from the Spanish term *piedra de ijada,* which loosely translated means "loin stone," inspired by the idea that jade could bring relief for kidney stones.

Although jade deposits aren't widespread in the United States, the stone has become a treasure worth searching for. In Big Sur, California, divers can hit the jackpot scouring Jade Cove.

UNCOMMONLY KNOWN ...

PUFFER FISH CIRCLES In 1995, divers off the coast of Japan found circular geometric patterns carved in the sand. They appeared almost like works of art. It took another decade for researchers to solve the mystery of how they were made. The sandy rings, which bring to mind infamous crop circles, turned out to be the work of a puffer fish in an elaborate attempt to attract a mate. This five-inch-long Romeo creates radially aligned peaks and valleys by dragging his fins back and forth in the sand, a task he must diligently keep up to prevent the current from destroying his creation before it can be appreciated. He also decorates the circles (measuring some seven feet in diameter) with shells and fine sediment, hoping the design will help win a female's attention. If a lady puffer fish is impressed—and no one knows how she makes her judgment—she will lay her eggs in the center of the circle.

Rain Forest Treasures

Dense, mysterious rain forests have always been places of hidden treasure. We have been continually astounded by the rich concentration of life and natural resources that yield bounty beyond measure. Rain forests have given us chocolate and vanilla, flavors that expanded our sweet-loving habits forever. They've given us influential medicines, such as malaria-fighting quinine, that became some of our earliest forms of protection against deadly diseases. Indeed, the forests themselves are among nature's greatest gifts, a trove that we must wisely protect.

Vanilla

THE FIRST AMERICAN RECIPE FOR VANILLA ICE CREAM WAS PUBLISHED NEARLY TWO CENTURIES AGO; TODAY IT'S RANKED AS THE MOST POPULAR FLAVOR.

It's ironic that we often describe something as "vanilla" when it's bland or plain, considering it takes only a fraction of a single vanilla bean, or pod, to transform an entire family dessert. And belying their shriveled appearance, vanilla pods are the proud fruit of a spectacular member of the orchid family native to southern Mexico and Guatemala. The Aztecs used vanilla to flavor their *chocolatl* (cacao) drink, a practice adopted by Spanish conquistadors, who brought it to Europe. That was vanilla's only known use until a 17th-century British apothecary, Hugh Morgan, invented vanilla-flavored sweetmeats for Queen Elizabeth I. Her love of the treats helped propel vanilla into fashion. The French used the pods to flavor ice cream, which is how the U.S. minister to France, Thomas Jefferson, discovered it. Vanilla went on to become a crucial ingredient in many American recipes, including the original formula for Coca-Cola.

Vanilla is one of the most expensive spices after saffron, because its production is a high-maintenance affair. The pods grow on vines that can stretch more than 300 feet. They produce lovely yellow-green flowers that open for only 24 hours. If they're not pollinated in that span, the flowers wilt and die, and there will be no fruit. Healthy pods must be picked by hand before they completely ripen and set out to dry for several months. Pure vanilla extract is made by macerating the dried pods with water and alcohol.

Artificial vanilla flavoring, found in many prepared foods, is synthesized from lignin, a by-product of wood pulp used to make paper. It's less expensive, but there's nothing like the real thing.

Lemongrass

THIS GRASS ISN'T ACTUALLY RELATED TO THE LEMON. THE SIMILARITY IN SCENT COMES FROM CITRAL, A COMPOUND ALSO FOUND IN LEMON RIND.

Walk into a mill where tough, fibrous stalks of lemongrass are being processed, and you won't be able to miss the floral, citrusy aroma. Fragrant lemongrass has been used for centuries across Asia as a favored ingredient in curries, soups, and other dishes to balance the taste of oil and meat. The tall, hardy grass grows wild in the tropical climes of India, Australia, and Southeast Asia. Its stalks are too tough to eat, so they are typically crushed to extract their oil. The pungent liquid was once used as a preservative on ancient palm-leaf scrolls in India. It kept the scrolls well conditioned and discouraged destructive insects. Lemongrass contains citronella, which finds wide use today in soaps and candles and is the plant component that helps keep bugs at bay—most bugs, that is. Ironically, some say that citronella attracts honeybees.

Antifungal, antibacterial, and generally considered soothing, lemongrass in various forms has traditionally been employed to ease aches and pains. In India, where it's also used to treat ringworm and purportedly lessens depression, it's frequently steeped to make a "fever tea" designed to cure whatever ails you. Across the ocean in Australia, Aborigines have used lemongrass to treat earaches and coughs.

Lemongrass oil makes a healthy, savory addition to dinner recipes and is a great way to perfume your house —or yourself: It's featured in environmentally conscious deodorants.

PEOPLE WHO CHANGED HISTORY

John Muir (1838-1914)

In 1867, working in a factory, John Muir suffered an eye injury that nearly blinded him. He recovered and was inspired to turn his gaze toward the natural world. California's Sierra Nevada captured him, and he worked for a time in the Yosemite Valley, where he spent years advocating for its protection. Called the father of the national parks, he was a driving force behind the creation of a host of wilderness areas and parklands. His 1901 book, *Our National Parks,* led President Theodore Roosevelt to visit Muir on location, a trip that prompted legislation that preserved Yosemite for future generations.

John Muir at Yosemite's Mirror Lake, California, 1902

Cocoa Butter

CACAO BEANS HAD RELIGIOUS MEANING TO THE AZTEC. THEY USED THEM IN COMING-OF-AGE CEREMONIES, AND WEDDING COUPLES EXCHANGED THEM.

Though they may seem like distant cousins, cocoa butter and chocolate are both born from the cacao bean. The cacao tree has grown in South America for centuries, but it had a long journey before it arrived to yield the cocoa butter we know today. The tree was first cultivated by the ancient Olmec people, and later the Maya and Aztec, who used the cacao bean as currency. They also used the beans to make a cacao drink. During the Spanish inquisition, Christopher Columbus brought cacao beans back to Spain in 1502, but the first record of cacao being introduced as a drink in Spain took place in 1544. Drinking chocolate spread across the continent as an increasingly popular delicacy and gave rise to Europe's first chocolate houses. By the end of the 16th century, chocolate was even believed to have curative powers.

Fat-rich cocoa butter is what makes chocolate melt in the mouth, but it wasn't until 1828 that it was extracted from the bean and had a chance to entrance on its own. That was the year Conrad J. Van Houten invented his cocoa press, which made it possible to separate cocoa solids from cocoa butter. The process made drinking chocolate cheaper, made it possible to manufacture solid chocolate confections, and allowed people to explore uses for cocoa butter.

The butter's combination of fats remains solid at room temperature and melts at body temperature, and it's resistant to oxidation (which helps keep chocolate bars from going bad).

An effective and pleasant-smelling lubricant, cocoa butter soon found its way into moisturizing cream, lip balm, and sun lotion. Cocoa butter maintains its reputation as a superior moisturizer, but recent studies unfortunately suggest it has little effect when it comes to preventing stretch marks.

Quinine

QUININE IS FLUORESCENT, WHICH MEANS THAT IF YOU PLACE A BOTTLE OF TONIC WATER UNDER A BLACK LIGHT, IT WILL GLOW FROM WITHIN.

From the rain forest of South America comes the cinchona shrub, which changed the face of medicine and altered our drinking habits. The Quechua people of Peru didn't know about the alkaloid quinine in the

UNCOMMONLY KNOWN ...

TARANTULAS They have a scary reputation, but in fact many tarantulas are docile creatures. They hardly ever bite, and when they do—though the bite can be painful—their venom is milder than a honeybee's. Experts will tell you not to handle tarantulas, but that's for the spiders' protection. Tarantulas—many of which live in rain forests—are surprisingly fragile. They have exoskeletons that they sometimes shed, leaving their water-filled abdomens vulnerable. If you drop the spider, it can be easily injured.

cinchona's bark, but they certainly understood that the bark could calm the raging fevers and chills of an often fatal disease—a scourge we know to be mosquito-borne malaria. Legend has it that a fever-mad Indian who got lost in the jungle stumbled on a pool of stagnant water surrounded by cinchona trees. He drank the bitter liquid and thought he was poisoned, but soon after, his fever disappeared. The people learned to peel the bark, grind it, and mix it with sweet water to temper its bitterness. It was, in fact, a lifesaving tonic. Today when bartenders grab the mixer gun for tonic water, they find it labeled "Q" for quinine.

Accounts differ as to how the remedy became known in Europe, but its introduction dates to the early 17th century. It was already renowned when French chemists Pierre-Joseph Pelletier and Joseph Caventou isolated and named the alkaloid in 1820.

Quinine was often mixed with wine and given to soldiers and sailors, making it the first successful use of a chemical compound to treat disease; it's said that success or defeat in battle often rested on whether the troops were drinking their quinine. British colonials in India, so the story goes, mixed gin with their tonic water to make it more palatable—and a classic cocktail was born.

Jute

JUTE IS ONE OF THE MOST ABSORBENT FIBERS IN NATURE. A JUTE RUG HAS THE ABILITY TO SOAK UP ABOUT A QUARTER OF ITS WEIGHT.

Jute has long played its humble part as familiar twine in kitchen drawers, but it's also been influential in trade, war, and the textile industry. It's native to the Bengal region of India and to Bangladesh, where it's still one of that country's most important exports. It grows in two varieties: white jute and tossa jute. Both are tall, grasslike relatives of the hemp plant. Jute fibers are unique in that unlike other textile fibers, they're made

WHAT'S INSIDE?

Quicksand

Despite what you see in movies featuring quicksand, this natural phenomenon isn't as treacherous as it seems. Quicksand is created when solid ground—usually sand or grainy soil—is bogged by water, forming a soupy paste. Water gets trapped, and the slurry can't support a person's weight. It's true that the more you struggle in quicksand, the faster you'll sink, but you won't sink past your waist. Human density is about one gram per milliliter, and quicksand's density is around two grams. The best way to escape quicksand is to slowly spread out your legs and try to bring them to the surface. Then carefully make your way toward firmer ground.

up of lignin as well as cellulose, meaning that jute is part fiber and part wood. The fibers are long—between 3 and 13 feet. Jute has been dubbed the "golden fiber" because of its flaxen color and its silkiness to the touch. It has been farmed in India and what is now Bangladesh for millennia, but the process of stripping and weaving it by hand is painstaking. By the 1830s, textile factories in Dundee, Scotland, discovered that treating jute with whale oil allowed it to be processed by machine. That discovery spawned an industry that brought droves of Irish immigrants to the area. Because women were the ones who did the spinning, the influx caused people to start calling Dundee "She Town." Jute went into everything from clothes to ropes to burlap sacks for bulk goods such as coffee beans. More than a billion sandbags made of jute protected the trenches during World Wars I and II. Jute products are entirely biodegradable, a winning attribute that continues to make them an environmentally friendly choice.

PEOPLE WHO CHANGED HISTORY

Jane Goodall (1934-)

At age 26—with her notebook, her binoculars, and little else—Jane Goodall traveled from England to the wilds of what would soon be the nation of Tanzania to study the chimpanzees she'd been interested in all her life. It was 1960, and Goodall became the first known person to befriend wild chimps and observe their behavior at close range. Over the course of decades, she discovered they were not so different from people in their habits and moods. Her patient observations challenged many prevailing assumptions about our closest primate relatives and sparked global interest in the animals that continues to this day. National Geographic documented her work, inspiring others to enter the field of primatology. In 1977 she founded the Jane Goodall Institute, which supports ongoing study of the chimps and sponsors conservation and responsible development projects in Africa. She later established a youth outreach program, Roots & Shoots.

Jane Goodall, Tanzania, 1962

Rubber

VULCANIZED RUBBER WAS USED TO MAKE CONDOMS IN 1843, PROVIDING THE WORLD'S FIRST RELIABLE FORM OF ARTIFICIAL CONTRACEPTION.

What do Batman, warships, and the industrial revolution have in common? All were fueled by vulcanized rubber. Like the movie superheroes whose suits were made from it, rubber's powers seem to have known no bounds.

Rubber was around as early as the Enlightenment, but it was mostly considered a curiosity. In the mid-19th century, the British government thought the substance was bulletproof. Thomas Hancock, who pioneered the rubber industry in Britain, knew better. The man who helped

WHAT'S INSIDE?

Termite Cathedral

Master engineers of the insect world, Cathedral termites found in Australia's Northwest Territory build massive, towering nest mounds that jut out of the landscape like dragon's teeth. The structures—made of mud, saliva, grass, and feces—can rise more than 15 feet. If converted to human scale, they would reach five times as high as the Empire State Building. The construction is accomplished by millions of tiny blind workers. Hollow columns they build inside the mound, plus the dried grass they use for its outer walls, create an impressive air-conditioning system that protects the occupants from the strong Australian sun.

produce the waterproof coats we call mackintoshes was horrified that soldiers might be sent to their deaths in rubber vests. Fortunately, he was able to show the powers-that-be that their confidence was misguided.

Rubber comes from tropical trees that produce latex, a sticky, milky substance they use in defense against insects. Humans learned to harvest latex by making diagonal cuts into bark and collecting the fluid that drains from the tree. Tapped latex is naturally malleable but unstable.

In 1839, American chemist Charles Goodyear figured out that adding sulfur stabilized latex, allowing it to stretch while holding on to its original shape. He called it "vulcanized" rubber (named after the Roman god of fire). It's been used to make products that have shaped the modern age: gaskets that enabled the industrial revolution's machines; fittings for submarines that influenced the outcomes of both world wars; tires that changed how we travel.

Rubber has made our lives more convenient, though not without human cost. On rubber plantations, mistreatment of workers and dire working conditions were commonplace: Fortunately this situation has improved over time.

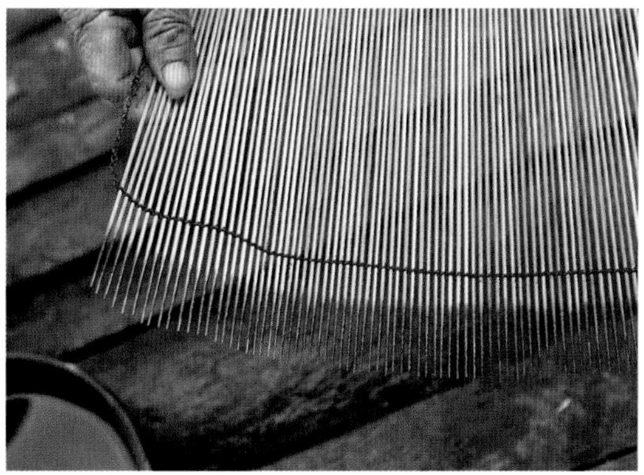

Curare

WHEN SCIENTISTS FIRST EXPERIMENTED WITH POISONOUS CURARE, THEY FOUND IT WAS USEFUL AS A MUSCLE RELAXANT AND ANESTHETIC.

Lethal and medicinal, curare is one of nature's most interesting contradictions. The alkaloid is found in woody vines of South America and was used for centuries as a poison by indigenous tribes. Hunters would dip darts and arrows in curare paste to paralyze prey—and, in strong enough doses, to kill it. When Spanish conquerors arrived, the Indians started using curare to attack the invaders. The unknown nature of the "flying death" was particularly frightening to Europeans. According to Sir Walter Raleigh: "there was never Spaniard . . . that could attain to the true knowledge of the cure . . . but [the Indians'] soothsayers and priests, who do conceal it." The secret of curare remained closely guarded until 22-year-old Charles Waterton, a British gentleman-adventurer, traveled to Guyana in 1804 to work on his family's plantation and brought samples back to England. By the mid-20th century, medical researchers learned to harness curare to relax patients' muscles during general anesthesia. In recent decades, natural curare has been replaced by manufactured synthetics.

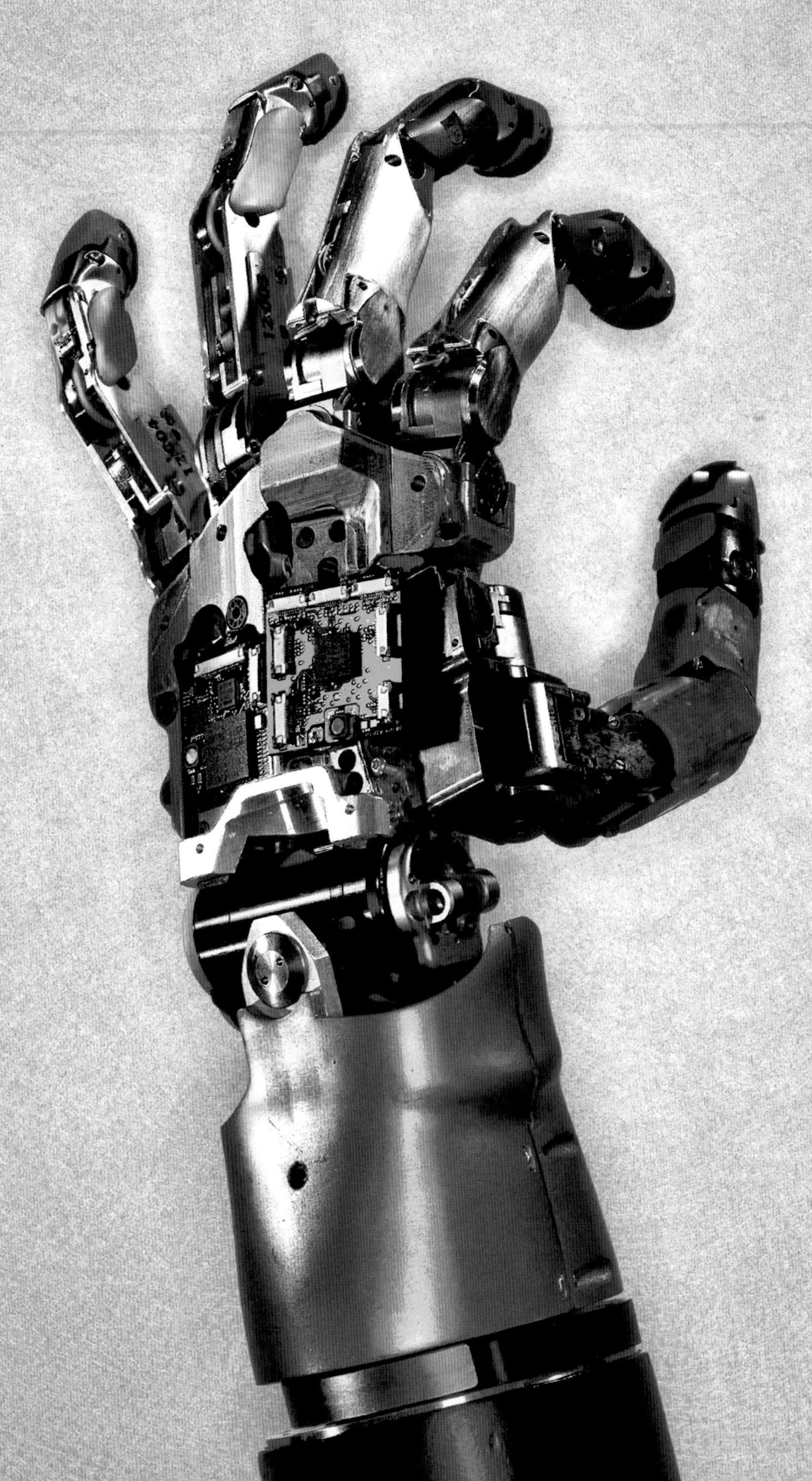

If at first the idea is not absurd,
then there is no hope for it.

–ALBERT EINSTEIN (1879–1955)

Weird Science

We celebrate the great scientists and inventors of the past. Everyone knows about Edison and his light bulb, Watt and the steam engine, and thanks to the electric car, Tesla and the induction motor. We're also grateful to the anonymous creative souls who came up with the wheel, the fork, and the hairbrush. But what about the odder corners of our technological history? Whose idea was it to turn smelly, sulfurous water into medicine? Why would you spin glass into ships' hulls? Who would fill a tooth with toxic mercury? It takes a particularly imaginative mind to see the practical uses of odd materials—and the odd uses of practical materials. Fortunately history is replete with such ingeniousness. In this chapter, we take a stroll through the curious origins and fascinating mechanics of all sorts of objects, fabrics, and mixtures. Some are high tech, such as surgical lasers, prosthetic limbs, and synthetic diamonds. Others have been around for a surprisingly long time. Asphalt has paved roads since the glory days of ancient Babylon. Bamboo, the original renewable resource, has been made into utensils and musical instruments for thousands of years. We'll take a look at strange composites, aids for our ailing bodies, recycled and reusable materials, and fabulous fakes. We'll also pay a visit to the greatest inventor of all: Mother Nature. Weird science doesn't get any weirder than a chameleon's tongue, a hummingbird's wings, or a dolphin's bifurcated brain. We may understand our own devices, but many of nature's creations remain a mystery to us. Scientists are just beginning to unravel how a polar bear stays warm under a coat of hollow hairs and why a hippopotamus appears to be sweating blood. Human history is full of invention, but it's got nothing on natural history.

Everyday Amalgams

Most of us know the term "amalgam" from the dentist's office. Our metallic fillings are amalgams, mixtures of mercury, silver, tin, and copper. But an amalgam is any combination of diverse elements. Chemistry has given us helpful amalgams in compounds ranging from laxatives to antifreeze. A mixture of sticky petroleum and gravel, resulting in an asphalt pavement, has provided a smooth ride to everyone from the charioteers of Babylon to today's commuters. When varied ingredients come together to make a new and useful substance, the world benefits.

Asphalt

LOS ANGELES'S FAMOUS LA BREA TAR PITS, GRAVEYARD OF MANY PREHISTORIC CREATURES, ARE NATURAL ASPHALT POOLS.

When Belgian chemist Edmund DeSmedt rolled out an asphalt pavement in front of city hall in Newark, New Jersey, in 1870, it marked a first for the United States but not for the world. Asphalt had been used in roads for thousands of years. In ancient Mesopotamia, according to a 625 B.C. inscription, "Nabopolassar, King of Babylon . . . made a road glistening with asphalt and burnt bricks." French engineers employed asphalt blocks to resurface the Champs-Élysées in 1824. By the 20th century, the transportation needs of World War II and the subsequent growth of automobile-dependent suburbs spurred the spread of asphalt highways.

Like Nabopolassar's roads, today's asphalt surfaces are a mix of sharp and sticky. Asphalt itself is a part of petroleum and can be found in natural pools or impregnated within rock or tar sands. It's as waterproof, dense, and gummy as taffy. The road material is a mixture of aggregate—sharp stones of various sizes—and the sticky asphalt, a binder. Today it accounts for over 90 percent of paved surfaces in the United States.

WHAT'S INSIDE?

OxiClean

OxiClean, a popular commercial stain remover, mixes a few common ingredients to jump-start a chemical process. In addition to detergents, the chief ingredient in OxiClean is sodium percarbonate, a product of mixing sodium carbonate and hydrogen peroxide, a bleach. Sodium carbonate, also known as washing soda or soda ash, is often extracted from the ashes of plants that grow in salty soils. When added to water, OxiClean starts a bubbling, oxygen-rich reaction that breaks down stains, leaving behind only biodegradable chemicals.

Antifreeze

ETHYLENE GLYCOL WAS ORIGINALLY USED IN DYNAMITE. IT ALLOWED THE EXPLOSIVE TO BE MADE IN SAFE, COOL SURROUNDINGS.

Early car engines used plain water as a coolant, and it worked like a champ—in the summer. In the winter, water doesn't just freeze; it expands as it freezes, and so it wasn't practical in an enclosed engine.

Car manufacturers began adding methanol, an alcohol, to the water. Methanol did lower the coolant's freezing point, but its tendency to evaporate and corrode the engine made it, too, less than ideal. So automakers turned to ethylene glycol, an organic chemical compound first synthesized in 1856 by French chemist Charles-Adolph Wurtz. Added to water, it not only lowers the freezing point but also raises the boiling point, making it an antiboil as well as an antifreeze. Automakers adopted the compound in 1926, and it continues to be used today.

Ethylene glycol is highly toxic as well as useful. Ethylene is a natural plant hormone, and ethylene glycol has a sweet, fruity taste that can entice pets and small children. Therefore, some manufacturers add a bitter flavor to the fluid, while others are turning to another chemical, propylene glycol. This form of antifreeze is so benign that it is used in toothpaste and ice cream.

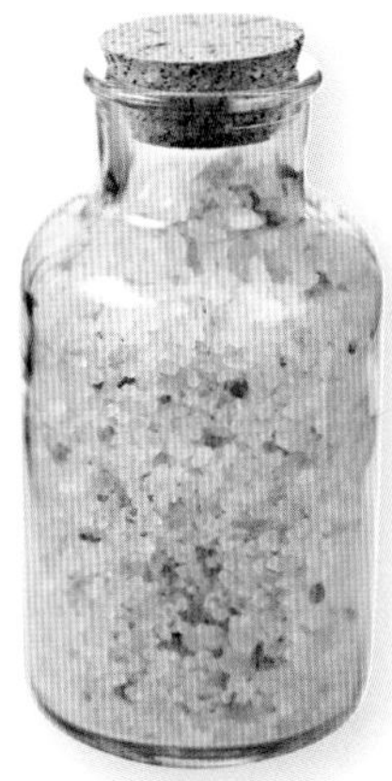

Epsom Salts

ACCORDING TO ITS PROPONENTS, EPSOM SALTS CAN EASE BACK PAIN, SMOOTH SKIN, HEAL CUTS, AND IMPROVE SLEEP.

A cow discovered Epsom salts, or so the story goes. According to local legend, in the early 17th century a resident of the English market town of Epsom, southwest of London, was out with his cattle on the village common when he saw water filling a cow's hoofprint. The next day, he sipped from the overflowing print and discovered that the water not only had a mineral taste, but was an excellent "purgative," as they said in those days—in other words, a laxative.

Word of the mineral water's benefits spread, and for a time, Epsom was a flourishing spa town. So many people flocked to the town that they kept drinking the wells dry. Soon chemists deciphered the secret of Epsom water: It contains the inorganic salt magnesium sulfate, a compound of magnesium, sulfur, and oxygen. In dried,

crystalline form, the compound was soon marketed as Epsom salts. Over the years, its purported benefits have expanded to include claims that when dissolved in water, the salts soothe muscle aches, help remove splinters, and leach toxins from the body. However, scientific evidence for these effects is lacking. As a medicine, magnesium sulfate is used intravenously to prevent eclampsia and ease asthma attacks. Orally it's still a great purgative. In a bath, Epsom salts may be merely a pleasant placebo.

Simple Green

SIMPLE GREEN IS OFTEN USED TO CLEAN THE FEATHERS AND FUR OF BIRDS AND MAMMALS CAUGHT IN OIL SPILLS.

Simple Green lives up to its name. It's a simple, literally, and ecologically green cleaning fluid that can be used on anything from machinery to pots and pans.

Inventors Bruce FaBrizio and his father developed the liquid in 1975 as a nontoxic, nonflammable way to remove tannic acid from commercial coffee roasting machines. They then expanded its use to other equipment and to floors, delivering it to businesses in 55-gallon drums. In time, Simple Green's biodegradable qualities gained it a following among a public that was becoming more attuned to environmental issues. Its parent company began to market it in grocery stores and club stores as an all-purpose, environmentally safe cleanser.

What's in it? Like most other cleaning products, it's mainly water, a universal solvent. Added to that are four chemicals, including ethoxylated alcohol, often used in detergents to pull up and remove dirt. Two secret ingredients give Simple Green its distinctive sassafras odor and dark green hue.

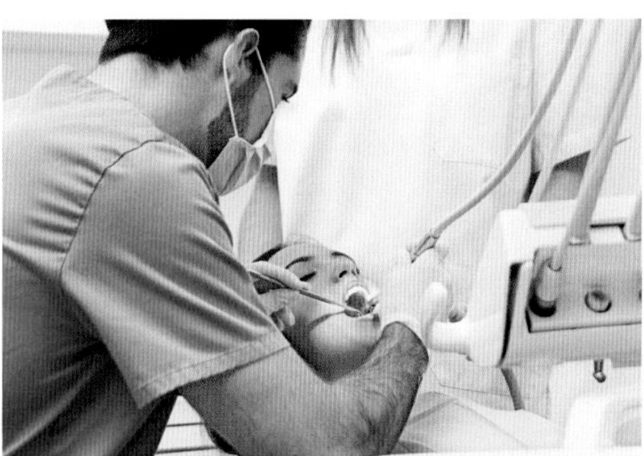

Dental Fillings

AN ELECTRIC CURRENT CAN FLOW BETWEEN ADJACENT GOLD AND SILVER FILLINGS, GIVING THE MOUTH A SHOCK.

Dental cavities can be repaired with gold, ceramics, or resins, but the most familiar filling is the silver/mercury amalgam. Commonly used now, when it was introduced to the United States, it caused an uproar known as the first amalgam war.

Amalgam fillings are about as old as cavities themselves. Chinese texts from the seventh century mention silver amalgams, as do medieval German texts. Then as now, the fillings were 50 percent mercury and 50 percent silver, tin, and copper. Although mercury is toxic on its own, in combination with the other metals it is harmless.

By the 19th century, however, many dentists preferred gold, a safe but costly material. When Englishmen Edward and Moses Crawcour introduced silver amalgams in New York State in 1833, their cheaper alternative aroused the ire of the American Society of Dental Surgeons, which banned its members from using the material. The controversy raged until 1859, when a new society, the American Dental Association, was formed and promoted the silver amalgam as its favored filling.

PEOPLE WHO CHANGED HISTORY

Ellen H. Swallow Richards (1842–1911)

Breaking barriers in American science, chemist Ellen Henrietta Swallow Richards pioneered sanitary engineering in venues ranging from state to kitchen. After earning a bachelor's degree from Vassar College in 1870, she was accepted as a "special student" at all-male MIT, becoming the first woman in the United States to attend a science school. Her bachelor's degree from MIT was matched by a master's from Vassar the same year.

Richards went on to promote the education of women in science and also to conduct a huge survey of water quality in Massachusetts, an endeavor that led to the first state water-quality standards in the nation. She applied the same scientific rigor to the household, writing *The Chemistry of Cooking and Cleaning*, setting up model kitchens, and establishing the field of home economics.

Ellen Richards, 1915

Milk of Magnesia

AS IRELAND'S FIRST INSPECTOR OF ANATOMY, JAMES MURRAY WAS REQUIRED TO KNOW THE CIRCUMSTANCES OF EVERY BODY BEING DISSECTED.

The brilliant heart surgeon or the inventor of a vaccine may get all the glory, but few doctors are more sincerely valued than those who can soothe a stomachache. In 1829 James Murray of Belfast, Ireland, earned a title and an elevated social position after he used a new fluid magnesia preparation to ease the digestive troubles of the marquis of Anglesey, lord lieutenant of Ireland.

Murray was an Irish apothecary and surgeon with an inventive mind. His preparation consisted mainly of magnesium hydroxide, an inorganic compound that in solid form is called brucite. Mixed with water and ingested, the cloudy liquid acts as an antacid and a laxative. Anglesey was so pleased with Murray's concoction that he had him knighted and appointed personal physician to him and two subsequent lord lieutenants.

Murray's liquid wasn't patented until after his death in 1873. Meanwhile, Anglo-American pharmacist Charles Henry Phillips created a similar preparation and marketed it under the name "Phillips' Milk of Magnesia," a brand still familiar today.

Bodily Functions

From aching muscles to failing hearts, from dirty diapers to severed limbs, many of the problems that plague the human body have met their match in human resourcefulness. More than a few remedies have their origins in centuries past. Prosthetic limbs appear in some of humankind's oldest writings. Medieval physicians peddled muscle liniments similar to those found on drugstore shelves today. However, modern miracles such as lasers, microchips, and plastics have taken old technologies to a new level, allowing us to shape an eyeball or safely stop a heart from beating while we move it from one chest to another.

Disposable Diapers

YES, ASTRONAUTS SOMETIMES WEAR DIAPERS UNDER THEIR SUITS. IN NASA-SPEAK, THEY'RE KNOWN AS MAXIMUM ABSORBENCY GARMENTS (MAGS).

The age-old problem of soggy diapers met a fed-up mother in the 1940s, and the disposable diaper was born. Into the 20th century, cultures around the world had taken a variety of approaches to keeping babies dry. Some Native Americans stuffed animal skins with moss or packed grass; other cultures used some kind of cloth wrapping such as linen. Laundry was such a chore that parents in early modern societies might change cloth diapers only once every several days, or perhaps hang them up to dry and then reuse them.

Even when washing machines and modern sanitation saved infants from these unsavory wrappings, cloth diapers, worn under rubber pants, were still prone to leaking or promoting diaper rash. American inventor Marion Donovan, who had two children of her own, grew tired of the constant struggle with wetness and crafted her own waterproof diaper cover from a shower curtain. Moving on to parachute fabric with snap

WHAT'S INSIDE?

Soylent Meal Replacement

For those who find cooking, or indeed, eating, to be a chore, there's Soylent. Created in 2012 by time-stressed software engineer Robert Rhinehart, the liquid meal replacement is touted as a quick, completely nutritional alternative to solid food. (Rhinehart says the name was inspired by the soy-lentil diet of the overcrowded population in Harry Harrison's science-fiction novel *Make Room! Make Room!*) Mixed with water, the Soylent powder becomes a bland, beige drink that is 43 percent carbohydrates, 40 percent protein, and 17 percent fat, plus vitamins and minerals. Maltodextrin, rice protein, and oat flour are the main ingredients.

fasteners, she began to sell her "Boater," which could be stuffed with absorbent paper, through the Saks Fifth Avenue department store in 1949. It was a huge success, so much so that she sold the rights to the Keko Corporation for one million dollars.

By 1961, Procter & Gamble merged the idea of a waterproof cover and disposable paper into a single disposable diaper, launched under the name Pampers. Donovan went on to file patents for about 20 other inventions, from facial tissues to a new type of dental floss.

UNCOMMONLY KNOWN ...

GEORGE WASHINGTON'S TEETH George Washington never wore a set of wooden teeth, as popularly believed, but the first president was plagued by dental problems and sported a variety of dentures throughout his career. The appliances bothered him: He complained they were "uneasy in the mouth and bulge my lips out." His most elegant set of false teeth, created by French dentist Jean-Pierre Le Mayeur, had bases carved from hippopotamus ivory inset with real animal and human teeth. Le Mayeur left a space for Washington's one remaining tooth.

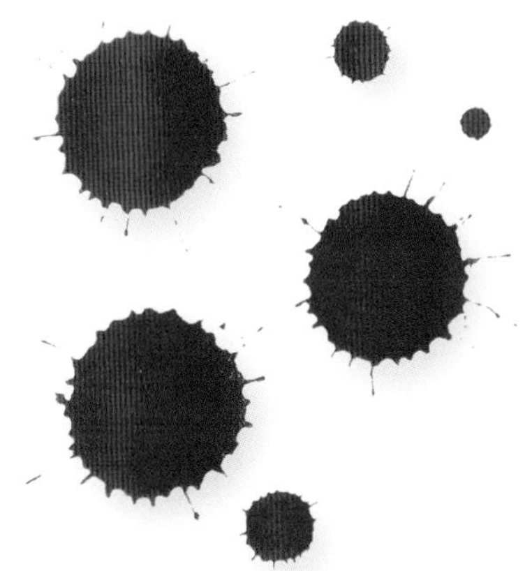

Artificial Blood

NEW VARIETIES OF ARTIFICIAL BLOOD ALWAYS HAVE THE BLOOD TYPE O NEGATIVE, CONSIDERED THE UNIVERSAL DONOR.

In 1878 gynecologist Theodore Gaillard Thomas published a paper reporting success using cow's milk as a blood substitute. Two out of his three transfused patients died, but Thomas claimed that their deaths were unrelated to the transfusion: As long as the milk was fresh, the transfusion was safe.

This did not turn out to be true, but the optimistic physician was just one in a long line of doctors attempting to solve the age-old problem of blood loss. Physicians have used beer, urine, and plant resins to replace blood, as well as blood taken from animal and human donors. Nonblood transfusions fail in large part because blood's main role is to supply the body with oxygen through the hemoglobin in red blood cells. Until the 1940s, blood-to-blood transfusions were risky due to problems with storage, blood-type incompatibility, and transfusion-transmitted infections. Even now, although complications are rare, blood transfusions occasionally transmit diseases or fail due to incorrect cross-matching. Donated blood has a short shelf life and can be in high demand, especially during wartime.

In the 20th century, researchers focused on new ways to introduce hemoglobin to patients needing a transfusion. Beginning in the 1980s, several companies tested hemoglobin-carrying blood substitutes with names like HemAssist and PolyHeme, but these had unacceptable mortality rates. Now, hopes ride on a new and promising source: stem cells. The all-purpose cells can be cultured and grown into mature red blood cells by the billions. Much work remains to be done, however. The next steps, before it's donation ready, are to produce the blood in large quantities and thoroughly test it.

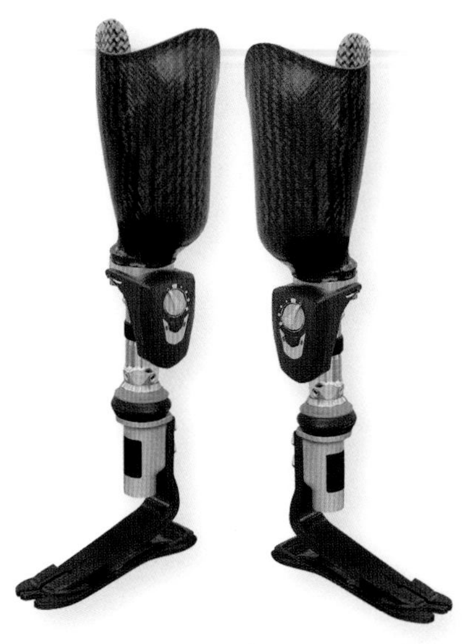

Artificial Limbs

MORE THAN ONE-AND-A-HALF MILLION AMERICANS HAVE LOST AT LEAST ONE LIMB, NOT INCLUDING FINGERS AND TOES.

Roughly 9,000 years ago, according to the sacred Sanskrit texts of the Rigveda, the warrior queen Vishpala lost her leg in battle. Undaunted, she donned an iron leg and returned to the fight. That particular prosthetic limb has never been found, but archaeologists have discovered a handsome wood and leather toe attached to a 3,000-year-old Egyptian mummy. Classical Greek and Roman writings also describe artificial hands and feet. One of the more dramatic stories related by the historian Herodotus tells of the Greek seer Hegesistratus. Captured by the Spartans, he cut off his own foot to escape his shackles, traveled for three days, and then made himself a new foot out of wood.

Although watchmakers and other craftsmen from the Middle Ages through the American Civil War devised clever joints that allowed artificial knees to bend or lock or fingers to curl, prosthetic limbs remained fairly crude mechanical devices until recently. The invention of strong, lightweight composite materials and the microchip have allowed manufacturers to custom-design prosthetics that feel more like the real thing. Some can even respond to electrical signals from the brain routed through the remaining limb's nerves.

Now in development are artificial limbs that can transmit the sensations of pressure and vibration from the prosthetic back to the wearer's muscles. Not only do these limbs feel more realistic, they can have the added benefit of eliminating the odd and unpleasant sensation that so many amputees experience—that of having a phantom limb.

PEOPLE WHO CHANGED HISTORY

Henrietta Lacks (1920-1951)

Reproducing deathlessly in laboratory cultures, the human cells known as HeLa have been used to develop drugs for polio and leukemia, map genes, perfect in vitro fertilization, and in myriad other ways. If all the HeLa cells ever grown were laid end to end, they would circle the Earth three times. The cells all come from one woman: Henrietta Lacks, a Virginia tobacco farmer who died of cervical cancer in 1951. Doctors harvested her cancer cells without her consent. Now, more than 60 years later, Lacks's descendants sit on a panel that approves access to data from the HeLa genome.

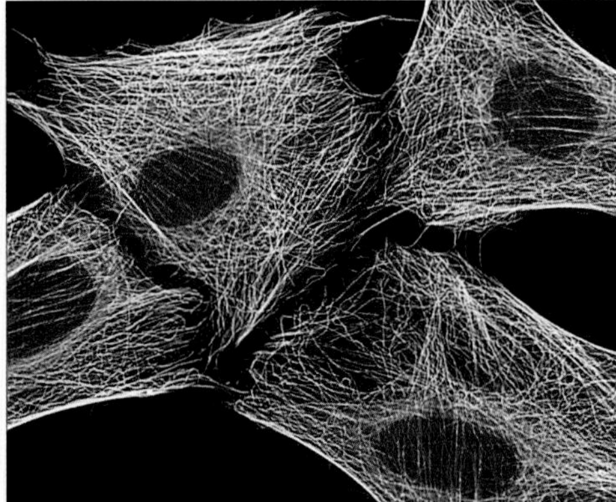

Magnified and colorized HeLa cells

Muscle-Rub Ointment

DRIED AND MIXED WITH SUGAR, OIL OF WINTERGREEN RELEASES A BRIEF BURST OF LIGHT (TRIBOLUMINESCENCE) WHEN SMASHED.

Massage a muscle-rub cream into a sore shoulder, and your skin feels cold and then hot. That's because most contain a counterirritant, a substance that makes pain recede by creating a competing sensation of coldness or heat. Some, such as Tiger Balm, rely on menthol for this distraction. In many others—ointments such as Bengay and Icy Hot—the primary ingredient is methyl salicylate, or oil of wintergreen. The compound is related to the active ingredient in aspirin and is produced by many plants, including the minty-smelling wintergreen, where it may deter browsing animals. Today the chemical can be synthesized, sparing the plant.

Liniments have been around a long time. Medieval physician Paracelsus created one called opodeldoc that contained camphor and wormwood and was still in use in the 20th century. Native Americans reputedly used wintergreen leaves to treat aches and pains; early colonists steeped the leaves in hot water to brew a soothing tea. In 1898, French doctor Jules Bengué introduced Bengay as a commercial preparation to the United States.

But user beware: A little methyl salicylate goes a long way. In large amounts it's toxic, and people who overdo the lotion have been hospitalized.

UNCOMMONLY KNOWN ...

DNA LEGOs DNA has often been called the building block of life. Now, it is literally the building block of . . . building blocks. Scientists at Harvard University exploited the genetic molecule's structure—the fact that each of its bases links only to one other base—to create LEGO-like DNA bricks. One day such microscopic blocks might form electrical circuits or drug-delivery devices.

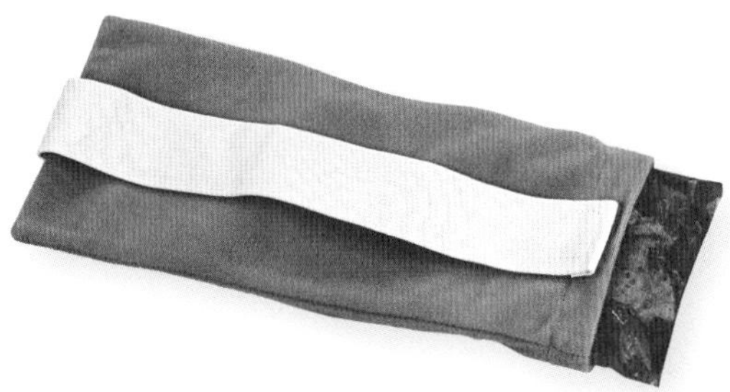

Hot and Cold Packs

SOME HOT AND COLD PACKS ARE FILLED WITH GRAINS OF WHEAT, WHICH HOLD HEAT AND COLD FOR A LONG TIME.

The first line of defense for an injured muscle or joint is often a cold pack to reduce blood flow and fight inflammation and swelling, followed by a hot pack to promote healing and relax muscles. Homemade therapies often employ bags of frozen peas and hot-water bottles to achieve the cold and hot effect. However, a handy hot and cold pack will do the same thing with less muss and fuss.

New York pharmacist Jacob Spencer was the first to invent a reusable soft pack that could go from cold to hot and back again. As a sales representative visiting hospitals, he saw doctors and nurses filling latex gloves with ice to make instant cold packs, with all the mess that entailed. In 1971, Spencer filled a tough plastic envelope with a neutral gel, dyed it blue simply

because it looked pretty, and marketed it as the first reusable hot and cold pack. Chilled in the freezer or warmed in the microwave, hot and cold packs are flexible enough to be bent around a sore arm or shoulder. Today they often come with sleeves that can be securely wrapped around the injured area to deliver relief exactly where it is needed.

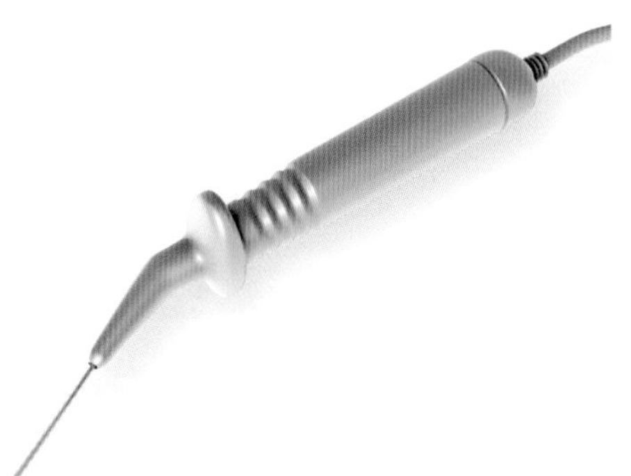

Laser Surgery

SEMICONDUCTOR LASER RAZORS OCCASIONALLY APPEAR ON THE MARKET, BUT A PRICE TAG IN THE HUNDREDS OF DOLLARS DETERS MOST MEN.

When American physicist Theodore Maiman invented the first working laser in 1960, many people joked that it was "a solution looking for a problem." Lasers had a science-fiction appeal but no immediate application. Doctors appreciated the fact that the devices produce a concentrated, high-intensity beam of light that cuts like the sharpest scalpel but with little blood loss. However, the early devices were inconsistent and hard to control.

The scientific world probably didn't anticipate that the first successful medical use of this high-tech device would be tattoo removal. In 1963, dermatologist Leon Goldman described successfully obliterating a tattoo. Within a year, ophthalmologists were using the beams to stop the spread of abnormal blood vessels in the retina.

Today lasers are widely employed in medicine. Directed through optical fibers, they can substitute for scalpels to cut away tumors or precancerous growths. They're a mainstay in eye and skin surgery, used to remove port-wine birthmarks or to weld detached retinas back in place. One of the most common kinds of laser surgery is LASIK (laser-assisted in situ keratomileusis), in which the cornea is reshaped to correct vision. After cutting a flap in the cornea, the surgeon removes tissue with a cool ultraviolet laser until the eyeball is the desired configuration. Each laser pulse removes less than 1/100,000th of an inch of tissue—precision no scalpel can match.

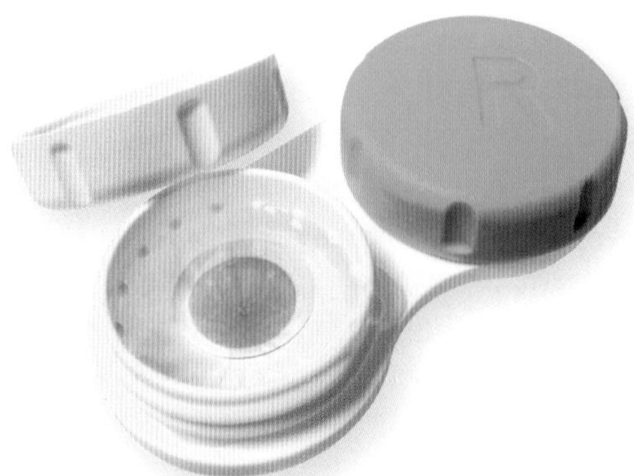

Contact Lenses

SCIENTIST RENÉ DESCARTES IN 1636 SUGGESTED CORRECTING VISION BY PRESSING A WATER-FILLED GLASS TUBE DIRECTLY AGAINST THE EYEBALL.

Comfortable contact lenses are a recent innovation, but the idea that something pressing on the eyeball could change vision has been around for a long time. No less an inventor than Leonardo da Vinci, in his 1508 *Codex of the Eye,* noted that a person might alter his vision by dunking his head into a bowl of water.

By the late 19th century, precision glass-cutting made actual contact lenses possible. Swiss physician Adolf Fick fitted the first such lens in 1888. They did correct vision, but the glass lenses were wide and heavy, covering the entire eyeball and blocking oxygen from the eye's surface. After a few hours, they were acutely painful.

The development of lightweight, scratch-resistant plastics in the 20th century spelled relief for lens wearers, though lenses still covered the whole eye. It didn't occur to lens makers that smaller lenses would stick to the eyeball until 1948, when English optician Kevin Tuohy accidentally broke off the outer rim of a lens. He tried it in his wife's or his own eye (stories differ) and discovered that it easily adhered to the cornea.

From that point on, advances in thin, soft, water-permeable materials such as silicone hydrogel have given us increasingly comfortable contact lenses. The latest tissue-thin lenses can be worn for a few weeks, tossed out, and replaced with a fresh, clean set.

WHAT'S INSIDE?

Decaf Coffee

Caffeine, possibly the world's favorite stimulant, is a natural component of coffee. For some people, it's the essential part. For others, it's a jitter-producing distraction. In 1906 German merchant Ludwig Roselius patented the first technique for removing the caffeine from coffee beans. His method used benzene (now known to be a carcinogen) as a solvent to extract the stimulant from the green, unroasted beans. Today coffee loses its kick in one of two ways. A water-based process filters out the caffeine, then returns the flavor-rich liquid to the beans. The direct solvent technique bleeds out the caffeine with chemicals, such as ethyl acetate or carbon dioxide, that target only caffeine and leave the flavor behind.

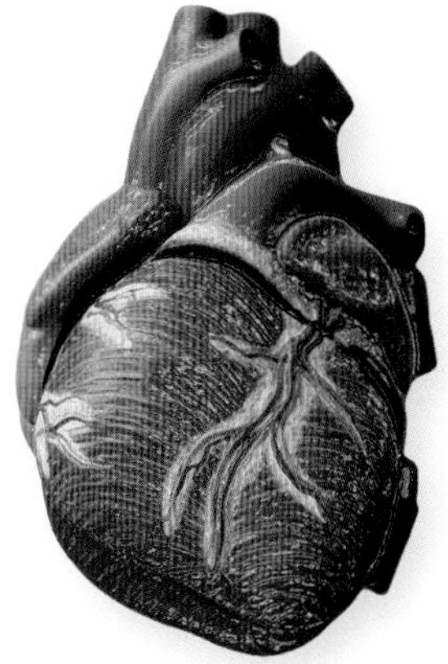

Heart Transplant

IN 1984 CALIFORNIA SURGEONS TRANSPLANTED A BABOON HEART INTO AN INFANT KNOWN AS BABY FAE. SHE LIVED FOR THREE WEEKS.

Two major problems stood in the way of the earliest heart transplants. First, surgeons needed to keep the organ and recipient alive while the heart was detached. In 1953 Philadelphia surgeon John Gibbon, Jr., used a heart-lung machine to sustain a patient for 27 minutes while his heart was being repaired.

More serious than the surgical challenges was the problem of tissue rejection. In the 1960s and 1970s, immunosuppressant drugs began to address that issue, sometimes at the patient's expense. In 1967, South African surgeon Dr. Christiaan Barnard won acclaim after he transplanted the heart of a 25-year-old accident victim into the chest of Louis Washkansky, a 55-year-old man with heart failure. Washkansky's immunosuppressives left him open to pneumonia, and he died 18 days later. In the years after, similar problems meant that the majority of transplant patients died within months.

In the 1970s and 1980s, better drug regimens began to boost survival rates. Today, average life expectancy for a heart transplant patient is 13 years.

Reduce, Reuse, Recycle

Recycling has a modern ring to it, but it's a practice as old as civilization. Aside from the occasional wasteful aristocrat, most people in history couldn't afford to throw away useful materials. They repaired them, reused them, or reworked them into new objects. This tradition has been revived in recent decades as our wasteful habits have caught up with us. Old tires now become springy playground surfaces. Soda bottles are spun into clothing. Compostable organic matter replaces plastic. We haven't yet gotten to the point where everything old is new again—but we're working on it.

Polar Fleece

MAKING POLYESTER FROM RECYCLED BOTTLES USES LESS ENERGY THAN MAKING IT FROM SCRATCH.

Once ridiculed as the source of double-knit suits, polyester fiber has made a comeback as an ecologically responsible fabric. Polyester fleece is not only a warm, practical cloth: It can be made from recycled soda bottles.

Polyester is a class of synthetic, petroleum-based polymers invented by British scientists and developed commercially by the DuPont corporation. In the form of polyethylene terephthalate (PET), it's used in a wide variety of products, including plastic bottles. Extruded into fibers, it becomes a wrinkle- and moisture-resistant fabric. In the 1980s, manufacturers found a way to use PET in the fluffy, warm fabric marketed as Polartec or polar fleece. However, PET's basis in fossil fuels and its nonbiodegradable qualities meant that it wasn't an environmentally friendly substance.

Polyester, however, is. In the 1990s the Patagonia company, one of the largest marketers of polyester fleece clothing, began to incorporate recycled soda bottles in its fabric; about 25 go into each fleece jacket. Bought from local recyclers, the bottles are sorted by color, sterilized, and chopped up. The chips are heated and

UNCOMMONLY KNOWN ...

PLASTIC ADDICTS Americans throw away 32 million tons of plastic a year, mainly in the form of containers and packaging, including many of the 29 billion water bottles we buy each year. Only 9 percent of plastic waste is recycled, though the percentage is higher for PET plastics: Thirty-one percent of those bottles and jars are reused. Recycling just one plastic bottle saves enough energy to power a 60-watt lightbulb for six hours.

pressed through spinnerets to make the polyester fibers, then dried and knitted into a fresh new fabric. The fleece itself can also be returned and recycled, gaining a second life as a blanket, cap, or cozy top.

Playground Surfaces From Tires

IN 1983 A MOUNTAIN OF TIRES NEAR MOUNTAIN FALLS, VIRGINIA, CAUGHT ON FIRE AND BURNED FOR NINE MONTHS. CLEANUP TOOK 20 YEARS.

Kids are hard on playgrounds, but not as hard as playgrounds are on kids. Each year, more than 200,000 children visit the emergency room with playground injuries, almost half of them serious ones such as fractures and concussions. Most of these traumas come from falls, so the playground's surface is a major factor in determining whether a child has a soft landing or a broken arm or cracked skull.

Playgrounds are found everywhere from the inner city to suburban adventure parks, and their surfaces range from utilitarian to luxurious. Dirt, grass, and asphalt make for cheap but rough terrains. More often, a well-maintained playground cushions falls with sand, wood chips, or, increasingly, rubber mulch made from ground-up tires.

In the United States alone, about 290 million tires are discarded annually. These bulky, nonbiodegradable items use up landfill space, breed mosquitoes, and sometimes catch on fire. Fortunately, most tires are burned for fuel or recycled, including the 8 percent that are ground up into springy nuggets. This rubber mulch is now widely used in landscaping and under recreational equipment. It cushions falls from up to 14 feet (as opposed to wood chips, which can handle a 6-foot drop) and makes an afternoon at the playground a happier experience for everyone.

PEOPLE WHO CHANGED HISTORY

Bill McKibben (1960-)

Bill McKibben is a writer and environmental activist whose 1989 book, *The End of Nature,* was one of the first popular works to lay out the facts of climate change. After an early career as a staff writer for the *New Yorker,* he began to work as a freelance writer covering the environment and technology. He is a founder of 350.org, a grassroots organization devoted to raising awareness of climate change (and named after the maximum desirable level, in parts per million, of atmospheric carbon dioxide). McKibben frequently leads rallies and spent three days in jail after protesting a proposed oil pipeline. He was awarded the Gandhi Peace Award in 2013.

Bill McKibben, 2006

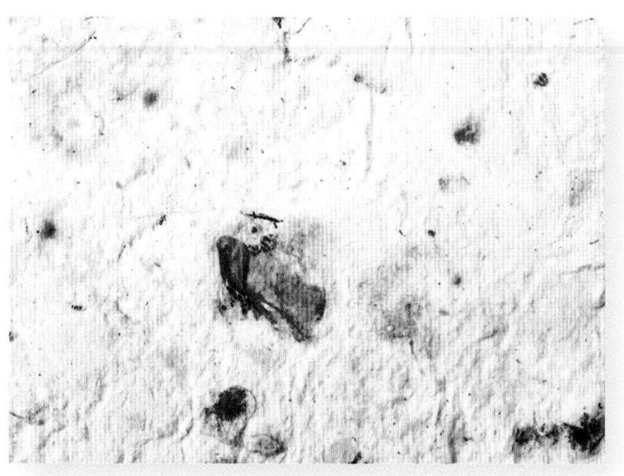

Rag Paper

RAGS FOR PAPERMAKING WERE IN SUCH HIGH DEMAND IN THE 18TH CENTURY THAT SOME COUNTRIES FORBADE THEIR EXPORT.

Long before *recycling* entered the modern vocabulary, papermakers were reusing cloth rags to make high-quality writing materials. Tradition credits Chinese court official Ts'ai Lun with inventing paper around A.D. 105. Previously, court scribes had written on heavy, expensive silk. Ts'ai Lun made his material from mulberry bark, hemp, cloth rags, and fishing nets that were pulped, soaked, and dried on a screen. From China, the craft spread to the Arab world, reputedly after Arab captors forced two Chinese prisoners to give up their papermaking secrets in 751.

By the Middle Ages, water-powered paper mills made the process practical on a large scale throughout Asia and Europe. Into the 19th century, hemp, linen, and cotton rags were the basis of most paper. Ragpickers, or rag-and-bone men, traveled the streets with their wagons, scavenging discarded rags and reselling them. Beginning in the mid-1800s, pulp paper mills, using cellulose from wood, took over paper production. Rag paper is now a luxury item, used for stationery and currency.

WHAT'S INSIDE?

Biodegradable Trash Bags

Handy and cheap, plastic trash bags are a boon to the household, but they are a serious bane to the environment. Americans alone toss out 200 millions tons of garbage each year, much of which ends up in landfills encased in polyethylene bags. Many estimates claim that it will take as long as a thousand years for buried plastic bags to break down.

Biodegradable or compostable trash bags provide a limited solution to this problem. Some have additives that force the plastic to disintegrate over time. Others are made from corn or potato starch and break down in a compost heap. However, virtually nothing, no matter what it's made of, will decay quickly in the airless depths of a landfill. The most ecofriendly option is to reduce waste as much as possible.

Compost

COCKROACHES CAN BE USED TO SPEED ALONG THE COMPOSTING PROCESSES, SINCE THEY INGEST ALMOST ANYTHING AND EXCRETE A RICH "FRASS."

Another ancient idea has become new again. The use of decaying, nutrient-rich organic matter as fertilizer is as old as agriculture itself. The Bible contains the parable of a man who instructs his gardener to cut down a barren fig tree. The worker tells him, "Sir, let it alone for one more year, until I dig around it and put manure on it." New England's settlers plowed thousands of rotting fish into their soil to enrich it; George Washington, a devoted farmer, experimented with different types of compost until he arrived at his favorite, a combination of sheep dung and "black mould from the Gulleys on the hillside."

After German chemist Justus von Liebig discovered in the 1840s that nitrogen is a key plant nutrient, chemical fertilizers began to supplant compost on big farms. But interest in more natural methods never died out on smaller farms and gardens. In the mid-20th century, British agronomists Sir Albert Howard and Lady Eve Balfour separately spurred a resurgence of interest in sustainable farming with their books on the best practices of composting. Howard's recipe of three parts plant matter to one part manure, layered and turned regularly, is still widely followed.

Entire cities have now gotten into the business, collecting biodegradable waste, composting it, and reselling it to gardeners and farmers at a profit. San Francisco alone composts about 250,000 tons of its citizens' garbage each year. Sold to local vineyards, yesterday's coffee grounds become part of tomorrow's cabernet.

UNCOMMONLY KNOWN ...

CLAY CHAI CUPS The ultimate in recycling, India's handmade clay teacups are designed to be used only once and then smashed. In some places, the cups are known as *pi ke puht*—"drink and chuck." Around the country, chai *wallahs*—young tea servers—on street corners and in train stations dispense the drink in these single-use vessels. Because they are used only once, the cups are more sanitary than glasses; returning to the clay from which they are made, they are better for the environment than plastic cups.

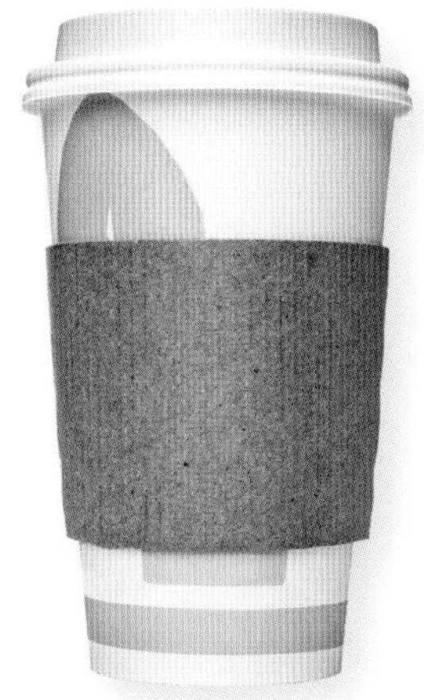

Compostable Coffee Cup

PLA PLASTIC IS USED NOT ONLY IN COFFEE CUPS BUT ALSO AS A KEY MATERIAL IN 3-D PRINTERS.

Pour hot coffee into a paper cup, and you'll soon find yourself with a handful of scalding liquid. Pour it into a plastic cup and you're safe, but you're also adding to the world's permanent trash. The more sustainable solution is a paper cup with a biodegradable plastic liner, now found in some ecologically conscious products.

A commonly used such liner is PLA resin, made from polylactic acid, which in turn is derived from cornstarch or sugarcane. PLA has been around for a long time. It was discovered in 1932 by DuPont chemist Wallace Carothers, famed for his invention of nylon, but it was too expensive to produce commercially. In 1989 American inventor Patrick Gruber discovered a cheaper way to make it after brewing it on his kitchen stove. Cups lined with PLA won't decompose in a backyard compost heap, but at the high heat of a city compost center, they'll return to the earth.

Fiberglass

CRUSHED WASTE GLASS IS KNOWN AS CULLET; THE WORD MAY COME FROM THE OLD TERM *COLLET,* A NECK OF GLASS LEFT ON THE BLOWING IRON.

Fiberglass is a versatile substance made from a versatile ingredient: spun glass. Fiberglass wool makes excellent insulation; formed into sheets, it can be molded into ceiling panels or boat hulls (as in a kayak). By incorporating glass waste, fiberglass also helps recycle glass containers.

Historically, glassmakers have guarded their secrets, but the pioneer of spun glassmaking had no such compunction. French 18th-century polymath René Antoine Ferchault de Réaumur—entomologist, industrialist, and inventor of the temperature scale that bears his name—developed the process for spinning molten glass into fibers using a rotating wheel. He was trying to make artificial heron feathers, not fiberglass, but he predicted that one day, flexible glass fibers could be woven into fabric.

By the 20th century, German manufacturers were producing fiberglass insulation, and in the 1930s the process was made more efficient by the U.S. company Owens Corning, which came to dominate the market. Today the industry is a significant buyer of the 11 million tons of glass that Americans discard each year.

Rain Barrel

ONE INCH OF RAIN, RUNNING OFF 1,000 SQUARE FEET OF ROOF, YIELDS 623 GALLONS OF FRESH, MINERAL-FREE WATER.

The household rain barrel has an old-fashioned air about it. American pioneers and Depression-era farmers were often pictured washing their laundry in the soft water collected in the barrel; water from rain barrels fed vegetable gardens and sluiced down dusty yards. The barrels have made a comeback in recent years, particularly among homeowners in drought-prone landscapes and those looking to conserve water in general.

Collecting rainwater is an ancient practice. Villagers built cisterns to gather runoff as long ago as the Stone Age. Ancient Roman villas typically collected rainwater in an *impluvium,* a basin built into the floor of the dwelling's open atrium. Beneath it, an additional cistern might collect overflow. Decorated with mosaics and marbles, these pools could be quite lovely—Pompeii has a building known as the House of the Beautiful Impluvium. The vast Basilica Cistern, built under the streets of Constantinople (now Istanbul) in the sixth century A.D., is also known as the Sunken Palace because of its grandeur.

In the developed world, modern sanitation and municipal water systems have put rainwater collection largely into the hands of city planners. However, conservation-minded homeowners often turn to small rain barrels to catch runoff from a downspout. The barrels may themselves be recycled from whisky or wine barrels or from plastic food containers. Cleaned and screened to keep out mosquitoes, they take on new life in the freshwater business.

UNCOMMONLY KNOWN ...

DUSTMEN Along with rag-and-bone men, England's cities also benefited from dustmen. These scavengers literally collected dust—ashes and cinders left over from household wood and coal fires and discarded on dust hills in the street. Larger cinders were sold to brickmakers, and the finer dust was added to manure. Far from being reimbursed for this service, dustmen themselves paid for exclusive collection rights. The word "dustman" later came to mean anyone hired to carry away garbage.

Bamboo

BAMBOO GROWS FAST BUT FLOWERS RARELY. ONE SPECIES FLOWERS AT THE SAME TIME IN ALL LOCATIONS EVERY 130 YEARS.

The very qualities that make bamboo a pest—its adaptability, its rapid growth and spread, its ability to rebound after cutting—also make it a versatile renewable resource. Part of the grass family, bamboo's 1,400 species are found around the world, though most flourish in Asia. It is the world's fastest-growing plant. The hollow stem is famous for shooting skyward at almost visible speed, up to three feet a day. Cultivated bamboo needs little water or fertilizer and few pesticides. With its weblike roots, it grows well on steep hillsides, stemming erosion.

Bamboo's utility is not news to Asian cultures. Bamboo furniture and weapons date back more than 3,000 years in China; bamboo strips were used to write on before the invention of paper. Today the material is increasingly found in the West in a wide range of products: flooring, fabric, utensils, laptop cases, bicycles, and more. Entire houses, flexible and earthquake proof, have been built from bamboo. The ancient plant is gaining a new and environmentally minded audience.

Fake It Till You Make It

Diamonds are forever, we're told, but so are fake diamonds. These days, expensive, high-quality materials have met their match in clever knockoffs. Silver plate looks like the real thing. Artificial fur is as soft and warm as its animal counterpart. Even ersatz champagne and caviar, though they might not fool a gourmand, are convincing and tasty as party treats. Faux materials are not only generally less costly, they're ecologically healthier for the planet as well. Only occasionally does the fakery cross the line: Don't try to make that counterfeit money at home.

Synthetic Diamonds

EVEN RARER THAN EARTH'S NATURAL DIAMONDS ARE THOSE FROM OUTER SPACE, FOUND IN DUSTLIKE SIZES IN SOME METEORITES.

Diamonds glitter nicely in a gold setting, but they have far more uses than engagement ring bling. As the hardest-known naturally occurring material, they make ideal drill bits and abrasives and form a part of many lasers and transistors. Natural diamonds are so rare and expensive, however, that inventors have long sought to make their own.

Natural diamonds are formed from carbon atoms, crushed and heated for at least a billion years in the enormous pressures of the Earth's mantle. In the 1950s, scientists at General Electric were the first to consistently produce synthetic diamonds, using a powerful press that induced 1.5 million pounds per square inch and temperatures of 2000°C (3630°F).

Today, high-pressure, high-temperature (HPHT) presses turn out diamonds chemically identical to those found in nature, at far less cost. A low-pressure method known as chemical vapor deposition is also gaining ground: It grows sheets of diamond crystals using carbon-rich gas. Though rarely larger than one carat, they shine just like the real thing, and on occasion have fooled even experienced jewelers.

WHAT'S INSIDE?

Counterfeit Money

Counterfeiting used to be a complex criminal enterprise requiring special printing plates and presses. Now, anyone with a scanner and a printer can make a middling $100 bill. Counterfeit currency requires two things: sharp printing and the specialized rag paper that gives greenbacks their characteristic feel. Some do-it-yourself counterfeiters get around this second problem by using real currency. After bleaching the ink off old $1 or $5 bills, they reprint them with scanned images of $20 or $100 bills. These won't have the anticounterfeiting features such as 3-D ribbons of real bills, but they can pass muster if not scrutinized closely.

Vegetarian Leather

THE MYTHICAL NAUGA, THE CREATION OF MADISON AVENUE ADVERTISING, SUPPOSEDLY SHED ITS SKIN ONCE A YEAR TO SUPPLY NAUGAHYDE.

Leather—tanned animal skin—is a versatile material, tough, soft, and water resistant. It makes great boots, coats, and handbags. People who won't wear anything that once had a face often turn to fake leather to gain the same advantages. This vegetarian "pleather," as it's often known, has come a long way since its beginnings as a particularly stiff form of upholstery.

Faux leathers are a blend of plastic and fabric. One of the earliest successes in the field was Naugahyde, a vinyl-coated fabric invented at the U.S. Rubber Plant in 1914 and once widely used as a tough, waterproof upholstery fabric. In the 1960s, ads featuring the supposed Nauga animals from which the upholstery was made were so popular that some people were convinced the creatures were real.

Most early faux leather fabrics were coated with polyvinyl chloride and were notorious for their stiffness and for trapping sweat. Increasingly the fabrics are imbued with polyurethane instead, which is softer, more natural looking, and friendlier to the environment. Under the name polyleather, vegetarian leather can be seen on the catwalk in designer outfits that sell for thousands of dollars.

UNCOMMONLY KNOWN ...

DIAMONDS AND GRAPHITE Diamonds are transparent and, at 10 on the Mohs hardness scale, are the hardest natural substance. Graphite is matte black and very soft, with a rating of 1 or 2 on the Mohs scale. And yet the two minerals are sisters under the skin, both made of pure carbon and chemically identical. The difference lies in their crystal structures. The carbon atoms in diamonds are arranged in strongly bonded tetrahedrons. Graphite's carbon atoms form hexagonal rings in layers that split apart easily, which is why graphite makes both a good lubricant and soft pencil lead.

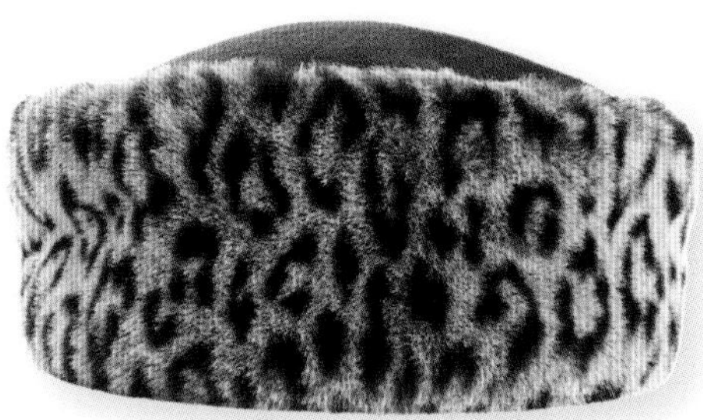

Fake Fur

HOW TO TELL REAL FUR FROM FAKE: THE TIPS OF REAL HAIRS SHARPEN INTO A POINT. ALSO, FAKE FUR SMELLS LIKE PLASTIC WHEN IT'S BURNED.

In the 1990s, nude celebrities in magazine ads declared, "I'd rather go naked than wear fur." The campaign, sponsored by People for the Ethical Treatment of Animals (PETA), marked a turning point in public attitudes toward wearing animal pelts.

Fake fur became the politically conscious choice.

For warmth, weather resistance, and sheer sumptuous comfort, it's hard to compete with the real thing. Though fur was humans' first covering, it evolved into a luxury item through the ages. By the 20th century, fur coats were coveted more as status symbols than as practical outerwear.

A federal tax on fur, imposed after World War I, spurred manufacturers to develop alternatives. Early versions of faux fur, dull and dense, were crafted from alpaca hair. In the 1950s, improved artificial fabrics took over. Acrylic polymers could be extruded in threads, cut, and dyed to look like the real thing. Today's soft, water- and fire-resistant modacrylics allow supermodels and ordinary folks alike to wear "fur" in good conscience.

PEOPLE WHO CHANGED HISTORY

Robert Jarvik (1946-)

Robert Koffler Jarvik, inventor of the first artificial heart, entered the field of medicine as a designer rather than as a clinician. At Syracuse University he studied architecture and mechanical drawing before eventually enrolling at the University of Utah for a medical degree. Joining the Division of Artificial Organs at the University of Utah Medical Center, he began crafting mechanical hearts. The Jarvik-7, jointly designed with Dr. Willem Kolff, became the first mechanical heart implanted in a human being. In 1982, it kept dentist Barney Clark alive for 112 days.

Dr. Robert Jarvik holding the Jarvik-7, 1984

Pergo

LAMINATE FLOORS CAN LOOK LIKE WOOD, STONE, OR TILE, COMPLETE WITH TEXTURES AND EDGES IMPRINTED INTO THE TOP LAYER.

It's not hardwood, but laminate flooring can pass for real wood if you don't look too closely. It achieves this realism thanks to photographic technology, which allows ultrasharp images of wood grain (or stone or other surfaces) to be printed on a film that forms part of the composite floor.

Pergo is the most familiar name in laminate floors; its parent company pioneered the material in the early 20th century. Founded as a beechwood refiner in Sweden, Perstorp Industrial Group originally produced laminate for use in radio cabinets in the 1920s. Not until the 1970s did laminate take off in flooring, and even then it looked plastic and false. Better printing improved the wood-grain look until, by the 1990s, it appeared authentic.

Laminate floors have four layers. The bottom layer is a moisture-proof backing. Above it is the core: high-density fiberboard imbued with resin.

Applied on top of that is the thin layer that contains the high-resolution image of the desired wood grain. Covering all is a transparent, waterproof, scratch-proof wear layer. All four sheets are stacked on an assembly line, fused together by a hydraulic press at 600 pounds per square inch and heated to 400°F. After the compressed sheets cool, they're cut into planks and shaped with tongue-and-groove edges so that even the most inept homeowner can fit them together.

UNCOMMONLY KNOWN ...

FOOL'S GOLD More properly known as iron pyrite, fool's gold has led many a would-be prospector astray. The shiny, brassy ore looks superficially like gold when embedded in rock, but a few simple tests distinguish it from its precious lookalike. Pyrite forms in sharp-sided crystals, unlike the nuggets or flakes of gold. Strike it with a steel hammer, and it gives off sparks; scratch it vigorously, and it smells like sulfur. If the mineral you find does these things, don't bother taking it to the bank.

Vermeil

ORMOLU IS SIMILAR TO VERMEIL, BUT AN ORMOLU OBJECT IS BRONZE, NOT SILVER, BENEATH A LAYER OF GOLD.

After Oliver Cromwell overthrew the British monarchy in 1649, his government melted down the gold in the crown jewels and sold off the gems. Officials were rather disgusted to find that Queen Edith's crown, an 11th-century heirloom, was "formerly thought to be of massy gold, but upon trial found to be of silver gilt." They assessed it at a mere £16.

Silver gilt objects, also known as vermeil, are in fact quite valuable. To be classified as true vermeil today, an object must consist of a sterling silver base coated with at least two and a half microns of ten-carat gold. Gold by itself is heavy and soft. By covering silver with gold, metalsmiths can create jewelry, utensils, and artworks that are lighter and stronger—not to mention cheaper—than solid gold.

Gilding silver is an ancient art. Homer's *The Odyssey* mentions the technique: "As when a man overlays silver with gold . . . even so the goddess shed grace upon his head and shoulders." Although an object can be gilded simply by applying hammered gold leaf onto its surface, a chemical process known as fire-gilding was the standard from ancient China into modern times. The metalworker dissolves gold into heated mercury, or quicksilver, then spreads the amalgam over the object's surface. The object is placed in an oven or over an open fire, and the mercury evaporates, leaving behind a thin gold coating that can be polished into smoothness. Unfortunately, this technique produces highly toxic mercury fumes, a well-known hazard of the gilding profession. John Webster's 1612 play, *The White Devil,* mentions "a gilder that hath his brains perished with quicksilver."

Today's vermeil is typically produced by far safer electrolysis. The silver object and a bar of gold are both immersed in a solution; when an electric current passes through the solution, gold ions attach themselves to the silver. Metalsmiths then burnish the vermeil object, smoothing and polishing to create a high-shine finish.

Sheffield Plating

THE SHEFFIELD COMPANY OF CUTLERS STILL EXISTS. IT IS HEADED BY A MASTER CUTLER, WHO HAS TWO WARDENS, SIX SEARCHERS, AND 24 ASSISTANTS.

Before electroplating took over as the process for adding a silver layer to cheaper metals, a canny English metalsmith from Sheffield named Thomas Boulsover devised the handy silverplating process that came to be known as Sheffield plating. Boulsover was a member of the Cutlers' Company, a guild of craftsmen who produced "Knives, Blades, Scissers, Sheeres, Sickles, Cutlery wares and all other wares and manufacture made or wrought of yron and steele."

As the story goes, in 1743 Boulsover was repairing a copper and silver knife when he accidentally melted its handle and the pieces fused. When Boulsover pressed the melted metals, they rolled out as one, although the copper and silver layers were still distinct.

Boulsover realized that he could shape this copper-silver substance into all sorts of plated objects—buttons, tea caddies, candlesticks, and the like—at a fraction of the cost of pure silver. When copper was sandwiched between two layers of silver, the resulting bowls or cups would be silver inside and out. The layered edges were then covered with silver wire.

Sheffield plate became a booming business, employing many metalworkers in the Yorkshire city. Apprentices would train for years, graduating to full-fledged craftsman status by creating a single masterwork on their own. After electroplating made Sheffield plating obsolete, "old Sheffield plate" became a collector's item. Aficionados know to look around the edge of an antique for the raised seam where the silver was folded over the telltale copper layer.

Alcohol-Free Champagne

THE JAPANESE COMPANY B&H LIFES MAKES A NONALCOHOLIC, CATNIP-SPICED WINE FOR CATS CALLED NYAN-NYAN NOUVEAU.

Many people enjoy a bit of the bubbly on special occasions. What's a New Year's party without a champagne toast? But sparkling wine contains—well, wine—and wine contains alcohol, and many

WHAT'S INSIDE?

Fake Crabmeat

Fake crabmeat doesn't contain any crab, but it does contain a host of ingredients that go through an elaborate sequence of mashing, flavoring, and coloring. The primary component is processed white fish, known as surimi. The fish, usually pollock, is cleaned and minced; sugar or sorbital keeps it from breaking down when frozen. Flavorings, egg white, and other ingredients are added as the fish is reduced to a paste. Rollers press the paste into sheets, which are cooked and sliced. Paprika, caramel, and other colorings give the surimi its pinkish-orange tinge. Finally, it's steamed and vacuum-packed, ready for sushi or salads.

folks can't or won't drink alcohol. For teetotalers, some wine producers make alcohol-free beverages that can stand in for the more intoxicating drinks.

Nonalcoholic wines had a poor reputation until the 1980s, when some producers began to compete more seriously against their alcoholic counterparts. In 1986, for instance, J. Lohr's ARIEL Blanc won a gold medal in a competition against traditional wines. Since then, a number of vineyards have added a nonalcoholic line.

Nonalcoholic wine starts as regular wine, proceeding through the entire fermentation process, which produces alcohol. To remove it, sometimes the wine is passed through a filter; other times it's spun in a cylinder to separate out the alcohol, which is then boiled off. At that point, water or grape juice is usually added to the flavorings to reconstitute the wine. To bring sparkle back to sparkling wine, the wine is fermented a second time. This second fermentation adds in a tiny amount of alcohol. In fact, all nonalcoholic wine made by these processes will retain a small but measurable percentage of alcohol. People who abstain completely should stick to alternatives, such as sparkling juice.

Fake Caviar

FAKE CAVIAR CERTAINLY BEATS REAL CAVIAR IN PRICE. RUSSIAN CAVIAR SELLS FOR AS MUCH AS $100 AN OUNCE; FAKE CAVIAR, ABOUT $2.

Caviar has long been synonymous with a certain kind of elite dining. Less glamorously known as fish eggs, or roe, by tradition the only true caviar comes from sturgeon, particularly the sturgeon of the Caspian and Black Seas. The salty little eggs have been coveted as a delicacy for centuries in the aristocratic households of Russia and Europe. So popular was it that the once plentiful sturgeon had been fished out of its traditional grounds by the late 20th century. For people who wanted to conserve fish species or just didn't eat animal products, an alternative arrived: seaweed caviar.

Seaweed caviar starts with kelp, a fast-growing underwater plant with a gelatinous texture. After it's harvested, the kelp is dried, ground into a powder, and mixed with salt, flavorings, and water until it becomes a thick liquid. Extruded through nozzles into black pearls that look remarkably like roe, the faux caviar is rinsed, pasteurized, and popped into elegant little jars. Consumers can choose from a variety of flavors, including spicy chili and ginger—though they would surely be considered heresy by the Russian royalty of old.

Beastly Facts

Human ingenuity has given us marvelous inventions, but no one beats Mother Nature when it comes to spectacular design. A shark's conveyor-belt teeth; a hummingbird's swiveling wings; a hippo's antibiotic sweat: These adaptations and countless more are testaments to the creativity of the natural world. It's hardly surprising. Human civilization has been around for only a few millennia, while animals have had millions of years to evolve into the array of shapes and abilities they now possess. As observers, we're just beginning to understand their infinite variety.

Chameleon Tongues

MANY CHAMELEONS HAVE SCALY MANES OR CRESTS ON THEIR HEADS; THEIR NAME COMES FROM THE GREEK FOR "LION ON THE GROUND."

Chameleons are famed for their color-changing abilities, but perhaps not enough appreciation is given to another remarkable characteristic: their extra-long, super-speedy tongues.

These lizards are found in warm regions around the world and live mainly in trees, where their five toes give them a firm grip. They excel as predators, with two adaptations giving them a particular advantage. Their pivoting eyes can focus on insects, their preferred food, up to 30 feet away. Once within range, they unleash their tongues. Accelerating from 0 to 20 feet per second in 20 milliseconds, the hollow appendage can unfurl to nearly twice the lizard's body

PEOPLE WHO CHANGED HISTORY

Joseph Priestly (1733–1804)

English chemist and clergyman Joseph Priestley was an independent thinker who applied the same scrutiny to religion and politics as he did to science. In the 1770s, while living next to a brewery with a handy supply of carbon dioxide, he began to study the nature of gases. Eventually he was the first to identify ten gases, most famously oxygen. His support of the American and French revolutions prompted a mob to destroy his house and laboratory in 1791. Priestley soon moved to the United States, whose government he thought "relatively tolerable." He died in Pennsylvania.

Joseph Priestley, 1795

length. Specialized muscles propel the tongue forward; the sticky end traps the unsuspecting insect; then retractor muscles pull it back into the chameleon's mouth, where the tongue folds up like an accordion. The tongues of some small chameleons are said to have the highest power output by weight of any other animal known.

Penguin Knees

SOME PREHISTORIC PENGUINS WERE AVIAN GIANTS, STANDING AS TALL AS SIX FEET AND WEIGHING 250 POUNDS.

A human watching a penguin waddle stiffly across the Antarctic landscape might wonder how evolution came to design such an incredibly awkward animal. A penguin is a bird that cannot fly. It has to clamber over challenging terrain, but it doesn't seem to have knees. When it wants to get somewhere fast, it flings itself down on its chest and toboggans down a slope. Where's the evolutionary sense in that?

The reason for all these odd adaptations becomes clear when a penguin enters the water. The birds are superbly adapted water creatures, their bodies beautifully shaped for life beneath the waves. Penguins broke off from other bird species at least 60 million years ago as their bodies began to adapt to an oceanic environment. Their bones became solid and heavy to give them negative buoyancy while diving. Wing bones fused together as the flight appendages became flippers. Feathers grew dense and waterproof, covering a generous layer of fat. Penguin blood evolved to hold enough oxygen to sustain a big bird underwater for 27 minutes. And, yes, penguins do have knees—but they're hidden beneath the bird's thick lower feathers. Only the bottoms of their legs and their clawed feet are visible. This helps a penguin's body keep its streamlined shape: comical on land but spectacularly graceful in the sea.

Shark Teeth

THE LARGEST SHARK TEETH ON RECORD—OVER SEVEN INCHES LONG—BELONG TO THE EXTINCT MEGALODON, A CENOZOIC-ERA PREDATOR.

When a great white shark opens its jaws for a savage bite, the sight is made even more terrifying by its row on row of serrated teeth. All sharks, ranging from top predators like the great white to gentle giants like the whale shark, have ranks of disposable

teeth that are replaced continuously throughout their lifetimes. This is possible because the teeth aren't embedded in the jawbone, but instead arise from a membrane in the gums. As each tooth grows, the newer tooth behind pushes the older one forward, conveyor-belt style, until it reaches the front ranks in the jaw. After anywhere from eight days to a few months of wear and tear, the forward tooth drops out and is replaced by the one behind it. (The cookiecutter shark, famous for its round bite, loses a whole jaw's worth at once.) Some sharks go through 30,000 teeth during their lives.

This rare arrangement may be a seal's nightmare, but it's a paleontologist's dream. Because sharks have cartilage, not bony skeletons, their teeth are the only part of their anatomy that remains in the fossil record.

WHAT'S INSIDE?

Squid Ink

When a squid needs to flee from a predator, it covers its tracks with a marvelous defense: a cloud of ink. Many different cephalopods, including octopuses and cuttlefish, possess ink sacs containing a combination of the dark pigment melanin, mucus, and chemicals that can affect an attacker's senses of taste and smell. A threatened squid will release the ink along with a jet of water from its siphon. In some cephalopods, the ink forms a kind of smokescreen that obscures the escaping animal. In others, it takes on a blobby squidlike shape known as a pseudomorph, or false body, which confuses the predator as the real squid zigzags away.

Polar Bear Skin

LEGEND HAS IT THAT POLAR BEARS COVER THEIR TELLTALE BLACK NOSES WHEN HUNTING, BUT RESEARCHERS HAVE NEVER OBSERVED THIS.

The far north has its fair share of white animals—arctic foxes, hares, even beluga whales—but none is more impressive than the polar bear. *Ursus maritimus* is the largest land carnivore, with some males growing close to ten feet long and weighing up to 1,600 pounds. Surviving in temperatures well below zero, the polar bear relies on several adaptations to keep from freezing, including a heavy layer of fat, thick fur, and coal black skin.

This black skin is the polar bear's secret, hidden beneath its dense coat. A black nose and the black pads of its paws are the only outward clues to its existence. The dark color may help keep the bear warm by soaking up any sunlight that eventually reaches the skin. Just as helpful is the bear's fur, the hairs of which are not actually white but transparent. Each hollow hair scatters visible light like snow to create a white effect. (In warm weather, a bear might turn green for a while as algae grows inside the hairs.) At one time, it was thought that the tubelike hairs served as mini-fiber-optic cables, channeling light and warmth directly to the bear's dark skin, but research has disproved this enticing theory. However, by trapping and scattering light so effectively, the hairs keep the bear's body heat close to its skin. In fact, researchers have difficulty spotting polar bears with heat-sensing night-vision goggles because the bears' fur traps heat so well. Chilly on the outside, the bears blend well into their chilly surroundings.

Tiger Stripes

UNLIKE ZEBRA STRIPES, TIGER STRIPES GO ALL THE WAY INTO THE SKIN. A SHAVED TIGER STILL SHOWS THE SAME PATTERN.

According to Hathi, the elephant in Kipling's *The Jungle Book II,* the earliest tiger was a peaceful, golden fellow: "In those days the First of the Tigers ate fruit and grass with the others. He was as large as I am, and he was very beautiful, in colour all over like the blossom of the yellow creeper. There was never stripe nor bar upon his hide in those good days when this the Jungle was new." From an evolutionary viewpoint, there may be some truth in this classic fiction. Tigers share a distant ancestor with stripeless, cat species such as lions and cougars. However, by the time tigers reached their current habitats in Asia and attracted the notice of wary humans, they had acquired the black-on-gold stripes that are their distinguishing characteristic.

The irregular markings probably serve as camouflage in a sun-dappled, grassy environment, helping the cats to sneak up on prey. Stripes vary in color and shape not only from one subspecies to the next, but also from one animal to the next. Just like humans and their fingerprints, no two tigers have the same pattern of stripes.

Researchers take advantage of this difference to track individual tigers. Using images of the elusive creatures captured by camera traps, scientists employ software to map each tiger's markings in three dimensions and compare them to images in a database. With this information, conservationists can monitor tiger populations and possibly catch poachers as well.

UNCOMMONLY KNOWN ...

CHOW TONGUES Most dogs have pinkish or spotted tongues, but the ancient Chinese breed known as the chow, or chow chow, sports a characteristic blue-black tongue. The only other dog with a similarly dark tongue is the shar-pei, also a Chinese breed. DNA studies of domestic dogs suggest that both breeds are ancient ones, more closely related to wolves than most other dogs. Whether this accounts for their black tongues is still a mystery.

Hippo Sweat

HIPPOS ARE ONE OF THE MOST DANGEROUS ANIMALS IN AFRICA. THE AGGRESSIVE CREATURES CAN RUN UP TO 20 MILES AN HOUR ON LAND.

The hippopotamus lives an in-between life. It's a land mammal most comfortable in the water, a social creature in the river but a solitary one on shore. (The Greeks called it the "river horse.") Although

it looks something like a big, stocky pig, its closest evolutionary relative is the whale. The ancestors of both hippos and whales split off from even-toed land animals some 60 million years ago.

Hippos spend up to 16 hours a day staying cool in rivers, lakes, or mud. Observers have long been puzzled by a strange phenomenon that appears when the animals come ashore to bask or to graze: They seem to be sweating blood. Roman naturalist Pliny the Elder suggested that the river horse, being "over-gross and fat," deliberately pricked itself on sharp reeds to let blood and relieve its "superfluous humours." On land, hippos' thick, almost hairless skin does exude a distinctly orange-red liquid that in time dries out and turns brown. Intrepid scientists who swabbed the faces and backs of the aggressive creatures have discovered that the thick secretions aren't sweat but a protective substance given off by glands under the skin. When the fluid emerges, it's colorless, but gradually orange and red pigments become visible to give it a bloody look. Chemical analysis shows that the secretions not only act like sweat to cool the hippo, but also work as a sunscreen and an antibiotic for the animals' vulnerable skin, inhibiting the growth of dangerous bacteria. Still, too much sun will crack a hippo's hide, so eventually even the best lubricated river horse has to return to the water.

UNCOMMONLY KNOWN ...

FEATHERIES The earliest golf balls were solid wood, but by the 1600s, British craftsmen came up with "featherie" balls. Three pieces of horsehide or cowhide were sewed into a sphere, leaving a small hole into which was stuffed enough chicken or goose feathers to fill a top hat. The ball, then soaked in water, hardened as it dried—and could cost as much as a golf club.

Hummingbird Wings

SOME HUMMINGBIRDS MIGRATE THOUSANDS OF MILES. THE TINY FLIERS CAN STAY IN THE AIR FOR UP TO 22 HOURS AT A TIME.

For sheer acrobatic skill, no other birds can match hummingbirds. They can fly at more than 30 miles an hour. The blurringly fast motion of their wings, beating up to 200 times a second, produces the zooming or humming sound that gives them their name. Courting hummingbirds can dive at 60 miles an hour. Unlike other birds, they can hover indefinitely in the air, fly backward, and even fly upside down.

Just how they do this wasn't evident until high-speed photography came along and researchers could study them in slow motion. They saw that hummingbird wing strokes were unlike those of other birds. Instead of flapping up and down, generating lift from each downstroke, hummingbird wings pivot forward and backward, rotating up to 140 degrees in a figure-eight motion. The birds are actually twisting their "wrists," which are located close to their shoulders inside the upper wing. Each downstroke gives them 75 percent of their lift; each upstroke adds 25 percent. Tiny variations in the angle of the wings allow them to change direction instantly, back up, or even fly inverted when they're fighting another hummingbird.

Other specialized body parts support this high-speed maneuvering. Hummingbirds' chest muscles make up more than a quarter of their weight, and their hearts are enlarged to support the heavy demand for blood. Their feet are tiny, keeping total weight down; hummingbirds can perch with them but not walk. They're designed for flight, and their flight is a thing of beauty.

Dolphin Brains

OTHER SPECIES, INCLUDING SEALS, SEA LIONS, AND BIRDS SUCH AS THE DOMESTIC CHICKEN, EXHIBIT ONE-SIDED SLEEP PATTERNS.

Some people are said to sleep with one eye open, alert to danger, but dolphins do this every day. In the 1960s, researchers noticed that the marine mammals closed one eye, then the other, but rarely both as they slept. Two decades later, using electroencephalographs, they discovered that only half a dolphin's brain entered slow-wave sleep at any one time. The other half registered normal waking activity. Typically dolphins sleep about eight hours a day, alternating brain hemispheres every two hours or so. They can even coordinate their sleep with other dolphins as they swim in pairs. One dolphin will keep an eye open on one side while its partner's eye is closed, and vice versa, switching when they change positions.

Sleep is a scientific mystery, and researchers aren't sure why any animal does it—but wakefulness is particularly important for underwater mammals. Not only do they need to be alert for predators, but they may need to be awake in order to breathe, a process that involves consciously opening their blowholes at the surface. The alternating sleep pattern seems to keep dolphins perpetually attentive and fresh. After five straight days of sleep observations, noted one study, "the dolphins were in much better shape than the scientists."

PEOPLE WHO CHANGED HISTORY

Jacques Cousteau
(1910–1997)

Known for his trademark red cap, ocean explorer Jacques Cousteau was instrumental in bringing undersea conservation to public awareness. During World War II, Cousteau gained early fame as the co-inventor (with Émile Gagnan) of the Aqua Lung scuba apparatus. After the war, he converted a minesweeper into the research vessel *Calypso* and began to travel and film underwater life. His book *The Silent World* (1953) and the documentary of the same name brought him worldwide attention, augmented by the hugely popular television series of the 1960s and 1970s, *The Undersea World of Jacques Cousteau*. Later in his life, Cousteau became a leader in the fight to restrict whaling and undersea nuclear dumping. After his death at the age of 87, a street in Paris was renamed "rue du Commandant Cousteau."

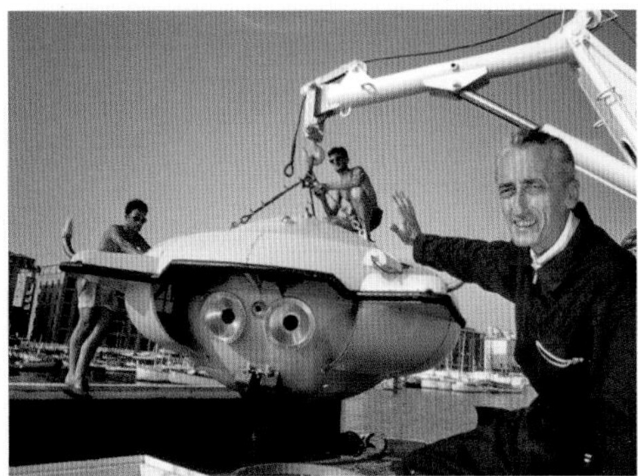

Jacques Cousteau with his research sub in Puerto Rico, 1960

I am not a glutton–
I am an explorer of food.
–ERMA BOMBECK (1927-1996)

Incredible Edibles

We're fairly discriminating about what we eat. A life-preserving defense that has evolved over thousands of years causes us to reject anything that looks, smells, or tastes "off." But fancy packaging, media hype, and long-standing tradition can short-circuit those defenses, telling us that even the most questionable-looking, -smelling, or -tasting foods are acceptable. Not all of the foods we look at in this chapter will appeal to everyone at first glance, sniff, or even taste, but each has proven highly edible over time—whether a few decades or several millennia.

Curious about junk food? You'll find out what really goes into a Twinkie and discover how a prohibition law led to the creation of Coke. You'll also learn that condiments are a multicultural lot. It's not surprising that soy sauce traces its roots to China—but so does ketchup. And maple syrup and sriracha were both born in the United States. We'll take some of the mystery out of "mystery meat" by revealing what goes into head cheese (head, yes; cheese, no), bologna, and sweetbreads. You'll find out that eating bugs isn't strange for many of the world's people, nor is it new. Eating dirt is common—and probably always has been. Then there's the matter of fugu, the Japanese fish so naturally poisonous that several people each year die after eating it. The sour taste of fermented foods like yogurt or sourdough bread would normally be a danger sign, but such foods have been safely consumed for thousands of years. And finally we look at the so-called good-for-you foods that seem new but aren't. The seitan in the vegetarian substitute for turkey, for example, was made in seventh-century China, and the kale that's a recent fad was familiar in ancient Rome. In this chapter you'll discover edibles that are incredibly diverse and can be incredibly appetizing. It's a matter of taste.

Junk Food

The Merriam-Webster dictionary defines junk food as "food that is high in calories but low in nutritional content." That is certainly true of every food featured in this section. Still, that hasn't stopped Americans from scarfing them down in epic amounts. On average, each American consumes about 44 gallons of soda per year, more than 20 pounds of candy, and maybe 150 hamburgers—and that's not counting the fat-laden cheese and special sauce on many of them. Cheese curls and Twinkies, like all the other foods in this section, aren't good for you. But they're so tasty that you might not care.

Cola Drinks

THE NAME OF THE TOP SELLER, COCA-COLA, COMES FROM THE MAIN INGREDIENTS IN ITS ORIGINAL FORMULA, KOLA NUTS AND COCAINE.

Colas are the world's most popular carbonated soft drinks, but they weren't the first ones. Parisians drank naturally carbonated spring water flavored with honey and lemon in the 1600s. By the 1800s several artificially carbonated drinks were available at drugstore soda fountains. Ginger ale and root beer were also around before the first colas were made in the 1880s. But those drinks and their inventors are footnotes in the story of an industry dominated by the beverage invented by an Atlanta physician and pharmacist.

Owner of a pharmaceutical company after the Civil War, John Pemberton wanted to produce new potions to improve health. He created French Wine Coca in the 1880s, describing it as "the most excellent of all tonics" and advertising it as a cure for a host of maladies. It was a mix of extract of coca leaves, wine, and kola nuts—a version of a similar French concoction. The drink was well received and established a customer base in the Southeast. Unfortunately for Pemberton, Prohibition came to Atlanta in 1886. He was forced to remove wine from the drink and sweeten it with sugar syrup. Pemberton also changed the name of the drink to Coca-Cola—and the rest, as they say, is history.

Several other cola drinks followed, including Pepsi in 1898 and Royal Crown in 1905. In today's colas, a mixture of citrus oils and spices stands in for the flavor of kola nuts, and caffeine is a legal substitute for the cocaine in the original recipe. But it hasn't hurt. Colas easily outsell every other type of soda worldwide.

Gummi Bears

HARIBO, THE FIRST GUMMI BEAR MAKER, IS A CONTRACTION OF THE INVENTOR'S FIRST NAME, HANS, LAST NAME, RIEGEL, AND CITY, BONN.

German confectioner Hans Riegel wasn't the first person to make soft candies. Centuries earlier soft candies made from sugar and rice starch were produced in Japan and China. Turkish Delight, a chewy candy formed from sugar and cornstarch, was well known in Europe from at least the turn of the 19th century. Several other soft, fruity candies were popular in Britain (Wine Gums) and in the United States (Chuckles) during the first decades of the 20th century.

Riegel quit a partnership in another confectioner to start his company, Haribo, in 1920. He set out to produce his own version of a soft, gelatin-based, fruit-flavored candy, and he had a singular idea to set his candy apart from the rest: make it in the shape of dancing bears. Gummi bears hit the market in 1922, and sales grew steadily. By World War II, Haribo's gummi bears were enjoying success across Germany. However, the candy business suffered during the war, and Riegel himself passed away in 1945. But the plant in Bonn was left intact, and his sons took over the business. During the postwar years, Haribo expanded as the bears gained popularity throughout Europe. That popularity spread to the United States by the 1980s. Several imitators have cropped up in recent decades, including the Jelly Belly gummi bear and Trolli's gummy worms in the 1980s. But Haribo remains the gummi candy leader, turning out 100 million of the tiny bears every day.

PEOPLE WHO CHANGED HISTORY

Ray Kroc (1902–1984)

As the founder of McDonald's restaurants, Ray Kroc changed the way Americans eat. In 1954, Kroc was selling industrial mixers and visited the California restaurant of two of his best customers, Maurice and Richard McDonald. Kroc was impressed by the assembly-line methods the brothers used to make their hamburgers, cheeseburgers, french fries, and milkshakes.

Kroc, an Illinois native, talked the McDonalds into allowing him to create a group of drive-in hamburger restaurants using their methods and name. The first of his restaurants opened in Des Plaines, Illinois, on April 15, 1955. By 1960 there were 200. Today there are more than 36,000 McDonald's in more than 100 countries worldwide, employing nearly 2,000,000 people.

Ray Kroc pioneered expansion of the fast food industry by standardizing and automating the production process. He created a chain of restaurants for people who wanted to eat out but didn't want to spend a lot of time or money doing it. Kroc didn't invent most of the methods that initially made McDonald's successful, but he recognized their importance when he saw them, and he applied them on a larger scale than ever before.

Ray Kroc, 1975

Popsicles

THE TWO-STICK POPSICLE WAS INVENTED DURING THE GREAT DEPRESSION SO TWO KIDS COULD SHARE A FIVE-CENT TREAT. IT WAS DISCONTINUED IN 1986.

Popsicles are enjoyed by kids—but they might also have been accidentally invented by one. In 1905, so the story goes, 11-year-old Frank Epperson was using a powdered mix and water to make a sweet drink. He left the cup containing the drink, along with the wooden stick he was using to stir it, outside on a chilly northern California night. In the morning he found the mixture frozen in the cup around the stick—the first frozen treat on a stick.

Epperson went into real estate as an adult, but made his "ice lollipops" on the side. After introducing the treat at an amusement park, where they were well received, he patented the "Eppsicle" in 1924. He later changed the name to "Popsicle," reportedly because that's what his children had nicknamed their father's frozen treat. In 1925 Epperson formed a partnership with a company to distributed his Popsicles. But needing money after the 1929 stock market crash, he sold his patent rights. Today the Unilever Corporation owns the Popsicle brand, but the word has entered the language as the generic term for all ice pops. Trendy shops now advertise flavors ranging from tangerine to beet to avocado. But the top-selling Popsicle remains cherry.

WHAT'S INSIDE?

Twinkies

The original 1930 recipe for Twinkies included natural ingredients. Over time, because of the need to extend the shelf life of the cakes, artificial ingredients were substituted for most of the natural ones. Today Twinkies contain some 39 ingredients—none of them milk or butter. Twinkies are sweetened with corn syrup, and held together by monoglycerides and diglycerides: emulsifiers that keep the ingredients from separating. Artificial butter flavors the cake, and artificial vanilla flavors the cream. Cellulose gum keeps the cream creamy; sorbic acid prevents mold.

Sandwich Cookies

OREOS ARE THE WORLD'S BEST-SELLING COOKIE. A STACK OF ALL THE OREOS EVER MADE WOULD REACH TO THE MOON AND BACK FIVE TIMES.

There were many kinds of cookies before sandwich cookies existed, and the exact origin of the sandwich type isn't known, but one of the earliest was likely the linzer cookie. It derived from the linzer torte,

UNCOMMONLY KNOWN ...

FIRST CAFFEINATED DRINK In Europe this first drink was chocolate, not tea or coffee. When Spanish conquistadors reached Mesoamerica in the early 1500s, the Aztec introduced them to a savory drink made with cacao beans. Spanish ships brought the beans back to Spain, but many Spaniards found unsweetened chocolate unpalatable. One wrote that it was "a bitter drink for pigs." Chocolate gained popularity after sugar was added, and by the 17th century, chocolate beverages were enjoyed all over Europe.

a nut cake with raspberry filling that debuted in Linz, Austria, in the 1600s. Some food historians believe the sandwich cookie may have descended from Victorian sandwich cakes, popular in the latter half of the 19th century, that combined two layers of sponge cake with jam in between.

For most of the past few hundred years, cookies were baked at home for special occasions. Because of the expense of ingredients and time required for preparation, they weren't the common treats they are today. By the early 1900s, new technology and cheaper prices for sugar and other ingredients made commercial cookie production possible. That's when sandwich cookies came into their own.

In 1908, Sunshine Biscuits introduced what it called an "upscale" confection—a creamy filling sandwiched between two crunchy, elegantly embossed chocolate wafers. It was called Hydrox. Four years later, National Biscuit Company made a knockoff and called it the Oreo. Sales of Oreos quickly surpassed Hydrox because of a superior publicity campaign—and a less clinical-sounding name.

Today there are several popular brands of sandwich cookies, including Kellogg's Vienna Fingers, Pepperidge Farm's Milanos, and the Girl Scouts' Do-Si-Dos.

Funnel Cake

TODAY MOST FUNNEL CAKES ARE DUSTED WITH POWDERED SUGAR. IN THE MIDDLE AGES, THEY WERE OFTEN DRIZZLED WITH SYRUP AND SALT.

Funnel cakes, a staple at fairs and festivals, take their name from the funnel that's used to create them. The ropes of fried dough that form funnel cakes are made from batter that is squeezed through a funnel into hot oil. No one knows when the first funnel cake was made, but a similar recipe was in circulation in medieval Europe. A basic recipe from an English cookbook circa 1390 instructs the cook to pour a batter into a bowl with a hole at the bottom, then let the batter fall into hot oil and "frye it wel."

It's likely that early settlers in North America were familiar with funnel cakes. They brought the recipe from Europe and made them occasionally. Enjoyed through the generations, they were still a treat in some American homes in the late 19th and early 20th centuries.

Many people now associate funnel cakes with the Pennsylvania Dutch. Some food historians believe that link was forged at the Kutztown Folk Festival in the 1950s, which highlighted the culture of the Pennsylvania Dutch. Originally

of German heritage, they commonly ate funnel cake as a breakfast or mid-morning pastry. Along with other traditional foods offered at the festival, funnel cakes helped fulfill the proclamation to "eat till ya ouch."

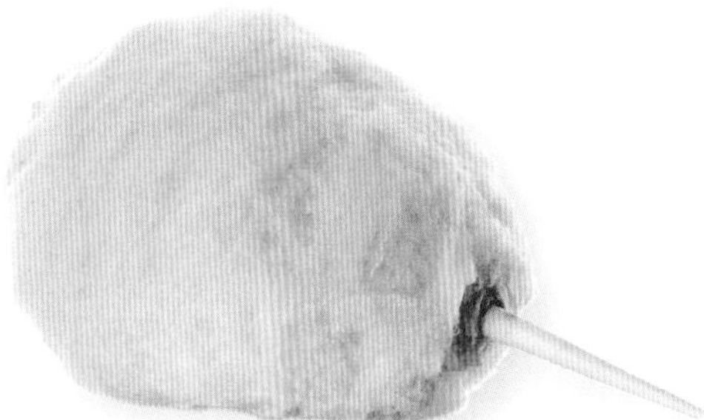

Cotton Candy

"COTTON CANDY" IS THE COMMON NAME IN THE UNITED STATES AND CANADA. IT'S "CANDY FLOSS" IN GREAT BRITAIN AND "FAIRY FLOSS" IN AUSTRALIA.

Cotton candy is basically spun sugar, which has been around since at least medieval times. Back then, confectioners melted sugar, then poured it in thin streams to create delicate strands that dried into beautifully intricate desserts. Until the turn of the 20th century, spun sugar was always produced by hand. However, the advent of machines that made the sugar-spinning process easier also made cotton candy possible. Invention of the first machine is usually credited to John C. Wharton and William Morrison, who developed it in the late 1890s. The spinning machine forced melted sugar through the small holes of a screen, creating thin filaments. A bowl-shaped barrier trapped the threads, which formed a pile of lacy fluff as they cooled. The confection, initially called fairy floss, was introduced at the 1904 World's Fair in St. Louis, where almost 70,000 servings of it were sold. By 1920 in this country, fairy floss had become cotton candy.

The machines that make the sweet treat have come a long way. Today they heat sugar to 300°F and spin it out at almost 3,500 revolutions per minute. The result is very thin filaments of spun sugar, undreamed of in the past. Cotton candy now comes in a rainbow of colors and in flavors ranging from traditional cherry to sour apple and bubblegum.

Cheese Curls

CHEETOS COME IN A VARIETY OF SAVORY FLAVORS, INCLUDING CHEDDAR JALAPEÑO, CHILI LIME, AND NOW CINNAMON-SUGAR SWEETOS.

The cheese curl is one of those foods that was created by accident and then became an American favorite. Cheese curls are basically cornmeal and water that is cooked and then extruded through a die. As the long puffy ropes come out of the machine, a knife cuts them into pieces. The pieces curl as they're baked or fried; then they get a spritz of oil and a dusting of salt and seasonings such as cheese powder.

Curls were born serendipitously in the 1930s during the making of livestock feed at Wisconsin's Flakall Company. To prevent the feed-making machine from clogging, workers periodically poured a slurry of cornmeal mush into it. When the machine got hot, it spit out the mush as puffy ribbons that hardened as they hit cooler air. A machine operator named Edward Wilson gathered some of the crunchy ribbons and took them home, where he added salt and flavorings. Recognizing the potential of Wilson's discovery, Flakall began to sell the ribbons as a snack called Korn Kurls. By the 1950s they'd become widely known. Today Frito-Lay produces the most popular cheese curls, Cheetos.

PEOPLE WHO CHANGED HISTORY

Gregor Mendel (1822–1884)

Gregor Mendel was a 19th-century botanist and cleric who discovered the key to plant heredity. In the mid-1800s, he experimented with pea plants to determine how physical traits pass from one generation to the next. The experiments established the basic rules needed to create a hybrid—a cross between two or more parent plants that creates a new variety with desired characteristics. Tangelos (tangerine and pomelo or grapefruit) and tayberries (blackberry and red raspberry) are delicious examples of hybrids.

Painting of Gregor Mendel in his garden

Candy Bars

THE WORLD'S MOST POPULAR CANDY BAR IS SNICKERS, WITH RECENT ANNUAL SALES OF 5.5 BILLION BARS EARNING $3.5 BILLION.

It's impossible to know precisely when and where the first candy bar was made. Thousands of years ago, people in places as widespread as China and Egypt made sweet treats from fruit, nuts, and honey. Today, though, when we think of candy bars, we generally think about chocolate. Until the mid-1800s chocolate was consumed only as a sweetened drink. In fact no one knew how to make solid chocolate until 1847, when Joseph Fry & Sons discovered a recipe for making a chocolate paste that could be molded into bars. Fry mixed Dutch cocoa (alkalized cocoa powder) with melted cocoa butter and sugar to create the first chocolate bar. Though they were more bitter and coarse than modern candy bars, Fry's innovation led the way for future chocolatiers.

The first commercially produced chocolate bars in America came from the factory of Milton Hershey in Pennsylvania. Hershey made chocolate coatings for caramels in the early 1890s. Then, after finding a formula for manufacturing milk chocolate cost-effectively, his factory began to churn out the iconic Hershey milk chocolate bar in 1900. Today in the United States, the Hershey's milk chocolate bar remains at the top of the chocolate heap.

Condiments

A condiment is used to enhance the flavor of food. That covers a lot of territory: everything from innocuous table salt to searingly hot sriracha. People have used condiments such as soy sauce and vinegar for thousands of years. Some newer condiments, such as Vegemite, are less well known—and far less widely loved. Ketchup and mustard are ubiquitous favorites, showing up on restaurant tables, food-truck counters, and in school cafeterias. Common or otherwise, condiments have interesting stories to tell—a smorgasbord of flavor-enhancement history.

Maple Syrup

IN THE 1950S THE UNITED STATES PRODUCED 80 PERCENT OF THE WORLD'S MAPLE SYRUP; TODAY IT'S CANADA THAT PRODUCES ABOUT 80 PERCENT.

Maple syrup is the concentrated sap of various species of maple trees, especially the sugar maple. European settlers learned about syrup from Native Americans, who tapped the maples in early spring when the sap started to rise. People collected the sap, which is 98 percent water, in hide or birch-bark buckets, then placed heated rocks in the buckets to steam off enough water to concentrate the liquid into thicker, sweeter syrup. Native Americans used maple syrup to sweeten their foods, and the regional cooking of New England reflects that history, with maple syrup–flavored dishes such as baked beans and squash and pumpkin casseroles.

Maple sugaring still occurs early each spring. The process is less labor intensive than in bygone years, but the commercial product remains expensive: It takes about 40 gallons of sap to make a single gallon of syrup. In the 1950s and 1960s, cheaper "pancake syrup," made mostly with substitute sweetener and artificial color, gained popularity. The recent emphasis on natural foods has meant increased demand for pure maple syrup.

UNCOMMONLY KNOWN ...

KETCHUP The Chinese created the first sauce called *ke-tsiap*, but it wasn't tomato based. It was a fish sauce made from salted, fermented anchovies; a recipe for ketchup dates to the sixth century. British traders brought it to Europe in the 1700s. Tomato ketchup didn't come along until the early 1800s—after Europeans and Americans lost their fear of the "poisonous" New World vegetable.

Sriracha

NASA SENDS THE CHILI SAUCE CONDIMENT INTO SPACE FOR THE ENJOYMENT OF ASTRONAUTS AT THE INTERNATIONAL SPACE STATION.

Sriracha is a hot sauce made of jalapeño chili peppers, garlic, vinegar, salt, and sugar. It's named for Si Racha, a town in Thailand that's home to a well-known chili paste. There are several brands of sriracha, but the first and best known in the United States was created in California in the 1980s by David Tran, a Vietnamese immigrant.

Tran began making hot sauce in his native country a decade earlier. It was a family operation, with his brother growing the peppers and Tran mixing up the sauce and bottling it for sale to local restaurants and retailers around Saigon. In the late 1970s politics caught up with him and his sauce business. An officer in the South Vietnamese army during the Vietnam War, Tran found it uncomfortable to remain in Vietnam after the communists came to power. He and his family immigrated to the United States, ending up in California in 1979. Unable to find a decent job, he fell back on what he knew best: making hot sauce. He began by producing the fiery, garlicky condiment on a small scale in his home. It caught on quickly, and by the early 1980s he was off and running. Tran expected his main clients to be Vietnamese restaurants, but his booming success has shown sriracha's wide appeal. The company's state-of-the-art factory in Irwindale produces 20 million bottles of sauce a year.

UNCOMMONLY KNOWN ...

FAT-FREE DAIRY It's a fact: Dairy products naturally contain fat. "Fat-free" products are those from which most—but not quite all—fat has been removed. Fat-free or skim milk has less than 0.5 percent fat. Nonfat sour cream starts as skim milk and is thickened with gelatin or starches.

Mustard

MUSTARD SEED IS ONE OF THE FEW SPICES FROM A TEMPERATE CLIMATE. THE UNITED STATES AND CANADA ARE ITS MAJOR PRODUCERS.

The use of mustard seed goes back at least 3,000 years to ancient India and Sumeria. The early Egyptians seasoned their food with the seeds and even stocked King Tut's tomb with a supply of the spice for the afterlife. Mustard was also known in ancient Greece and Rome. Upper-class Romans mashed up mustard seeds and mixed them with wine. In Greece, the famous physician Hippocrates used mustard plasters to treat toothaches.

Various types of mustard grow in many parts

of Europe. In the early 1600s Dijon became the mustard-making capital of France. Two local men, Maurice Grey and Antoine Poupon, founded their company in 1777. Mustard came to America in the 1700s, and Americans took to it, primarily the savory brown variety. Charles Gulden, after a stint with a Union regiment at Gettysburg, began producing his iconic spicy mustard in New York City in 1862. Today there are scores of mustards of all shades, but Americans' favorite is yellow—especially at baseball games.

Soy Sauce

BASED ON SALES, SOY SAUCE IS THE THIRD MOST POPULAR CONDIMENT IN THE UNITED STATES, FOLLOWING BEHIND MAYONNAISE AND KETCHUP.

For untold millennia, the people of China preserved meat for the winter by packing it in salt. Juices that leached from these meats were used to enhance the flavor of other foods. The emergence of Buddhism in the first century B.C., with its emphasis on vegetarianism, created a need for a meatless version of the seasoning. Soybeans and grains were substituted for meat, and the resulting fermented sauce was salty and pungent and grew popular even among meat-eaters.

According to legend, a Japanese priest studying in China developed a taste for the sauce and took samples of it back to Japan. The Japanese people enjoyed it widely and began to brew their own around the 6th century. The saucemakers of Japan changed the recipe over time, and it eventually became a major component of Japanese cuisine.

The importation of soy sauce into the United States began in the 1800s, along with an increasing number of Asian immigrants. Chinatowns sprang up in many urban areas in the latter part of the century, and most non–Asian Americans got their first taste of soy sauce in the Chinese restaurants that opened in the following decades. Today soy sauce, once exotic, sits firmly in America's culinary mainstream.

Vegemite

VEGEMITE HAS YET TO CATCH ON IN THE UNITED STATES, BUT JARS OF IT CAN BE FOUND IN FOUR OUT OF FIVE HOMES IN AUSTRALIA.

Vegemite is a salty yeast spread developed in Australia after World War I as a substitute for Marmite, the same type of spread, which is produced when brewer's yeast from the beermaking process is removed

WHAT'S INSIDE?

Movie Popcorn Butter

It's hard to know what's really in the popcorn "butter" offered at most movie theaters, since theaters don't generally disclose the ingredients. Still, one thing is fairly certain about the yellow liquid: None of its ingredients has ever seen a cow. Movie popcorn butter is basically oil, with artificial butter flavoring added. The oily substitute does have at least one practical advantage over the real thing: It doesn't soak into the popcorn as much as actual butter does because its water content is lower; that keeps the popcorn from getting too soggy.

and concentrated. The Marmite Extract Company began producing it in England in 1902. The factory was located in Burton-upon-Trent, home to several breweries. Marmite became popular in early 20th-century Britain, which exported it to several other countries around the world, including Australia, where it quickly took hold. But German U-boat attacks on Western European shipping during the war disrupted trade, making it virtually impossible for Marmite to reach Australia. Suddenly there was a niche in the nation's food market to be filled.

Several attempts failed before Australian scientist Cyril Callister and his colleague, Fred Walker, teamed to develop a Marmite substitute in 1923 that they called Vegemite. The newcomer was not an instant success. It finally became a beloved staple during World War II, when the government included it in the ration packs of Australian soldiers. Posters featuring the homegrown spread went up all over the country with the slogan, "Vegemite: Keeping fighting men fighting fit." The condiment came to be associated with health, nationalism, and support for the war effort. Today it's the Aussie version of ketchup.

Vinegar

HENRY J. HEINZ MANUFACTURED VINEGAR ONLY TO PRESERVE THE PICKLES HE SOLD—UNTIL HE REALIZED THE CONDIMENT COULD SELL ITSELF.

The word "vinegar" comes from the French words *vin aigre*—"sour wine." Traces of the versatile liquid have been found on casks in Egypt and China that are thousands of years old. It's likely that the first vinegar was a fortuitous accident—a keg of wine might have been improperly stored, letting in oxygen. A biochemical reaction then created acetic acid, the sour wine. Vinegar has found myriad uses from ancient times onward as flavoring, medicine, preservative, and of course as a condiment. It was used to treat illness in early Babylon. In ancient Greece, wounds were disinfected with vinegar—as they were on U.S. Civil War battlefields.

What eventually becomes vinegar begins as fermented alcohol: cider, wine, or even beer. When bacteria overwhelms the alcohol, inadvertently or otherwise, vinegar is the acidic result. The label on a vinegar bottle usually tells what it's made from; red wine vinegar is made from red wine and apple cider vinegar from cider, for example. However, distilled white vinegar starts out as industrial alcohol.

Mystery Meat

Though we may laughingly choose to call them mystery meats, their ingredients are certainly not unknown to their producers or to many of their enthusiastic consumers. For others of us, to know them is not necessarily to love them. Less knowledge can sometimes be more appetizing (that might even apply to a nonmeat entry, tofu, that often stands in for meat; it is actually derived from plants). But by shedding light on how these underappreciated "mystery" foods are produced, some people may decide to investigate their primary selling point: their taste.

Head Cheese

A MEDIUM-SIZE SLICE OF HEAD CHEESE CONTAINS ONLY 45 CALORIES, THOUGH TWO-THIRDS OF THOSE CALORIES COME FROM SATURATED FAT.

Head cheese is a somewhat unappealing name for what many might consider a somewhat unappealing food. It's made from the boiled head of a pig or cow and has nothing whatsoever to do with cheese. Researchers have found recipes for head cheese dating from 17th-century Europe, where it's widely believed to have originated as far back as the Middle Ages. Unable to obtain the best cuts of meat, peasants learned to make use of animal parts that rich landowners spurned. The people used animals' heads, along with other bits and pieces, to make a hearty, nourishing meal.

Although it looks similar to sausage and cold cuts such as bratwurst and bologna and can be sliced in the same fashion, head cheese is made in a different way. An animal's head (minus eyes and brain) is simmered for several hours with onions, celery, and spices.

The meat is then pulled away from the skull, chopped, and placed in a sided container. The broth in which the meat cooked is poured on top, covering the meat. The broth contains collagen from the head's cartilage and bone marrow. Collagen causes the liquid to gel around the chunks of meat when the dish cools. Head cheese is generally served chilled or at room temperature.

Myriad cultures feature their own versions of head cheese, and it goes by many different names. In southwest Louisiana, Cajuns know it as "hog's-head cheese." The Pennsylvania Dutch pickle the meat first and call it souse. In Mexico it's *queso de puerco*. In France it's *fromage de tête*, in Germany *presskopf*, in Denmark *sylte*, and in England brawn. In Scotland, head cheese is known as potted heid.

Tofu

SOY AND QUINOA ARE THE ONLY TWO PLANTS THAT CONTAIN ALL NINE OF THE ESSENTIAL AMINO ACIDS THAT HUMANS NEED EACH DAY.

Tofu, also known as bean curd, is essentially curdled—spoiled—soy milk. It has been around for at least two millennia, and probably longer. A Chinese mural from the Han dynasty (206 B.C. to A.D. 220) depicts the making of soy milk and tofu. Historians believe tofu reached Japan sometime around the eighth century, introduced by priests who had journeyed to China to study Buddhism. (In Chinese, the *t* in "tofu" is pronounced as a *d*.) Bean curd became an important part of the vegetarian diet of the priests. On their return, Japanese nobility and the samurai warrior class enjoyed tofu as well. Beginning in the early 17th century, tofu gradually became popular throughout Japanese society.

The first printed reference to tofu in the West was found in a Spanish book from the 1600s, when Europeans were increasing trade with Asian countries. In the late 19th century, tofu was produced on a small scale in both France and the United States. The first commercial production of tofu outside Asia occurred in California in 1929. But the bean curd didn't gain broader appeal until the 1960s and rising public interest in healthful eating.

Tofu is made by soaking, crushing, and boiling dried soybeans. The mash is strained to yield soy milk, and coagulants are mixed with the milk to curdle it. Curds (solids) are separated from whey (liquid) and transferred into molds. Additional whey drains from the molds, leaving behind a soft, solid substance that can be cut into squares and stored in water. Tofu, which sometimes substitutes for meat, is considered healthful because it's high in minerals such as potassium, iron, and calcium. It's also a major source of protein, especially for the people of East Asia, where it's considered a staple.

PEOPLE WHO CHANGED HISTORY

Thomas Jefferson
(1743–1826)

When Michelle Obama became the First Lady, she started a program to encourage American children to eat healthier by incorporating more vegetables into their daily meals. Part of that program was the planting of a White House garden, inspired by the garden Thomas Jefferson planted at Monticello, his hilltop home in Virginia. Jefferson, who ate mostly vegetables, thought it was important for people to cultivate their own food. He kept a daily "Garden Kalendar" between 1809 and 1826, noting every change in his crops between planting and harvest. A section of the Obama White House garden is dedicated to our third president and contains plants grown from seeds or cuttings from Monticello. They include some of Jefferson's favorites: tennis ball and brown dutch lettuce, prickly seeded spinach, choux de milan cabbage, and green globe artichoke.

Portrait of Thomas Jefferson by Rembrandt Peale, 1805

Sweetbreads

SWEETBREADS NEVER ORIGINATE FROM OLDER ANIMALS, BECAUSE THYMUS GLANDS ATROPHY BY THE TIME THE ANIMALS TURN SIX MONTHS OLD.

Sweetbreads sound like a dessert but aren't. They are actually the thymus and, less often, pancreas of young calves, lambs, and pigs. They're considered offal—the internal organs that are left after an animal is butchered. The first recorded mention of sweetbreads dates back to 1578 in England, but humans have probably eaten sweetbreads for as long as hunters have eaten animals.

From written history, we know that disadvantaged people ate offal such as sweetbreads when they couldn't afford any other type of meat. But for people of means, offal was awful. They either threw it away or sold it for not much money to anyone who would buy it. Over the centuries, poor people of many cultures learned how to turn sweetbreads and other innards into surprisingly tasty dishes.

It's an understatement to say sweetbreads have never been wildly popular in the United States, but that's not the case elsewhere in the world. Today sweetbreads are savored across nations as diverse as France, Argentina, and Turkey, where they are grilled or barbecued. Although sweetbreads are a good source of protein, they are not the most healthful part of an animal to consume. For starters, they're high in saturated fat and cholesterol. What's more, they pack on calories. A single four-ounce serving of grilled beef sweetbreads contains 360 calories. By comparison, the same-size portion of sirloin has only 145.

UNCOMMONLY KNOWN ...

FREEZE DRYING Without changing the composition and structure of food, freeze drying removes water content, thereby retarding spoilage or making food lighter for camping or space travel. Archaeologists have found naturally freeze-dried food left centuries ago by the Inca in high mountain larders. Commercial freeze drying was developed during World War II to preserve blood plasma and medicines.

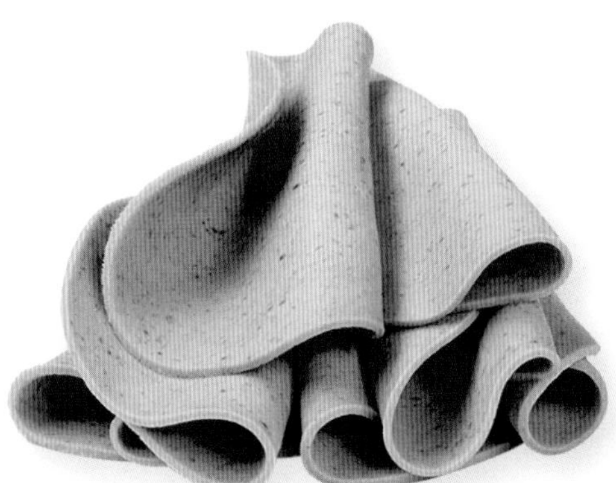

Bologna

BOLOGNA INCLUDES SPICES AND CHUNKS OF FAT, BUT THEY'RE GROUND UP SO SMALL THAT THEY ARE NOT INDIVIDUALLY RECOGNIZABLE.

The history of bologna begins with a European predecessor that made the city of Bologna, Italy, famous. Centuries before the cold cut we know today existed, there was mortadella, an Italian sausage made

WHAT'S INSIDE?

Tenderizers

Meat tenderizers are made of enzymes called proteases. They break the bonds between amino acids in complex proteins such as collagen, commonly found in the skin, bones, and connective tissue of animals. When collagen bonds are broken, the meat softens. Enzymes derived from fruit are the most common tenderizers. Actinidin, for example, originates from kiwis. Bromelain is extracted from pineapples. When they are processed into a powder and sprinkled on meat, the chemical reaction goes to work, taking some of the workload off our jaw muscles.

from pork that's traditionally ground into paste in a mortar. It's infused with bits of fat, peppercorns, and sometimes pistachios that are easily visible in slices of the meat.

Historians trace mortadella back to Bologna in the 1300s. But it's probable that even prior to that, similar sausage was prepared in the kitchens of monasteries and the wealthier classes; during the Middle Ages, mortadella was a fancy food reserved mostly for feast days and banquets. The first written recipe is dated 1557, and by the 1600s Bologna the city was renowned.

The bologna we eat in the United States is an inexpensive lunch meat made from scraps of pork or beef or both. It contains fat, salt, and a mix of spices similar to those in mortadella—including black pepper, celery seed, allspice, myrtle, coriander, and nutmeg. It's likely that the Americanized version of mortadella was created by Italian immigrants looking for a meat that could be sold cheaply to working-class customers. It was hardy stuff: Bologna sandwiches could be held for lunch all day with no refrigeration and still not spoil. During the Depression, the affordable cold cut became more widely available and remains a popular sandwich option today.

Ham Hocks

PIGS ARE NOT NATIVE TO THE AMERICAS. COLUMBUS BROUGHT SWINE WITH HIM TO THE NEW WORLD IN 1493 ON HIS SECOND VOYAGE.

Ham hocks are the lower hind leg of a pig, often sold smoked or cured. They are an important element in the traditional cuisine of the American South and have been since the 1600s, when pigs were introduced to the Atlantic colonies. The settlers from Europe were familiar with raising pigs and prepared simple dishes from various parts of the animal, including ham hocks. Dishes that featured ham hocks were common in many of the colonists' former homes in northern Europe, from Poland and Hungary to Germany and the British Isles.

Historically, ham hocks have also been associated with the cuisine of African Americans. During slavery, the best parts of the pig were reserved for the wealthy planters. The less desirable parts, such as ham hocks and chitterlings—intestines—were made available to the servants and slaves. These cast-off cuts became a cooking staple, enriching the regional cuisine of the South. The hocks have a large center bone, thick skin, and generous fat surrounding small nuggets of meat. The meat is pulled out and eaten, or shredded and added to vegetables, beans, or other dishes. Ham hocks, combined with herbs and spices in boiling water, are the foundation of a savory, multipurpose stock.

Deviled Ham

THE UNDERWOOD COMPANY PATENTED ITS RED DEVIL LOGO IN 1870. IT NOW REIGNS AS THE OLDEST FOOD TRADEMARK IN THE UNITED STATES.

Deviled ham is a seasoned ham spread produced by grinding up the meat, then adding a variety of ingredients including herbs and spices such as cayenne pepper and tarragon, along with sour cream, mustard, and hot sauce. The term "to devil" in connection with food dates back at least to the 18th century. The *Oxford Companion to Food* relates that "deviling" meant to cook a food "with fiery hot spices or condiments." Most of us have had savory deviled eggs; other foods such as shrimp and crab are also frequently deviled.

The first commercial maker of deviled ham was the William Underwood Company. The firm began life in Massachusetts in the early 19th century producing condiments such as mustard and ketchup and selling them in glass bottles. The company grew substantially during the Civil War when it supplied canned goods to the Union Army: The glass-packed foods stayed unspoiled longer. Underwood first manufactured deviled ham in 1868. Shortly after, the firm started marketing the spread in small cans stamped with a little red devil holding a pitchfork. Family owned until the latter part of the 20th century, the Underwood Company is now a subsidiary of B&G Foods. But the little red devil lives on in supermarkets everywhere.

UNCOMMONLY KNOWN ...

OLDEST SOUP One of the easiest types of meals to prepare, soup undoubtedly is also one of the oldest. Throwing many ingredients into one cooking pot is a simple food preparation that would have been known to people in every culture. Archaeologists have found evidence that some 6,000 years ago, hippopotamus soup was on the menu for people in Africa. Along with hippo, the soup contained sparrow meat, lentils, vegetables, and spices.

Oxtail

ABOUT HALF THE CALORIES IN A SERVING OF OXTAIL COME FROM FAT, BUT OXTAIL IS ALSO A GOOD SOURCE OF PROTEIN AND IRON.

Oxtails once came from actual oxen—big steers generally trained as draft animals to pull plows and wagons. Today, what's called an oxtail is most likely to be from any type of cow or bull. Butchers cut the tail into sections, each with a large

PEOPLE WHO CHANGED HISTORY

Lafcadio Hearn
(1850–1904)

Born to Greek and Irish parents, Patrick Lafcadio Hearn was a widely traveled 19th-century journalist and author. He is perhaps best known for his writings on Japan. But in the United States, he's remembered for introducing the world to the Creole culture of New Orleans. A seasoned reporter, Hearn arrived in New Orleans in 1876 and fell in love with the city. He covered its captivating way of life, penning articles on its food, music, architecture, language, and people. His stories were often accompanied by woodblock illustrations. Hearn wrote the first cookbook to feature Creole recipes, *La Cuisine Creole*, and he compiled a volume of Creole proverbs.

Lafcadio Hearn, circa 1889

marrowbone at the center surrounded by a fatty portion of meat.

Oxtails were once generally considered to be peasant food. Though they're clearly not internal organs, they were nevertheless categorized as offal because the tail was deemed a throwaway part of the animal—virtually worthless. Many butchers in the past would simply give away oxtails for free to customers who made a small purchase. Over time, lower-income people of many cultures who couldn't afford more desirable cuts of beef learned to prepare and enjoy the discards such as oxtails.

Bony oxtails are still not a choice cut for most people. What meat there is starts out tough. Yet because of the generous amount of fat and marrow in oxtail, the meat does become tender after several hours of braising or stewing. Oxtails are often used today as a base for flavorful beef stock. Oxtail soup is a traditional offering in England and Jamaica, among other countries.

Chicken Nuggets

DURING THE 2008 OLYMPICS IN BEIJING, JAMAICAN RUNNER USAIN BOLT ATE ABOUT 1,000 CHICKEN NUGGETS AND WON THREE GOLD MEDALS.

McDonald's introduced its Chicken McNuggets in 1980, but the fast food chain didn't invent them. That distinction goes to Robert C. Baker, a Cornell University professor of poultry science. Baker and a group of graduate students came up with dozens of ways to process chicken into new products, including chicken hot dogs, meatballs, and cold cuts. In 1963 Baker had the idea for what he called breaded chicken on a stick—basically a nugget.

McDonald's says it developed its McNuggets independently as a response to the federal government's dietary guidelines recommending less fat and less red meat. McNuggets were meant to give customers an alternative to the chain's signature hamburgers. After rejecting chicken potpies and fried chicken parts, the company settled on chunks of fried breast meat. The meat is first ground and then mixed with, among other ingredients, water, sugar, salt, and preservatives. Nuggets-to-be are formed into four shapes—ball, bell, boot, and bow tie—then dipped in batter and fried in vegetable oil. With more than 69 million customers a day, McDonald's locations worldwide produce an astounding number of nuggets.

You Can Eat That?

Fried grasshoppers might not seem like a tasty treat to everyone, but millions of people around the world happily eat grasshoppers and other insects without batting an eye. Among the offbeat edibles—at least by most Americans' standards—featured in this section are eggs buried in mud, the flesh of poisonous fish, moldy cheese, jelly-like fish soaked in lye, and dirt. How did people come to eat this strange-sounding smorgasbord? In most cases it's just a matter of habit and culture, but attitudes about food often change over time.

Seaweed

CHINA IS THE LEADING PRODUCER OF EDIBLE SEAWEED, FOLLOWED BY KOREA AND JAPAN; THE THREE ARE ALSO THE LEADING SEAWEED CONSUMERS.

Seaweed was an important part of the culinary traditions of China, Korea, and Japan for centuries. It still holds a prominent position in East Asian countries. In Japan at least 20 species of seaweed are found in commonly eaten dishes. In Korean culture, birthdays are traditionally celebrated with a soup containing seaweed, and women eat seaweed for three weeks after having a baby.

Historically, seaweed has been consumed by coastal residents of certain Western countries as well, though its importance has diminished with time. Centuries ago, Irish coastal dwellers added a red seaweed called dulse to their oatmeal porridge. Seaweed became a welcome food for Scots forcibly relocated to the coast at the turn of the 19th century to make way for sheep farms. In the mid-19th century, Irish families turned to seaweed during the great potato famine.

Seaweed has become more commonly available in the United States in recent years as its nutritional value has gained public awareness. Seaweed is low in calories and high in fiber and vitamins, including A, B_{12}, and C. It's also a good source of calcium and is especially prized for its iodine content, a mineral not found in many other foods.

For now, seaweed wrapped around a sushi roll (a 1,500-year-old Japanese tradition) or floating in miso soup is probably the most likely encounter for many Americans. But seaweed snacks are fast becoming popular; stores now stock chips made from the seaweed nori right beside pretzels and corn chips. Raw seaweed is less commonly found, except in Asian specialty shops. But as Asian-American culture expands, the role of the versatile aquatic vegetable will grow along with it.

Grasshoppers

MICHINOMIYA HIROHITO, EMPEROR OF JAPAN FROM 1926 TO 1989, DIDN'T EAT GRASSHOPPERS, BUT HE ENJOYED WASPS WITH SOY SAUCE.

Grasshoppers aren't appetizing to most Americans. But many cultures don't share that attitude toward sitting down to a plate of insects. In parts of Mexico, grasshoppers are a traditional dish. One Oaxaca recipe calls for grasshoppers with fried onions, tomatoes, and peppers. The consumption of insects was certainly known in ancient civilizations. Eating grasshoppers was sanctioned in the Old Testament, along with locusts, crickets, and beetles. The ancient Romans enjoyed beetle larvae.

UNCOMMONLY KNOWN ...

FUGU A single puffer fish, or *fugu* in Japanese, contains enough of the lethal poison tetrodotoxin to kill about 30 people. That doesn't stop diners from relishing it in seafood-loving Japan, where the flesh of the puffer fish has been a traditional delicacy for centuries. Chefs who prepare it must be carefully trained to remove all of the deadly poison. Nevertheless, several people in Japan die each year from improperly prepared fugu.

Insects remain a cheap source of protein and are widely available in developing countries, where other protein can be out of reach. Fried caterpillars are popular in parts of Africa, and the eggs of half-inch-long water boatmen stand in for caviar in Latin America. As a growing number of people from cultures where eating bugs is common settle in the United States, insect dishes are starting to appear on menus. Mexican farmers are raising grasshoppers especially for the U.S. and other emerging markets. You can now order grasshopper tacos at restaurants in New York and San Francisco, and a Houston eatery serves the hoppers with guacamole.

Dirt

A TYPE OF CLAY CALLED KAOLIN IS USED TO TREAT DIARRHEA AND INFLAMMATION AND IS AN INGREDIENT IN THE MEDICATION KAOPECTATE.

For $110, people in Tokyo can dine on salad with dirt dressing, sea bass with dirt risotto, and enjoy a dessert of dirt ice cream. Eating dirt might be a current fad in developed nations, but elsewhere it's not new. Known to science as geophagy, dirt eating has been around for millennia. Hippocrates is credited with the first written mention of the practice about 2,000 years ago.

Modern anthropologists have observed it in many cultures around the world. Eating dirt is most common in tropical areas, where microbes both helpful and harmful thrive.

Some researchers think geophagy could be a protective evolutionary adaptation acquired over thousands of years to be medically beneficial. The population most likely to eat dirt—children and women of childbearing age—is also the one most susceptible to bacterial infection. Dirt when eaten might protect the stomach and prevent the absorption of pathogens. Components of dirt might also ease stomach upset, supply nutrients, and increase a fetus's immunity to certain illnesses.

1,000-Year-Old Eggs

IN THAILAND THE EGGS ARE CALLED *KHAI YIAO MA*, WHICH MEANS "HORSE URINE EGGS." THE EGGS' PUNGENT ODOR INSPIRED THEIR NAME.

Thousand-year-old eggs aren't nearly that old. They're also called—only slightly less exaggeratedly—century eggs. In fact the eggs have been preserved from just a few weeks to a few months. However, though their exact origin is uncertain, their history in Asia stretches back many centuries. According to one account, the first 1,000-year-old eggs were discovered accidentally during China's Ming dynasty (1368–1644). Duck eggs that had been gathered and carelessly discarded in a limewater pool were found transformed in color and texture. Someone tried the eggs, enjoyed them, and obviously lived to tell the tale.

Since then, to create the eggs on purpose, a hole is dug in the ground and a mixture of clay or ash, salt, lime, rice husks, tea, and straw is poured in (this can also be done in a crock). Fresh duck, quail, or chicken eggs are buried in the mixture. During the time the eggs are buried, the mixture is gradually absorbed through the eggs' shells, and chemical changes take place. The egg yolks turn dark green, and the whites turn a dark brown or amber color. Along with the changes in color comes a strong smell of sulfur and changes in texture. The yolks of the eggs turn creamy, much like soft cheese, and the whites become gelatinous. The eggs are said to have a rich, sharp, cheesy flavor—an acquired taste.

Roquefort

FARMERS ONLY GET ABOUT 16 GALLONS OF MILK FROM EACH LACAUNE EWE PER SEASON, ONE-THIRTIETH THE AMOUNT THEY GET FROM A COW.

Roquefort is a type of blue cheese produced in southern France. To be officially designated Roquefort, the cheese must be made from a certain kind of milk, aged in a certain group of caves for a certain amount of time, and contain a certain type of mold.

WHAT'S INSIDE?

Fruit Leather

The first fruit jellies and pastes were produced in the Middle East, made from figs, apricots, dates, and other fruits. The people of southern Europe knew fruit pastes as early as the 16th century, and the basic recipe has remained unchanged for hundreds of years. Fruit is first pureed, then spread out in thin sheets and dried. The dried sheets can be rolled up for storage and easy eating. Modern commercial fruit roll-ups began to appear on supermarket shelves in the United States in the early 1980s. Store-bought roll-ups often contain less actual fruit and a great deal more sugar (along with chemical additives) than homemade fruit leather. But natural fruit leathers are higher in certain vitamins and have a lower percentage of sugar than many other sweet, candy-like snacks.

Only milk from Lacaune ewes can be used to make true Roquefort. The ewes, which graze on the high plateaus of Aveyron, are the result of extensive crossbreeding to produce animals with the desired characteristics. They give only a limited amount of milk, restricting the amount of authentic Roquefort that can be made each year.

The cheese must be aged in the limestone caves around Mount Combalou for at least three months. The cool, moist environment is perfect for the growth of the blue mold, *Penicillium roqueforti,* that creates the characteristic blue-green spots in the final product.

Roquefort is one of the oldest known varieties of cheese. Pliny the Elder, the great Roman scholar, remarked on its deep aroma in A.D. 79. Seven centuries later, it was a favorite food of Charlemagne, emperor of France.

The cheese and its name became forever linked in 1411 when Charles VI of France granted official right to produce the aromatic cheese to the people of the small town of Roquefort-sur-Soulzon.

Lutefisk

A QUARTER-POUND OR SO OF LUTEFISK HAS ABOUT 50 CALORIES. IT'S LOW IN SALT AND HIGH IN SELENIUM AND OTHER VITAMINS.

Lutefisk, or lyefish, is literally fish that's been preserved in highly alkaline lye. It has been a traditional winter holiday dish in Norway, Sweden, and Finland from as early as the 1300s. Lutefisk traveled to the United States with Scandinavian immigrants, and it's less popular today in its countries of origin than in the Upper Midwest, where many people of Scandinavian descent settled. In fact the "lutefisk capital of the world" is in Madison, Minnesota.

Strong-tasting lutefisk has its detractors, but holiday festivals and fundraising dinners at Lutheran churches in the Midwest traditionally feature it. The dinners customarily include side dishes of potatoes, green beans, and rutabagas, along with platters heaped with *lefse,* a Scandinavian flat bread made from potatoes.

Lutefisk starts out as dried cod. It's first soaked in water and then a lye solution. The fish puffs up as it absorbs water and softens into a jelly-like state as it's broken down by the lye. The fish is soaked in water again for several days to remove the caustic lye, then boiled or steamed.

Fermentation Station

The broad range of foods in this section share one thing in common. They are all formed by way of fermentation, a process that breaks down sugars and converts them into other compounds such as alcohols and acids. Fermentation using yeast can create bubbles of carbon dioxide that put the fizz in root beer and the holes in bread that make it rise. Fermentation using bacteria produces acids that yield yogurt, sauerkraut, and sourdough bread their characteristic sour tastes. Even though these featured foods are all fermented, each has a distinctive history.

Sauerkraut

NEARLY 400 MILLION POUNDS OF SAUERKRAUT ARE CONSUMED ANNUALLY IN THE UNITED STATES—WELL OVER A POUND FOR EACH MAN, WOMAN, AND CHILD.

If you think sauerkraut was invented in Germany, you're probably not alone. After all, *sauerkraut* means "sour cabbage" in German. It's true that German immigrants originally brought sauerkraut to America in the 19th century, but the history of fermented shredded cabbage traces back much further.

For millennia, people have been preserving food by fermenting it. Shredded cabbage fermented in rice wine was a staple in China 2,000 years ago, commonly eaten by workers building the Great Wall. When trade links were established between China and Europe in the Middle Ages, foods were exchanged along with other goods. People living in what is now Germany were introduced to Chinese fermented cabbage and made it their own.

In the mid-1800s a wave of German immigrants brought their traditional foods to the United States, including their fermented cabbage. Sauerkraut was readily accepted by mainstream America. By the mid-1900s it had become one of America's favorite toppings. Most sauerkraut available today is pasteurized in brine and then packaged for sale.

WHAT'S INSIDE?

Rumtopf

The word literally means "rum pot" and refers to a crock filled with layers of rum-soaked fruit. Rumtopf was a method of preserving summer fruit for winter in European countries such as Germany and Denmark and was brought to the United States by immigrants. A rumtopf is started in summer and finished by early fall. Strawberries are traditionally included; raspberries, plums, peaches, and grapes are also favored. As each type of fruit ripens through the season, it's layered with rum and sugar. The fruit must remain immersed in rum, and a proper rumtopf must sit for at least two months after the last fruit is added before eating.

Sourdough Bread

SAN FRANCISCO IS FAMOUS FOR ITS SOURDOUGH. BAKERS CLAIM THAT SOME OF THE STARTERS IN USE HAVE BEEN AROUND FOR MORE THAN 100 YEARS.

Sourdough is thought to be the oldest type of leavened bread. It was made thousands of years ago in ancient Egypt; evidence of it goes as far back as 1500 B.C. Historians think the method of making sourdough was discovered by accident: Unleavened bread dough was left out in the open air, giving wild yeast a chance to infiltrate, causing the dough to rise. Bakers preferred the lighter bread and continued the practice.

The base of sourdough bread is the starter, which begins with flour and water. Exposed to the outdoors (or now with store-bought ingredients), the mixture becomes permeated with yeast and bacteria. The bacteria break down the flour's complex carbohydrates into simple sugars, producing lactic acid and acetic acid—primarily responsible for the bread's sour taste. Yeast in the dough also feeds on these simple sugars and gives off carbon dioxide. The gas creates bubbles in the dough, causing the bread to rise. Flour is added periodically, providing the microorganisms more to eat and allowing the starter to live indefinitely. Without sourdough starter, settlers headed to the frontier West in the 19th century would not have had pancakes and biscuits for breakfast.

UNCOMMONLY KNOWN ...

CARBONATION Carbon dioxide dissolved in a liquid beverage creates a fizzy–carbonated–drink. It can occur naturally, when spring water absorbs carbon dioxide underground. Joseph Priestly discovered how to carbonate beverages artificially in 1767 by infusing the gas into still water.

Root Beer

ALTHOUGH ROOT BEER IS A POPULAR SOFT DRINK IN THE UNITED STATES AND CANADA, IT'S NOT PARTICULARLY WELL LIKED OUTSIDE NORTH AMERICA.

Root beer has been known since the 18th century, one of a group of beverages in colonial America called "small beers." The small beers were made from various roots, barks, and saps, including sassafras (root beer) and birch (birch beer). They were lightly carbonated from the fermentation of sugars. Although small beers were popular hot weather drinks, some were more popular than others. Early root beers contained a bit of alcohol and were used to treat sore throats.

A Quaker pharmacist from Philadelphia, Charles Hires, was the first to make what was formerly a home brew into a commercial success. Hires introduced artificially carbonated root

beer at the Philadelphia Centennial Exposition in 1876. By 1893, he was selling root beer in bottles. During Prohibition in the 1920s, some breweries produced root beer instead of orthodox beer to stay in business.

The original sassafras flavoring in root beer came from the safrole oil in the root. However, in 1960 safrole was identified as a carcinogen, and the federal government banned its use in food. Today the taste of root beer derives from a medley of flavorings.

Miso

THE COLOR OF MISO VARIES, DEPENDING ON THE INGREDIENTS AND LENGTH OF FERMENTATION; LIGHT MISOS ARE MILDER THAN DARK ONES.

Miso is a traditional Japanese bean paste created through the fermentation of soybeans, rice or barley, salt, water, and a mold (*koji*). The mixture is poured into wooden barrels and aged, sometimes for several years. Miso's forerunner, *chiang*, was known in China as early as the fourth century B.C. It too was a paste made from fermented soybeans, plus wheat, alcohol, and salt. Koji was used to season other foods. Precisely when miso was introduced to Japan is unclear, but historians believe it traveled there with Chinese Buddhist monks in the seventh century A.D. At first miso was enjoyed by the Japanese upper classes but gradually spread to become a staple of the national cuisine. Over time, regional variations of miso developed.

Miso was introduced to the West in the 1960s; most Americans know it as the base of a savory soup. Miso's increasing popularity is due in part to its salutary probiotic benefits. Probiotics are bacteria and yeasts that thrive in the human body and promote health, especially health of the digestive system. They grow in miso during fermentation. Probiotic foods such as miso are thought to contribute beneficial microorganisms, not only aiding digestion but offering a measure of protection against harmful bacteria. Miso is also an excellent source of several B vitamins.

Yogurt

CONSUMPTION OF YOGURT IN THE UNITED STATES HAS MORE THAN DOUBLED IN THE PAST DECADE. NEARLY A THIRD OF ALL AMERICANS EAT YOGURT.

Yogurt is one of those foods that seem to have been around forever. Its roots are traceable back some 9,000 years to Central Asia. The word itself is Turkish, and yogurt is a fixture in the Turkish diet. Whenever yogurt first appeared, food historians believe its discovery was likely accidental, possibly made by shepherds or nomads when milk curdles in its container. Bacteria in the milk caused it to ferment and thicken, taking on its characteristic sour taste. Over the millennia, yogurt became an important part of cuisines across Europe and Asia. In India it's eaten plain, or served as *raita*—a mixture of yogurt, cucumbers, cilantro, and spices. Greeks make a tangy dip of yogurt, cucumbers, and garlic called tzatziki.

When yogurt is produced commercially in large batches, bacteria (*Streptococcus thermophilus* and *Lactobacillus bulgaricus*) and sometimes yeast *(L. acidophilus)* is added to the milk to cause fermentation. The milk then sits for several hours at a constant temperature—about 110°F—until it begins to form the curds that give yogurt its creamy texture. Many Americans include yogurt as part of a healthy diet. Yogurt is low in calories and high in calcium and protein.

PEOPLE WHO CHANGED HISTORY

Louis Pasteur (1822–1895)

Groundbreaking French chemist and microbiologist Louis Pasteur is responsible for major discoveries that led to the germ theory of disease. He's probably best known for developing the process of pasteurization in the 1860s, in which foods are subjected to high heat to kill harmful microorganisms. Pasteurization was first applied to wine and later to milk and beer. Many of our most common perishable foods, such as fruit juices and dairy products, are now required by law to undergo pasteurization or to be produced using pasteurized ingredients.

Pasteur pictured in an advertisement circa 1900

Salsa Verde

IN 1997, MAY WAS DECLARED NATIONAL SALSA MONTH IN THE UNITED STATES TO RECOGNIZE THE CONDIMENT'S UNIQUE HERITAGE.

In the United States, salsa verde, or green sauce, is associated with both traditional Mexican cuisine and cuisine of the American Southwest. The basic ingredient is the tomatillo, a small, green, fruit native to Mexico and Central America. Records from 16th-century Spanish invaders show that the Aztec were enjoying salsa by the time the Spanish arrived. Bernardino de Sahagún, a missionary in what is now Mexico, documented many aspects of Aztec culture. His writings mention the foods available at Aztec markets, including salsas made with tomatillos.

In the 20th century, Americans outside the Hispanic community were introduced to salsa during the 1940s, when the first commercial salsas made their appearance in Texas. The taste for salsa spread to all compass points as the culture from south of the border fanned out. By the early 2000s salsa was a fixture in kitchens and restaurants across the country. In Latin America, salsas vary from nation to nation. Argentine salsa verde, for example, is called *chimichurri;* it's a parsley-based sauce with garlic, shallots, and spices.

Good for You

Most Americans are increasingly conscious of their diet, looking for ways to eat healthfully. And if indeed we are what we eat, a lot of us are better off these days than even the recent past. Each of the foods in this section helps fill the bill. Avocado is loaded with healthful monounsaturated fat. Kale is a powerhouse of antioxidants. Oat bran can lower serum cholesterol, decreasing the risk of cardiovascular disease. Carob stars as a low-fat, caffeine-free chocolate substitute. All the foods have intriguing stories behind their nutritional benefit. It's a formidable menu.

Carob

CAROB IS USED AS A SUBSTITUTE FOR CHOCOLATE IN DOG TREATS BECAUSE UNLIKE CHOCOLATE, IT'S NOT TOXIC TO MAN'S BEST FRIEND.

Carob comes from the seedpods of a large evergreen tree native to the Mediterranean region. Once the pods are harvested, their slightly sweet pulp is roasted and ground into a dark brown powder that's similar in appearance to cocoa powder.

Carob trees have been cultivated in the Middle East for some 4,000 years. They were also grown in ancient Greece and Rome. The Greeks' word for the carob was *keration,* and it is believed that carob seeds were used as a unit of measurement for gemstones and gold. That association still exists today. The weight of gems is measured in carats, while the purity of gold is measured in karats.

Carob has never been a common food in the United States, but it gained popularity in the 1970s as a healthful alternative to chocolate.

PEOPLE WHO CHANGED HISTORY

Marcus Virgilius Eurysaces (circa 50–20 B.C.)

In ancient Rome most people baked their own bread in home ovens, until the second-century B.C., when professional bakers became more common as wealthier women sought to avoid the chore of daily breadmaking. A freed slave of Greek background named Marcus Virgilius Eurysaces is credited with inventing the first labor-saving device for bakers: a mechanical dough mixer. Eurysaces attached horses or donkeys to mixing paddles inside a large stone basin. As the animals circled around the platform, the paddles mixed and kneaded the bread dough.

Carving of bread bakers on Marcus's tomb

Carob is lower in fat than chocolate, contains dietary fiber, and is a good source of B vitamins, calcium, and potassium. And unlike chocolate, which has caffeine, carob won't keep you awake.

Seitan

OUNCE FOR OUNCE, SEITAN HAS MORE PROTEIN THAN A NEW YORK STRIP STEAK AND ONE-QUARTER THE FAT—BUT IT'S GOT MORE CALORIES.

Seitan is a Japanese word for a food that's made from cooked, seasoned wheat gluten. It is frequently substituted for meat. Vegetable meat substitutes like seitan can be traced back to ancient Chinese Buddhist culture. Because Buddhism encouraged vegetarianism, monks sought stand-ins for meat. They discovered they could make a dense food rich in protein by soaking wheat flour dough in water. The food was later introduced to Japan, where it was typically flavored with soy sauce and ginger to create what we know today as seitan.

Making seitan the traditional way starts with a flour and water dough that is kneaded and rinsed under water simultaneously for perhaps 30 minutes to leach out wheat starch. When the process is complete, only gluten remains. Seitan gained prominence in the West in the 1970s with the growing popularity of vegetarian and vegan diets. High-protein seitan is also high in iron and low in fat.

As with tofu, seitan on its own is rather bland but readily acquires the flavor of whatever other foods are prepared with it. Because it's dense and chewy, seitan can mimic the texture of some meats. In fact, it's occasionally called "wheat meat." Innovative products made from seitan, such as vegetarian "turkey," often called tofurkey, have become popular with people who enjoy the taste and feel of meat but maintain diets that don't include it. Tofurkey is seitan that has been shaped appropriately and coated with oil and spices. When tofurkey is hot out of the oven and slathered with gravy, aficionados can't wait to gobble it up.

Muesli

MUESLI TRADITIONALLY IS UNSWEETENED; MANY KIDS' BREAKFAST CEREALS ON STORE SHELVES CONTAIN OVER 50 PERCENT SUGAR BY WEIGHT.

Muesli was invented by physician Maximilian Bircher-Brenner in the early 20th century for patients at his clinic in Switzerland. Their daily routine focused on outdoor activity and healthful eating, and a cornerstone of the program was Bircher-Brenner's special diet. To retain nutrients, food was eaten raw or cooked slowly over low heat. Breakfast, lunch, and dinner would start with a dish of muesli, an unsweetened medley of raw apple, nuts, and oats, all soaked in milk

or cream. The word *muesli* derives from a term in German dialect meaning "mash-up." The recipe today hasn't changed much: It typically calls for oats, nuts, seeds, and dried fruit eaten with milk. Muesli is distinct from granola, an American invention created in the 1890s containing many of the same ingredients. Unlike muesli, however, granola is sweetened and baked and often eaten dry.

Kale

A SUPERFOOD IN MANY RESPECTS, RAW KALE ALSO CONTAINS CHEMICALS THAT CAN BLOCK ABSORPTION OF IODINE, CAUSING HYPOTHYROIDISM.

Sometimes it seems as though kale was discovered only recently, but in fact people have been eating this green leafy vegetable for thousands of years. Writings from early Rome refer to *brassica,* a group of plants in the mustard family that includes broccoli, cabbage, and kale. By the Middle Ages, kale was known across Europe and Asia. Scots, Italians, and Russians, among others, developed their own varieties of the hardy plant.

Kale has been grown in America since colonial times. Thomas Jefferson, an avid gardener, raised several varieties of it. Through most of the 20th century kale was a constant but not particularly sought-after offering in the produce sections of many supermarkets. Around the turn of the millennium, health consciousness—and interest in kale—increased. Indeed, it's a powerhouse of nutrients: vitamins such as K, A, and C as well as minerals that include manganese, calcium, and iron. Kale is high in dietary fiber, low in calories, and has more antioxidant qualities than almost any other vegetable or fruit.

WHAT'S INSIDE?

Protein Shake

Protein shakes are drinks used mainly by athletes to get more protein into their diets. The protein can come from various sources, including casein and whey from milk, soybeans, eggs, or even rice. The shakes are available in many flavors and are sold in powdered form or ready-to-drink containers. The percentage of protein in a shake varies widely, from nearly pure protein to a small amount added to mostly carbohydrates and some fat. People trying to build muscle opt for a high-protein shake, while those who are seeking to increase endurance, such as distance runners, choose one higher in carbs. Directions for all: Shake well, enjoy.

Oat Bran

IDENTIFYING OATS AS HEALTHFUL HUMAN FOOD IS A RELATIVELY RECENT DEVELOPMENT. IN MANY COUNTRIES, THEY WERE LONG FIT ONLY FOR ANIMALS.

Oats have been cultivated for at least four millennia, with the earliest known evidence found among Egyptian artifacts some 2,000 years old. Oats are a small grain that grows especially well in wet, cool areas of the temperate zone. Because they can thrive in poor soil, they often flourish in places where other crops struggle to grow.

European settlers coming to North America brought oats with them in the 17th century. The grain was heavily cultivated on the East Coast, but production moved west to the prairies and plains as the nation expanded.

Oats have traditionally been considered a livestock feed. Aside from occasional bowls of breakfast oatmeal, they didn't play a large role in the diets of most Americans for much of U.S. history. But that changed in the 1980s. Following news that oat bran, the outer layer of hulled grain, was particularly "heart healthy," eating the bran became something of a fad. Oat bran, high in soluble fiber, appeared in a wide range of food products, from cereals to muffins to breads. Soluble fiber reduces the amount of LDL (low-density lipoprotein, or "bad" cholesterol) in the blood and has therefore been associated with lowering the risk of cardiovascular disease.

Oat bran and whole oats retain much of the nutritional value of the unhulled grain. Rolled oats lose some nutritional value while in processing. A one-third cup of oat bran contains about five grams of fiber; processed oat cereal might have little more than a single gram of fiber in the same serving. Steel-cut oatmeal contains the whole oat kernel, chopped into pieces, and is chewier than oatmeal made from rolled oats.

UNCOMMONLY KNOWN ...

LOW-CALORIE FRIED FOOD High in both fat and calories, fried food is delicious but unhealthy. Yet low-calorie fried food is possible. The first step is to choose oil that's low in saturated fat, such as peanut oil, canola oil, or even olive oil. The oil must be very hot to limit the amount the food absorbs. Cooks must also limit batter and breading, which add calories. Draining food on towels before serving removes excess oil.

Avocado

AVOCADOS ARE SURPRISINGLY HIGH IN POTASSIUM. HALF A MEDIUM-SIZE AVOCADO PROVIDES AS MUCH POTASSIUM AS AN AVERAGE BANANA.

The avocado we love in salads, sandwiches, and especially in guacamole has been cultivated in what is now Mexico for some thousands of years before Europeans arrived in the New World. The plant spread south from Mexico, and in the 16th century, Spanish conquistadors found the fruit growing from central Mexico to northern Peru. An avocado-shaped jar dating to A.D. 900 was reportedly discovered in the pre-Inca city of Chan Chan. Spanish conquistadors saw avocados in Aztec markets in the 1500s, and Hernán Cortés may have been the first European to taste one. After their conquest of Mexico, the Spanish took the avocado to the Caribbean and beyond.

There are three basic varieties of avocado. The pear-shaped Guatemalan avocado has dark green, bumpy skin. The West Indian avocado is the largest, with smooth, light-green skin. The hardy Mexicana is the smallest and has brownish purple skin when it's ripe. Despite their long history of cultivation, avocados didn't see large-scale production until the 20th century. Today Mexico remains the world's top producer. Other extensive commercial operations take place in Indonesia, Chile, and the Dominican Republic. In the booming U.S. market, avocados are harvested in California, Florida, and Hawaii.

We shape our buildings;
thereafter they shape us.

—WINSTON CHURCHILL (1874-1965)

Building Blocks

For the earliest human dwellings, mobility rather than permanence was the foremost feature. Scientists believe that Stone Age hunter-gatherers made collapsible huts from animal skins; later, nomadic herders in Asia and American Indians on the Great Plains used similar tentlike structures to follow their food source across the land. The development of agriculture gave rise to more permanent settlements, with buildings of masonry and timber.

The Egyptians were the first to build monumental structures. The pyramids were such a feat of engineering that for nearly 4,000 years, no one managed to build anything taller. Not until the Middle Ages were they topped by the great cathedrals of Europe. With cast-iron building methods in the 19th century came the skyscraper, and cities have been competing to build the tallest ever since.

Advances in building technology created a need for rigorous regulations. Ancient Greeks and Romans are supposed to have instituted the earliest construction inspections, but it often took a disaster to produce an effective set of building standards. After the Great Fire of London destroyed the city in 1666, stringent new guidelines finally addressed concerns that had been mounting in the city for a century.

The history of the world's building blocks would fill many volumes. This chapter only grazes the surface, from a look at primitive structures that kept people out of the cold, to modern skyscrapers that reach new heights—literally—of excess. It touches on the technologies that keep buildings standing when nature would have them topple, and peers at the enterprise that made moving people and building materials possible in the first place: transportation. Finally, it examines building frontiers we are only on the fringes of exploring—the oceans and outer space.

At Home

Early societies had limited options when it came to building a shelter. They needed to convert materials near at hand into housing of some kind, and to do so took imagination and resourcefulness. Grass, sod, mud, caves, abandoned structures—all were potentially useful. In the 20th century, advances in transportation expanded the supplies available to most people, and industrialism brought a wave of mass-produced and prefabricated housing. Nonetheless, in some places, people continue to live in updated versions of homes their ancestors built centuries ago.

Floating House

FLOATING REED HOUSES COULD BE CONSTRUCTED IN AS LITTLE AS THREE DAYS WITHOUT NEED FOR NAILS, HAMMERS, WOOD, OR GLASS.

On a spot believed by some to have been the biblical Garden of Eden, the Ma'dan, or Marsh Arabs, lived a waterborne existence for more than 5,000 years. They built villages of reed houses that floated at the confluence of the Tigris and Euphrates Rivers. These basket homes rested, half-supported and half-floating, on marshy islands of mud and rushes. Well-cared-for reed houses could last up to 25 years, but what they couldn't survive was Saddam Hussein. In 1991, convinced that the marshes were sheltering opponents of his regime, the dictator drained the marshes and torched the reed houses. In 2003, when the United States invaded Iraq, the dikes Saddam had built were broken and the wetlands again flooded. A smaller community of Arabs repopulated them, though the ecosystem is much altered and the wildlife populations diminished.

Centuries earlier and half a world away in Peru, Uro Indians—threatened by invading Inca and Colla Indians—abandoned their lakeside settlements on Lake Titicaca. They decided the middle of the lake was as safe a retreat as any and built floating islands they could live on. They wove long reeds to create buoyant homes, then lived afloat in isolation for the next several hundred years, fishing and birding in peace. A community of Uros still resides on a string of floating islands on the lake, though tourism now supports them. Floating homes aren't only relics of the past. Modern houseboats—some quite luxurious—are a novelty for some and a way of life for others, with at least 2,500 houseboats in Amsterdam, Netherlands, alone.

Russian Dacha

THE DACHA HAS HOUSED CREATIVITY AND TYRANNY: BORIS PASTERNAK WROTE *DOCTOR ZHIVAGO* IN ONE; STALIN CONDUCTED BUSINESS IN HIS OWN.

The Russian summer retreat known as the *dacha*—from the verb meaning "to give"—dates back to Peter the Great, who presented courtiers with plots of land on the outskirts of St. Petersburg. In the 19th century, dachas became suburban refuges for the rich and middle class of Russia, who fled the hot, crowded cities in the summer to spend time in relatively rural isolation. Some of these dachas were lavish; others were simple wooden cottages.

In Soviet-era Russia of the 1950s, a severe postwar food shortage spurred the government to distribute tiny parcels of land—six to an acre—to citizens to use as subsistence garden plots. Occupants built wooden huts on part of the site and used the rest for their gardens, which they cultivated prodigiously to have food supplies for the long Russian winter. These working-class dachas were basic shelters, constructed of whatever wood people could find. Despite their simplicity—or perhaps because of it—the dacha was important to Russian morale. In addition to providing an important food source, it was a refuge from the oppressive Soviet regime for residents of cities like Moscow and St. Petersburg.

Dachas are still an important part of Russian culture, though traditional ones now stand next to moneyed modern versions—megacottages of stone or brick, where swimming pools and lawns have replaced vegetable gardens.

PEOPLE WHO CHANGED HISTORY

Sarah Susanka (1958-)

Sarah Susanka is an author and architect whose work has sought to turn the modern mini-mansion building culture on its head. Her Not So Big series of books espouses a new architectural philosophy for building and remodeling homes. She contends that there is no need to build a so-called McMansion for a family of three. Good design and intelligent use of space are the keys to creating a home that is gracious, functional, and comfortable. Money saved by constructing a modestly sized house can then be invested in finishing details that will make the home beautiful and lend it personal character.

Sarah Susanka in Toronto, Canada, 2010

Prairie Sod House

SOD HOMES WERE CHEAP. ONE FRUGAL, ENTERPRISING SETTLER REPORTED THAT HE SPENT A TOTAL OF $2.78 CONSTRUCTING HIS IN 1870.

Building materials were scarce for settlers looking for a better life on the American prairie. The Homestead Act of 1862 sent floods of land-seeking pioneers west, but when they staked a claim, it was often far from any ready source of timber or stone. So they built homes with what was available to them in great abundance: prairie sod. It was not as flimsy a construction material as one might suppose. The prairie grasses had a tight, dense root system that created a mat that was strong but flexible. Homesteaders—with considerable effort—cut the tough sod into wide bricks and laid them in courses to form the walls of the "soddies," usually no bigger than 16 by 20 feet. The still living root systems of the bricks would then begin growing into each other to give the walls and roof added strength.

Modest soddies weren't the gracious New England clapboards some settlers had left behind, but their thick walls kept their inhabitants mostly dry and comfortable in a harsh prairie climate that matched bitter winters with searing summers.

The homes had their shortcomings: They showered dirt on their occupants, rodents and snakes burrowed into the walls, and the roofs were prone to collapse when they became soaked with rain or snowmelt. As settlers became more prosperous, they built frame houses, but they often kept their sturdy soddies around for use as barns or storage buildings.

UNCOMMONLY KNOWN ...

JAPANESE "RICE SKIN" HOUSE Rice grains are sheathed in hard, silica-rich husks that are inedible to humans and removed after rice is harvested. Japanese farmers mixed the husks into a paste and formed it into bricks, from which they built "rice skin" houses. Rice husks remain a significant agricultural by-product, incorporated into insulation, composite building material, and even car tires.

Cave Dwelling

EARLY CHRISTIAN MONKS DECORATED THE WALLS OF CAVE SANCTUARIES WITH BYZANTINE FRESCOES THAT HAVE LASTED FOR CENTURIES.

An eerie landscape of gnarled rock pinnacles and badlands has been home to countless generations of troglodytes in Cappadocia, a region of east central Anatolia in Turkey. People didn't live among these

UNCOMMONLY KNOWN ...

MODERN CAVE DWELLINGS A cave home usually has to be chiseled out of existing rock or perhaps retrofit in hollows left behind by industrial mines. The residents of Coober Pedy in South Australia have made their homes in the caverns of an old opal mine since the early 20th century. And in China, people have been living in the cliffs of Loess plateau in Shaanxi province for thousands of years. Some 30 million residents still live there today.

formations; they lived *in* them. Prehistoric volcanic eruptions left behind a soft rock, called tuff, that water and wind carved into tortuous formations. The qualities that made tuff vulnerable to the elements made it convenient for human burrowing too.

The history of people living in the caves is ancient. In the fourth century A.D., Christians fleeing Roman persecution established monastic communities in Cappadocia by tunneling into the rock and hollowing out spaces for monasteries and dwellings.

To escape attack by later Arab invaders, they burrowed even deeper, forming subterranean towns that concealed them from the raiding parties. It was a compelling subterfuge—attackers would arrive to find the area deserted, its inhabitants vanished. Unknown to the raiders, their quarry were quietly hidden below, sealed inside a subterranean complex with enough provisions to sustain them for weeks.

Some of these clandestine cities housed thousands of people and went down eight levels, with underground living quarters, stables, storehouses, and chapels linked by secret passageways. The cave dwellings were inhabited well into the 20th century, and a few people still live in them today. The honeycomb rock caves of Cappadocia are recognized by the United Nations as a World Heritage site.

Yurt

THE EARLIEST ARCHAEOLOGICAL EVIDENCE OF YURTS COMES FROM BRONZE AGE ROCK ETCHINGS THAT WERE DISCOVERED IN SIBERIA.

The yurt has been home to simple herders and great Mongol warlords alike. The cylindrical portable tent has been the dwelling of nomadic communities on the Central Asia steppes for millennia. Composed of wool felt fixed over a frame of flexible wood, the yurt was an efficient mobile shelter for herders who moved their flocks across the grasslands. Yurts could be broken down or set up in a couple of hours and be transported on the backs of yaks, horses, or donkeys. The felt that composed the wall of the tent was often woven from hair of the herders' own animals. And the circular form of the yurt broke the near-constant winds of the steppes from any direction.

In the early 13th century, Genghis Khan commanded his entire Central Asian empire from a *ger,* the Mongolian version of a yurt. His was a mobile mini-mansion, pulled by 22 oxen and guarded at all times by cavalry and foot soldiers.

Today, remaining nomadic groups in Central Asia still rely on these portable homes, and sheepherders in Kazakhstan and Mongolia continue

to use these temporary shelters. In the Western world, some high-end camping outfitters are offering luxury yurts as part of their adventure travel packages.

Prefabricated Home

A SEARS, ROEBUCK HOME KIT CONTAINED ABOUT 30,000 PIECES AND AN INSTRUCTION BOOK, AND COST FROM $650 TO A FEW THOUSAND DOLLARS.

A dismantled house shipped from England to Massachusetts in the 17th century to oversee a fishing fleet was the earliest known "prefabricated" home. During the gold rush in the mid-19th century, prefabricated kits were shipped to California so that prospectors could erect quick shelters.

The impetus for modern prefab housing was the assembly line—mass-produced building materials offered the construction industry a cheaper, faster alternative to custom home building. Prefabricated homes were sold in kits via catalogue, most famously by Sears, Roebuck and Company starting in 1908. They were a hit: Durable and well engineered, the kit homes were nearly indistinguishable from custom-built houses. By 1940 Sears had shipped more than 70,000. Mobile prefab homes were used during and after World War II to address housing shortages, but by the 1970s they had lost steam, partly because people associated them with the hasty, sometimes flimsy construction of the war years. Recently prefab has reemerged on the home front as people seek attractive and affordable, ecofriendly houses.

WHAT'S INSIDE?

Plaster

Plaster is an age-old building material. The Egyptians used it in the pyramids, the Greeks used it for interior decor, and medieval Londoners employed it all over the city as a fire retardant. The composition of plaster has varied through history. It was mixed from whatever people had available to make into a paste, including clay, mud, animal hair, and even Spanish moss. Today, in its primary use as an interior building material to cover walls and ceilings, its basic composition is simple and fairly standard: water, with some combination of sand and gypsum or lime.

Loft Apartment

IN ALL LIKELIHOOD, THE ENGLISH WORD "LOFT" IS DESCENDED FROM THE OLD NORSE WORD *LOPT*, WHICH CAN MEAN EITHER "AIR" OR "SKY."

These trendy apartments have an upscale cachet today, but their roots were far from luxurious. The original lofts were little more than salvaged spaces in derelict industrial buildings, appropriated by

PEOPLE WHO CHANGED HISTORY

Jane Jacobs (1916-2006)

Jane Jacobs was not a formally trained urban planner and didn't have a college degree, but her grounded, intelligent views on community planning changed the way Americans thought about cities. In her 1961 book, *Death and Life of Great American Cities,* Jacobs advocated pedestrian-friendly, human-scale neighborhoods featuring short city blocks and mixed-use buildings that encouraged resident interaction. She also staunchly opposed high-rise developments and expressways that bisected neighborhoods, arguing that they disrupted a city's urban fabric and damaged its social cohesion.

Jane Jacobs, 1962

cash-strapped artists. After World War II, manufacturing in New York and other large cities began to shrink as factories moved to the suburbs, leaving behind shuttered buildings in neighborhoods like Lower Manhattan's SoHo. The areas were not zoned for residential use, but the open floors and large windows of the old factories appealed to artists. They moved in, jerry-rigged utilities, and turned the spaces into hybrid living/working studios, illegally at first.

The concept of these open-plan, minimalist spaces caught the public imagination, and property values in areas such as SoHo went through the roof, pricing out the artists and replacing studios with boutiques. The conversion of industrial buildings into loft apartments became a hallmark of gentrified urban areas. Lofts became so popular that new buildings of loft-style apartments are now erected, substituting what they've lost in authenticity with every imaginable amenity.

Housing Development

THE CURVING STREETS OF MANY MODERN SUBDIVISIONS COME FROM DESIGN STANDARDS INSPIRED BY THE WORK OF FREDERICK LAW OLMSTED (SEE P. 130).

Americans' migration to the suburbs and the age of the housing development go hand-in-hand. Through the Depression and World War II years, the residential construction industry in the United States lay dormant. After the war, a flood of returning veterans and the resulting baby boom created a severe housing shortage. To meet the demand, developers starting buying land on the outskirts of cities, dividing it into individual lots, and building mass-produced, single-family houses. They were perfect for young families and were financially manageable for veterans, who received a housing subsidy from the GI Bill.

The earliest and most famous developments were the Levittowns, communities created by real estate developer William Levitt outside Philadelphia and New York City. Rigidly planned, their streets lined with modest, identical homes, they became an emblem of America's postwar suburban landscape and the archetype for countless housing developments that followed.

Old and New Heights

The towering Lighthouse of Alexandria signaled ships approaching the Egyptian harbor; the medieval spire of Salisbury Cathedral pointed toward heaven. Today skyscrapers are built partly to maximize urban space, but increasingly just to be really, really tall. If it's crowned tallest, a skyscraper is lucky to hold on to the title for more than a few years. Thereafter the most it can hope for is to achieve the iconic status of the Eiffel Tower or the Empire State Building. In a global skyscape crowded with gleaming towers, the competition is fierce.

Empire State Building

THE EMPIRE STATE BUILDING WAS THE TALLEST BUILDING IN THE WORLD FOR NEARLY 40 YEARS BEFORE THE WORLD TRADE CENTER DISPLACED IT.

When the Empire State Building was completed in 1931, New York had won a fierce competition among U.S. cities as to which of them could build the tallest skyscraper in the world. A humbler model of the 102-story, 1,454-foot New York tower had appeared two years earlier on the skyline of a North Carolina city. The architecture firm behind the Empire State Building had tried out their art deco high-rise design on the 314-foot Reynolds Building in Winston-Salem; the prestigious award they won for that project helped them snag the plum New York City commission.

Though it has achieved iconic status today, the Empire State Building was more highly hyped during its construction than after its completion. In the Depression-era climate of the 1930s, the construction project employed 3,400 workers, who received excellent pay and finished the building in just over a year, ahead of schedule and under budget. But the tower had always been conceived as an architectural landmark first

UNCOMMONLY KNOWN ...

GREAT WALL OF CHINA The wall, 2,000 years in the making, spans 5,500 miles, and under specific conditions, can be visible from orbit. Yet for all that, it owes its mass and longevity in part to a rather humble bonding agent. Workers built sections of the wall using a mortar that was mixed with sticky rice soup, an ingredient sourced locally that gave the structure great mechanical strength and proved to be more resistant to water than traditional mortar.

and a functional space second. After the initial hoopla following its opening, it remained largely vacant for years, prompting jaded New Yorkers to dub it the "Empty State Building."

One World Trade Center

FROM THE GROUND TO THE TIP OF ITS SPIRE, THE BUILDING RISES 1,776 FEET, MATCHING THE YEAR THE DECLARATION OF INDEPENDENCE WAS SIGNED.

When the World Trade Center towers collapsed as a result of the September 11, 2001, terrorist attack, it left a 16-acre wound in lower Manhattan. Almost immediately the decision to rebuild on the site was clear: A new skyscraper would attest to America's resilience. Completing the task, however, took far longer than expected. For almost five years, plans for the new tower inched through a snarl of red tape and debates over its design, security, and financing. In 2006 ground was finally broken, but for several more years, work on the tower was all below street level—discouraging to a public that expected to see it rise like a phoenix.

The footprints of the original towers were preserved for a landscape memorial, but the excavation of the new building site turned into a veritable archaeological dig. Predictably, workers uncovered human remains and debris from the 9/11 attacks, yet they also uncovered an 18th-century Philadelphia-built cargo boat and bones from a 19th-century slaughterhouse.

In 2009, aboveground construction finally began. The building slowly climbed skyward as an army of ironworkers pieced together floor after floor of the 104-story structure. By 2012 the tower was up with a building height of 1,362 feet. The observation deck at 1,250 feet is scheduled to open in 2015. The cubic base has a footprint equal to the original twin towers. Crowned with a 408-foot spire, One World Trade Center is now the tallest building in the hemisphere.

WHAT'S INSIDE?

Artificial Turf

Synthetic turf is used mostly for athletic fields. It's a durable, low-upkeep alternative to grass turf, and it doesn't require water, which is important in drought-prone areas. Artificial turf is a sandwich made up of plastic grass blades on top that are rooted into a cushioned infill layer usually composed of sand or recycled rubber and underlaid by a drainage layer that wicks away moisture. The infill layer is critical. The first artificial turf systems in the 1960s and 1970s were hard, and this cushioning now gives athletes a much softer, safer landing. In full sun, synthetic surfaces heat up much more than natural grass does, meaning activities on artificial turf should be scheduled to avoid the hottest times of day.

Shanghai Tower

TO QUAKE-TEST THE TOWER, ARCHITECTS BUILT A 43-FOOT SCALE MODEL AND SHOOK IT TO SIMULATE A 7.5-MAGNITUDE EARTHQUAKE.

Prior to 1970, Shanghai didn't have a single building over 20 stories high. Today it has dozens. The country's tallest—at least temporarily—is Shanghai Tower, completed in 2013. You might think its 128 stories could make it time-consuming to navigate, but the tower boasts the fastest elevators in the world, whizzing between floors at 40 miles an hour.

The building's rounded, tapering form is not just a visual accent but a structural insurance policy. Engineers designed it to counter the typhoon-strength winds that it might have to withstand. The skyscraper's sculptural profile curves at a fixed angle of exactly 120 degrees (the form determined to best bear wind loads) as the structure climbs to 2,073 feet.

From the outside, Shanghai Tower appears to be implacable glass and steel, but it's softer on the inside. The architects sheathed the tower with a second glass skin and installed nine vertically stacked atrium lobbies in between. The light-filled spaces recall Shanghai's historic landscaped courtyards, and they give the high-rise's occupants the pleasure of stepping into a garden without having to descend a quarter mile or more.

PEOPLE WHO CHANGED HISTORY

Antoni Gaudí (1852–1926)

Antoni Gaudí created a new kind of architecture in his home country of Spain. His whimsical building designs avoided straight lines, and he adorned facades with richly colored textures. Gaudí began working on the famous Church of the Sagrada Família in Barcelona, in 1883, building on a Gothic structure started a year earlier by architect Francesc de P. del Villar. When Gaudí died in 1926, the cathedral was less than a quarter finished. The basilica is a brilliant, bizarre tangle of fluid forms and biblical tableaux. Work on the church continues, but many fear that without Gaudí's imagination, it will never truly be the sacred spectacle he envisioned.

Gaudí's Sagrada Família, Barcelona, Spain

Eiffel Tower

ALMOST SEVEN MILLION PEOPLE VISIT THE ICONIC FRENCH TOWER EVERY YEAR, AND IT HAS INSPIRED MORE THAN 30 REPLICAS AROUND THE WORLD.

The Eiffel Tower has staying power. Meant to stand for only 20 years, the latticed iron tower was designed and built by Gustave Eiffel as the entrance piece to the 1889 World's Fair. Parisians did not unanimously embrace the structure. French writer Guy de Maupassant is said to have taken his dinner every day in the Eiffel Tower's restaurant because it was the only spot in Paris from which he was spared the sight of it. The tower was permitted to overstay its 20-year welcome when officials realized it had benefits as a radio mast, and it was used to intercept and transmit radio signals during World War I.

The tower was a world-famous landmark by the time Germany seized Paris in World War II, and even Hitler, on his only visit to Paris in 1940, could not resist posing in front of it. The photo op notwithstanding, he ordered the city reduced to rubble as the Allies advanced in 1944. Hitler's order—for reasons that have never been clear—was ignored, and the Eiffel Tower was granted another reprieve. It was the scene of one final sensational World War II episode the same year, when an American fighter pilot chased a German plane through its arch during a dogfight, thrilling and reinvigorating weary Parisians and French Resistance fighters.

Burj Khalifa

THE ELEGANT FORM OF THE BURJ KHALIFA IN DUBAI NARROWS AS IT RISES. WIND BREAKS AROUND THE FORM, REDUCING STRESS ON THE TOWER.

Constructing the world's tallest building involved many firsts. It was the first time anyone had built so many stories (160); the first time an observation deck had been at such a height (the 124th floor); the first time elevators had traveled such a distance; the first time people had occupied floors so high. It was certainly the first time anyone had built such a mammoth structure so near a web of geologic fault lines. Though Dubai is not considered at high risk for earthquakes, it feels the tremors from Iran's sometimes deadly quakes from across the Persian Gulf. Constructed over a period of five years and opened in 2010, the Burj Khalifa, named after the president of the United Arab Emirates, opened in the wake of a real estate

crash in Dubai. The tower is mostly occupied today, but its debut was not unlike the Empire State Building's: a heralded engineering feat culminating in lots of vacant office space in the years before an economic recovery.

Though the stunning tower reflects the shift of supertall skyscraper architecture from the West to Asia and the Middle East, Western architects and engineers were closely involved in its creation. The design team was the same Chicago-based architectural firm that designed One World Trade Center. And the Burj tower bears a striking resemblance to Frank Lloyd Wright's 1956 design for the Mile High Illinois, a fantastical skyscraper proposed, but never built, for Chicago.

UNCOMMONLY KNOWN ...

THE STATE HERMITAGE MUSEUM Not to be discounted in the giant-building discussion are structures that sprawl rather than soar. The Hermitage in St. Petersburg, Russia, is one of the largest museums in the world. It occupies six buildings that cover some 57 acres and house more than three million objects. To see everything, you would have to walk about 15 miles of corridors and browse the exhibits 8 hours a day for 11 years.

Space Needle

SIX PEOPLE HAVE SAFELY PARACHUTED OFF SEATTLE'S SPACE NEEDLE. FOUR OF THEM HAD PERMISSION; THE OTHERS WERE TAKEN INTO CUSTODY.

The first rendering of Seattle's futuristic tower was a scrawl on a paper placemat by a man more inclined toward business than design. Edward Carlson, the president of Western International Hotels, was organizing the 1962 World's Fair in Seattle when he doodled his idea for an architectural showpiece that would embody the exposition's "21st Century" theme. His idea, inspired by the Stuttgart Tower in Germany, resembled a crude lollipop.

The concept was passed along to architect John Graham, and from a flurry of refinements and revisions emerged the Space Needle, a sort of flying saucer on stilts with a rotating restaurant at the top. Graham was an enthusiastic proponent of rotating restaurants: He was fresh from designing America's first at the Ala Moana Hotel in Honolulu.

Planning and construction were rushed. Builders found a suitable site in the nick of time, and the construction was completed in just over a year, a few months before the fair opened.

For a tower that appears so top-heavy, the Space Needle in fact is quite the opposite. To anchor its 30-foot-deep base, a fleet of 467 trucks poured concrete continuously for an entire day, producing a foundation as heavy as the entire rest of the 605-foot edifice. The center of gravity is just 5 feet above the ground to prevent any earthquake less than magnitude 9.0 from toppling the tower. The design was put to the test in 1965 when a 6.5 tremor rocked the Needle but reportedly did little more than smash a couple of liquor bottles.

Petronius Oil Platform

AT 2,001 FEET, PETRONIUS STANDS AMONG THE WORLD'S TALLEST MAN-MADE STRUCTURES. AND AT 43,000 TONS, IT'S NO LIGHTWEIGHT.

As surely as many of the world's tallest buildings were built for spectacle, the Petronius oil platform (tapping the oil field named for a Roman writer) was engineered for sheer utility. Like an iceberg, most of it lies underwater: Of the platform's 2,000 vertical feet, only about 250 rise above the Gulf of Mexico. The bulk of the rig, constructed in the late 1990s and in operation by 2000, descends to the seafloor, secured there by giant footers. The platform's wells reach another mile and a half into Earth's crust, then tentacle out laterally for several more miles in their quest for crude.

The superstructure of Petronius that's visible above the water is an unsightly tangle of valves, pipes, rotors, and generators that power the rig. The machinery emits an incessant roar—a constant companion for the dozens of men who both work and live on the offshore oil rig.

The platform's engineers were not even faintly concerned with making it attractive; their goal was to make it massively productive. At full capacity, Petronius can pump 60,000 barrels of oil and 100 million cubic feet of natural gas each day. Considering the potential profits from such output, construction of the rig was a bargain—at $500 million, it cost less than a third of what it took to build Dubai's Burj Khalifa tower.

As a freestanding underwater structure, Petronius has other qualities that its giant terrestrial counterparts lack. It's a so-called deepwater-compliant platform, meaning that it's built to give and sway much more than earthbound towers. When the ocean is choppy, Petronius can move side to side with the swells as much as 25 feet.

WHAT'S INSIDE?

Aerogel

Aerogels are among the lightest solids known to humans. They are essentially the framework of a gel that is left behind after moisture is removed. That result is achieved through supercritical drying, a process that dehydrates a gel without shrinking it or altering its form. The pores that once held the gel's moisture are instead filled with air, and because air conducts heat very poorly, the light, flexible material is an excellent insulator. NASA sent aerogels into space to insulate the Mars rovers and help collect comet dust. Aerogels are now beginning to find use in more earthly endeavors such as in the construction industry, though their fragility and their current high cost can limit their applications.

Deep Space, Deep Seas

The exploration of space wasn't undertaken until Earth was pretty well charted. Exploring the oceans started earlier; crude submarines ventured underwater by the 1600s. But even with modern technology, those frontiers are so vast that forays into them are still relatively superficial—spacecraft have explored the nearer reaches of the solar system, and shallow coastal waters are sprinkled with man-made reefs and islands. It's easy to imagine more centuries passing before humans are comfortable enough in ocean depths or deep space to really build in them.

Space Station Mir

MIR HAD FIVE MODULES ATTACHED TO ITS CORE UNIT, WHICH INCLUDED AN ASTROPHYSICS OBSERVATORY AND SEVERAL SCIENCE LABS.

In March 2001, what looked like a flaming meteor arced across the sky over the South Pacific and plunged into the ocean. It was in fact the guided demise of the Russian space station Mir, whose 15-year tour in space came to an end. Beyond outliving its projected five-year mission, the versatile space laboratory outlasted even the Soviet regime that launched it in 1986. Mir orbited Earth 86,000 times at nearly 18,000 miles an hour. More than 100 visitors and crew rotated through it over the years, shuttling between Earth and Mir, their supplies transported on robotic cargo space ferries.

Mir's career in orbit was not without drama. In the late 1990s, a fire broke out on board, and in a separate incident, the station collided with a cargo vessel. In 2012, a Mars probe launched from Mir failed and crashed into South America. But ultimately Mir ended its mission without any real catastrophe. Its death knell came when the Russian government decided its money was better spent on the new International Space Station.

UNCOMMONLY KNOWN ...

WIELICZKA SALT MINE Sometime in the 13th century, miners began carving salt from caverns near Krakow, Poland. In 2007, some 700 years later, mining operations finally ended, but the subterranean chambers retained a life of their own. Today, nestled nine levels belowground and reached by descending 800 stairs, it is a large complex of health spas, art galleries, chapels, and a museum. The old mine also boasts an underground salt lake and caverns large enough to host concerts, weddings, and other events.

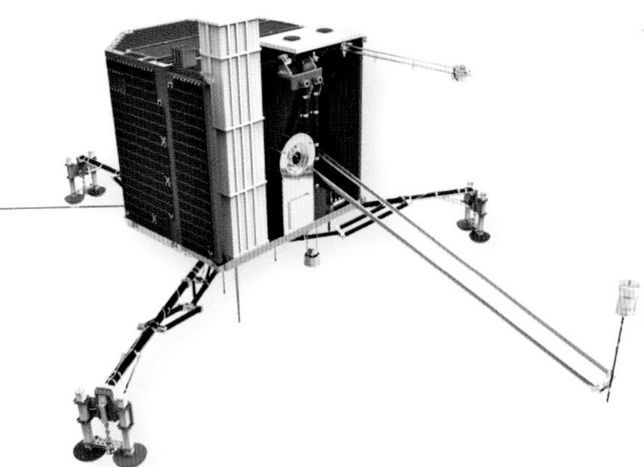

Spacecraft Philae

PHILAE BROKE ITS DRILL PROBING THE SURFACE OF A COMET. SCIENTISTS THINK THE COMET WAS FROZEN SOLID RATHER THAN SOLID ROCK.

In November 2014 a tubby, washing machine-size probe named Philae became a hero—and nearly a martyr—in the exploration of space. Philae was the first probe to land on a comet, with the goal of giving scientists a close-up look at the comet's surface and composition. Wads of ice and rock, comets are particularly intriguing because they are remnants from the formation of the solar system and may offer clues to how our planet was formed.

Philae hitched a ride to the comet on the unmanned spacecraft Rosetta, which chased the comet for ten years and four billion miles before finally drawing near enough to deploy Philae. Floating down to the surface, the little probe had a rough landing. Part of its anchoring system failed, causing it to bounce twice and settle against a cliff, out of sight of Rosetta and, worse, out of sight of the sun, which powered its batteries. Nevertheless, the probe collected and transmitted data for 56 hours before its batteries died and it fell silent.

Even with Philae in hibernation, Rosetta's mission continued. The spacecraft will stay with the comet as it approaches the sun. On June 13, 2015, Philae had caught some solar rays and begun to emerge from hibernation.

Artificial Reef

ABOUT 2,000 YEARS AGO, THE PERSIANS BUILT SOME OF THE EARLIEST ARTIFICIAL REEFS ACROSS THE TIGRIS RIVER TO FEND OFF PIRATES.

In its first life, remaining afloat was paramount for the U.S.S. *Oriskany*. The aircraft carrier earned battle stars in the Pacific during the Korean and Vietnam Wars. Today it rests on the floor of the Gulf of Mexico. In 2006, the decommissioned ship was scuttled off the coast of Pensacola, Florida, to perform new service as an artificial reef. The old hulk provides a surface on which coral and algae can grow, and it offers shelter that attracts and supports a host of marine life. Almost two centuries ago, South Carolina fishermen tried to build artificial reefs with logs, but metal refuse eventually prevailed. Ships, tanks, and even subway cars have been sunk along the Atlantic, Pacific, and Gulf coasts to form reefs that boost recreational and commercial fishing. While repurposing junk for reef construction is frugal, it's not the only way. The Japanese, who have been using artificial reefs since the late 1700s, have made a modern industry of designing and building special structures dedicated as reefs.

Underwater Museum

SCULPTURES DESIGNED TO BE SUBMERGED IN SALT WATER ARE MADE FROM A SPECIAL PH-NEUTRAL CEMENT THAT ENCOURAGES CORALS TO COLONIZE.

Vacationers to Cancún, Mexico, are usually not seeking a cultural experience. Spring break crowds descend there looking for a party; sun worshippers crowd its beaches. Just off the coast, the Mesoamerican Reef attracts snorkelers by the thousands each year, threatening the fragile marine environment. On nearby Isla Mujeres, an artist named Jason deCaires Taylor found an unlikely way to coax the snorkelers away from the natural reef: He built an underwater museum, the Museo Subacuático de Arte. Hundreds of concrete statues, sunk in 12- to 25-foot-deep water, form a spectral underwater gallery that diverts tourists from the natural reef to this unusual artificial one.

The statues become crusted with coral and algae soon after their submersion, and they grow a halo of waving seaweed that makes them appear to be long-waterlogged artifacts. In reality they have a modern, local resonance—the artist modeled some of them on people from the fishing village where he lives. He molded his neighbors' features in plaster, and then converted the molds to concrete figures. There are now more than 500 statues. The artist's underwater sculptures also appear off the coasts of Grenada and the Bahamas, and in the United Kingdom, among other watery locations.

Channeling Water

SCENIC WINDMILLS ONCE PUMPED WATER OUT OF HOLLAND'S LOWLANDS BUT HAVE SINCE BEEN REPLACED BY POWERFUL INDUSTRIAL PUMPS.

The Netherlands, a major seafaring nation with bustling ports, would like to have little to do with water inland from its coast. Unfortunately, that isn't an option: A quarter of its land, with half the country's population, lies below sea level. River flooding and ocean surges are a perennial worry.

For more than a thousand years, the Dutch have battled that reality. They constructed dikes to hold water back, mounded up land to build on, pumped water out, and shortened and walled their coastlines. They haven't always been successful. On a catastrophic night in 1953, the North Sea crashed over its barriers and killed 1,835 people.

Ultimately the sea will win, especially as sea levels rise. So the new Dutch approach is to coexist with the water rather than try to master it. Much of the Dutch population living below sea level is on polders—low-lying wetlands walled off behind dikes. Traditionally, to keep the polders dry, water is pumped out of them and returned to the sea via canal. Now dikes are being strategically breached to create spillways that channel floodwater over the lowlands in a controlled manner and thus prevent it from rising in contained waterways and potentially overwhelming the dikes. The tactic will also protect densely populated cities sitting behind levees downstream. The change has meant that some low-lying farms have been displaced and their occupants relocated, but the government is working on an innovative solution: Engineers are experimenting with buildings that float in place, so that if water rises, homes just rise with it.

UNCOMMONLY KNOWN ...

KANSAI INTERNATIONAL AIRPORT Built on an artificial island in Japan's Osaka Bay, the airport was hailed as a geoengineering achievement when it opened in 1994. It was the first large-scale commercial airport to be situated on reclaimed land, and it was carefully designed to weather sea surges. But no one expected it to sink like a stone. During its first several years, the airport settled rapidly into the seafloor. Billions in Japanese dollars were spent on a giant retaining wall, which successfully shored up the airport.

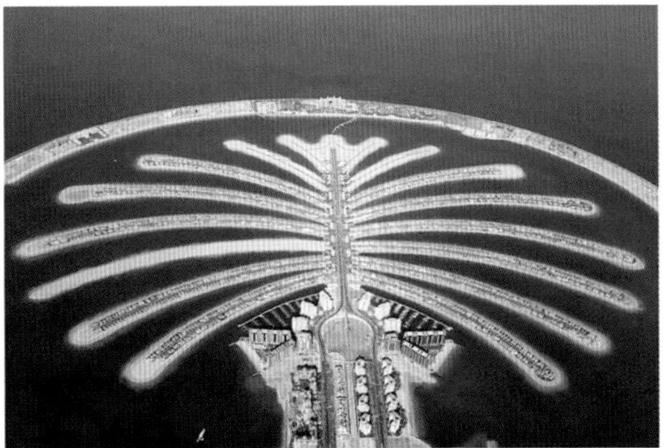

Artificial Islands

THESE ISLANDS HAVE BEEN DISCUSSED AS A MEANS TO BLUNT THE STORM SURGES THAT THREATEN COASTAL CITIES SUCH AS MANHATTAN.

Mexico City sits on the remains of one of the earliest known artificial islands, the 14th-century Aztec capital of Tenochtitlan. In the swampy Lake Texcoco, the Aztec engineered an island metropolis that at one point contained a population of 400,000. Early artificial islands were often hubs of political power and status. In Micronesia the city of Nan Madol, thought to be the seat of an ancient dynasty, is composed of 92 artificial islands built between 500 and 1,000 years ago. The remains of artificial rock islands in the lochs of Scotland and Ireland held dwellings called *crannogs,* which until the 17th century were used as defensive fortresses and symbols of status.

Modern artificial islands are often status symbols, but they tend more toward commercial extravagance. Dubai's Palm Islands, built from dredged sand, were constructed in the elaborate design of palm fronds, a spectacle best admired from above. From a practical point of view, the long, narrow fronds maximize space for beachfront property, and the islands are jammed with high-end villas and hotels.

Restorations and Preventions

Hammurabi, king of Babylon from 1792 to 1750 B.C., established one of the earliest building codes by stating that a builder whose faulty construction resulted in a death would meet the same fate. Repercussions are not so extreme today, but rigorous structural standards still govern much new construction. When possible, buildings are designed to withstand the stress a natural disaster could be expected to place on them. But that doesn't mean a structure will escape a disaster unharmed; it just means that it shouldn't collapse, at least not until everyone gets out.

Earthquake-Proof Buildings

FLEXIBLE BUILDING MATERIALS SUCH AS STRUCTURAL STEEL CAN HELP A BUILDING WITHSTAND GROUND MOTION IN A QUAKE.

After major earthquakes in Japan and Italy in the late 19th century and the devastating 1906 San Francisco earthquake, engineers began to factor seismic activity into the design of new buildings. Some of the measures were as basic as considering soil condition at the site and keeping designs symmetrical. More advanced techniques included the development in the 1960s of base isolation, a technology that stabilized a building by "floating" it over its foundation on springs or rubber bearings that absorbed the ground's rocking rather than transferring it to the building above.

On May 12, 2008, visitors to Taiwan's 1,671-foot skyscraper, Taipei 101, appreciated another earthquake technology, a mass damper. As the historic 7.9-magnitude quake in Sichuan, China, sent ripples through Taipei, a 728-ton pendulum suspended near the top of the tower countered the swaying of the building by swinging gently in the opposite direction.

WHAT'S INSIDE?

Self-Healing Concrete

Concrete has been in use for millennia despite a persistent problem: cracks. Now scientists have come up with a remarkable advance: concrete that heals itself. Bacteria are embedded, along with starches. As long as the concrete stays in one piece, the bacteria lie dormant. But if it cracks, air wakes the bacteria, and they begin consuming the starch. Then they reproduce, and as they do so, they excrete calcite, a mineral that bonds to the concrete and eventually fills and seals the crack, giving the healed concrete nearly all its original strength.

Hurricane Netting

HURRICANE NETTING WAS DESIGNED TO BATTEN DOWN HOUSES, BUT IT CAN PROTECT BOATS, CARS, SIGNS, AND JUST ABOUT ANYTHING ELSE.

Tropical disturbances that form off the west coast of Africa travel across the Atlantic gathering force. Often Florida is one of the first landmasses the storms hit as full-blown hurricanes. In 1992, Hurricane Andrew ravaged the Bahamas before slamming into the Florida coast with a violence that broke all the National Hurricane Center's wind gauges. Andrew was only the third documented Category 5 hurricane to make landfall in the United States It leveled buildings and killed 26 people. In its wake, the state revised its building codes and stepped up homeproofing.

In the face of gales that exceed 100 mph, a homeowner's most basic concern is keeping the house together. Lose a window, and the house may be lost too. A gale, once inside, seeks a weak point for its exit, which is often the roof. Homeowners often anchor windows and roofs with clips and shutters.

In 2004, a structural engineer was inspired by the tarps securing the loads of dump trucks traveling at high speeds. He and a shutter manufacturer came up with a similar concept for tying down houses with strips of polyester fabric, forming a net that wrapped over the roof and anchored in the ground. The system secures the house and deflects the force of the wind by half. Combined with shutters and roof bracing, it can help a hurricane-battered home live to see another storm.

Concrete Fabric

CONCRETE CLOTH WAS DESIGNED FOR USE BY THE MILITARY, BUT IT'S NOW AVAILABLE FOR CIVIL ENGINEERING PROJECTS AND PRIVATE CITIZENS.

A tornado leaves behind a relatively narrow ribbon of destruction. Building codes in tornado country are generally more relaxed than in hurricane-prone areas because it's not economically feasible to shore up every house to withstand a twister. The more important structure—the one that can save its occupants—is a storm shelter. The most secure shelter is underground, but in the absence of that, a new material may provide a sound alternative. Concrete cloth is a cement-impregnated fabric that when wetted, exposed to air, and draped over a frame hardens into a strong, bunker-type shell. For owners of mobile homes or others without basements,

it could beat waiting out a twister in an interior closet. Far less expensive than an excavated shelter, it can quickly form a low fireproof structure that resists high winds and projectiles. Concrete cloth might just save some lives in Tornado Alley— the twister-prone area that extends from west Texas to parts of Oklahoma and Kansas.

Shipping Container Buildings

PEOPLE DON'T BUY CONTAINERS AT THE PORT. DISTRIBUTORS ACQUIRE THEM FROM SHIPPING COMPANIES AND TRANSPORT THEM TO CUSTOMERS.

An industrial freight unit, treated with chemical pesticides and often having an unknown cargo history, the shipping container is not an obvious home-building solution. It gained popularity as a modular housing unit mostly because it was so available. Thousands of empty containers stack up at U.S. ports. The steel boxes, with an 8-foot opening and 20 or 40 feet long on average, are a 1950s invention that revolutionized the global shipping industry. There's no way to identify exactly when a shipping container first officially became someone's home, but a 1987 U.S. patent filed by a man named Philip C. Clark lists a "method for converting one or more steel shipping containers into a habitable building."

The containers, with minimal modifications, have been put to use in low-income housing, mobile clinics, and schools. The military has used them as administrative and training buildings.

Recently shipping container architecture has graduated from utilitarian to hip, becoming a green alternative to traditional home building. Though the repurposed containers have a modernist simplicity many people find attractive, the price of conversion—including installing electricity and plumbing—can be daunting.

Avalanche Protection

AVALANCHES ARE SO SUDDEN AND POWERFUL THAT PEOPLE IN THE MIDDLE AGES SIMPLY ACCEPTED THEM AS UNAVOIDABLE ACTS OF GOD OR THE DEVIL.

The Alps were one of the first densely populated mountainous regions, and Switzerland and Austria did much of the trailblazing in protecting people and property from the deadly snow slides. Among the frustrating challenges was how arbitrary avalanches could be. Although some occurred almost annually, others, owing to a set of complex climate and snowpack conditions, occurred only once in centuries. In 1951, a particularly terrible winter for avalanches in the Alps, 200 people died and houses that had stood unharmed for 500 years were destroyed.

Historically, avalanche protection mostly involved damage control. People built mounds of earth against the mountain-facing side of a house to divide and divert the snow roaring down the slope. They were the earliest versions of modern avalanche-deflection dams. Not until the beginning of the 20th century did people explore ways to stop an avalanche from even starting by installing rugged fences that anchored snow high in the start zone. Defensive structures like deflection dams are often cheaper; so too are retention dams—large pits that can bring an avalanche to a halt.

Roadways in avalanche-prone regions of the world are commonly sheltered by variations of a structure that originated during the early days of the U.S. Transcontinental Railroad. In 1869, rail workers in the Rocky Mountains built timber galleries over the tracks with slanted roofs that mirrored the slope of the mountain and dumped cascading snow safely beyond the tracks.

UNCOMMONLY KNOWN ...

INCA ROPE BRIDGES The South American Inca people wove mountain grasses into thick cables for bridges they anchored on either side of wide, deep gorges in the Andes Mountains. The swaying, sagging suspension bridges were deceptively strong–Spanish conquistadors rode horses over them in the 16th century. Today nearly all the rope bridges have been replaced with modern truss spans, but one remains, near Huinchiri in Peru. Each year the bridge is lovingly restrung with grass cords woven by families from four local villages.

Fireproof Building Material

STEEL CAN FAIL AT TEMPERATURES HIGHER THAN 1000°F. SOME MODERN BUILDINGS CIRCULATE WATER IN THEIR STRUCTURAL COLUMNS.

Emperor Nero supposedly played his fiddle as Rome burned in A.D. 64, but he wasn't too cavalier to guard against another conflagration. The regulations he drew up for rebuilding the city walls required that they be fireproof. In general, fire protection engineering has been a process of trial and error. After the Great London Fire of 1666 destroyed 80 percent of the city—built principally of wood—a sadder, wiser city rebuilt with stone and brick. During the industrial revolution, concrete and steel began to replace combustible materials, and in the United States the sprinkler system was born following devastating fires in New England textile mills.

The Chicago Fire of 1871 brought another fireproof material to the fore: terra-cotta. As the blaze advanced through the city, the architect of the Palmer House hotel stowed the blueprints for the building under a layer of sand and clay in the basement. The hotel burned but the plans survived, and terra-cotta was hailed as viable fireproofing.

Reuse and Repurpose

Recycling was as natural to earlier generations as rewearing a shirt or washing a dish to use again. Before mass production made goods widely available and easily replaceable, people had to make careful use of what nature provided them, conserve their belongings, and extend the life cycle even of broken things by putting the remnants to other uses. Green living is a modern movement, but its tenets aren't—people were practicing them centuries ago, just to survive. Societies today are merely rediscovering the example of their resourceful ancestors.

Living Roof

GREEN ROOFS AREN'T JUST FOR HIGH-RISES. FORD MOTOR COMPANY'S VAST TRUCK PLANT IN MICHIGAN IS TOPPED WITH FIELDS OF SEDUM.

Around 600 B.C., King Nebuchadrezzar II built the Hanging Gardens of Babylon near his palace, allegedly to placate his homesick Median wife. The gardens were legendarily stunning, but the use of greenery later in building history was motivated more by self-preservation. The Vikings built turf and stone homes in Iceland and Greenland to shield themselves from the frigid winters. Similarly, in the 19th century, settlers on the American frontier built and roofed homes with insulating prairie sod.

The benefits of green roofs eventually trickled down to the 20th century, which had seen the rise of dense, asphalt-bound urban centers. The green-roof industry first took off in Germany in the 1960s and began to gain traction in the United States around the turn of the millennium. Living roofs offer a host of practical benefits—insulation, energy savings, storm-water infiltration—but urbanites also began to see them as precious oases of green space, and everything from crop farms to lavish gardens is now sprouting from city rooftops.

WHAT'S INSIDE?

Solar Panels

A lot of invisible activity goes on inside a solar panel. The panels are made up of a series of connected photovoltaic cells. Each cell is composed of two silicon layers sandwiched between a thinner metal backing and a metal conductor strip that sits on top. An electric field is generated between the silicon layers, and when photons from the sun hit the panel, they force the electrons into motion. As the electrons bounce around and hit the metal conductor strip, they generate energy that flows through wires and provides electricity that can warm—or cool—a house, heat water, and power appliances that need to be plugged in.

Straw Bale Home

A STRAW HOUSE WOULD SEEM TO PRESENT A DANGEROUS FIRE HAZARD. ACTUALLY, IT'S MORE LIKELY TO ROT FROM EXPOSURE TO MOISTURE.

In the Nebraska Sand Hills, early settlers were surrounded by little but sand and grass. They turned to an unlikely building material: straw. The invention of the steam-powered baler in the 1890s led the straw bale to become a significant construction material. Homesteaders stacked them to create not only houses but also churches, stores, offices, and schools. It was a surprisingly effective remedy for the absence of timber. The straw buildings were quick to put up, sturdy, provided good insulation, and even dampened the noise of the ceaseless prairie wind.

One of straw-bale construction's more unusual challenges was bovine—hungry cattle reportedly ate at least one early straw building, an unfenced one-room schoolhouse, in 1902. The use of stucco or plaster to cover straw walls alleviated that threat, and for well into the 20th century, straw-bale buildings were a common sight in the Sand Hills.

The practice waned in the 1950s as mass-produced building materials became common. But in the past decade, straw has been making a resurgence for more or less the same reasons the settlers liked it: It's a good insulator, it's cheap, and it can almost always be locally sourced.

Plastic Composite Lumber

COMPOSITE LUMBER WAS INVENTED BY BUSINESSMAN ROGER WITTENBERG. "RECYCLING," HE SAID, "IS THE BEST WAY I KNOW TO MAKE MONEY."

People have been tinkering with wood for millennia to make it stronger and more durable. Archaeologists discovered evidence of the most primitive version of engineered wood, plywood, in the tombs of Egyptian pharaohs. But the invention of

UNCOMMONLY KNOWN ...

ECOFRIENDLY SKYSCRAPERS A critical item on any engineering checklist for skyscrapers is making the towers able to withstand winds that blow far above the ground. But some new skyscrapers have begun to turn the wind into an environmental and economic advantage. Large-scale wind turbines are integrated high up in a tower's structure, where they can catch and harvest the wind. The energy is converted to power that helps run the building's electrical and mechanical systems.

plastics in the 20th century ushered in a whole new era of manufactured lumber. In 1988 an organic chemist and entrepreneur named Roger Wittenberg discovered a way to combine shredded plastic bags with sawdust to create a product that mimicked wood but was more durable. The company he eventually founded, Trex, started an industry that turned this formula into plastic composite lumber.

To gather the principal ingredients for its product, the company collected billions of plastic bags (in 2003, it scooped up about half the grocery bags recycled in the United States). For the sawdust, it gathered millions of pounds of wood scraps from furniture manufacturers and ground them down, eliminating the need for any trees to be felled. The ingredients were then mixed, heated, pressed, and sliced into boards for use in decking, benches, and walkways. It's usually conceded that plastic composite lumber does not rival wood aesthetically—but its rot resistance, low maintenance, and competitive pricing are their own attractions.

PEOPLE WHO CHANGED HISTORY

Frederick Law Olmsted (1822–1903)

Frederick Law Olmsted was regarded as the father of landscape architecture in the United States. He designed some of the country's most famous urban parks by applying his philosophy that dense urban centers need to include an oasis of pastoral landscape. Along with British landscape architect Calvert Vaux, Olmsted designed and constructed New York City's Central Park. Olmsted integrated naturalistic features such as wooded areas, meadows, lakes, and lawns, among which New Yorkers could take refuge from the crowds and clamor of their city. His influence went beyond parks. The curving streets of modern subdivisions draw from his designs for planned communities such as Riverside, Illinois, which avoided right angles and aligned roads to the land's contours.

Olmsted, 1860s

Recycled Steel

STEEL CAN BE MELTED AND RE-FORMED INDEFINITELY, AND THE NEWLY FORGED OBJECTS WILL REMAIN AS STRONG AS THE ORIGINALS.

Tossing articles away permanently was often a luxury that previous generations didn't have. In the 1930s people made a living out of collecting and selling scraps of metal, especially iron and steel. During World War II, scrap recycling was an important part of the war effort—metal remnants were melted down and turned into ships, tanks, and weapons.

Recycling became an environmentally focused concern only when mass production resulted in a flood of cheaply produced goods that were more easily disposed of and replaced than reused.

As more and more waste headed to landfills and incinerators, a broad awareness of conservation took root with a renewed sense of urgency. In some cases, recycling became compulsory:

All of the steel products in the United States today contain a minimum of 25 percent recycled steel.

For decades, an enormous amount of steel has been salvaged from old cars, which are crushed, hauled to a steel mill, and then pulverized in a matter of seconds by powerful shredders. Huge magnets separate out the steel from the plastic and upholstery, and the metal is melted down and sold to become new products.

Beyond cars and curbside bins, scrap metal is big business. Steel is salvaged from unlikely places—even from the most stunning disasters. In 2001, the wreckage of the World Trade Center yielded hundreds of thousands of tons of high-grade steel, some of which was used to build the U.S.S. *New York*.

UNCOMMONLY KNOWN ...

BEER-BOTTLE JACKPOT It's no surprise that the Las Vegas Strip generates empty beer bottles. Rather than ship them to a landfill, an environmental design firm converted 500,000 of them into a composite material it calls GreenStone and used it to build the Morrow Royal Pavilion, a 30,000-square-foot replica of an English manor. The firm estimates the bottles would have occupied 400,000 cubic yards of space in a landfill. The pavilion's function is eco-minded: it houses GreenStone manufacturing operations.

Salvaged Wood and Stone

CENTURY-OLD BRICK PAVERS, 200-YEAR-OLD EUROPEAN COBBLESTONES, ANTIQUE FIREBRICKS: ALL HAVE BEEN SALVAGED AND REUSED.

During World War II, most of the country's metal resources were put to work making weapons, so factories and warehouses were often constructed of wood instead. Such old industrial buildings, along with barns, are the biggest sources of reclaimed lumber today. They aren't the only ones: In 2010, huge, centuries-old timbers were retrieved from a saltwater pond at the Charlestown Navy Yard in Boston. They had been preserved there since at least the 1800s, awaiting use in a warship and forgotten when shipyards turned to iron for constructing ships. On Flathead Lake in Montana, a sawmill once made railroad ties from logs floated down the Flathead and Swan Rivers during spring drives. Now sunken logs are retrieved from the bottom of the lake and used to make furniture.

Stone too is recovered from old buildings and abandoned public works. When an 1885 masonry reservoir in Ohio was dismantled in 2010, an Iowa company salvaged 6,000 tons of sandstone, which it peddled as ready-made landscaping stone.

Reclaimed wood and stone have advantages. Lumber reclaimed from old buildings often originated from old-growth trees and has a mass and strength virgin timber cannot match. Salvaged stone has already been quarried and cut; both activities consume considerable time and money. Unlike steel or plastic, though, reclaimed wood and stone are limited resources. The supplies will last only as long as there are reserves of old buildings and structures from which they can be salvaged.

Transportation Systems

Transportation is the circulatory system that supplies the modern world with lifeblood. It is integral to widespread human settlement. Until established transport systems could convey people to places efficiently or deliver things they needed to build communities, economic development was stymied. Cities certainly found that to be true: If an efficient system of pedestrian movement is in place, downtowns stay economically viable. Large-scale building doesn't begin until it happens, and communities have trouble sustaining themselves if it goes away.

New York City Subway

ON ITS FIRST DAY OF OPERATION, OCTOBER 27, 1904, THE LONG-AWAITED NEW YORK CITY SUBWAY CARRIED 150,000 PASSENGERS IN FIVE HOURS.

When the New York City subway opened in 1904, the concept of a mass underground transport system was no longer new. The London Underground had opened its first Tube line nearly 40 years earlier, in 1863, and Boston had rushed to open America's first subway in 1897. But if New York didn't have the oldest subway system in the world, it did have the oldest subway tunnel. The pre–Civil War Atlantic Avenue Tunnel was built to carry passengers on the Long Island Railroad under a densely crowded section of Brooklyn. Then in 1870 an inventor named Alfred Ely Beach constructed a 300-foot demonstration subway tunnel; his so-called Beach Pneumatic Transfer was an effort to drum up interest in underground transit for New York. The novelty line had only a single track and passenger station and traveled the distance of a city block. The public was intrigued, but the grim economic climate of the 1870s prevented Beach's experiment from going any further.

The city finally broke ground on its full-scale subway system in 1900 and opened it four years later. Another set of routes and stations was planned and partially constructed in the 1920s before the Great Depression and war years put an end to the expansion; some remnants still exist today. Along with these unfinished portions are dozens of other tunnels and stations that were opened, used, and then abandoned because of finances, declining ridership, or route changes. Ironically, sitting derelict today is the very platform where it all began. The grand Romanesque Revival-style City Hall Station, from which the first subway train departed amid great fanfare in 1904, has been closed and deserted since 1945.

Underground Cities

IN 50 YEARS MONTREAL'S UNDERGROUND COMPLEX WENT FROM A SINGLE PASSAGE TO A 20-MILE NETWORK CONNECTING MORE THAN 1,600 BUSINESSES.

The planners of Montreal (above) were building up rather than down when the idea for underground pedestrian corridors occurred to them. In the late 1950s, urban planner Vincent Ponte and architects I. M. Pei and Henry Cobb were collaborating on Montreal's first skyscraper when Ponte thought an underground passage from the building to the central train station would be welcome in the city's cold climate.. This initial segment launched a rambling, mazelike network of underground tunnels and stairs that connected metro stations, stores, hotels, and offices.

The tunnel system was constructed somewhat haphazardly over the decades. Private developers went to great lengths to complete the tunnels, in some cases making wild diversions around the property of recalcitrant landowners. At one point, the entire 19th-century Christ Church Cathedral was supported on stilts while footings for the pedestrian complex underneath it were poured.

Montreal's underground network is the world's largest, but far from the only subterranean city. Toronto boasts 19 miles of underground shopping arcades, and cities such as Osaka and Tokyo, Japan, have extensive underground networks.

Airports

THE EARLIEST "FLYING FIELDS" WERE LARGE, VERSATILE GRASS EXPANSES SO AIRPLANES COULD ALWAYS FACE INTO THE WIND TO TAKE OFF.

Before there were airports, there were airfields, and they were little more than that: grass plots that planes landed on and took off from. Until the 1930s most airplanes and airfields were used by the military, but between the world wars, air travel started to become available to civilians. With that development came the need for formal departure and arrival terminals: Enter the airport and, with it, innovations like paved runways and runway lighting. In the 1960s and 1970s, air travel became accessible to the masses, and airports mushroomed into the massive concrete mini-cities we know today. The fourth busiest in the United States, Dallas/Fort Worth International, for instance, covers 27 square miles, moves 170,000 people a day, and employs 60,000.

To build these sprawling complexes, cities had to commandeer thousands of acres of private land, and they never knew what they might encounter during construction. In 1961, workers at Seattle-Tacoma International Airport unearthed a beautifully preserved 12,500-year-old sloth skeleton. And embedded in one of Savannah–Hilton Head's runways are two gravestones that workers reverently replaced after they built over a 19th-century family cemetery in the 1970s.

Shipping Ports

SHANGHAI WAS A SMALL FISHING VILLAGE IN 1842. TODAY THE GIANT PORT CITY HANDLES SOME 30 MILLION SHIPPING CONTAINERS A YEAR.

Shipping is economical. That age-old discovery has made the industry not only durable but massive. The Egyptian pharaoh Khufu, best known for building the Great Pyramid at Giza, also built the first known port in the world on the Sinai Peninsula 4,500 years ago. A couple of millennia later, Rome supplemented its commercial port, Ostia, with the even mightier Portus, composed of two engineered deepwater harbors. Portus was a marvel, but it was also the hub of import, distribution, and warehousing for Rome. The success of the empire depended on it. At its height, Portus was a mile wide and could accommodate hundreds of ships at a time.

Yet Portus pales in comparison to today, in large part due to the introduction of the shipping container. The modern port of Rotterdam is 25 miles long; the wharves alone of the world's busiest port, Shanghai, cover 1,000 acres. These great hubs load and offload container ships that are up to a quarter-mile long and as tall as a 20-story building. Modern ports do still have in common one thing with Rome's: Civilization might collapse without them. Ninety percent of everything we use day-to-day arrives on ships from teeming container ports.

Railroads

IN 1804 IN WALES, THE FIRST STEAM-POWERED TRAIN PULLED 70 PASSENGERS AND A LOAD OF IRON NINE MILES AT ABOUT FIVE MILES AN HOUR.

Ancient Greeks cut parallel tracks across the isthmus of Corinth in the sixth century B.C. to form one of the earliest known track systems. Miners in Europe began using tramways with wooden tracks in the 1500s, but the modern mechanized railroad on steel tracks didn't come along until the 1800s in Britain.

Construction of the first transcontinental railroad across North America was a defining moment in America's westward expansion. Starting in Sacramento, California, in the West and Council Bluffs, Iowa, in the East, crews worked for six arduous years laying about 1,800 miles of track over harsh terrain. They met in Promontory, Utah, in 1869 to national fanfare and an elaborate ceremony to drive the final spike. Embarrassingly, the heads of both the Union and Central Pacific railroad companies swung and missed the spike. With poetic justice, an actual railroad laborer stepped up to drive home the spike that opened the United States to transcontinental passage.

PEOPLE WHO CHANGED HISTORY

I. M. Pei (1917-)

The Chinese-born architect has famously used angular geometries to design landmark buildings that are greatly admired and sometimes controversial. Signature works include the glass pyramid entrance to the Louvre in Paris, the Holocaust Museum in Washington, D.C., and the Museum of Islamic Art in Qatar. Pei's vision has extended to structures less avant-garde but no less influential. He was the architect of a terminal at John F. Kennedy International Airport in New York City that was eventually demolished. Today many air-traffic control towers are based on his designs.

Pei in front of his pyramid at the Louvre, in Paris, France

Climate-Connected Cities

MINNEAPOLIS BOASTS THE LARGEST PEDESTRIAN SKYWAY SYSTEM IN THE U.S., WITH 8 MILES OF WALKWAYS THAT CONNECT 80 CITY BLOCKS.

Harsh weather, coupled with post–World War II migration to the suburbs, made cities such as Minneapolis (above) anxious for the health of their downtowns. In the 1950s a businessman named Leslie Park pitched the idea of enclosed walkways above street level that would link offices and shops. His idea wasn't new; in Chester, England, elevated galleries had been keeping people out of the rain since the Middle Ages. Nonetheless, Minneapolis residents were skeptical until the first climate-controlled skyway opened in 1963. It was an instant hit. By 1972 Minneapolis had established itself as a second-story city. Today, the Plus 15 network in Calgary, Alberta, Canada, has trumped Minneapolis's Skyways as the world's most extensive elevated pedestrian walkway, with more than ten miles of bridges connecting the city.

Similar models have been a bust in more temperate locales. Baltimore, Maryland, invested in elevated walkways in the 1960s, but later dismantled them, because removing foot traffic from street level damaged the downtown economy.

U
S
Die Sitze bitte nicht festhalten

Anyone who tries to make a distinction between education and entertainment doesn't know the first thing about either.

—MARSHALL MCLUHAN (1911–1980)

That's Entertainment

From the earliest days of civilization, human beings have sought out pastimes that have helped us celebrate the best in ourselves and in others. These various activities are representations of our strengths and weaknesses, our good times and bad. Whether watching actors play out their roles on stage or on screen, we love to root for the heroes and cheer the downfall of the villains, all the while reveling in the joy of a story well told. When it comes to music, we dance and sing along with our favorite songwriters, whether live or recorded, knowing that music is perhaps the purest expression of the soul.

As civilizations developed, people devised ever more ways to express their creativity and passions. They invented new pastimes and diversions, including games and competitions that tested their hand-eye coordination—skills required today to master the latest electronic video games. Modern amusement parks have sprouted across the country and around the world, showcasing death-defying rides and attractions that get our adrenaline pumping and our hearts racing.

Indeed at the very heart of our nature is a desire to transcend boundaries and push our bodies to their physical limits—at least perhaps to watch others try their luck. At great sporting events, we thrill to the athletic feats of the top competitors. We witness what the human animal is currently capable of and begin to think about the possibilities of even greater achievements in the future. Drawing inspiration from sports and games and amusements, we come to know ourselves and our fellow human beings a little bit better. We may even be inspired to dream of escaping the bonds of gravity itself—before the dream takes flight and we wake up firmly anchored in the safety and comfort of our living rooms.

Got Game?

Pinball wizards of the 1940s and 1950s and their flashing, clattering, joyous machines were pioneers of a vast galaxy of gaming that's been expanding ever since. And while pinball gained a reputation for naughtiness—and worse—its successors by and large have become mainstream, including an arcade staple from Japan that munched its way into 1980s history, a steampunk CD-ROM that sold millions of copies, and two consoles that could be played at home. From the arcade to the living room, here are some games people can't get enough of. No quarters required.

Pinball

THE ORIGINAL WOODEN PINBALL MACHINE WAS DESIGNED IN 1931, BUT THE ALL-IMPORTANT FLIPPERS DIDN'T COME ALONG UNTIL 1947.

The first pinball machines encouraged tilting. The original version of the game, named Whiffle Board, took its inspiration from a French diversion called bagatelle, which was similar to billiards. Whiffle Board and other games that followed had flat surfaces balanced on four wooden legs. With no flippers to keep the ball in play, players physically maneuvered the playing field to score points. Since that made pinball more a game of chance than skill, many cities banned it, likening it to gambling and believing, often correctly, that it was associated with organized crime. In 1942 New York City's mayor, Fiorello LaGuardia, went so far as to have thousands

PEOPLE WHO CHANGED HISTORY

Shigeru Miyamoto (1952-)

Growing up near Kyoto, the Japanese native was inspired by nature, especially a sprawling cavern he discovered as a child in the mountainous forest near his home. He never forgot the awe he felt exploring it, and as an adult he channeled that into his pioneering work creating video games. Miyamoto is responsible for one of the most iconic characters in gaming history, Mario—the hero in *Donkey Kong*, *Super Mario Bros.*, and *Mario Kart*. He also helped mastermind *The Legend of Zelda*, *Star Fox*, and others. And the list keeps growing.

Shigeru Miyamoto with Mario, Los Angeles, 2014

of the machines rounded up and turned into scrap for the war effort. Well into the 1970s, pinball was associated with corrupting youth and inspiring hooliganism. An 80-year pinball ban in Oakland, California, was finally lifted in 2014.

Foosball

IN 1978 FOOSBALL WAS ONE OF THE MOST POPULAR SPORTS IN THE UNITED STATES, WITH TOP PLAYERS COMPETING FOR A MILLION-DOLLAR PRIZE.

Foosball has many fathers—and even more variations. Three men have been credited with inventing the game: French engineer Lucien Rosengart, who also claimed to have invented the seat belt; Spain's Alexandre de Finesterre, who said he invented the game after being inspired by table tennis; and England's Harold Searles Thornton, who was the first person to patent the notion of attaching playing pieces to a pole. His uncle Louis liked the idea so much that he brought it to the United States, where he got his own patent in 1927.

The rules of the game are as vague as its history, and foosball tables are constructed differently in various regions around the world. Some tables use plastic players, some use hardwood, and some incorporate different playing fields. The first foosball leagues began springing up in Belgium in the 1950s, marking the increased popularity of the game. Foosball tables became a staple of bars and gaming halls across the United States in the 1960s and 1970s, but the advent of arcade video games signaled the end of the foosball explosion. Nevertheless, ardent fans persist, staging foosball tournaments across the globe—even if no one can agree exactly on the formal rules of the game.

Pac-Man

IT TOOK GAMER BILLY MITCHELL SIX HOURS ON JULY 3, 1999, TO ACHIEVE THE WORLD'S FIRST PERFECT SCORE IN PAC-MAN: 3,333,360.

Pac-Man creator Toru Iwatani was 27 years old and working for the Japanese video game company Namco when one day he took a hard look at the pizza he was eating. With two slices missing, the pizza resembled a mouth. According to Iwatani, that was the inspiration for the game that ate its way through untold quarters and singlehandedly ignited the arcade revolution of the 1980s. Called *Pakku-Man* in Japan (after the Japanese word for the sound of a mouth opening and closing), it was only a modest

hit until it was introduced in the United States. Video games predate *Pac-Man,* but none before it rode as intense a wave of cultural popularity. It's reported to have earned more than one billion dollars in its first year of release in the United States alone. It inspired 16 sequel games, including *Ms. Pac-Man* in 1981 and *Jr. Pac-Man* in 1983. Other games succeeded *Pac-Man* in popularity over the years, but nostalgia for the original remains strong.

Myst

MANY SOUND EFFECTS FOR *MYST* WERE RECORDINGS OF EVERYDAY SOUNDS—CAR TIRES RUNNING OVER GRAVEL EMULATED A CRACKLING FIRE, FOR EXAMPLE.

In 1993 a steampunk video game released on CD-ROM changed the nature of gaming forever. Constructed by two brothers, Rand and Robyn Miller, then 35 and 27 years old, respectively, *Myst* was revolutionary most notably because it provided virtually no narrative before users started playing. Instead, the game immersed the player in the story immediately and asked them to figure it out as they went along. A player took on the role of "the Stranger," who has landed on a mysterious island known as Myst. The players then had to sift through multiple screens collecting content, such as journals and other objects, using them to help move to different worlds called "Ages." In these new worlds, the player continued to unravel the ongoing narrative of the game and complete various puzzles. Though the story was complex, navigating the game was fairly simple: An on-screen hand represented the player, and clicking on objects revealed hidden details.

In creating the elaborate story and settings in which they plunged their players, the Miller brothers took inspiration from an immensely popular role-playing game of the 1980s, *Dungeons & Dragons. Myst,* initially released for Macintosh computers only, later moved to multiple platforms including Windows, PlayStation, and Sega Saturn. The game eventually sold more than six million copies and inspired five sequels as well as three novels. In 2014 a TV series based on the game was announced. The company that the Miller brothers formed to release *Myst,* Cyan, Inc., is still developing video games.

WHAT'S INSIDE?

Video Game Controllers

The devices are engineered thoroughly, inside and out. In many ways they're little changed since Atari's Stephen Bristow received a patent for his "improved joystick" in 1978. It used a ball-and-socket joint and potentiometers around circuit elements. When a player pushed the joystick up, for example, a circuit would be completed and register on the screen. Designers have added high-tech features such as LED light bars that the consoles can track, a motor to provide vibration, and wireless transmitters. On the outside, new and better ergonomics allow controllers to fit more comfortably in a player's hand.

Wii

NINTENDO HAS NEVER EXPLAINED WHAT *WII* MEANS, BUT PEOPLE SPECULATE IT STANDS FOR "WE"—WITH EACH *I* REPRESENTING A PLAYER.

As the video game marketplace heated up in the 2000s, producers were looking for ways to make games better, faster, more interactive—and to continually improve graphic quality. In 2006 industry giant Nintendo unveiled a different kind of game system. Wii was innovative on many levels—it featured a wireless controller, the "Wiimote," with an accelerometer and an optical sensor that allowed the console to track its every motion—but its graphics were not cutting edge, and it wasn't designed solely for enthusiastic gamers. Instead, it had broad appeal for non-game-players, a demographic that most video game makers ignored. The new controller used motion-capture technology to put players virtually inside the game and interact with the video system in a way that had never been done. The *Wii Fit* was just one of the games designed for the system; it has sold 37 million copies and inspired a fitness craze. Wii reenvisioned video games and inspired a new audience, young and old, not merely to sit in front of a screen but to take part and get moving.

Atari

BEFORE VAST MULTIPLAYER ONLINE GAMES, BEFORE PLAYSTATION AND WII, ATARI REVOLUTIONIZED VIDEO GAMES, IN HOMES AND IN PUBLIC.

When Nolan Bushnell and Ted Dabney met in 1969, video games didn't have a big audience. But the two young engineers saw the future, and in 1971 they sold their first game, *Computer Space*. That year, with $500, they started the company that became Atari (Japanese for "success") and changed the industry with one stroke: *Pong*. The video tennis game featured two solid bars and a darting ball. The machine kept score while producing distinctive "boink" sounds. When *Pong* debuted at a bar in Sunnyvale, California, it proved so popular that patrons would line up before the bar even opened for the day.

Atari sold $3 million worth of *Pong* cabinets in two years, then introduced a home version that helped spark the home video game craze. Warner Communications bought Atari in 1976; sales reached $415 million in 1980. Three years later, as competition soared, the end was near. But during Atari's brief reign, it was the winningest video system in the world.

Music to Your Ears

"If music be the food of love, play on." So wrote William Shakespeare in *Twelfth Night,* and so say we all when we hear melodies we love. Taking music with us wherever we are is a relatively new concept, first made possible by transistors that fulfilled our desire to keep the beat going far from home. After that breakthrough in technology came ways of storing music on computers, along with new devices for listening. And music is no longer just for our ears, as videos prove we love to watch our favorite music makers as well as hear them.

Portable Record Players

THESE RECORD PLAYERS OFTEN LOOKED LIKE SMALL SUITCASES, COMPLETE WITH HANDLES. MODERN VERSIONS STILL FREQUENTLY COPY THAT VINTAGE LOOK.

It took 40 years after Edison invented the phonograph for a company to make a portable record player. The British firm Decca produced small hand-cranked players used by troops in World War I. The 1924 Swedish Mikiphone folded down to a remarkably small size but required assembly and didn't have a loudspeaker. More portables followed, including the RCA Victor Special Model K in 1935. In the 1950s teens danced to the sounds produced by Britain's popular Dansette. Transistor technology made record players and radios even more portable, and Henry Kloss's 1962 KLH Model 11 became the first portable stereo: It contained an amplifier and two speakers. But that same year saw the release of the compact cassette tape, signaling the beginning of the end for portable record players—at least until the resurrection of vinyl in the 21st century.

WHAT'S INSIDE?

Harmonica

Harmonicas are framed free-reed wind instruments, which means the reeds inside are encased in a frame. Tuned to a particular key, harmonicas produce sound when air passes through external holes and vibrates the reeds. In most harmonicas, the outer cover encloses two brass reeds—one for when the player exhales and the other for when the player inhales. A comb, made from plastic, wood, or metal, is sandwiched between the blow reed and the draw reed. The comb defines and separates the instrument's holes, often 10 or 16, each correlating to an individual note.

Transistor Radio

BUILDING ON TECHNOLOGY FROM WORLD WAR II, TRANSISTOR RADIOS LET US TAKE MUSIC ON THE GO IN AN INCREASINGLY MOBILE SOCIETY.

It wasn't music that led to the creation of the transistor radio. Instead, the quest to build smaller, more efficient radio-controlled bombs during World War II drove its invention. Bombs guided by vacuum tubes were tactical energy hogs, and the military wanted something compact, more durable (at least before they went off), and less energy draining to conduct the flow of electrical currents in them. It was 1947 before three scientists at Bell Labs came up with a solution: the transistor. A few years later, transistor technology was open to everyone, and companies were searching for ways to make it profitable. A partnership between Texas Instruments (TI) and Industrial Development Engineering Associates did just that, making music history in the process: Regency fit four TI transistors into a radio five inches tall and four inches wide—a truly portable radio. The Regency TR1, released in October 1954, sold 100,000 models in one year alone, despite a relatively high cost ($50, or more than $400 today). Other companies saw the potential and immediately began licensing the patented technology, leading not just to more models of transistor radios but also to

UNCOMMONLY KNOWN ...

"WHITE CHRISTMAS" Bing Crosby's 1942 version of Irving Berlin's "White Christmas" sold more than 50 million copies, making it Guinness World Records' highest-selling single of all time. Elton John's tribute to Princess Diana, "Candle in the Wind," is second, at 33 million copies.

smaller computer chips, helping pave the way for home computers followed by laptops and ever smaller devices.

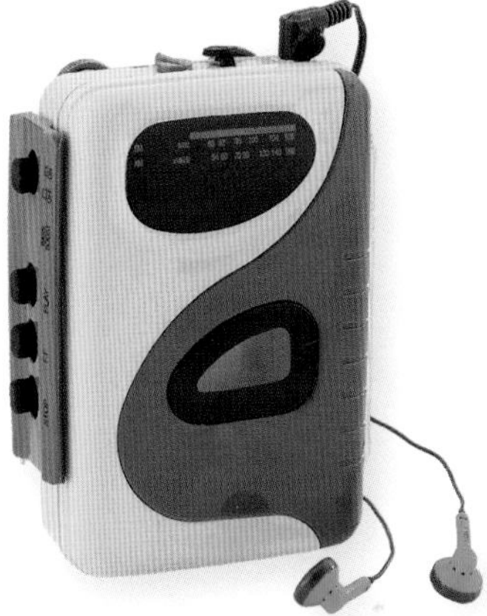

Walkman

THE WALKMAN COULD ENTERTAIN TWO LISTENERS WITH ITS TWO HEADPHONE JACKS. AFTER ITS RELEASE, SALES OF CASSETTE TAPES SOARED.

With the portable record player firmly established and cars being sold with cassette and eight-track players built in, could a portable cassette player be far behind? In fact, the portable players showed up only a few years after their vinyl-playing counterparts, but what made the Walkman, which debuted on July 1, 1979, so special was its diminutive size, smaller than any previous music-making technology. The Walkman was born when Sony co-founder Masaru Ibuku asked his deputy

(and future Sony president), Norio Ohga, to design a cassette player that would use only headphones. The next challenge was to choose a name. After trying out suggestions such as the Sound-About and the Stowaway, Sony finally settled on the Walkman. Americans liked the sound of it and snapped up millions. Although cassette tapes are outmoded, Walkmans are still being made, now playing MP3s and DVDs and doubling as phones.

iPod

A COPYWRITER COINED THE NAME AFTER NOTICING THE GADGET BORE A RESEMBLANCE TO THE POD-BAY DOORS IN *2001: A SPACE ODYSSEY.*

The first iPod advertised itself as "1,000 songs in your pocket" and was hailed by the late Apple founder Steve Jobs as a "breakthrough." But the iPod was not an innovation in and of itself. Rather, it was an improvement on existing technology, using a battery from Sony, computer chips from Texas Instruments, and a newly developed hard drive from Toshiba. Moreover, iPod wasn't the first MP3 player invented. In 2000, almost two years before the release of the iPod, came the debut of iTunes, which managed MP3 files and acted as a virtual jukebox. Other portable players at the time worked with digital files, but Jobs wanted something better, and he wanted Apple to produce it, even though music had never been part of the company's traditional business model. Toward the end of October 2001, Jobs previewed Apple's new 5GB gadget amid great fanfare, but it wasn't until the second-generation iPod was released in July 2002 that the device began to realize its potential—doubling and quadrupling capacity with 10 gigabyte and 20 gigabyte versions. By 2003 the company had released still another update, and sales of iPods had topped one million units. That number vaulted to ten million a year later and today totals nearly half a billion. Early iPods, now rare, regularly fetch hundreds of dollars from collectors.

Headphones

MA BELL IS THE MOTHER OF THIS INVENTION, AND IT CAME FROM NECESSITY: HEADPHONES WERE DESIGNED IN 1881 FOR TELEPHONE OPERATORS.

Businessman John C. Koss created the modern headphone in 1958, but he was hoping to be known for something else. Koss had an idea to develop a new type of portable phonograph that would offer stereo playback. To highlight the stereo component,

PEOPLE WHO CHANGED HISTORY

Sean Parker (1979-)

Born in 1979, Sean Parker has played a key role in Internet history. He partnered with Shawn Fanning during development of Fanning's file-sharing service Napster. One year after Napster started, it had tens of millions of followers. Parker left Napster to start another successful company, Plaxo. When he met Mark Zuckerberg, Parker joined Facebook's founder and served as its first president for a year. He then moved on to such sites as Spotify and Airtime. Parker is a catalyst who makes things happen.

Internet wizard Sean Parker, 2011

he and engineer Martin Lange added an innovation: the SP3 Stereophone.

Prior to that time, headphones had been bulky, heavy contraptions used mostly by telephone operators and pilots. In 1910, electrician and inventor Nathaniel Baldwin developed a compressed-air sound amplifier and used it to create a receiver that he in turn shrank down to create what he called Baldy Phones. Baldwin sold 100 of the headphones to the U.S. Navy for use in World War I.

What Koss invented was far lighter and more efficient. Once plugged in to the phonograph, the Stereophone allowed people to listen in private, with a full range of high and low notes. Sadly, Koss's phonograph was a bomb, but the Stereophone was a smash hit, leading to better headphones and eventually earbuds, for us all.

MP3 File

RELEASED IN 1995, THE COMPRESSION TECHNOLOGY THAT CHANGED THE MUSIC INDUSTRY TOOK ITS NAME FROM MPEG-1, AUDIO LAYER 3.

The MP3 owes its existence to two disparate things: a century's worth of research by telephone companies and Suzanne Vega's a capella song "Tom's Diner." Beginning around 1910, phone companies conducted extensive research on the limits of human hearing, focusing on the highs and lows of audibility. In 1988 mathematician and audio engineer Karlheinz Brandenburg was using data from that research to help create a way to condense music into small computer files. Because our ears can hear and process only a certain number of sounds at any given time, huge amounts of audio are lost that could be condensed, Brandenburg theorized. But when he heard Vega singing, he realized that his work so far would not be effective on that particularly warm vocal.

Brandenburg was part of a team known as the Motion Picture Experts Group (MPEG), and as a result of that one song, the group changed its algorithms, leading to creation of the MP3. The MP1 and MP2, two previous versions, were termed more "lossy"—they lost more sound while compressing files. The MP3 offered a solution, and it coincided with the expansion of Internet availability in homes. The MP3 team even gave the technology a birthday: July 14, 1995.

Tell Me a Story

It's often been said that one picture is worth a thousand words, but in the case of a lavishly illustrated picture book, their value may stretch far beyond that. As printing technology has expanded, the ways we enjoy books have grown as well. Young readers delight in picture books and pop-up books, and comic books and innovative graphic novels have stepped in to entertain readers of all ages. These days we sometimes don't need a book to be physically printed to enjoy it. For many people, audiobooks and e-books have changed the very nature of how they read.

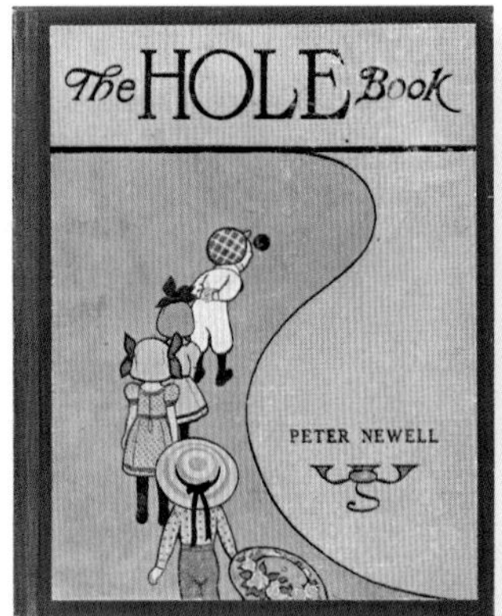

Picture Book

IN 1908 PETER NEWELL'S *THE HOLE BOOK* FEATURED A HOLE ON EVERY PAGE—THE RESULT OF AN ERRANT BULLET FIRED BY A YOUNG BOY.

Orbis Sensualium Pictus, a 1658 work by Czech John Amos Comenius, is considered the first children's book and the first picture book. Featuring 150 drawings, it sold well and was often taught in classrooms. However, for the next two centuries the format floundered. It wasn't until British illustrator Randolph Caldecott began marrying art and story that publishers and readers began to see the full potential of picture books. Beginning in 1878 and until his death in 1886, Caldecott released two books every Christmas season, many of them instant best sellers eagerly anticipated by children around the world. Picture books took another leap forward in the early 20th century, when printing technology began to catch up with the

PEOPLE WHO CHANGED HISTORY

Jeff Bezos (1964-)

In 1994, 30-year-old investment banker Jeff Bezos came across a startling statistic: Internet use was growing at an incredible 2,300 percent every month. Bezos saw enormous sales potential there, and he knew he wanted to be part of it. He quit his lucrative job, raised $1 million, hired five employees, and in July 1995 launched his Seattle-based online venture: Amazon.com. Concentrating initially on bookselling, the business earned nearly $16 million in sales in its first year alone. Today it's the largest online retailer in the world with a staggering array of products and offering original programming to watch online. And Amazon still sells lots of books.

Jeff Bezos, 2013

innovative ideas of illustrators such Peter Newell, who topped his *Hole Book* with his next: A runaway baby carriage rolls its way through *The Slant Book*, which is shaped like a rhomboid. Picture books have been creatively evolving ever since.

Audiobook

THOMAS EDISON WANTED TO MAKE A RECORDING OF CHARLES DICKENS'S *NICHOLAS NICKLEBY*, BUT RECORDING ON WAX PROVED TOO DIFFICULT.

Without audiobooks, the history of the recording industry might have been very different. During the Depression, few families could afford record players, and even if they could, most records played for only a few minutes. The 1930 development of the long-play (LP) record changed things only slightly. Sales of LPs were sluggish until 1933, when they became the recording method of choice for Talking Books—recordings for the blind. With $10,000 of federal funds, recorded books were born, albeit only for the blind (for years sighted people weren't allowed to buy them). But in 1952 two entrepreneurial women fresh out of New York's Hunter College, Barbara Holdridge and Marianne Roney, went to a lecture by Dylan Thomas and convinced him to record some of his poems as well as his then little-known *A Child's Christmas in Wales*. It was a hit, and Caedmon Records was born. Soon T. S. Eliot, Gertrude Stein, W. H. Auden, and others were making recordings. The company also brought in actors, including Richard Burton, Albert Finney, and Maggie Smith, to read authors' works. Audiobooks were now made for sighted and nonsighted people alike. The advent of the cassette tape in the 1960s meant commuters could listen to a selection on their way to work, driving up demand for an ever broader range of audiobooks.

E-Reader

ABOUT A QUARTER OF ALL AMERICANS HAVE READ AN E-BOOK. E-FANS READ 24 BOOKS A YEAR; THEIR PRINT-ONLY COUNTERPARTS READ 15.

The first e-book came about long before the first e-reader—almost 50 years earlier, in fact. A teacher in Galicia, Spain, named Ángela Robles envisioned an easier way for her students to carry textbooks. In 1949 she invented the Mechanical Encyclopedia, powered by compressed air and working off spools loaded with content. The patented device even allowed readers to zoom in on text. Two decades later, on July 4, 1971, University of Illinois graduate student Michael Hart keyboarded the Declaration of Independence. Since he made it available for download—and started a resource for free online books, Project Gutenberg,

in the process—he is widely credited with creating the first e-book, but he was building on a tradition that Robles began. Stand-alone e-readers didn't arrive until 1998, when Nuvo Media released the Rocket eBook and SoftBook Press debuted the SoftBook. Both partnered with publishers at a time when all involved, including authors, were trying to figure out the impact of digital distribution on copyright, a debate that continues.

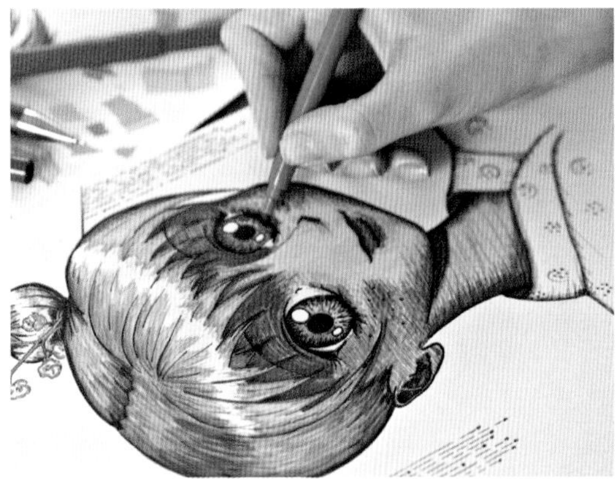

Graphic Novel

IN 1992, ART SPIEGELMAN'S *MAUS*, ABOUT HIS FATHER'S SURVIVAL OF THE HOLOCAUST, WAS THE FIRST GRAPHIC NOVEL TO WIN A PULITZER PRIZE.

Comic books are usually thought of as being mostly for kids, but adult fans of the format have been taking issue with that for decades. When critic Richard Kyle came up with the term *graphic novel* in 1964, he was envisioning longer narratives encompassing mature stories, and he was predicting where the industry was headed. While they are not considered true graphic novels today, early prototypes of the format include Gil Kane and Archie Goodwin's 1971 book *Blackmark*, George Metzger's 1976 *Beyond Time and Again*, and Phil Yeh's 1977 *Even Cazco Gets the Blues.*

The first time a book described itself as a graphic novel was on the dust jacket of Richard Corben's illustrated adaptation of Robert E. Howard's *Bloodstar* in 1976. Two years later, comic book legend Will Eisner, creator of *The Spirit,* would use the term for his *A Contract With God.* Eisner was seemingly unaware of the term's having been previously coined. Though not the format's originator, he's largely responsible for popularizing it and reaching new audiences with his work. In 1985 Eisner chose another term to describe how comic books and graphic novels told stories: *sequential art.* Arguably human beings have been telling stories with sequential art since cave dwellers, and comic books and graphic novels are two more examples.

Pop-Up Book

KIDS' BOOKS WEREN'T POPULAR UNTIL JOHN NEWBERY'S 1744 *A LITTLE PRETTY POCKET-BOOK.* A PRESTIGIOUS AWARD NOW BEARS HIS NAME.

Pop-up books are synonymous with early childhood, giving young minds a chance to explore a story through moving parts and artful paper construction. But the history of the pop-up book begins with

WHAT'S INSIDE?

Permanent Paper

In 1990 President George H. W. Bush signed the Permanent Paper Law, ensuring that all federal records and publications would henceforth be printed on acid-free paper. The law was enacted to prevent the erosion of important historical documents that eventually occurs with the use of traditional paper. The growing popularity of scrapbooking has also increased the demand for acid-free paper. The acidity in paper is activated by lignin, which is found in wood pulp. Paper is considered acid free, or neutral, if it has a pH of 7 or greater. To achieve that level, acid can be removed (though the process is often expensive) or its effects can be countered with a calcium-carbonate filler. Alternatively, paper can be made from a material other than wood, such as cotton, hemp, or linen.

philosophy and spirituality. The first known examples of the books date back to the 14th century, when a Franciscan priest and poet from Majorca, Ramon Llull, employed revolving discs on paper to teach principles of thought. Over the centuries, "lift-the-flap" books followed and were used for education (particularly to help medical students learn anatomy) and for children's stories. Artists and paper engineers such as Germany's Lothar Meggendorfer helped develop new methods for interlocking movable parts and came up with new designs to entertain both children and adults. What we would consider the first modern pop-up book appeared in 1929 with the publication in England of the *Daily Express Children's Annual No. 1* by Louis Giraud and Theodore Brown. Since then, innovative paper engineering has resulted in ever more elaborate constructions and taken the form to new heights—literally. In 2010, Pearle Opticiens in Belgium created the world's largest pop-up book, spanning roughly 20 feet by 13 feet and featuring pop-ups over 7 feet high.

Comic Book

THE *HOGAN'S ALLEY* COMIC STRIP WAS SO POPULAR THAT IT INSPIRED THE FBI TO BORROW THE NAME FOR A TRAINING FACILITY IN OHIO.

From the earliest cave paintings to Egyptian hieroglyphics to Michelangelo's *The Creation of Man* on the ceiling of the Sistine Chapel, art has told stories in narrative form. Swiss writer Rodolphe Töpffer created the first narrative tabloid in 1833, *Histoire de M. Jabot,* by combining pictures and text in a historical tale.

But it was the popularity of editorial cartoons throughout the 1800s that primarily inspired American comic strips, which in turn led to the popularity of comic books. In 1895 Richard Outcault created *Hogan's Alley* for Joseph Pulitzer's newspaper, *New York World.* Other popular strips followed.

In 1933 entrepreneur Maxwell Gaines convinced Eastern Color Printing to reprint some in a size and format that would create the modern comic book. Gaines put *Famous Funnies* on sale for ten cents each, giving birth to an industry that would, in just five years, generate Superman in *Action Comics* #1, followed by soon-to-be classics, such as Batman, Wonder Woman, Captain America, Spider-Man, and a galaxy of others.

Moving Pictures

When the lights go down, the stories begin. But in the past, the movies themselves weren't the only attraction. Newsreels kept the public informed of the events of the day at a time when many households had no televisions. The film industry grew in technological leaps and bounds, from the silent era to talkies to color to mind-blowing IMAX 3-D. Music videos have taught us that watching music can be as fun as listening to it, and today's widespread distribution of video cameras has inspired the creation of a website devoted to sharing our home movies.

Newsreels

IN 1937 PERHAPS THE MOST DRAMATIC NEWSREEL IN HISTORY CAUGHT THE FLAMING CRASH OF THE *HINDENBERG* AT LAKEHURST, NEW JERSEY.

At a time when most homes had no television set and maybe one radio with which to receive word of important events, newsreels helped keep the populace informed. Five independent companies produced the ten-minute-long films, which were divided into segments focusing on national politics, international affairs, sports, entertainment, and more. Newsreels with fresh content were produced and distributed twice a week. They became particularly important during such information-starved times as the Great Depression and World War II. Week after week, they reached more than 40 million American moviegoers. Newsreels were so popular with some viewers that New York City's Embassy Theater showed them exclusively—running all five editions in a continuous loop every day. Eventually, of course, the newsreel was doomed by the explosion of television. As TV news became more pervasive, newsreels faltered and finally faded out for good in the mid-1960s.

In the newsreels' heyday, the most popular series was *The March of Time,* which ran from 1935 to 1951. At its peak, 20 million people a month viewed it in some 9,000 theaters. Its news reporting even earned it a special Academy Award in 1936. In 2014 one of the five major producers of newsreels, the British firm Pathé, released its digitized archived content, totaling 3,500 hours of footage, thus bringing glimpses of the past to a whole new generation of viewers: those who watch the newsreels on the Internet.

Music Video

THE BIG BOPPER–AKA J. P. RICHARDSON –ONE OF THE EARLY ICONS OF ROCK-AND-ROLL, COINED THE TERM "MUSIC VIDEO" IN 1959.

Long before the birth of rock-and-roll, the first music videos were making their own noise. In fact the *Dickson Experimental Sound Film,* widely recognized as the oldest known musical video, dates back to the mid-1890s. In it, two men dance while inventor William Dickson plays the violin nearby—not quite the over-the-top production most people are used to today.

In the early years of the 20th century, illustrated song slides were developed to run between vaudeville acts as well as to promote sheet music. Since sound was recorded separately and the films were never publicly released, such illustrated songs are often considered true ancestors of the modern music video. They featured live acts providing musical accompaniment to projected images. And that led in 1925 to the animation-pioneering Fleischer brothers' debuting "follow the bouncing ball" sing-along videos—other precursors to music videos.

In the 1940s, "soundies"—short videos featuring music and dancers—were a hit in bars and restaurants around the world. But it was the legendary Big Bopper, J. P. Richardson, who ten years later saw the potential for video to pair with pop music, filming videos for three songs, including "Chantilly Lace" in 1958. He predicted that video and music would merge to create a modern art form.

Tragically, he died in a plane crash in 1959 before seeing his prediction become reality. Performers such as Ricky Nelson, the Beatles, the Rolling Stones, and many other music artists used videos to promote their songs from the late 1950s onward, leading ultimately to the birth of a television channel devoted to the art form, MTV, in 1981.

WHAT'S INSIDE?

3-D Glasses

The first full-length 3-D movie, *The Power of Love,* was released in 1922, and it worked because of simple anatomy. Human eyes are spaced approximately two inches apart and therefore see the world from different angles. Movies shot in 3-D, and the glasses required to watch them, exploit this. Two cameras film roughly two inches apart; when the images are projected on movie screens simultaneously, audience glasses filter out one side for each eye, creating the illusion of a single three-dimensional view. Older 3-D movies used different hues–red along with blue or green–to create the 3-D effect, but since that affected the color quality of the movie itself, a new method was developed. Modern 3-D projectors use polarizing filters, one for each of the two reels of film and their slightly different images. Viewing glasses have plastic polarized lenses that reverse the images and bring them together, fooling our brains into believing we're immersed in a three-dimensional world.

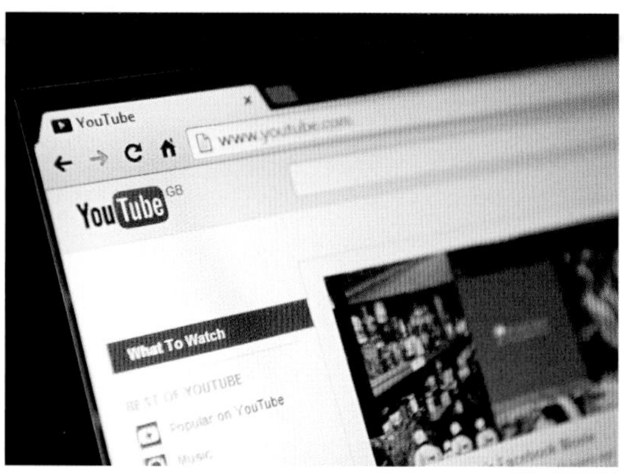

YouTube

JAWED KARIM, ONE OF YOUTUBE'S CO-FOUNDERS, POSTED THE FIRST VIDEO TO THE SITE: 19 SECONDS OF HIM AT THE SAN DIEGO ZOO.

For three former employees of the online payment service PayPal, Valentine's Day 2005 held a labor of love. That's the date Chad Hurley, Steve Chen, and Jawed Karim created YouTube, the world's most popular video-sharing site. According to Karim, they were inspired by two 2004 events, one epically tragic and one simply controversial: the Indian Ocean tsunami that killed more than 225,000 people and Janet Jackson's "wardrobe malfunction" during the Super Bowl halftime show.

Witnesses to the events had made video recordings on various devices, but the videos were hard to find online. The three men came up with a plan for a central website to host such videos, as well as many others, while attending a dinner party. The idea was a good one, and in May 2005 they launched a beta version of the site. By September, one of YouTube's videos (a Nike ad) had reached one million views, and in October 2006, the site was so popular that Google made an offer and acquired it in a billion-plus-dollar deal. The next year, YouTube made history when it partnered with CNN to air a live presidential debate.

As of 2015, YouTube accounts for nearly 15 percent of all downstream traffic on the Internet during peak evening hours, and 300 hours of new video are uploaded every minute. People around the world each month watch six billion hours of videos on the site.

UNCOMMONLY KNOWN ...

THE FIRST MOVIE In 1906, while American film producers worried that audiences couldn't sit still through a long movie, Australian writer and director Charles Tait made what is considered to be the first full-length feature film. The hour-long movie, *The Story of the Kelly Gang,* focused on the notorious outback bank robber Ned Kelly, who to this day some Aussies view as a folk hero and others as a murderer.

Silent Films

NEARLY 11,000 AMERICAN FILMS WERE MADE DURING THE SILENT ERA, BUT BARELY A THIRD HAVE BEEN PRESERVED. THE REST ARE LOST TO TIME.

The silent film era began in the 1870s with single scenes, such as Eadweard Muybridge's *Sallie Gardner at a Gallop* in 1878—just two dozen still images in all—and the two-second-long *Roundhay Garden Scene* in

WHAT'S INSIDE?

Gorilla Glass

Developed by Corning, Gorilla Glass is used on cell phones, mobile devices, televisions, and more, all of which need screens strong enough to resist scratching and cracking. As with regular glass, Gorilla Glass begins with silicone dioxide–sand–but it also contains aluminum, oxygen, and sodium, forming an aluminosilicate. The glass is melted and shaped, then immersed in 752 degree Fahrenheit potassium salt, just hot enough to break the bonds of the sodium ions in the aluminosilicate. Potassium ions then move in and form permanent bonds, compressing the glass and making it more durable.

1888. The former film captured a horse running, the latter, made by Louis Le Prince, is often considered the first narrative film, despite its brevity. It wasn't until the 13-minute *Le Voyage Dans La Lune* in 1902 that longer films began to appear. Some of the most celebrated names of the silent era are Buster Keaton, D. W. Griffith, Charlie Chaplin, and Sergei Eisenstein, who made the 1925 silent epic *Battleship Potemkin,* which included one of the most influential scenes in film history, a massacre on the Odessa Steps in Ukraine. The first American feature film, *Birth of a Nation,* was made in 1915 by Griffith; the Civil War tale is rightfully recognized as shamefully racist.

The true spirit of silent films lives in more lighthearted fare, such as Harold Lloyd performing death-defying stunts in 1923's *Safety Last* (opposite). Lloyd went on to make twice as many movies as better-known contemporaries Keaton and Chaplin. One of the first "talkies, " movies with sound, was *The Jazz Singer,* starring Al Jolson and released in 1927. Silent films continued to be produced for several years following that, but the talkies heralded the end of an era. In 1936 Chaplin made one of the last silent films, *Modern Times.*

Netflix

NETFLIX'S PATENTED RED ENVELOPES WERE DESIGNED TO STAND OUT AS WELL AS TO PROTECT DVDS AS THEY SPED THROUGH POSTAL SORTING MACHINES.

Digital video discs—and DVD players—hit American shores in 1997. A few months later, Netflix was born, offering subscribers DVD rentals through the mail. The company was founded by two Californians, Reed Hastings and Marc Randolph. While the business model was simple—customers queued their movies online and received new ones when they returned previously rented DVDs—the software was innovative. The company developed algorithms for making suggestions to users, based on which movies they had watched previously and how they and others rated those films. (The company currently breaks its movie offerings into 79,000 categories to help gauge subscribers' preferences.) Slowly, Netflix began having an impact on the entertainment world. In 2012 when executives at the AMC cable-TV channel noticed that ratings for the show *Breaking Bad* had doubled, the jump was attributed to new viewers getting hooked on earlier seasons through Netflix DVD rentals. Recently the company has turned to more streaming content and now serves 50 million subscribers in 40 countries.

Each month, Netflix viewers watch more than two billion hours of content on the site. During peak hours, a third of all downstream Internet traffic is on Netflix.

IMAX

DERIVING ITS NAME FROM THE WORDS "MAXIMUM IMAGE," THE GIANT-SCREEN FORMAT DEBUTED AT THE EXPO '70 WORLD'S FAIR IN OSAKA, JAPAN.

The great white screen was born in the Great White North. In 1967, the Fuji Group tasked Canadian filmmakers Graeme Ferguson, Roman Kroitor, and Robert Kerr with a project of unprecedented magnitude: create an enormous theatrical experience to unveil at Expo '70. The filmmakers had dabbled with a large-screen format at the '67 Expo in Montreal, but they would create something far grander for Osaka. First, they used a special camera that filmed in 65mm rather than the standard 35mm (today, IMAX is filmed in 70mm). And instead of using multiple projectors to play films on the big screen, their invention would require just one. For that, they brought in an old friend, engineer William C. Shaw. IMAX launched as planned at Expo '70 with the film *Tiger Child.* The first people ever to experience IMAX saw it from a rotating platform that moved through the theater. In the decades since, more than half a billion people have witnessed an IMAX film. After Expo '70 the historic projector was installed at the Cinesphere in Toronto's Ontario Place.

UNCOMMONLY KNOWN ...

PERSISTENCE OF VISION Motion pictures are a series of still images shown in rapid succession, but why do we perceive them as a single continuous movement? Filmmakers often cite persistence of vision, the theory that the brain retains images for a fraction of a second after they're captured by the retina. Additionally, psychologists credit the phi phenomenon, an optical illusion wherein the brain fills in the blank spaces between images.

Green Screen

WHY GREEN? IT WORKS MORE EFFECTIVELY WITH DIGITAL CAMERAS AND ALLOWS MORE DETAILED IMAGES TO BE CAPTURED THAN DO OTHER COLORS.

In the world of special effects, green is the new black. But Hollywood magic makers have covered the spectrum. In 1898 filmmaker George Méliès used black mattes to prevent parts of the frame from being exposed; he'd film another scene to "fill in the blanks." The use of a so-called

PEOPLE WHO CHANGED HISTORY

The Lumière Brothers (Auguste Lumière: 1862-1954; Louis Lumière: 1864-1948)

Louis and Auguste Lumière, from Lyons, France, are considered the founders of modern cinema because of their breakthrough invention, *le Cinématographe*. Sons of a painter, they began experimenting with photographic processes in the 1870s. Their greatest achievement would come following their father's 1894 trip to the United States, where he saw a demonstration of Thomas Edison's new Kinetoscope. The elder Lumière returned to France with some sage advice for his sons: Get into the business. Louis and Auguste began working on a device to make filmmaking easier and less expensive. Their innovative idea combined a lightweight movie camera, projector, and printer all in one, which was quieter and used less film. Patented in 1895, the Cinematograph allowed filmmakers to easily carry their equipment, which meant the art form could truly take root. The invention gave us the word "cinema."

Lumière brothers, 1920

traveling black matte in 1933 kept *The Invisible Man* out of sight. That same year saw the advent of the Dunning process, which brought *King Kong* to life. The process used one blue shot and one yellow to create a traveling matte for black-and-white films. A huge leap forward arrived with a 1940 color movie, *The Thief of Bagdad,* the first to use a chroma key, meaning it overlaid three shots: green, red, and blue. Filmed against a blue screen, the action could be imposed over different backgrounds, creating startling—for their time—special effects. Later, Hollywood tried a yellow screen and an ultraviolet matte. Today green screens rule. Among other virtues, they reduce the challenge of filming against a blue sky. For modern special effects, it's just easier being green.

Foley Pits

ONE OF THE SINGULAR CRAFTS USED TO MAKE MOVIE MAGIC IS NAMED AFTER JACK FOLEY, A PIONEER OF ADDING EVERYDAY SOUNDS TO FILM.

Foley artists create sounds that often go unnoticed by movie audiences. Big explosions and the like are the work of a sound effects team. Foley artists' work is subtle—footsteps, closing doors, clinking glasses, jangling car keys, perhaps breaking bones. Creation of the sounds occurs in a Foley pit, where they're recorded and synced to the appropriate scene. The pit may be large or small, but it usually contains several kinds of flooring, from wood to concrete, to mimic walking. Not everything an actor walks on can be in the pit, however: Snow and grass are hard to maintain, so Foley artists have to innovate. They might choose material such as cornstarch to convey the sound of snow crunching underfoot. Using myriad props, they produce the swish of fabrics, the squeaking of hinges, and on and on. Jack Foley wanted his craft to blend into the background. It's fitting then that his full name never appeared in any film credits—yet nearly every movie today has an artist working in his name.

Sports Fans

"Sports," playwright Neil Simon once wrote, "is the only entertainment where, no matter how many times you go back, you never know the ending." You can, however, know some of the beginnings that shaped how the games are played, including how those referees and the team mascots made it onto the field. Before you get taken out to the ball game, discover a bit about the history of baseball diamonds and the stadiums that house them; and prior to the next hockey face-off, find out why the players hit a puck instead of frozen cow dung. Let the games begin!

Noisemakers

BEFORE THEY FOUND FAVOR AT SPORTING EVENTS, NOISEMAKERS OFTEN ENLIVENED SUCH RELIGIOUS CELEBRATIONS AS PURIM AND HOLY WEEK.

Loudly jeering an opponent is probably as old as cheering for your side. Historically, such behavior hasn't been confined to sports. Yelling has been a part of many religious ceremonies for thousands of years, and ancient noisemakers such as bone whistles were developed for sacred rites. Meanwhile, horns, drums, and other instruments have been used for centuries by militaries around the world.

It's no wonder that noisemaking excitement carried over to sporting events. In modern times, perhaps the best known noisemaker is the cowbell, used at college football games since the late 1930s. Eventually they created such a din that in 1974, the Southeastern Conference banned all artificial noisemakers.

Elsewhere noisemakers are still prevalent at many sporting events, whether fans want to hear them or not. The *vuvuzela,* based on a South African horn, distracted soccer players at the 2010 World Cup so much that it was nearly banned. By 2014 the vuvuzela had been replaced by the Brazilian *caxirola* percussion rattle—or it would have had it not been banned before the games began.

UNCOMMONLY KNOWN ...

FASTEST TENNIS SERVE Whizzing by at 163.4 miles an hour—roughly the speed of a Boeing 757 at takeoff—Sam Groth's serve at the 2012 Busan Open Challenger Tennis in South Korea became the fastest in tennis history. The Australian player was just 24 years old when he achieved the distinction, beating the former record, 156 mph, set by Croatian Ivo Karlovic in 2011. Despite the record, Groth lost the match to Uladzimir Ignatik of Belarus.

Jumbotron

THE LAST MAJOR LEAGUE BASEBALL TEAM TO ADD A JUMBOTRON WAS THE CHICAGO CUBS, WHO FINALLY IMPLEMENTED THE TECHNOLOGY IN 2015.

Sony unveiled a whopper of a display at the 1985 World's Fair in Japan: the JumboTron, measuring 82 feet tall and 131 feet wide. Five years earlier, Mitsubishi Electric had created the 875-square-foot LED Diamond Vision for the 1980 All-Star Game at Dodger Stadium. And before that, in 1973, came the birth of the Telscreen, a big four-sided monitor where fans in attendance could see instant replays and scores from other games. Electronic scoreboards have been evolving since 1950, when the New York Yankees debuted a board that the *New York Times* hailed as an "electronic miracle." With the Jumbotron, Sony took a giant step forward but also a step back—the huge picture was not as sharp as an old VHS video. But advances in imagery have changed that. The largest high-definition video board, at EverBank Field in Jacksonville, Florida, boasts 11.8 million pixels on each of its twin 21,700-square-foot screens. Sony got out of the Jumbotron business in 2001, and the company no longer owns the trademark, but for sports fans around the world, this is truly the Jumbo Age.

UNCOMMONLY KNOWN ...

FIRST FEMALE PARACHUTIST On October 12, 1799, in France, 24-year-old Jeanne-Geneviève Garnerin became the first woman to use a parachute when she jumped from the gondola of a hot-air balloon operated by her husband, André-Jacques, the father of modern parachuting, nearly 3,000 feet up.

Referee

THE FIRST REFEREE WHISTLE WAS BLOWN AT AN 1870S SOCCER MATCH BETWEEN ENGLAND'S NOTTINGHAM FOREST AND SHEFFIELD NORFOLK.

Before referees, sports teams as we know them were responsible for supervising themselves. Since it was assumed a gentleman would never intentionally commit a foul and that team captains could resolve most disputes between themselves, game monitors seemed unnecessary when teams began to organize. In the 19th century; however, rules were written down so that games, particularly English football (or soccer, as Americans would say), could be standardized. As a result, formal officiating became necessary. In the 1840s, football teams in the United Kingdom nominated umpires—one for each team—to monitor games, but since their loyalties were often to the team that nominated them, a neutral third party—someone who could be "referred" to when disagreements arose—became necessary.

To convey authority, referees often wore white shirts and sometimes a beret or other hat. The

zebra stripes referees typically wear now were born in 1921. During a Michigan State–Arizona football game, a quarterback threw a pass to referee Lloyd Olds, whose white shirt made him resemble one of the players. Afterward Olds asked a friend to help him design a shirt so that would never happen again. The striped look wasn't popular with fans at first, but it worked. It soon caught on and was adopted by referees in other sports.

Baseball Fields

THE FIRST STEEL AND CONCRETE STADIUM WAS PHILADELPHIA'S SHIBE PARK. IT OPENED APRIL 12, 1909; THE PHILADELPHIA ATHLETICS BEAT THE RED SOX 8 TO 1.

Baseball took its inspiration from two popular British inventions, cricket and rounders, a children's game. The very earliest forms of the game date back to Revolutionary days, which is fitting considering how the sport has become quintessentially American.

The fields that baseball is played on have their own history. The baseball diamond was invented by Alexander Cartwright, owner of the New York Knickerbockers, who also helped formalize the game's official rulebook. He came up with the notion of foul territory as well as the distance between bases—90 feet. In fact Cartwright's rules remain the foundation for the way the game is played today. The rules were put to the test for the first time on June 19, 1846, at Elysian Fields in Hoboken, New Jersey, where Cartwright's team lost to the New York Nine, 23–1, but modern baseball, and the field it is played on, are said to have been born that day. In 1862 developer William Cammeyer built the first enclosed baseball field, Union Grounds, in Brooklyn, New York. The stadium could accommodate up to 15,000 cheering fans. Cammeyer charged 25 cents for admission and filled the seats, correctly sensing that people would line up to pay to watch America's pastime.

Hockey Puck

FEBRUARY 7, 1876, IS CONSIDERED THE BIRTHDAY OF THE TERM "PUCK," WITH THE FIRST KNOWN USE OF THE TERM IN THE *MONTREAL GAZETTE*.

Hockey is seen as a quintessentially Canadian sport, but it's played all around the world. Though its origins do lie in Canada, with a game played by the Mi'kmaq tribe in Nova Scotia as early as the 1800s, Canada can also lay claim to the first organized hockey game, which was played in Montreal in 1875. Scholars disagree on the origin of the word "puck"; it may derive from "poke," a term used in the sport of hurling, or it could come from the Middle English word "puke," which referred to the devil.

The earliest hockey pucks were made from wood, rubber, or, in a pinch, frozen cow dung. Today they are all made of highly vulcanized rubber and are largely produced in four countries: Canada, Russia, China, and the Czech Republic. All official game pucks are one inch thick and three inches in diameter, and they weigh roughly six ounces. Pucks are black to stand out on the ice and must be kept frozen before all games to reduce friction, so they can travel farther faster. During game play, pucks regularly reach speeds of 80 to 90 mph; the hardest slap shots can exceed 100 mph. Despite the dangers the whistling pucks present to the game's goalkeepers, the first full hockey face mask wasn't worn until 1959.

PEOPLE WHO CHANGED HISTORY

International Olympic Committee

The International Olympic Committee's 102 members "represent and promote the interests of the IOC and the Olympic Movement," according to the Olympic Charter. The committee was created in 1894, the start of the modern Olympics, to ensure the games were organized every four years (they're now staggered every two years between summer and winter games). The IOC promotes ceremonial events, such as the UN's International Day of Sport for Development and Peace, but refrains from politics while ensuring the safety of athletes and maintaining the integrity of the games.

The first Olympic Committee, Athens, Greece, 1896

Mascots

THE UNIVERSITY OF GEORGIA IS ON ITS NINTH BULLDOG MASCOT NAMED UGA. EIGHT PREVIOUS UGAS ARE BURIED IN THE COLLEGE STADIUM.

The word "mascot" derives from slang used by French gamblers and has been used for centuries to describe an animal or thing that conveys good luck. The word was popularized in a French opera, *La Mascotte,* in 1880, but it really took off when sports teams started bringing live animals to events, hoping their barks, snorts, or roars would intimidate opponents. These days, mascots are often costumed creations, animal or otherwise. The NFL's Minnesota Vikings have Ragnar the Viking, the San Francisco 49ers have Sourdough Sam, and the Tampa Bay Buccaneers have Captain Fear. Perhaps the most revered mascot in the United States, though, is Uga from the University of Georgia. The good-luck pup has been played by an actual bulldog since 1956, when a local family began volunteering their own pets for the position. Uga has a car (and driver) that delivers him to his personalized hotel room before each game, and he rides a golf cart to Sanford Stadium, where he watches the contest from his own on-field air-conditioned doghouse. It's a dog's life, and it's nothing to howl at.

Very Amusing

Step right up! This is your ticket to the little-known stories behind the wild rides found at theme parks around the world. Take a spin through Herbert Sellner's kitchen, birthplace of the Tilt-A-Whirl, hop onboard the Ferris wheel and learn how it was designed to compete with the Eiffel Tower, and then see if you would be brave enough to "shoot the chutes" (if not, just play it safe and stick with the log ride). These time-tested amusements have been providing thrills, chills, and smiles for decades. See how they all began and why they endure.

Tilt-A-Whirl

NO TWO RIDES ON A TILT-A-WHIRL ARE EVER QUITE THE SAME. PHYSICISTS DETERMINED IT CREATED WHAT THEY TERMED CHAOTIC MOTION.

Herbert Sellner had a simple way of entertaining his young son: He placed him securely on a chair set atop the family's kitchen table and then shook and spun the table. The wild movements provided seemingly endless delight. In 1926 the Faribault, Minnesota, woodworker converted that idea into what would soon become a carnival classic: the Tilt-A-Whirl. Sellner was a toymaker and furniture builder who had already begun designing amusement park rides when he came up with the idea.

Originally made out of wood, the ride had nine cars that freely spun while attached by a long "arm" to a center platform. In his application for a patent, Sellner aptly described his invention as an "amusement apparatus wherein the riders will be moved in general through an orbit and will unexpectedly swing, snap from side to side or rotate without in any way being able to figure what movement may next take place." The first Tilt-A-Whirl (left) opened at an amusement park in White Bear Lake, Minnesota. In 1927 it was an instant hit at the Minnesota State Fair, and the ride remains popular to this day. Tilt-A-Whirl has a legion of fans who love the ride's unpredictability. Its motion and speed are determined largely by the weight and movements of the people in each car.

Sellner 's company eventually built more than a thousand Tilt-A-Whirls. Over the decades, wood was replaced by aluminum, steel, and fiberglass, and the number of cars was reduced to seven. The firm remained a family-operated business and continued making half a dozen of the rides a year until it was purchased by Larson International in 2011. Tilt-A-Whirls are still mainly sold to amusement parks, but individuals can buy them too. That new-Tilt-A-Whirl smell will set you back about $300,000.

Ferris Wheel

THE FIRST FERRIS WHEEL HAD A SECOND LIFE AT SEA: ITS IRON AND STEEL HELPED BUILD THE WORLD WAR I BATTLESHIP U.S.S. *ILLINOIS*.

In anticipation of the 1893 Chicago World's Fair, engineer George Washington Gale Ferris, Jr., an Illinois native, wanted to design a breathtaking structure that would rival France's Eiffel Tower, which had just premiered at the 1889 World's Fair. How to top a landmark that had already redefined the City of Light? Ferris came up with an idea for a giant wheel that would provide rotating views of the Windy City's landscape for more than 2,000 riders at a time.

When completed, it stood 25 stories tall and cost a whopping $300,000 (almost $8 million in today's dollars). Customers paid 50 cents for the chance to climb aboard, and when all were loaded into the 36 cars, they enjoyed a ten-minute ride. After the fair and nearly 1.5 million riders, Ferris's wheel moved to Chicago's North Side, where its owners fought a decade-long losing battle to attract enough riders to offset costs. St. Louis bought the wheel in 1903, but there too the ride remained a tough sell, not earning enough to keep it profitable. It was finally demolished in 1906.

While the big wheel cost more money to maintain and operate than it brought in, design improvements such as smaller cars and less obstructed views made more cost-efficient Ferris wheels possible. Over the following century and beyond, the carnival staple has entertained millions of people. Ferris wheels were the inspiration for dozens of adrenaline-pumping thrill rides as well as majestic city-observation wheels. But the original's simple design that Ferris imagined remains a classic.

PEOPLE WHO CHANGED HISTORY

Walt Disney (1901-1966)

Born on December 5, 1901, Walt Disney left Kansas City in his 20s and followed his dreams to Los Angeles. He formed an animation company with his brother, Roy, and friend Ub Iwerks. In 1928 they released their first film, *Steamboat Willie*, starring the iconic Mickey Mouse. The company's first full-length feature, *Snow White*, released in 1937, took five years to create; 1940's classic *Fantasia* required a thousand people to produce. Walt Disney has received more Academy Awards than anyone else—26. By 1954 he was ready to tackle a new medium: television. When *Disneyland* premiered, it drew half of the total TV audience. Disney used money from the show to help fund more dreams that would entertain the world: theme parks. Disneyland opened in 1955, welcoming 28,000 guests its first day, including Ronald Reagan.

Walt Disney, 1955

Bumper Cars

IN 2014 ROYAL CARIBBEAN'S *QUANTUM OF THE SEAS* BECAME THE FIRST CRUISE SHIP TO OFFER BUMPER CAR RIDES TO ITS PASSENGERS.

Buckle up—the history of bumper cars is bumpy indeed, beginning with who exactly should get credit for their invention. They may have originated with a man named William Thursten, who headed a company that developed carnival rides. Or perhaps General Electric employee Victor Levand was their creator. While their origins are murky, it can be said that bumper cars truly began to hit the road in 1919, when Max and Henry Stoehrer's Dodgems first appeared in Massachusetts. Despite being notoriously hard to drive (*Scientific American* called them "highly unmanageable"), they soon caught on with collision-happy carnival-goers. Dodgems began to run out of gas in the 1970s, when Philadelphia cousins Joseph and Robert Lusse developed their Auto-Skooters. The Auto-Skooter was easier to drive and operated on metal floors; a metal pole extending from the cars touched the metal ceiling, completing an electrical circuit and powering the motor. Today bumper cars are still amusement park favorites. Six Flags Great America in Gurnee, Illinois, boasts the largest bumper car pavilion, covering nearly 6,500 square feet. Called Rue Le Dodge, it changes its name every Halloween season to Rue Le Morgue. Drivers beware.

WHAT'S INSIDE?

Calliope

Calliope was the Greek muse of epic poetry. The music her namesake instrument makes may not be poetic, but it's certainly epic. The incessant clamor can travel for miles, making it the perfect siren song to attract crowds to riverboats or to promote a carnival or circus. The nostalgic instrument is probably most associated with a favorite childhood ride, the carousel. Since its invention in the 1850s, little has changed in the inner workings of the "steam-whistle keyboard organ"—except, that is, for steam. In the original design, the keyboard directed steam from a boiler into the whistle pipes. Today most calliopes use compressed air.

Monorail

IN 1823 BRITISH ENGINEER HENRY ROBINSON PALMER PUBLISHED HIS SEMINAL WORK, *DESCRIPTION OF A RAILWAY ON A NEW PRINCIPLE.*

All aboard! Monorails roared into popular culture with the 1959 launch of Disneyland's transport and later with the Seattle World's Fair in 1962, when Seattle's monorail debuted. But the history of

UNCOMMONLY KNOWN ...

SANTA CLAUS LAND While fairs, carnivals, and amusement parks in one form or another have been around for centuries, the first true theme park was Santa Claus Land, which opened in August 1946 far from the North Pole in Santa Claus, Indiana. It was dedicated to all things Santa, including rides, toys, shops, and the merry old elf himself. It operates today under the name Holiday World, spanning 40 acres and boasting a water park.

the monorail extends much further back. The first monorail appeared near Moscow in 1820, designed by Ivan Elmanov, who built a track for a horse-drawn vehicle. That same year, Britain's Henry Palmer received a patent for a monorail. His one-track vision came to life at two notable locations in England: first at Deptford Dockyard near London in 1821 and then at Cheshunt Railway in Hertfordshire in 1825. The latter became the first monorail to transport passengers, though it was principally designed for moving quarry stones.

The first suspended monorail was developed in the 1890s by Germans Nicolaus Otto and Eugen Langen. In Ireland, a nine-mile monorail system between Listowel and Ballybunion designed by Frenchman Charles Lartigue ran from 1888 to 1924; it was steam powered and even turned a profit, carrying passengers and livestock as well as other freight. In more recent times, the Alweg company, founded by Swedish industrialist Axel Lennart Wenner-Gren, popularized the most common version of the monorail, the straddle beam. In it, the train rides an A-frame concrete or steel track, usually two to three feet wide.

Monorails, while not as prevalent as their two-track brethren, have been built around the world and grown in popularity as maglev—magnetic levitation—technology expands the boundaries of high-speed rail travel.

Log Ride

STUDYING HYDRODYNAMICS, KARL BACON, WHO DESIGNED RIDES FOR DISNEYLAND, CHANGED HOW FLUMES OPERATE—FASTER AND MORE THRILLING.

Log rides, or flumes, as they are more appropriately called, trace their beginnings to the popular water chutes of the early 20th century that put riders in flat-bottomed boats to slide down a ramp into a waiting pool. But the inspiration for log rides harks back further to the timber industry's method of driving logs downstream from mountain ranges to sawmills. In 1884 J. P. Newburg tapped into this inspiration for his Shoot the Chutes ride at Watch Tower Park in Rock Island, Illinois. The ride proved popular enough that other parks began to construct their own versions, including one at America's first modern amusement park, Paul Boyton's Water Chute in Chicago. The main drawback of water-chute rides, however, was they usually consisted of a single fast descent, which meant they offered a limited thrill—and were often unsafe. In 1963 Bud Hurlbut designed

El Aserradero at Six Flags Over Texas to simulate real logs moving downstream, capped by a final splashdown. Customers lined up to take the ride and get soaked. Hurlbut later created the classic Timber Mountain at Knott's Berry Farm in 1968, crowning him the log-ride king. The tallest log flume in the world stands at Indiana's Holiday World and Splashin' Safari, sending riders down a 131-foot drop at a 45-degree angle reaching speeds of 50 mph.

Waterslide

THE TOWN OF WISCONSIN WELLS, BOASTING MORE THAN 200 WATERSLIDES, CALLS ITSELF THE WATER PARK CAPITAL OF THE WORLD.

Historically, waterslides are as old as aqueducts, but the first waterslide created for public entertainment was Henry Sellner's Water-Toboggan Slide, which he constructed entirely out of wood in his native Minnesota in 1923. When riders hopped in a sled at the top of the slide, they began a thrilling journey that would shoot them to the bottom of the slide and beyond—skidding up to 100 feet across the top of the water. Sellner (who also invented the Tilt-A-Whirl) inspired many future water-based amusement park rides, several of which took his idea further, adding bends, loops, and even water cannons as riders made the plunge.

The tallest waterslide in the world has been certified by the *Guinness Book of World Records* as Verrükt in Kansas City's Schlitterbahn water park, which sends bathers careening down a 168-foot drop. Waterslides are divided into several variations: Body slides allow users simply to ride the water down on their own; tube or sled slides provide a craft for the journey, much like Sellner's first toboggan ride. Speed slides feature heart-stopping acceleration, and serpentine slides offer thrilling curves. In 1974 George Millay, one of the four founders of San Diego's SeaWorld, opened the first official water park, Wet 'N Wild, in Orlando, Florida. Since then, nearly 2,000 water parks have fountained around the world.

Aquariums

THE WORD "AQUARIUM" CAME TO US FROM THE FIELD OF BOTANY. IT DESCRIBES A PLACE IN WHICH TO GROW UNDERWATER PLANTS.

The first aquariums were constructed more for dietary reasons than aesthetic ones. Ancient Sumerians constructed man-made ponds for keeping fish at least 4,500 years ago. Many years later in ancient Egypt and China, fish were bred in tanks, leading to some of the varieties, including koi, that aquarium visitors enjoy viewing today.

In 1986 a 2,000-year-old shipwreck was discovered off the coast of Grado, Italy. In its remains, historians discovered what is believed to be an ancient aquarium, used to keep fish alive as they were transported to market for sale. The idea of modern aquariums where visitors can marvel at myriad forms of underwater life didn't take off until the 18th and 19th centuries, as people developed a better understanding of aquatic biology. In the 1700s, exotic goldfish from Japan were imported to France for public viewing. Then, in 1832, French naturalist Jeanne Villepreux-Power constructed a large glass aquarium in which to keep sea creatures. But aquariums were generally viewed as temporary fish quarters rather than long-term habitat until 1853, when British naturalist and writer Philip Gosse constructed the world's first public aquarium at the London Zoo. The next year, he wrote a book about his research, popularizing the word in his title: *The Aquarium*. Other aquariums soon began to appear, including one designed by P. T. Barnum at New York's American Museum of Natural History.

WHAT'S INSIDE?

Fun House Mirror

Never have looks been more deceiving. Like their flat counterparts, fun house mirrors are made from glass coated with metal. But fun house glass is first molded into a curved shape. A silver nitrate solution is poured over the glass and smoothed out; when it dries, silver deposits adhere to the surface—just as with any other mirror. On a flat mirror, light from the reflective surface hits our eyes at no particular angle, giving us the image we expect. But with curved mirrors, the angle of reflection is distorted. Concave mirrors elongate the viewer's image, while convex ones shrink it, giving us the amusing—and sometimes horrifying—results.

Fun House

THE ORNATE HALL OF MIRRORS CONSTRUCTED BY LOUIS XIV AT THE PALACE OF VERSAILLES INSPIRED THE CREATION OF FUN HOUSE MIRRORS.

Whether spooky or just goofy, fun houses boast an array of features that can throw visitors off balance, such as spinning disks, rotating barrels, sloping floors, wacky mirrors, dark hallways, and more. Fun houses come in two types: active or walk-through. In the former, visitors move through the structure at a set pace, either on foot or in a vehicle; in the latter, they are encouraged to take their time wandering around.

Fun houses originated at the turn of the 20th century at New York's Coney Island. The first one on the grounds, Katzenjammer Castle, opened in 1906; others quickly followed, incorporating various themes. Optical illusions inside the houses often made it seem as if objects were rolling uphill, and jutting walls added to visitors' happy disorientation. As more amusement parks began constructing fun houses, a host of versions arose, including ghostly haunted houses, others that kept visitors completely in the dark, and still others based on movies and nursery rhymes. One of the most creative variations was inspired by Noah's Ark and became popular throughout the United States and the United Kingdom in the 1930s.

Any sufficiently advanced technology is equivalent to magic.

—ARTHUR C. CLARK (1917–2008)

Gadgets and Gizmos

Most of us don't give a lot of thought to how we arrived at the fancy gadgets we use today. How did we figure out how to send satellites into space that can pinpoint our exact location back on Earth? How did we ever go from candles to LED lanterns, from clunky metal file cabinets to storing all our data in an invisible "cloud," and from peering at a patient's head to 3-D reconstructions of the person's brain? The answer is: keen observation, fortuitous discovery, careful trial, and (sometimes major) error. These pieces of technology all have interesting stories and have changed our lives in ways our forebears would have mostly found hard to fathom, though—surprisingly—some of them did. Many of our modern gizmos began their journeys with the ambitious ponderings of great thinkers such as Leonardo da Vinci, Thomas Jefferson, and Benjamin Franklin, who dreamed up some of the earliest known health monitors, personal scales, and swim fins. Even further back, ancient visionaries such as Greece's Ptolemy were able to produce advances such as the first geographical description of the world (built from rumor and other people's writings) that still serve as foundations for things we use today. Some gadgets, such as the hydration pack and the backpack, are ancient tools remade in a modern image. And then there are breakthroughs, such as the blood glucose meter, that took centuries of discovery, scientific inquiry, and technological innovation to evolve to their current state. No matter how far back their history goes or how they've progressed, these gadgets were all born out of the human desire to make the world a better, safer, and more convenient place. And while they may reach beyond our ancestors' imaginations, it's difficult for us to imagine how we ever lived without them.

Outdoor Adventure

The idea of sleeping outdoors to "get away from it all" would have puzzled ancient cultures; for most of human history, people didn't camp out just for fun. The innovations in this section didn't spring from a desire for recreation but from the need for warmth, clean water, and shelter. Gear like backpacks, sleeping bags, and camping stoves were made for, tested, and improved by field-bound soldiers and early explorers and mountaineers. When the automobile made weekend adventuring a popular pastime, these gadgets were ready to provide the comforts—and essentials—of home.

Hydration Pack

HUNTER-GATHERERS OF THE KALAHARI HAVE PUNCHED HOLES IN OSTRICH EGGSHELLS AND USED THEM AS CANTEENS SINCE THE STONE AGE.

Wineskin, bladder, flask, canteen: They've gone by many names, but portable water carriers have been essential since prehistoric times. We tend to take clean, drinkable water for granted now, but for early nomads, the ability to carry it with them could be a matter of life or death. They had to be able to quench their thirst as they moved their herds from one location to another, and reliable water sources weren't guaranteed. To transport water, they used what logically came to hand: animal bladders. Once properly cured, the bladders could hold not only water but other liquids, most significantly wine.

Through the centuries, people who stayed on the move tried out various other methods for carrying water, beer, and wine (alcohol was often safer to drink than water), including horns and clay pots. Shepherds tending their flocks carried hollowed-out gourds.

Canteens were an important item for soldiers, helping them stay hydrated while out on the long march. The earliest ones were heavy, made of wood and leather; later metal versions were generally more lightweight. Civil War soldiers carried canteens of tin and pewter, wrapped in cotton and wool to keep water cool. But the containers were awkward, prone to denting, and easily contaminated.

In recent years hikers and runners have come back around to the bladder-style water carrier. Designed for a backpack-style frame, the bladders are constructed of lightweight rubber and plastic, well insulated, and fitted with a hose and bite valve so thirsty users can sip hands free.

Battery-Powered Lantern

IN ANCIENT CHINA, LANTERNS WERE MADE OUT OF SILK, PAPER, AND SOMETIMES ANIMAL SKIN, ALL WITH FRAMES OF BAMBOO AND WOOD.

Long before electricity and battery power, we used lanterns to push back against the dark of night. Ancient people used them not only for illumination but also for ritual. The Greeks employed burning lanterns in augury—the practice of interpreting omens.

Ancient clay lamps were kept alight with oils and fats such as olive oil and whale oil. Eventually candle lanterns came into circulation, fashioned of wood and horn. For centuries, these two methods—oil and wax—were what everyone used to light their homes. But the lights overall were weak, and fire was a constant danger. A Nova Scotia doctor invented a kerosene lantern in 1846: It threw more light but still wasn't entirely safe.

Onto the lighting stage in 1896 came the first portable batteries, bringing with them tools like the "electric hand torch." The torches were used by the New York Police Department and met with great enthusiasm, but they had a habit of flickering off and on—hence the term "flashlight." In 1905 W. C. Coleman was inspired by a liquid-fuel version that was brighter, safer, and less likely to smoke than its predecessors. He built a company around these lanterns, which were used mostly by farmers but later became campers' light source of choice. The latest lanterns have swapped out liquid fuel for high-tech batteries and LEDs. The lights are brighter, hardier, and last longer, ensuring that no camper needs to be afraid of the dark.

PEOPLE WHO CHANGED HISTORY

Kurt Hahn (1886-1974)

Kurt Hahn was an innovative educator who embraced new approaches. In 1934 the school he founded in Scotland was doing something radical by emphasizing experiential knowledge. He believed young people should have a chance to learn by doing: to experience triumph, defeat, self-discovery, and the power of imagination.

When war broke out across Europe, Lawrence Holt, the father of one of Hahn's students, lamented that faulty training and a lack of practical knowledge were the reasons so many young soldiers were dying. Hahn and Holt started a program focused on "physical fitness, enterprise, tenacity and compassion among British youth," which they called Outward Bound. Today Outward Bound courses around the world turn nature into a classroom, teaching students not only how to survive but also how to problem-solve and work toward a common goal.

Kurt Hahn, 1952

Sleeping Bag

EARLY SLEEPING BAGS, STUFFED WITH HOLLOW CAMEL HAIR, PROVED A GUIDING PRINCIPLE: TRAPPED AIR MAKES EFFECTIVE INSULATION.

Like most other camping equipment, the sleeping bag started as a piece of military gear and a necessary item for adventurers. Designs of the 1880s featured sheepskins turned inside out, reindeer hides, and blankets rubberized on one side to roll up in. They made life a little more comfortable, but they didn't always keep out the cold and rain, and they were awkward to exit for middle-of-the-night bathroom calls.

In 1876 Welsh inventor Pryce Pryce-Jones debuted an upgrade he called the Euklisia Rug, a wool blanket that folded over and fastened at the side. He made 60,000 of them for the Russian Army. When the Russians canceled part of the order, leaving Pryce with 17,000 rugs, he started marketing them as a cheap bedding option; their popularity took them as far as the Australian outback.

Sleeping bags had improved drastically by the outbreak of World War II and the introduction of down-filled mummy-shaped bags. They were lighter and body hugging and able to hold in more heat. Most sleeping bags today still employ the design, but now they're usually stuffed with synthetic materials that make them water-resistant. You can even choose a sleeping bag by its temperature rating, so you can stay as toasty as you want.

WHAT'S INSIDE?

Sterno

Sterno, also known as canned heat, can make a handy source of fuel or for those who don't feel confident in their ability to build and start a fire. These cans of jellied alcohol first appeared in 1893 but didn't take off until World War I, when they started being advertised as a great present for soldiers deploying overseas. Sterno contains ethanol, the alcohol in liquor, as well as methanol, which makes the product so poisonous that no one should be inclined to drink it. That's not always been the case, however. Sterno has proved lethal to people who have tried straining it through cheesecloth for the ethanol.

Water Purification Pens

THE GREEK PHYSICIAN HIPPOCRATES INVENTED A BAG FILTER FOR PURIFYING WATER THAT BECAME KNOWN AS THE HIPPOCRATIC SLEEVE.

Water may be the source of life, but it can also be a source of disease. Ancient peoples didn't realize that when they sought ways to make water taste better,

UNCOMMONLY KNOWN ...

WALLET CAMERA Even with a fancy smartphone, snapping a covert picture of a fellow camper accidentally using poison ivy as toilet paper can be a difficult feat. Cold War spies of the 1960s didn't have smartphones, but they did have nifty cameras invented by their intelligence agencies, such as the KGB's wallet camera. All a Soviet spy had to do was roll it against a document to expose the film, even in low light, allowing agents to smuggle secrets without stealing the papers themselves.

they also happened to increase its safety. As long ago as 2000 B.C., Egyptians and Greeks were boiling and straining water to improve its taste and banish grit. That said, it wasn't until the 1700s that water filters—made of wool, charcoal, and sponge—found their way into European homes, and not until 1804 that the first municipal water plant opened, in Paisley, Scotland. The plant used sand as a filter and a horse-drawn cart to move water around.

In 1854 British scientist John Snow made a discovery as a cholera epidemic was being spread through contaminated water pumps. He applied chlorine to disinfect the pumps, and wide-scale water filtration was born. Before long, though, people began to realize that chlorine was less than ideal as a decontaminant. Too much chlorine was linked to respiratory problems, so scientists had to consider alternate ways to purify water.

Enter ultraviolet (UV) light. The practice of using UV light to decontaminate drinking water stretches back to around the turn of the 20th century, when the tactic was applied mostly in municipal plants. Today UV pens are a convenient way to get clean water on the go. The pens bombard water with UV light, zapping harmful bacteria. Purification that used to take hours can now be accomplished in seconds.

Chemical Toilet

THE FIRST U.S. PATENT ISSUED FOR A PLASTIC PORTABLE COMMODE WAS HANDED OUT IN THE 1960S FOR WHAT WAS CALLED A TOILET CABANA.

We might see today's portable lavatories as primitive, but outhouses have come a long way since the earthen holes they once were. Before flush toilets became widespread in the 1850s, all of history's commodes were some variation on the outhouse: communal spaces with rows of seats that gave little privacy and chamber pots that provided small comfort. Portable johns didn't emerge until the 1940s, when California shipbuilders complained about how far they had to walk from the job to relieve themselves. The first model was hardly more than a wooden cabana built around a holding tank, but its portability made it convenient. The issue with early outhouses (and nonflush toilets today) is the smell: Their wood and metal absorb odors and are hard to clean. In the 1970s, polyethylene and fiberglass versions helped but didn't entirely eliminate the odor issue. That's what made the chemical toilet such a big leap. Ammonia and other chemicals break down and deodorize waste, all in one flush. It might not seem fancy to

us, but kings and queens of old would no doubt appreciate the chance to mount this modern-day throne.

Camping Stove

A PORTABLE STOVE OF THE 1850S WAS CALLED THE ROB ROY, INSPIRED BY SCOTTISH EXPLORER JOHN "ROB ROY" MACGREGOR'S ADVENTURES.

From time immemorial, open fires were the only means to cook a meal or boil water in the wilderness. And while fire remains essential, open fires are smoky and sooty, and their temperature isn't easy to control. Those issues were merely inconvenient for nomads and cowboys but could be dire for mountain climbers and soldiers in the field. They needed something weatherproof, reliable, and easy to carry on their backs.

The portable stove showed up in the mid-19th century when a noted chef, Alexis Soyer, invented the "Magic Stove." It worked much like a kerosene lamp, with a wick that drew fuel from a tank. Such kerosene- and alcohol-based stoves set the standard until World War II. Halfway through that conflict, the U.S. Army put out an urgent call for a small, portable stove. It had to be field ready: light, compact, hardy under all conditions, and able to burn any fuel on hand. And the army wanted 5,000 of them delivered in 60 days. The Coleman Company, founded by the man who revolutionized the camping lantern, rose to the challenge. His portable "pocket stove," which could withstand temperatures of -60°F and 150°F, became one of the most influential noncombat innovations of all time. After the war, as recreational camping came into vogue, camp stoves became fancier; some had two or even three burners. Today you can buy a compact propane camp stove with a top so small you can hold it in the palm of your hand.

Backpack

WHEN THE FIRST U.S. CLIMBERS TOPPED MOUNT EVEREST IN 1963, THEY USED THE KELTY FRAME PACK TO GET THEIR GEAR UP THE MOUNTAIN.

For a seemingly simple device—a sack with handles meant to be slung over the shoulders—backpacks have come a long way in their shapes and materials. When early hunters began carrying them, they were made of animal skins.

Rucksack (from the German der *Rücken*, meaning "the human back") was the term used for military bags until the early 1900s, when the term "backpack" was introduced. They were a staple for soldiers, but it took backpacks a surprisingly long time to be geared for hikers.

When outdoorsman Dick Kelty tramped around the California hills in the 1950s, he didn't like the bulky surplus military backpacks that he and other hikers were using. He figured out that adding a hip belt and distributing the pack's weight away from the shoulders made long-distance toting a lot easier. Frame packs weren't new, but Kelty was the first person to introduce them commercially, inspiring the array of high-tech packs available today.

PEOPLE WHO CHANGED HISTORY

Yvon Chouinard (1938-)

In the 1950s French Canadian Yvon Chouinard followed his passion for rock climbing to Yosemite National Park. He was unhappy with the iron climbing pitons available, so he learned to blacksmith and made his own. That pastime turned into an outdoor gear company. When Chouinard traveled to Scotland and brought back a rugby shirt, he saw the potential to create robust clothing beyond the drab wool shirts of the day. His company, renamed Patagonia, has shaped the way many people dress for the outdoors.

Yvon Chouinard rock climbing in Colorado, 1994

Fire Starters

VIKINGS THOUGHT FIRE STEELS, THAT IS, STEEL FIRE STARTERS, HELD MAGICAL POWER. THE SPARK PRODUCERS WERE SO VALUED THEIR OWNERS WERE OFTEN BURIED WITH THEM.

The history of human development is irrevocably tied to our ability to make fire. Fires have shaped us: They've allowed us to gather together, cook our meals, and stay warm. Consequently, people have always sought quick and reliable ways to start them.

One of the earliest methods was through the friction of rubbing two sticks together—not easy and not quick. Another age-old method was to use flint and steel, wherein the sharp edge of a flint or similar stone struck sparking steel flakes onto tinder that could then be fanned into flame. Ancient people often carried flint-and-steel fire kits with them. But starting fires this way didn't tend to work well in wet weather.

That's where producing fire with petrochemicals and man-made materials came into its element, though the principles remain the same. The lighter you wield to ignite your charcoal grill uses ferrocerium, a man-made mixed metal patented in 1903, to strike a spark and butane gas for fuel. They light instantly time after time even if it's windy or raining. Fire-starter bricks are foolproof kindling pressed from sawdust and clean-burning combustibles that don't rely on the skill—or persistence—of the person making the fire.

Directionally Challenged

Until the 1700s we only knew about half of what Earth's surface looked like, and explorers had to get their bearings as best they could. They had the compass, but to really know where they were and chart the world, they needed more instruments. Devices such as sextants and others may seem outdated now, but they are pillars on which modern navigation was founded. Indeed, wayfaring tools have guided our history: They sparked an age of discovery, created empires, defined political boundaries, won wars, and now map the landscape of our consumer choices.

GPS

AFTER AN AIRLINER THAT STRAYED INTO SOVIET AIRSPACE IN 1983 WAS SHOT DOWN, THE U.S. DECLASSIFIED GPS FOR THE PUBLIC.

For those of us who rely on the global positioning system (GPS), it's difficult to comprehend how people ever arrived at their destination before technology revolutionized how we get to it. Historically, some people never did get there; ships veered off course in questionable weather because their navigation systems were based on the ability to determine position by the stars.

It wasn't until the 1960s that we developed the capabilities that made GPS possible. The space program, together with the military's need to respond to threats swiftly and accurately, led scientists to figure out how to combine radio-wave and satellite technologies to determine location. In 1973 the U.S. Defense Department's NAVSTAR GPS was built; the first satellites were launched soon after and were eventually joined by a full complement of more than two dozen. Your navigation-equipped car and smartphone receive signals from the satellites, which are constantly transmitting from space. At any given time, it takes at least three to pinpoint your location.

GPS was originally reserved for the military. Out of security concern, the government

UNCOMMONLY KNOWN ...

GEOCACHING It's treasure hunting for the 21st century. Instead of a faded paper map where X marks the spot, digital maps show geocachers, who sign up for the adventure online, the way to hidden bounty. Because GPS is accurate to within a few meters horizontally and a few more vertically, players can use their smartphones to zero in on a fixed point and cache-in on whatever tokens await there.

reduced the system's precision for nonmilitary uses with a protocol called Selective Ability. When that was lifted in 2000, GPS became ten times more accurate, and now we can't imagine finding our way without it.

Location Tagging Systems

TO LOCATE LAND, VIKING SEAFARERS WOULD RELEASE A BIRD. IF IT DIDN'T COME BACK, THEY KNEW LAND WAS CLOSE, JUST OVER THE HORIZON.

It wasn't always easy to put your finger down on a map and know where you were, let alone how far you were from somewhere else. Navigators of yore didn't have electronic tracking. They had tools such as the astrolabe and sextant, used to plot location by sun, moon, and stars.

In World War II scientists figured out that radio waves could do more than communicate: They could help technicians with quick math skills triangulate a place's position and pinpoint where to drop bombs or parachute to safety. With a wave of relatively inexperienced pilots heading for the sky, accurate location tagging was a crucial advantage in determining the outcome of the war.

UNCOMMONLY KNOWN ...

BLUETOOTH The name was inspired by tenth-century King Harald Blåtand of Denmark—Harold Bluetooth—who united warring factions the same way this technology wirelessly connects different devices, such as your phone and car audio system, so you can get directions without using your hands.

The 1940s also saw radio used for espionage. Léon Theremin created a covert listening device that retransmitted incoming radio waves. It was one of the earliest uses of passive data collection, which is how location tagging works today. Programs such as Foursquare passively collect GPS information and cell tower signals to figure out exactly where you are, provoking discussions about privacy—a concern that navigators of the past might not share.

Online Maps

DURING THE CIVIL WAR, BOTH SIDES USED HOT-AIR BALLOONS TO GET BIRD'S-EYE VIEWS OF BATTLEFIELDS IN ORDER TO CREATE GOOD MAPS.

People have always been interested in exploring, but there weren't always good maps to help them do so. For early explorers, the world was mostly a blank canvas. Ptolemy, the ancient Greek who worked

in the Library of Alexandria around A.D. 150, is considered the father of cartography. He used the contributions of scholars before him—the first to postulate that the Earth was round—to create a picture of the world. Although his original map has not been found, reconstructions have shown that it was remarkably close to accurate. Some 1,350 years later, Christopher Columbus carried a map based on Ptolemy's when he sailed west.

As exploration expanded, maps became more detailed. But it wasn't until the advent of GPS and the Internet that they became instantly available and interactive, accurately reflecting changing boundaries and turning us all into cartographers.

WHAT'S INSIDE?

Smartphone

Break open your smartphone and you'll find a dense world of metal and other elements. A typical smartphone holds about 300 milligrams of silver and 30 milligrams of gold. Then there's the rechargeable lithium ion battery, which uses lithium cobalt (or manganese) oxide for the positive side and carbon or graphite for the negative side to power your phone calls and Internet searches. The touch screen contains so-called rare-earth elements—things most people have never heard of, such as terbium and yttrium. They help create the crisp bright colors that make online maps look like moving works of art.

Compass

A COMPASS'S TYPICAL FLEUR-DE-LIS MARKING NORTH IS ACTUALLY A STYLIZED *T* FOR *TRAMONTANE*, FROM THE LATIN FOR "NORTH WIND."

The compass may seem nonessential now that we have GPS, but it remains one of humanity's most influential inventions, even though we don't know who invented it. The magnetic compass likely originated in China in the second century B.C. It was simply a spoon-shaped instrument placed on a cast bronze plate. The instrument was made of a naturally magnetized rock called a lodestone. The compass would always point toward one of Earth's two magnetic poles. The earliest compasses were reportedly used in fortune-telling, but by the 11th century A.D., they were adapted for navigation. For the first time, sailors could head out to sea less worried that weather would obscure the stars they steered by.

The compass slowly spread from Asia to the Mediterranean and Europe and helped enable the age of discovery. By the time it reached Europe around 1300, it had become a glass-covered box with a needle fixed to spin on a card marked with notches indicating direction. The devices were now accurate enough to be considered the mainstays of naval navigation. One challenge encountered was the presence of what we today call magnetic variation. The difference between geographic, or "true," north and magnetic north wasn't significant at lower latitudes, but it increased as explorers ventured too far north. Christopher Columbus noticed this oddity during his first voyage to the Americas but didn't mention it for fear of spooking the crew.

It's safe to say the compass helped spark many of the greatest technological innovations. In 1820 it prompted Denmark's Hans Christian Ørsted to realize that an electric current run through a wire produced a magnetic field, a discovery that paved the way for telegraphy, electric power generation, and wireless communication.

Rearview Cameras

THE NATIONAL HIGHWAY TRAFFIC SAFETY ADMINISTRATION PROPOSED THAT THESE CAMERAS BE STANDARD IN ALL NEW VEHICLES BY 2018.

When we talk about wanting to see what's behind us, we often say we wish we had eyes in the back of our heads. With rearview cameras in our cars, it can feel as if we do. People have long used mirrors and other reflective surfaces to see what's going on behind them, but on the road these days, cameras and sensors are taking the "blind" out of blind spots.

Cameras have come a long way since the camera obscuras of more than a thousand years ago that projected an inverted image as light passed through a tiny aperture. Portable cameras that appeared just before World War II were small enough to fit in a hand, making them ideal for covert surveillance; closed-circuit television, invented in Germany a few years later, was used to monitor V2 rocket launches. After the war, people began thinking about putting video cameras to peaceful uses.

In the 1970s rearview cameras were designed for big construction vehicles such as bulldozers and dump trucks, whose blind spots were so daunting and work sites so vast that mirrors alone weren't safe enough. The cameras were small—about the size of a nickel—and attached to the outside of a vehicle. A monitor screen in the cab allowed drivers to see whatever was behind them as they backed up. With time, the cameras became more sophisticated. Some have sensors that alert drivers if their vehicle is too close to an object. Rearview cameras are now becoming common in private vehicles, so it shouldn't be long before we all have eyes in the back of our heads.

Astrolabe

MECHANICAL ASTRONOMICAL CLOCKS, SUCH AS THE 15TH-CENTURY CLOCK IN PRAGUE' S OLD TOWN SQUARE, WERE INSPIRED BY THE ASTROLABE.

Before the compass found its way to the Middle East and Europe, there was the astrolabe. The flat brass instrument with a projection of the heavens that helped travelers find their way was the laptop computer

of ancient times. By putting the sun or moon between its two sights, users could determine an important list of variables, including latitude and the times of day and year. Displaying apparent distance between astronomical bodies and the horizon, the astrolabe let users calculate actual distance, height, and depth. Depending on the particular design, the back of an astrolabe might also include handy conversion charts.

Evidence suggests that the ancient Greeks had astrolabes, or at least thought up the intellectual framework needed to create one. Around 180 B.C. Hipparchus, who puzzled out the movement of the equinoxes and helped found trigonometry, refined the projection theory that made the astrolabe possible. More evidence of Greek involvement comes from Ptolemy, the father of mapping, whose writings suggest astrolabes were being used. Even so, no one knows when the first astrolabe was made, but we do know that the device was refined in the early Muslim world. The more detailed the engravings of the stars on the astrolabe, the easier it was to find the precise direction of Mecca to pray.

Until the compass and other inventions gained momentum, the astrolabe was crucial for navigation—and for education. In 1391 Geoffrey Chaucer wrote about it, reflecting the belief that astronomical knowledge was synonymous with good breeding.

UNCOMMONLY KNOWN ...

SENSE OF DIRECTION IS INNATE Studies of rats show their brains have a basic spatial framework by the time they leave the nest, suggesting that at least some sense of direction is built in. Human brains come equipped with three kinds of navigation neurons: place cells, grid cells, and head-direction cells. We have yet to figure out why—if humans share the rats' ability—we always seem to need directions.

Sextant

TWO MEN INDEPENDENTLY INVENTED THE DEVICE IN THE 1700S, BUT A DESIGN WAS ALSO FOUND IN ISAAC NEWTON'S UNPUBLISHED WRITINGS.

There was a time when finding one's way at sea was a matter of constant, anxious checking; it was also a matter of life and death. That's why innovations such as the sextant were so important. Its name comes from its scale—60 degrees, or one-sixth of a circle. Like the astrolabe, sextants were generally made of brass and measured angles between celestial objects and the horizon. Unlike the astrolabe, they used mirrors to be able to observe two objects simultaneously and calculate the distance between them. Invented in the 1730s, the sextant made it easier for Captain James Cook and Antarctic explorer Ernest Shackleton to approach their adventures with confidence. On his first Pacific voyage, Cook even used his sextant at night to make calculations based on the moon, which helped him check the accuracy of his other navigation tools.

A distinct advantage of the sextant is that should weather obscure the horizon, the device can create an artificial one for mathematical purposes. That's why sextants didn't become obsolete as did some old-school navigational equipment. Their appearance changed with time, but their usefulness remained. As we took to the air and into the deep sea, the need to calculate distances based on artificial horizons became that much more important. Tens of thousands of sextants were used during World War II, and sextants have even been used for taking measurements in space.

Globe

GLOBES WERE ONCE COMMONLY GIVEN AS GIFTS BETWEEN RULERS. THE SPHERES WERE BOTH BEAUTIFUL AND SYMBOLIC OF HUMAN DOMINION.

Globes, derived from the Latin word for sphere, were a prized innovation. We use them now mostly for educational support, but they started out as revelatory vehicles of discovery for our world. Globes first appeared in ancient Greece after scholars began realizing that the Earth was round. The oldest existing globe, held aloft on the marble shoulders of a statue of Atlas, dates back to A.D. 150.

Along with much else, globes fell into obscurity until the age of discovery. Columbus's voyages in the 15th century created an explosion of interest, and advances in printing made it easier to produce readable globes. They were constructed variously of wood, marble, and metal, then sheathed in either hide or paper to chart the world. Until the 17th century, California was thought to be an island, but globe mapping helped bring cartographers up to date. By the 18th century, globes were proving useful in mapping newly discovered islands in the Pacific, and in England compact globes became status symbols. In the 1800s, students could buy inflatable globes that were easy to carry around with them. In today's electronic age, globes might seem somewhat clunky, but they're still a great way to grasp the world.

PEOPLE WHO CHANGED HISTORY

Copernicus (1473-1543)

This Polish mathematician and astronomer changed the way we see our place in the universe, but what he set out to do was to restore the classic Greek sense of harmony. In the course of his studies, he read works by Greek philosophers and realized Ptolemy's Earth-centric organization of the cosmos didn't make sense. Copernicus moved the sun to the center, made the distance between planets relate to the size of their orbits, and sent Earth spinning on its axis. Though driven more by aesthetics than observation, his heliocentric universe helped launch a science renaissance.

Copernicus observing an eclipse in an 1876 drawing

To Your Health

Technology has revolutionized health management in ways that would boggle ancient minds. We have gadgets that automatically do things physicians themselves were unable to do: analyze a drop of someone's blood; scan patients' bodies and create 3-D maps of their insides; jump-start a person's heart. It's taken a long time for these modern lifesavers to replace what was once mostly messy guesswork. The devices featured here represent major medical breakthroughs and the ingenuity of doctors and patients who refused to take health challenges lying down.

Sterilization Machine

EARLY AUTOCLAVES WERE USED FOR COOKING BUT WEREN'T ALWAYS SAFE; THEY WERE PRONE TO BURSTING OPEN AND SPRAYING BOILING LIQUID.

This machine, also called an autoclave, is essential in medical settings because it's what makes tools like scalpels and forceps safe to use more than once. It works like a pressure cooker. A tight lid traps steam as water boils, raising the temperature and pressurizing the air inside, which gets hot enough to kill off bacteria. The autoclave didn't start out as a means of cleaning medical gear, though. It was actually promoted as an innovative way of preparing foods. In 1679 French physician Denis Papin maintained that using his "steam digester" made food easier to digest. Because the steam tended to unseat the lid (prompting him to add a safety valve), Papin suggested that the steam could be channeled to power an engine. He never built one, but the idea ultimately inspired what became the locomotive steam engine. Papin's "digester" didn't kick off a fast food culinary craze, but the machine clearly had potential. By 1820 in London, M. Lemare had refined it and was calling it an "autoclave," which he confidently claimed helped him cook meat in half an hour or less.

It was Louis Pasteur's studies around food—namely, an investigation into how to keep beer and wine from spoiling—that led him to discover that bacteria start to die when temperatures reach 120°F. Charles Chamberland, who was working with Pasteur in 1879, is credited with taking that knowledge and using it to turn the autoclave into a vital medical device. Sterilized instruments prevent infection, saving the lives of countless patients.

Breathalyzer

BREATHALYZERS WERE DEVELOPED DURING THE 1920S TO ALLOW FRUSTRATED WIVES TO TEST THEIR HUSBANDS' LEVELS OF DRUNKENNESS.

Drunk driving remains a serious problem, yet it's not as pervasive as it once was. Roughly 30 percent of all traffic fatalities today involve someone who's drunk behind the wheel. But until the 1960s, that number was closer to 50 percent. The ability to test for intoxication has helped reduce the booze-fueled carnage.

Prohibition made alcohol a political issue. When it became legal to drink again in 1933, most Americans rejoiced with liquid celebrations. Big cities saw a huge jump in drunk-driving deaths; in Chicago in 1934, for example, they quadrupled in just six months. Authorities needed to find ways of keeping intoxicated people from driving cars, which were no longer just the rich person's plaything.

Scientists had been working on alcohol-detection devices even before automobiles were a common feature of American life, but it wasn't until 1927 that they made inroads. That's when Emil Bogen discovered that neither blood nor urine was needed to test for inebriation; air worked just as well for getting an accurate reading of BAC (blood alcohol concentration). That same year, chemist W. D. McNally touted an apparatus that would change color if a drunk person blew through it. Next came the "Drunkometer," invented in 1938 by Rolla N. Harger. Subjects blew into a balloon, and the air was forced through a chemical solution. The public didn't much trust the tests, and indeed they weren't always trustworthy, which made it difficult for results to stand up in a court of law. In 1954 Robert Borkenstein came up with the first reliable roadside breathalyzer. Though it worked well, certain factors could still occasionally invalidate it. Today most police test for alcohol with virtually foolproof infrared and computer technology, giving drinkers ample cause to think twice before they drive.

PEOPLE WHO CHANGED HISTORY

Jane Fonda (1937-)

Jane Fonda is famous as an Oscar-winning actress and political activist, but her book *Jane Fonda's Workout Book* (1981) turned her into a health and fitness icon. Though it may seem strange now in an age when workout studios abound, 30 years ago they were a new concept. In 1979 Fonda decided to found a women-focused gymnasium in Los Angeles because she felt that existing gyms were geared toward men. Her enterprise did so well that it inspired the book that stayed on best-seller lists for two years and created whole new sections in bookstores for fitness-oriented literature. In 1982 she released a pioneering video, which was eventually followed by a score of others. They featured lots of spandex and showed women how they could stay fit in the comfort and privacy of their own homes. All told, Fonda sold 17 million copies, making them the best-selling home video of all time and game changers in the health and fitness realm.

Jane Fonda, 1985

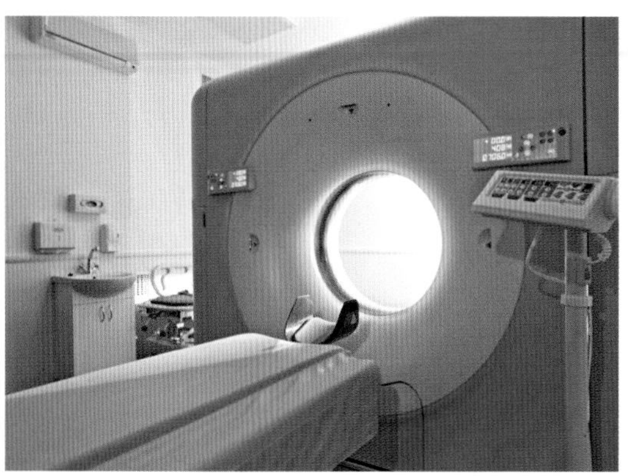

CT Scanner

THIS INVENTOR OF THIS GADGET WORKED FOR THE COMPANY THAT OWNED THE BEATLES' MUSIC; RECORD SALES HELPED FUND ITS CREATION.

When x-rays were invented in 1895, they revolutionized our ability to see inside the body without first having to cut it open. However, they're mostly ineffective for use on soft tissue, and even their images of solid structures like bones and teeth can leave a lot to be desired. Black-and-white x-rays are essentially shadows, which in their shades of gray can't do justice to the body's living-color complexities.

The CT (computerized tomography) scan changed all that. The man in charge of England's first business computer, Godfrey Hounsfield, developed the scanner in the 1960s when he looked for new uses for the technology. He investigated a technique that, unbeknownst to him, was first proposed by Austrian Johann Radon in 1917—to use multiple projections of an object to construct a 3-D image. That's essentially how Hounsfield's prototype worked: It made images of thin "slices" of brain, then meshed them into a 3-D model. Because intact human brains were hard to come by, Hounsfield's team procured cow brains from a local butcher.

Early scanners were frustratingly slow, demanding nine days of continuous operation for a single scan. But advances were on the horizon. In 1971 when doctors scanned a woman's brain for a suspected tumor, the process took only five minutes per scan. Today a CT scanner can crunch data for an image slice in three-tenths of a second.

UNCOMMONLY KNOWN ...

INFOMERCIALS These TV pitches can be seductive. They make tempting promises, but what you see isn't always what you get. Studies suggest that there's a science behind why infomercials are effective. They're often on late at night, when we're more vulnerable to persuasion, and they're scripted in a problem-and-solution format designed to raise our dopamine levels, which makes us feel happy.

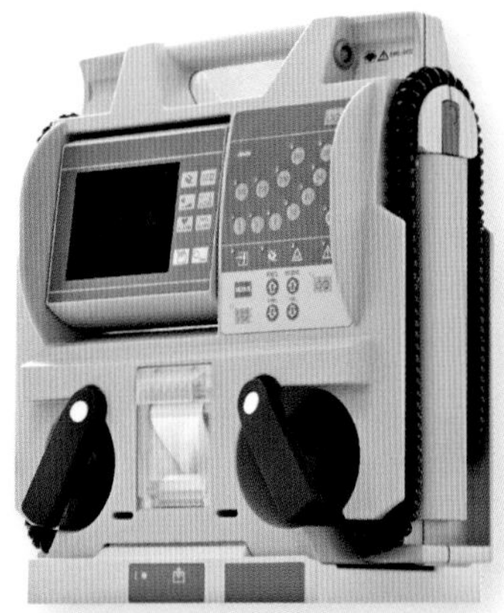

Defibrillator

IN THE 1950S, WILLIAM KOUWENHOVEN INVENTED A DEFIBRILLATOR FOR EXTERNAL USE, AN ADVANCE THAT ALSO LED TO THE DEVELOPMENT OF CPR.

Defibrillators conjure up images of TV dramas with doctors pressing paddles against an emergency heart patient and yelling, "Clear!" Those may be fiction, but the lifesaving power of the devices is entirely

WHAT'S INSIDE?

Touch Screen Technology

Indium, tin, and oxygen put the touch in touch screens. The three elements make up the transparent film that conducts electricity, which is what you're wielding each time you swipe your finger across a screen. There are two types of touch screens: restrictive and capacitive. When you press a restrictive touch screen, your finger pushes conductive and resistive layers against each other to trigger a function. When you touch a capacitive screen, a tiny electrical charge transfers to your finger, completing a circuit that creates a voltage drop that's turned into action.

real. AEDs (automated external defibrillators) can make a victim's heartbeat regular again. It's like giving the heart a jump start—a literal lifesaving spark.

It took a great deal of trial and error for the apparatus to evolve into its current form. In 1775, Danish doctor Peter Christian Abilgaard figured out that electricity could be used to stop and restart a chicken's heart. In the 1840s, scientists discovered that electricity could cause ventricular fibrillation (uncoordinated heart-muscle contraction) in dogs, but that a certain charge could also reverse that process. By the 1900s, researchers started making machines that were safe enough to try on humans. In 1947 cardiac surgeon Claude S. Beck was operating on a 14-year-old boy whose heart stopped during the procedure. Beck used a defibrillator he designed to restart the boy's heart and save his life.

It wasn't until the 1960s that defibrillators for external use became portable enough to be installed outside of hospitals. Now many come with technology that will talk users through the process, so nearly anyone can operate the device. Surgeons will sometimes implant a small, internal defibrillator that can automatically jump-start a stopped heart.

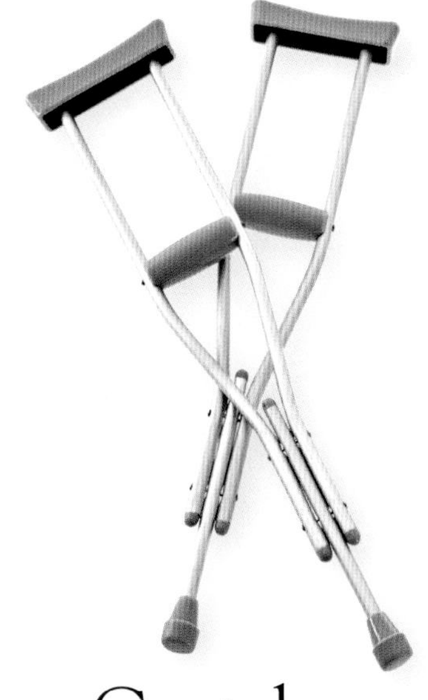

Crutches

SO MANY SOLDIERS LOST THEIR LEGS IN THE U.S. CIVIL WAR AND THE TWO WORLD WARS THAT CRUTCHES WENT FROM SPECIALTY TO COMMODITY.

Crutches have no doubt existed in one form or another since humans first hobbled across the Earth and an unknown inventor picked up a tree branch for extra support. Egyptian carvings from around 2830 B.C. suggest that their basic design hasn't changed much since the days of the pharaohs, though modern enhancements have made them more comfortable and easier to wield.

Most crutches had to be custom made until 1917, when mechanical engineer Emile Schlick patented the first commercial offerings, which looked like walking sticks with upper-arm support. The familiar wooden *T* has long tended to cut off circulation under the arms, so makers finally turned to bow-shaped designs. A. R. Lofstrand, Jr.'s 1940s crutches were height adjustable, an important refinement. New crutches are made of aluminum, light and strong, with soft grips and nonskid tips. But even the finest crutches will never be a joy to use, though

they're a vast improvement over the sad example Tiny Tim leaned on in Charles Dickens's *A Christmas Carol.*

Blood Glucose Meter

ANGRY THAT MONITORS WEREN'T AVAILABLE FOR AT-HOME USE, DIABETIC DICK BERNSTEIN CAMPAIGNED UNTIL THAT CHANGED IN THE 1980S.

Ancient Greek physician Aretaeus noted an ailment that brought on thirst, weight loss, and frequent urination. He called it diabetes: "a flowing through." Of course he had no way of knowing the cause or how to treat it. In medieval times, doctors relied on testing urine's sediment, color—even taste—to diagnose illness, but it took until the 1770s for the sweetness in urine to be identified as a high sugar level, the telltale sign of diabetes. In 1850 chemist Jules Maumené developed a strip that changed color if sugar was present in urine. That test and a strict diet were mainstays for those with diabetes.

In the 1920s when scientists discovered the hormone insulin, which regulates blood sugar, they learned that it's what those with diabetes lack. They could inject it, yet having no meter to measure blood sugar made injection a guessing game. Meters arrived in the 1970s, but hospitals and insurance companies were reluctant to support at-home testing. Their resistance halted progress until the 1980s. Today meters are common and small enough to fit in a pocket.

UNCOMMONLY KNOWN ...

BLOOD VESSELS The circulatory system is a contradiction–it's both fragile and robust. Researchers have discovered that emotional distress can cause stress cardiomyopathy, which can actually "break" your heart. On the other hand, the extent of blood vessels in the system is incredible. If you could lay all your capillaries, veins, and arteries end-to-end, they would stretch more than two times around the Earth–some 60,000 miles.

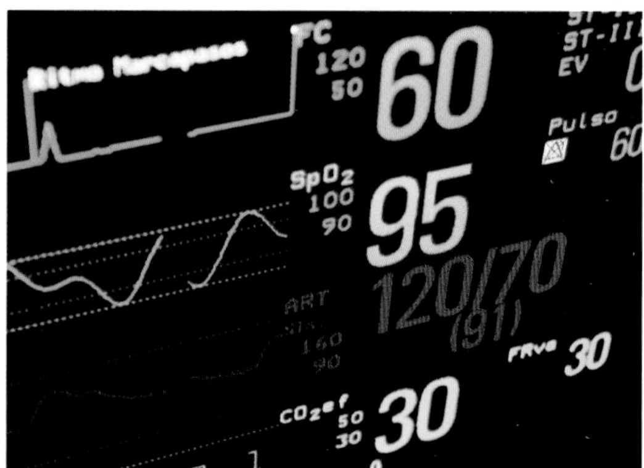

Vital Signs Monitoring System

NEW KNOWLEDGE OF THE CIRCULATORY SYSTEM INSPIRED STEPHEN HALES TO TAKE THE FIRST BLOOD PRESSURE MEASUREMENT IN THE EARLY 1700S–OF A HORSE.

Vital signs—body temperature, pulse, blood pressure, and respiration rate—have always been the body's way of letting us know how we're doing. In recent centuries physicians have understood their significance but haven't always had the implements to accurately measure and track them. Early home-visit doctors examined patients with few tools other than their eyes, ears, or touch to gauge vital functions. Then in 1816 René Théophile Hyacinthe Laënnec, apparently inspired by watching children play with a wooden trumpet, invented the stethoscope. He experimented with hollow tubes of cedar and ivory that allowed him to hear percussive sounds inside a patient and differentiate between them. Combined with other inventions such as the blood pressure cuff—the sphygmomanometer—sophisticated digital monitors now record all our vital signs simultaneously.

PEOPLE WHO CHANGED HISTORY

Marie Curie (1867-1934)

Born Maria Sklodowska, she was not allowed to go to Warsaw's male-only university in the late 1800s, so she studied math and science on her own, working as a governess to support herself. She moved to Paris and excelled at the Sorbonne, where she received degrees in physics and mathematics and met her physicist husband, Pierre Curie. Together they discovered polonium and radium. Marie came to understand the origin of x-rays and coined the term "radioactivity." In 1903 she was the first woman to win the Nobel Prize in physics. During World War I, she pioneered portable x-ray machines that were nicknamed "Little Curies." Sadly, in 1934 Marie Curie died from long-term radiation exposure.

Marie Curie in her Paris lab, circa 1900

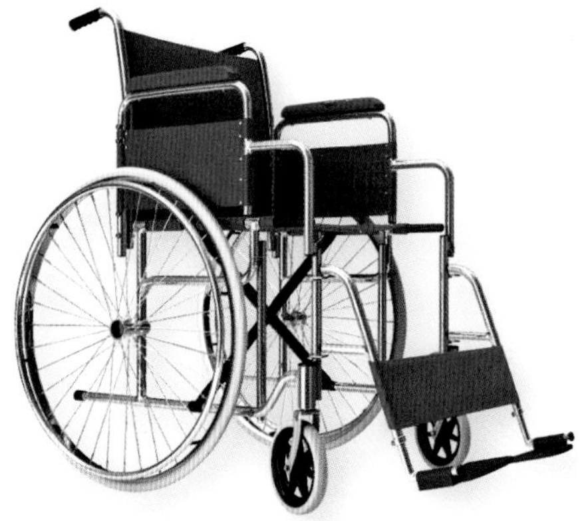

Wheelchair

PRESIDENT FRANKLIN D. ROOSEVELT HAD THE SECRET SERVICE BLOCK ANYONE WHO TRIED TO PHOTOGRAPH HIM WHILE IN HIS WHEELCHAIR.

The wheelchair was known in ancient times but didn't get much use; for millennia, the mobility of the disabled wasn't a priority. When prominent historical figures began to make use of them, the devices gained traction—literally. King Philip II of Spain had a reclining "invalid chair," and France's Louis XIV of France was confined to a wheelchair after surgery. Seeing royalty thus enthroned encouraged the acceptance of wheeled chairs, but they still had to be built to order.

Mid-18th-century England produced the "bath chair," with two large rear wheels and a smaller front wheel that could be steered with a tiller by the occupant. The first U.S. wheelchair was patented in 1869, but it wasn't until 1932 that the country saw a collapsible chair, invented by Harold Jennings and Herbert A. Everest for a disabled friend who was not able to take his chair on car trips. With postwar commercial expansion, wheelchairs got cheaper and more technologically advanced, including motorized versions allowing greater independence for people in need.

Work It

For many of us, it can often feel as if we live in our offices. Whether the office is a coffee shop, a cubicle, or a corner suite, it's a place we spend untold hours laboring—and dreaming. The inventions in this section make our work lives easier, faster, and more productive. Some modest officemates, such as the elegantly simple paper clip and thumbtack, have retained their original usefulness over their long history. Newer arrivals such as the calculator and the flash drive are the culminations of innovative technology. All of them support the bottom line.

3-D Printers

IMAGINE NEEDING A KIDNEY AND HAVING A MACHINE PRINT ONE OUT FOR YOU. THAT'S WHAT 3-D PRINTERS ARE STARTING TO MAKE POSSIBLE.

Printing technology has taken some surprising turns since Gutenberg's time in the 1400s. Back then, a compositor had to set pieces of wooden type by hand before they were slathered in ink and pressed to paper. A good compositor of the 15th and 16th centuries century might set 2,000 characters in an hour. Today a personal computer organizes the same number in roughly two seconds. Up until the 19th century and mechanized typesetting, the job of a pressman was mostly hand labor. In the latter half of the 20th century the printing process changed radically with computer technology, but the end result was more or less the same: ink on flat paper.

The 3-D printer has changed our notion of what printing is and what sorts of things it can produce. Called "additive manufacturing," 3-D printing takes a computer's instructions about the composition of an object and "prints" it out, layer by layer, from wells of plastic, ceramic, or metal. The first successful patent for what its inventor Charles Hull called stereolithography was granted in 1986.

Though the technology has grown and become more sophisticated over the years, most people are unfamiliar with 3-D printing. Its potential seems unlimited—and thereby potentially controversial as well. For example, it's possible to print weapons, including nonmetal firearms that could be difficult for security forces to detect. In 2013 doctors used a 3-D printer to make a partial skull piece and implanted it in a patient. The devices have been used to produce jewelry, hardware, and architectural models of houses. At some point 3-D printers may enable us to print full-size, livable houses.

Thumbtacks

THAT LITTLE "PIN IT" BUTTON THAT ALLOWS YOU TO ADD A PICTURE TO A PINTEREST BOARD? THAT WAS INSPIRED BY THE HUMBLE PUSHPIN

Throughout history, people used sharp objects like needles and straight pins to tack battle plans, maps, and grand ambitions to tables and walls. Those people were probably also pricking themselves frequently as they tried to rearrange items or put up new ones. It wasn't until the early 1900s that the first actual thumbtack (also called a pushpin or drawing pin) was invented. Sometimes the most brilliant inventions are also the simplest.

In 1900 Edwin Moore, a New Jersey photo lab technician, sought a tool that seemed basic enough—a pin with a handle—but couldn't find one, so he made his own. His first pushpins had glass handles and steel points, and he felt confident enough to start a company and devote himself to producing them, selling whatever he'd made the day before. His first sale totaled about $2.00. Soon, he would sell $1,000 worth of his pushpins to the Eastman Kodak Company. By 1903 he was proudly advertising his products in the *Ladies' Home Journal.*

While Moore was getting his company up and running, German clockmaker Johann Kirsten was designing what he termed a drawing pin—a flat-headed thumbtack for use on drawing boards. The only real difference between Moore's invention and Kirsten's was the shape of the head. Moore thrived after patenting his pushpin and went on to create such useful items as the picture hanger. Kirsten sold the rights to his thumbtack to a man who patented the device and made a fortune. Kirsten died poor.

UNCOMMONLY KNOWN ...

FIRST COMPUTER MOUSE Once upon a time, there was no point-and-click method of interacting with a computer; you had to keyboard your commands. The invention of the trackball in 1946 paved the way for the first computer mouse. Bill English and Douglas Engelbart collaborated on the mouse in 1963, so called because of its round body and thin tail-like cord. The first mouse was more the size of a rat but led the way for the sleek mice we use today.

Videoconferencing

WORKERS WHO CAN'T BE SEEN DURING TELEPHONE CONFERENCE CALLS TAKE THE OPPORTUNITY TO COOK, SEND E-MAILS—AND VISIT THE BATHROOM.

Meetings are among the least popular duties of corporate life. They're often long and tedious and can have a negative impact on morale. Though studies suggest that meetings aren't an effective use of time, workers are still obliged to come together and try to get things done. People now are

traveling and working from home more than ever before, but that doesn't mean meetings happen less frequently. They just occur in a different medium, usually a telephone conference call, and in fact often while people are away from their desks. Calls can be confusing and frustrating when you can't see the people you're talking to. That's why videoconferencing is such a beneficial innovation.

The invention of television made the videoconference possible by using two closed-circuit TV systems connected by cable or radio. Videoconferencing was introduced at the 1964 World's Fair in New York, but the staged presentation was so futuristic looking that people found it difficult to imagine the technology taking off. A decade later, newer videophones still seemed impractical and too expensive for regular use.

Nevertheless, the ability to feel connected to people through video was changing our world. TV altered how we perceived politicians and other newsmakers of the day. And research supported the idea that when people can see each other, they are more likely to feel engaged and invested in a conversation. In 1991 IBM had brought out the first PC-based video system, heralding the shift from television to computer-based video conferencing. Today conferees need to think twice before using the hour to paint their nails.

UNCOMMONLY KNOWN ...

EDIBLE PRINTING With edible ink you can turn a photo into a fun cake topper; 3-D printers take the concept to a whole new level. NASA has been working on a 3-D printer that would allow astronauts to print their own food. Seemingly far-fetched, that kind of printing is already happening on Earth. Firms have used printers to make chocolates and other candy, as well as cocktail garnishes—even crackers that sprout miniature salads.

Paper Clips

PAPER CLIP DESIGNS HAVE COME AND GONE SINCE THE ITEM'S INVENTION, BUT THE STEEL GEM CLIP REMAINS THE ALL-TIME BEST SELLER.

If you stepped back to the latter part of the 19th century, you'd find yourself navigating a strange world: hopping into a horse-drawn carriage, wondering whether the house of the friend you were visiting would have indoor plumbing. If you walked into an office, though, there is one thing you would recognize: the small but mighty paper clip.

For as long as there have been sheets of paper, we've needed ways to keep those sheets properly organized. Paper was a luxury item in ancient times, so people often sewed papers together or sealed them with wax. In the early 19th century, as paper became more prevalent, harried office clerks had more and more bundles they needed to fasten with string or sort into various boxes. People could also choose straight pins, but they were made of iron and had a tendency not only to rust but to pierce both paper and the unsuspecting finger. In 1855 the availability of strong, flexible steel changed how we thought of metal. Steel could be bent into rust-free hooks, hangers, and—of course—the paper clip. William Middlebrook's patent in 1899 wasn't for the clip itself, which had been around for some years, but for the machinery that produced it. He later sold it to a company that produced the iconic Gem clips. Since then, despite an increasingly technological world, the paper clip has remained basically unchanged.

Calculator

THE 1886 BURROUGHS ADDING MACHINE MADE THE FAMILY RICH. THE FORTUNE SUPPORTED BEAT GENERATION WRITER WILLIAM S. BURROUGHS.

It's amazing what today's calculators can solve, but they've been around in some form since ancient times. In the beginning, there was the abacus. Starting in the third century B.C., mathematicians in Egypt and Sumer figured out problems by sliding beads along rods. The abacus remained the calculator of choice for some 3,600 years, until the slide rule came onto the scene in England in the 17th century. The rule used logarithmic scales, making multiplication and division much faster.

France's Blaise Pascal built the first mechanical calculator in 1642, aimed at providing all four arithmetic functions without requiring much effort. That goal wouldn't be fully realized until the 19th century when adding machines became more widely available. The four-function Arithmometer and Comptometer were push-button ready but bulky. In the first half of the 20th century, the Curta was small enough to fit inside a pocket.

World War II prompted realization of the need for faster and more accurate ways to calculate distances between locations, including where to drop bombs, giving rise in part to the computers that would ultimately change the calculator calculus. By 1961 computer parts were small enough to produce the first all-electronic devices. They required a lot of power to operate, but microchips allowed calculators to fit in the palm of a hand.

Hewlett-Packard's 1974 "personal computer" was given a tapered shape so it would fit inside a shirt pocket. It blasted off aboard the U.S.-Soviet spaceflight in 1975, making it the first handheld calculator to orbit Earth.

WHAT'S INSIDE?

Ink-jet Color Cartridge

When you boil down their basic components, ink cartridges are 95 percent water and just 5 percent color. Those colors come from three dyes—red, blue, and yellow—each in its own chamber. But the chambers also hold a host of compounds that help the cartridges do their job. Ethylene glycol is mixed in with the colors to keep them blended with all that water. There's also Ethylenediaminetetraacetic acid (EDTA), an acid that snatches metal ions left by the cartridge's adhesive packaging to keep them from clogging the ink nozzles. Ethoxylated acetylenic diols help keep the surface tension of the ink just right, and the solvent cyclohexanone helps the ink bond to glossy paper. Butyl urea keeps the paper from bunching and warping once the ink dries. All told, those tiny costly drops of ink pack a complex punch.

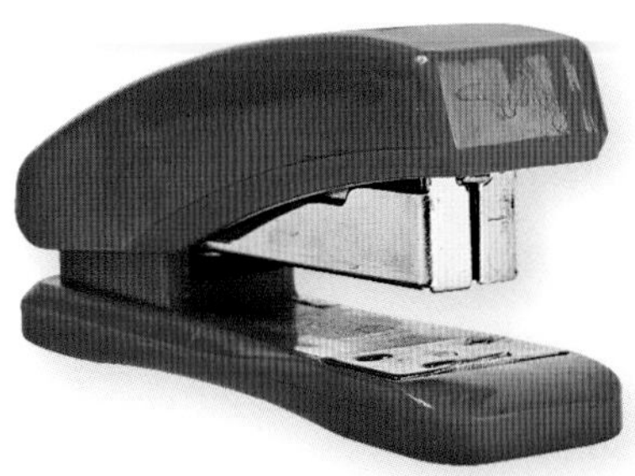

Stapler

WE TALK ABOUT CUTTING THROUGH BUREAUCRATIC RED TAPE BECAUSE THAT'S WHAT BOUND PAPERS BEFORE THE STAPLER CAME ALONG.

Prior to the stapler, there was no truly efficient way to bind thick documents together. Straight pins and string were finicky; glue and stitchery were time-consuming and messy; paper clips had their limits. Generally this was a problem only for people wealthy enough to be able to afford stacks of paper. But as paper grew more widely used, the stapler became, and still is, the paper binder of choice.

Vexed by the problem of paper binding, academics in A.D. 1200 started using wax and ribbon. Though we don't use such methods now, we echo their result when we attach papers in the upper-left corners. Legend has it that King Louis XV commissioned the first stapler, a gold-and-jewel-encrusted tool, but no device was patented until 1877. Philadelphian Henry Heyl's stapler did the previously impossible: bind papers in one fluid action. By 1879 George McGill had created commercial staplers that could drive a half-inch wire through paper; not only that, they could crimp the staples' ends. But those staplers looked more like industrial machinery and required frequent reloading. Then in 1895 came the E. H. Hotchkiss Company's "No. 1 Paper Fastener," which was so fast and convenient it became, well, a veritable stapler. The Japanese word for stapler is still *hochikisu,* inspired by what was soon known as "the Hotchkiss."

It wasn't until the 1920s that staplers became smaller, lighter, and capable of holding hundreds of staples at one time. In the 1930s Jack Linsky and the Swingline company revolutionized the business by designing compact staplers that allow users simply to open the hatch and drop staples in, making the whole process quick and easy. The company is still thriving, and countless Swingline staplers grace office desks.

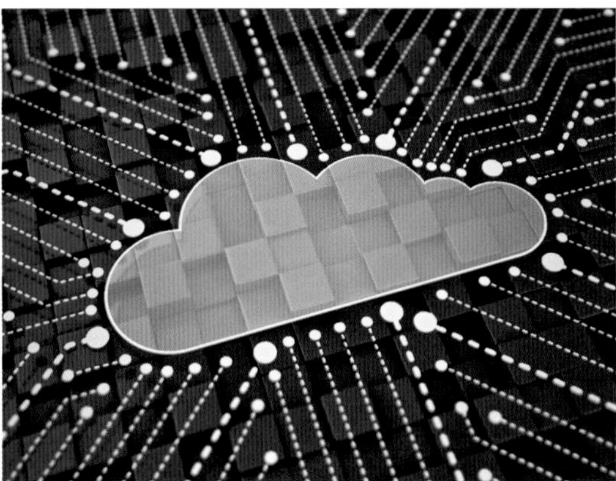

Cloud Computing

IT HAS BEEN PROJECTED THAT 50 BILLION OBJECTS MAY CONNECT TO THE INTERNET BY 2020, MAKING CLOUD COMPUTING MORE CRUCIAL THAN EVER BEFORE.

File sharing has long been a troublesome issue, so cloud computing is a welcome innovation. Before computers, important papers had to be gathered and sent by courier or mail; if the carrier dropped the documents in the mud, the sender and receiver were out of luck. Even when computers first appeared, most file sharing relied on exchanging floppy disks and faxes. These days we can send digital documents "into the cloud," enabling instant collaboration across a room or across the world.

In the 1950s there was time sharing, which allowed businesses and universities to access information at separate computer terminals, but it was expensive and didn't permit them to be on the mainframe simultaneously. By 1969 J. C. R. Licklider was introducing an "intergalactic computer network" that he hoped would one day let people access data from anywhere. His file-sharing vision was ahead of the technology; we had to wait for Internet bandwidth to broaden in the 1990s before we could begin sharing files en masse. In 1999 Salesforce became the first site to offer such a service over the Internet. It took about a decade for other companies to ramp up, and now it seems that for cloud technology, the sky's the limit.

PEOPLE WHO CHANGED HISTORY

Steve Wozniak (1950-)

Steve Wozniak designed the personal computer that set the standard, revolutionizing the way we do business. He founded Apple in 1976 with Steve Jobs, whom he met while Jobs was still in high school. Their first computer was the Apple I, built partly in Jobs's garage. Wozniak later designed the innovative Apple II, building the hardware and software himself while holding down a day job at Hewlett-Packard. The new design shaped what computers would come to look like and how we interact with them. Apple II had a keyboard, a slot for a disk, and color graphics. After leaving Apple in the 1980s, he went on to found or play important roles with other cutting-edge companies, and he became a leading advocate for technology education. Wozniak continues to be an influential voice in the tech world.

Steve Wozniak with an Apple IIe computer, 1983

Flash Drive

THE LATEST USBS CAN HOLD OVER A HUNDRED GIGABYTES OF DATA—ABOUT A THOUSAND TIMES MORE THAN THEIR ANCESTOR, THE FLOPPY DISK.

In 1969 when military analyst Daniel Ellsberg decided to copy the 7,000-page study later called the Pentagon Papers, he had to scan them through a photocopier. Imagine trying to pull off a covert operation in the bright light and whirring of a copy machine, a single page at a time. Such was not the case in 2013 for information leaker Edward Snowden, who could load documents onto a flash drive in seconds and slip it up his sleeve.

It used to be that floppy disks, DVDs, and CDs carried data, but they were bulky and easy to break. And anyone who's ever attempted to load large files onto them can attest to their frustratingly meager storage space.

The flash drive, or USB (Universal Serial Bus), changed all that. It was designed in 1996 to plug into any device, thus offering universal data exchange. From time to time since then, the government has attempted to ban flash drives. They're so small and USB ports so ubiquitous that it's not hard to imagine old-school spies being envious of the technology.

Getting Fit

For centuries humans got their exercise in the course of daily life. Hunting, gathering, and farming kept us fit. With technological progress, we slid into sedentary ways, and fitness became the precinct of athletes and soldiers. In the last few decades, though, we've become more interested in physical fitness. Many of these inventions were first used for other things—the scale for weighing goods and the skates for novelty. Some, like the pedometer, have been around for longer than you might think. They all promise to help us stay healthy and keep fit.

Pedometer

AVID WALKER THOMAS JEFFERSON INTRODUCED THE PEDOMETER TO THE AMERICAN PUBLIC. SOME PEOPLE CALLED IT THE "TOMISH METER."

Some of the greatest minds in history have turned their attention to creating contraptions that can count someone's steps. In the 15th century Leonardo da Vinci sketched out plans for a counting device inspired by the idea of documenting how far soldiers marched in a day. Some people suggest that 18th-century Swiss watchmakers and their motion-sensitive timepieces were the forefathers of the pedometer. We know Thomas Jefferson worked on one and popularized it but never patented his design. The step monitors really gained traction in the 1930s, when the Hike-o-Meter became popular with long-distance trekkers.

In 1965 Y. Hatano's *manpo-kei,* which translates to "10,000 steps meter," found favor in Japan. Hatano suggested 10,000 was the number of steps people need to take daily to balance their calorie intake and stay at a healthy weight. At that point in the pedometer's history, steps were recorded using a small lead-ball pendulum. It had to be held upright to work, which posed problems for people who might bend while they walked. Modern pedometers use sensors to track steps and

WHAT'S INSIDE?

Apple Watch

This smart watch takes the pedometer and turns it into a personal trainer. It uses GPS technology to track where you are and how far you've gone. An accelerometer marks your every move, and a sensor measures your heart rate. Syncing the watch to your phone means you can get real-time details about your movements and see whether you've reached your goals. Customization lets the watch get to know you so it can offer individualized encouragement. Combine that with its ability to check e-mail and organize your calendar—and tell time, of course—and you've got a small command center that will never let you forget to get up and get moving.

are accurate to within about 5 percent. Syncing them with a computer means you can now track metrics such as how energetically you're moving and whether you're climbing stairs. You can even encourage friends to keep going if you've opted to track their steps too.

Scales

WHEN SOULS ARRIVED AT THE GATES OF THE AFTERLIFE, THE EGYPTIAN GOD ANUBIS WEIGHED THEIR HEARTS TO DETERMINE THEIR FATE.

For most of human history, scales used comparison weights; an object was weighed against a counterweight to determine its relative heft. In order to make the calculations consistent, counterweights needed to be uniform and predictable, which is why the ancients relied on grains of wheat or seeds. Seeds from the carob tree gave us the term *carats,* which we use today to specify the weight of precious gems. A relative weight system can be effective, but it's also easy to scam. Even so, balance scales became symbols of fairness: Egyptian and Greek goddesses held scales to indicate the quest for justice.

Around 400 B.C. a weighing apparatus called a Bismar appeared, made of a wooden rod slung from a free-moving pivot, with a fixed weight on one end and a hook at the other. Goods were slung from the hook, and the pivot was slid along the rod until the two sides balanced. Greek philosopher Aristotle condemned the device as faulty and unfair, but it remained popular through the next millennium. The European counterweight unit, the stone, dates to antiquity, but a stone's weight varied wildly until the 14th century, when King Edward III decreed it to be 14 pounds. Leonardo da Vinci came up with plans for a self-indicating scale, but one wasn't manufactured for centuries.

Balance scales stayed in use until the first spring-driven scales came along in the 1700s. By the 1840s postal workers found their jobs becoming much easier with the accuracy of the candlestick spring scale, which measured tension or pressure to figure out an object's weight. Public spring scales began popping up in the streets of Europe, bearing slogans such as, "He who often weighs himself knows himself well. He who knows himself well lives well." In the 20th century, mechanical scales of all types declined with the development of electronics. Today's scales are often digital, and some can connect to the Internet and provide highly accurate results—no hooks or stones required.

UNCOMMONLY KNOWN ...

WEARABLE TECH It isn't a fantasy of the future. It's already here, and it goes way beyond smart watch monitors. Companies are developing products that promise to change the way we live, especially when it comes to fitness. An increasing number of smart garments are aimed at measuring movements: a glove to analyze golf swing, a waistband that vibrates when you let yourself slouch, and socks that deliver data about your running form directly to your phone. There are even temporary tattoos that promise to measure your salt and pH levels.

Elliptical

THE ELLIPTICAL IS A WELCOME ALTERNATIVE TO THE VIBRATING BELTS OF YESTERYEAR, DESIGNED TO VIGOROUSLY SHAKE FAT AWAY.

There was a time when many of us didn't need to work out. We were so busy defending ourselves, catching prey, and gathering supplies that we never had to worry about being out of shape. But ever since we started sitting more and moving less, we've been inventing machines to help us work up a healthy sweat.

Fitness to a degree was important as far back as ancient Egypt and Rome, though mostly for full-time athletes and soldiers readying for war. In the 19th century in the United States, fitness programs were introduced, but machines were still scarce. A few existing contraptions featuring seats and pulleys, such as the Gymnasticon, invented in 1796, looked more like exercises in torture.

The treadmill was invented in 1818. It was made for putting prisoners to work pumping water and grinding corn—hence the "mill" in its name. While it was outlawed as a punishment in 1898, cardiologist Robert A. Bruce started using treadmills to conduct human stress tests in 1952.

UNCOMMONLY KNOWN ...

HOW MUCH WATER SHOULD WE DRINK? The old "eight cups a day" rule is outdated. More is often better. It depends where we live, how much we exercise, and how much we weigh. Hydration can come from sources other than plain water too: coffee, juice, and foods with high water content can all help fill the need.

It wasn't long before they were marketed for fitness, capitalizing on a growing national trend. The elliptical machine, named for the shape feet inscribe as they pedal, didn't come onto the scene until the 1990s. It was born out of the quest for a low-impact workout—an apparatus easy on the joints. The elliptical quickly became a popular treadmill alternative, and one you're less likely to fall off of.

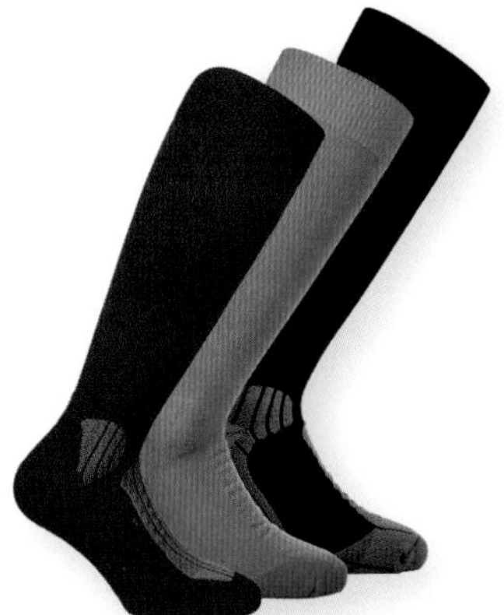

Compression Socks

BEFORE STRETCHY LYCRA WAS INVENTED IN 1959, HOSE WERE MADE OUT OF RUBBER-BASED THREADS, WHICH WERE NOT STRONG ENOUGH FOR GOOD COMPRESSION.

Engineer Conrad Jobst helped develop many innovations: the retractable car top for one, as well as gun sights used in both world wars, but his compression socks were the most personal. Jobst struggled from venous insufficiency, which causes blood to pool in the legs. When he took up swimming, he found that the water pressure made his legs feel better. Working on that principle, in the 1950s he created the first compression stockings—tight hosiery that would ease the discomfort of circulation problems—and founded a company to produce them.

Eventually the garments caught the attention of fitness professionals, who started experimenting with their own versions of the stockings. Some distance runners now swear by compression socks, saying their legs are far less sore after exercise. Indeed, studies suggest that wearing compression socks leads to improved recovery times and fewer injuries, but whether they can increase endurance is debated.

PEOPLE WHO CHANGED HISTORY

Jack LaLanne (1914-2011)

When François Henri (Jack) LaLanne was born in 1914, recreational fitness hadn't taken off. Nonetheless, his love for it inspired him in 1936 to open the first fitness studio in the United States. Over the years he pioneered such innovations as healthy snack bars at gyms, workout machines, and exercise TV shows. LaLanne pushed fitness boundaries. In 1954 at age 40, he swam the length of the Golden Gate Bridge—underwater—towing 140 pounds. The next year, he was crowned Mr. America. He walked the walk to the end: He did his daily workout the day before he died in 2011 at the age of 96.

Jack LaLanne photo shoot, California, 1960

Inline Skates

ACCORDING TO A PLAUSIBLE ORIGIN MYTH, A DUTCH MAN WANTED TO SKATE IN SUMMER, SO HE ATTACHED WOODEN SPOOLS TO HIS SHOES.

The first person to officially invent skates with wheels, John Merlin, made the bold choice to wear his custom-crafted novelty to a posh London masquerade party in the 1760s. He may have been a great inventor, but he apparently was not a very good skater: He crashed into a mirror and injured himself. Credit for the first true inline skates, where the wheels run in a single row, not two, goes in 1819 to a Frenchman, Monsieur Petitbled. His skates featured a wooden sole, leather straps, and three wheels of metal, wood, or ivory.

From the time wheeled skates first appeared until the second half of the 19th century, all incorporated some form of inline design—and all were hard to maneuver. They went forward just fine, but turning and stopping was another matter. In the 1860s American James Plimpton rocked the skating world with his front-and-back, four-wheel roller, or "quad," skates that could turn. It took inline skates another century to find their wheeled footing. In 1979 hockey player Scott Olson adapted skates to train in the off-season. The company he founded would

become Rollerblade, producing inline skates that could maneuver and brake, and transforming a novelty into a popular sport.

Swim Fins

TAHITIANS WHO DIPPED PALM FRONDS INTO HOT TAR AND THEN SWAM WITH THEM INSPIRED AMERICAN SWIM FIN DEVELOPER OWEN CHURCHILL.

Human bodies may not be designed for life in the water, but that hasn't stopped us from looking for ways to swim efficiently through it. The earliest swim fin design dates back to the 15th century and Leonardo da Vinci. He toyed with several inventions that borrowed mechanics from the animal world, including wings for flying and fins for cutting through water. Though his designs ended up being impractical, his ideas provided a foundation for later dreamers to build on. Benjamin Franklin, for example, often dreamed about sailing the high seas when he was growing up. An avid swimmer, young Franklin tinkered with fins shaped like lily pads designed to be strapped on hands.

Though less fanciful "swimming propellers" were invented in the early 1900s, it wasn't until 1940, after a trip to Tahiti, that gold-medal-winning yachtsman Owen P. Churchill elaborated on a French design, and vulcanized rubber "swim fins" (as he named them) started looking much the way they do today.

Churchill's fins became standard issue for divers in the U.S. Navy as well as for British frogmen. After World War II, commercial diving and recreational use of dive equipment slowly increased. These days it's common to see swim fins littering the decks of commercial dive boats or waiting to be donned at pools and beaches.

Resistance Pools

AT THE START OF THE FOURTH CENTURY A.D., ROMANS BUILT A 900,000-SQUARE-FOOT BATHING POOL HEATED BY FIRES FROM BELOW.

We start out life as innate little swimmers. When submerged, babies reflexively open their eyes and hold their breath. Later in life, many of us return to the water for exercise because its density creates a resistance-based, low-impact workout. And we just like to swim. Whether or not they had any concept of low impact, our ancestors were clearly fond of swimming; the Latin word for "pool," *piscina,* relates to the fish ancients sometimes put in their fancier baths and ponds. Greeks built pools specifically for swimming and encouraged the activity as a martial art. Plato believed youths should include the study of swimming along with their studies of math and astronomy; by 400 B.C. learning to swim was standard practice in Greece. Across the world in Japan, the first recorded swim competition occurred in 36 B.C.

Competitions were introduced to Britain in the 1800s, held in indoor pools in London. In 1896 swimmer John Trudgen showed off his "front crawl" (called the Trudgen stroke and later known as freestyle), which quickly outpaced breaststroke and sidestroke. The first pool to come to the United States actually sailed over the Atlantic on a White Star cruise ship that docked in 1907 (there was one on the *Titanic* too).

As swimming pools burgeoned and swimming for health and fitness grew, people started looking for ways to work out in water at home. To accommodate limited space, compact resistance pools, introduced in the 1970s and since refined, function as watery treadmills, allowing swimmers to exercise in place.

WHAT'S INSIDE?

Sports Gel

The contents of gooey sports gels might seem a mystery (and unappetizing to boot), but what they offer runners is quite simple: carbohydrates. When running, the body draws on supplies of fat and carbohydrate for fuel. Fat turns into energy slowly, making it a less-than-ideal fuel source when running for long periods at more than 60 percent of one's aerobic threshold. Performance often equates to how much glycogen–a form of glucose–is stored in muscles and blood. When runners open these small packs of nourishment midstride, they're gulping glycogen and other carbohydrates that wake up the brain and keep their legs driving.

Kettlebells

IN RUSSIA SOLDIERS CONTINUE TO BE JUDGED ON HOW MANY SNATCHES–SMOOTH QUICK LIFTS–THEY CAN DO WITH A 50-POUND KETTLEBELL.

Though many workout buffs today have never used a kettlebell, people have been hefting the bulbous weights since the days of ancient Greece. They really came into their own as a workout tool, though, when they made their way to Russia at the beginning of the 18th century. In 1704 the word "girya"—kettlebell—entered the Russian dictionary. The teakettle-shaped device was originally designed as a counterweight for measuring grain, but laborers found it a fun way to exercise (and prove their might) during their downtime. It didn't take long for demonstrations of kettlebell strength to be featured at festivals and fairs.

In the late 1800s Russian physician Vladislav Kraevsky traveled across Europe to research other nations' methods of exercise. When he returned, he introduced formal kettlebell and barbell routines.

Kraevsky is considered the father of weightlifting in Russia, where the sport is greatly revered. Lifting weights fuels the fitness goals of enthusiasts the world over—including the United States, where kettlebells in a wide range of weights can be found in practically every gym.

ENTRY TO THE TRAITORS' GATE

History never looks like history when you are living through it.

—JOHN W. GARDNER (1912-2002)

Perfectly Preserved

Great art, immortalized in the world's foremost museums or concert halls, uplifts us with its glimpse of the heights of human accomplishment. But when we see the ordinary objects of daily life collected and preserved with care, we feel a more intimate connection between ourselves and the rest of the human family. Sometimes the fact that the item has been collected is itself remarkable. Toilets, for instance, have their own fine institution in India. Badminton shuttlecocks merit display at England's badminton museum. Sometimes the very age of a common item, well preserved, is startling. Bone flutes survive that might have been played by Neanderthals. Bread from Herculaneum still bears the mark of the slave who baked it.

The entries in this chapter remind us how much we owe to the learned, passionate, and occasionally unusual folks who devote their lives to assembling and protecting everyday treasures. Famous scientists such as Charles Darwin and magnates like J. P. Morgan contributed to the collections described here—but so too did skateboarders, barbed wire collectors, the hobo king known as Steamtrain Maury, and Frances Glessner Lee, creator of tiny replicas of real crime scenes. Decades of devoted work went into Samuel George Morton's assortment of human skulls. Rattlesnake admirers put themselves at risk to nurture the twitchy inhabitants of Albuquerque's rattlesnake museum. Sports, too, breed their own zealous fans, as we are reminded when we trace the history of the soccer ball, trophies huge and tiny, or the once derided hockey mask, first worn by a female goaltender. The chapter concludes with historical monuments such as the Taj Mahal and the Tower of London. Among the most visited structures in the world, each is part of humanity's common cultural heritage.

Compelling Collections

Museums around the world preserve the artistic and scientific glories of their cultures: paintings and sculptures, fossils and gems. Tucked into quieter corners of the world are different sorts of collections, more homely but no less compelling. These are museums, galleries, or modest houses devoted to life's under-appreciated, ordinary objects. Who knew, for instance, that barbed wire came in more than 2,000 varieties, and is prized by collectors? This section samples some of the most noteworthy of these collections, ranging from toilets to tea accoutrements.

Timeless Toys

HALL OF FAME TOYS INCLUDE SUCH BASICS AS BALLS, BUBBLES, BLANKETS, CARDBOARD BOXES, MARBLES, PLAYING CARDS, AND STICKS.

In the 1950s, Joe McVicker, a maker of wallpaper cleaning paste, found his business was waning. The coal-darkened wallpapers of previous decades had given way to vinyl fabrics. One audience, however, loved his product. Local schoolchildren discovered that they could mold the flour-based compound into a variety of shapes without the effort required by stiffer modeling clay. McVicker took the compound to an educational convention, attracting commercial attention under a new name: Play-Doh. Its red-and-yellow can became instantly recognizable, now a classic of the playroom.

In 1998, Play-Doh and ten other toys, including teddy bears, Crayola crayons, and Monopoly, were inducted into the first class of the National Toy Hall of Fame. The hall is just one facet of the Strong Museum of Play in Rochester, New York, an institution devoted to the study of toys, games, and their role in society. Families can take a tour, but for the Strong Museum, play is serious business. The institution hosts researchers and sponsors one of the more entertaining journals in the academic world: the *American Journal of Play.*

WHAT'S INSIDE?

Nonglare Glass

The glass that guards art and artifacts in museums needs to protect the works without hiding them behind glare or reflections of their surroundings. That's why museums turn to nonglare or antireflective glass. Nonglare glass has a slightly matte surface, etched in such as way that reflected light is scattered in different directions. Antireflective glass, preferred by most artists, has one or more microscopically thin coatings that create a kind of destructive interference in the reflected light, reducing reflection while keeping a clear view of the art beneath.

Tea

A SONG DYNASTY TEXT SAYS THAT THE SEVEN NECESSITIES FOR STARTING THE DAY ARE FIREWOOD, RICE, OIL, SALT, SAUCE, VINEGAR, AND TEA.

A soothing cup of tea is an essential part of the day for hundreds of millions of people around the globe. Worldwide, three cups of tea are consumed for every one of coffee. To fully appreciate the ancient roots of the herbal beverage, a visit to the China National Tea Museum might be in order. The institution is steeped in history.

Located in Shuangfeng, near Shanghai, the museum occupies a serene, parklike setting. Inside, halls depict the story of tea, its ceremonies, and its wares. Records of tea drinking date as far back as the tenth century B.C. in China. Originally the leaves were baked into a brick, a portion of which could be broken off and ground into a powder. Tea spread into northern China by the Tang dynasty (A.D. 618–907); by the Song dynasty (960–1279) it had acquired a loose-leaf production as well as the elaborate ceremonies that made its consumption an art form. Scholars and monks wrote poems about tea tasting as a meditative exercise.

The art of tea extended to its exquisite containers, on display at the museum. Gracefully rounded kettles date back 5,000 years; celadon tea bowls from the Tang dynasty have a beautiful simplicity. Today visitors to the museum can observe a tea ceremony that might be enough to convert even the most ardent coffee drinker.

UNCOMMONLY KNOWN ...

CLEOPATRA? In 1512 Pope Julius II installed the statue of a beautiful woman in the Vatican. The snake curling around her arm led many to identify her as Egypt's Cleopatra. In the 18th century, experts realized the statue in fact depicted Ariadne, the mythical figure who helped Theseus defeat the Minotaur and escape the Labyrinth.

Barbed Wire

NINETEENTH-CENTURY RAILROADS, TIRED OF HAVING THEIR FENCING STOLEN, INVENTED THEIR OWN IDENTIFIABLE VERSIONS OF BARBED WIRE.

For such an unfriendly substance, barbed wire has a surprising number of fans. "The devil's rope," as it's sometimes known, was invented as cheap and practical fencing in America's post–Civil War years, when western farmers began to fence off grazing grounds and railroads needed to define their right-of-way. The form that's most familiar today—two strands of wire, twisted together, with a bar with two points wrapped around one strand at intervals—was invented by Joseph Glidden of Illinois. In 1874 he

won a patent on his version, known as Glidden's Winner and still widely used today.

Glidden's patent covered only his own design, so in later years, many others patented or simply sold their own variations. Today collectors recognize more than 2,100 designs with names such as the Ellwood Reverse Spread and the Brinkerhoff Opposed Lugs Lance Point. At least two U.S. museums are devoted to the fencing: the Kansas Barbed Wire Museum in La Crosse, Kansas, and the Devil's Rope Museum in McLean, Texas.

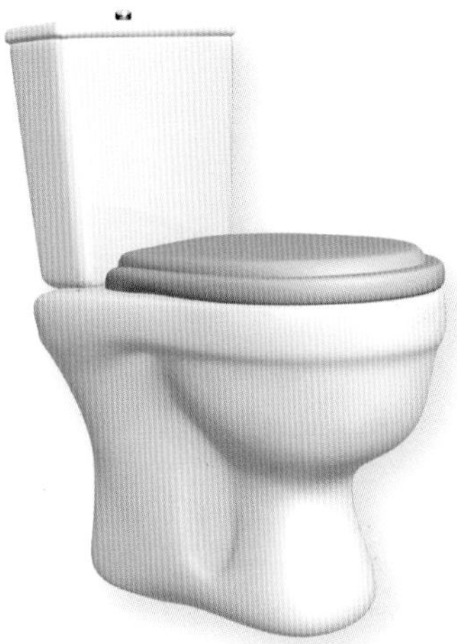

Toilets

THE SECOND-CENTURY ARYAN CODE OF TOILETS REQUIRED USERS TO CHANT A MANTRA ASKING ALL INVISIBLE SOULS TO VACATE THE AREA.

Museums of art are all very well, but few things are closer to our—um—hearts than toilets. These necessary agents of civilized life have a long and creative history worth memorializing, or so say the founders of New Delhi's Sulabh International Museum of Toilets.

Begun by Bindeshwar Pathak, leader of an Indian sanitation movement, the museum has a wide collection of chamber pots, privies, bidets, and toilets from the Middle Ages to the present. Documents trace the history of the toilet from the sophisticated brick bathrooms of India's Harappan civilization, 2500 B.C., to modern electric devices that turn human waste into ash. Cultural history is evident in Louis XIV's thronelike seat of ease and in the French commode shaped like a stack of classic English literature. Toilet-related humor and cartoons are not neglected, but the spiritual side of the excretory experience is also reflected in displays of poetry and ritual texts. Poetry aside, Pathak hopes the museum will highlight the need for sanitation in his country, where 70 percent of villagers live without a toilet in the household.

Paris Sewer Museum

UNTIL THE 1980S, LETTERS AND TELEGRAMS WERE DISPATCHED THROUGHOUT PARIS VIA A SYSTEM OF PNEUMATIC TUBES IN THE SEWERS.

"Paris has another Paris under herself; a Paris of sewers; which has its streets, its crossings, its squares, its blind alleys, its arteries, and its circulation, which is slime, minus the human form." In *Les Misérables,* Victor Hugo became the bard of the Paris sewers,

UNCOMMONLY KNOWN ...

THE HOBO FOUNDATION The traveling culture of the American hobo has found a permanent home at the Hobo Foundation in Britt, Iowa. Incorporated in 1974 by three hobos—"Steamtrain" Maury, "Hood River" Blackie, and "Feather River" John—the foundation supports a small museum in what was once a movie theater. There, visitors can view hobo memorabilia, listen to hobo music, and learn about the hobo lifestyle, which reached its peak during the Great Depression. The foundation also maintains a small cemetery in Britt, where those who were elected Kings and Queens of the Hobos can rest forever without charge.

immortalizing what is quite possibly the most famous municipal sanitation system in the world. Constructed in stages beginning in the Middle Ages, the city's sewers were so extensive by the early 1800s that even their dimensions were hard to pin down. Hugo's friend Pierre-Emmanuel Bruneseau, Paris's inspector of sewers, undertook to map them from 1805 to 1812; Hugo claims that Bruneseau found jewels in the sludge as well as the skeleton of an orangutan that had escaped from the Paris zoo. Beginning with Napoleon III the sewers were modernized, but today they remain so cavernous that they can accommodate not only boats but even a museum.

The Paris Sewer Museum (Musée des égouts de Paris) provides tours and information about the ancient system. A slightly malodorous path takes visitors along grates above the wastewater. Galleries display machinery used to clean the sewers, including a gigantic iron ball that rolled, Indiana Jones–style, through the tunnels. Classic Parisian street signs tell which street runs overhead, while models of intrepid, helmeted sanitation workers testify to the work that goes into maintaining the system's 1,300 miles of tunnels and cables. At the gift shop, tourists can buy a stuffed Parisian rat as a souvenir.

Hearses

PRESIDENTIAL CASKETS ARE TRADITIONALLY TRANSFERRED FROM HEARSES TO OPEN HORSE-DRAWN CAISSONS FOR PROCESSION TO THE CAPITOL.

The rituals of death are a part of human culture, dating back at least 100,000 years. Early remains have been found with traces of flowers in their graves. How those bodies were conveyed to the grave is unknown, but by Roman times, the funeral procession had become a key part of the ceremony surrounding interment. Funeral carriages grew ever more elaborate over the centuries, resulting in the decorated vehicles of the 19th century and the imposing limousines of modern times. For those with an appreciation of hearses and all things hearse related, a collection of luxury carriages is displayed at the National Museum of Funeral History. The Houston, Texas, museum was founded in 1992 to educate the public about "death care." Its hearse collection ranges from an 1850 horse-drawn German carriage, bedecked with wooden scrollwork, to a motorized Packard funeral bus from 1916, large enough for a casket, pallbearers, and 20 mourners. Hearses used for the funerals of Presidents Reagan and Ford are there, as is the one that carried Grace Kelly's coffin. Not everyone will go out in a similar style, but contemplating the elegant final rides can be a morbidly satisfying experience.

Nature's Bounty

Something about the natural world inspires ardent collectors. Perhaps it's nature's infinite variety. Maybe it's a quest to learn more about ourselves as living creatures. Whatever the reason, naturalists and enthusiasts of various stripes have devoted themselves to putting both the living and the dead on exhibit. Some collections are grand, as in the botanical expanses of London's Kew Gardens and the shining insect displays at the Natural History Museum. Others are fascinating and just a tad scary. Rattlesnakes, anyone? How about skulls?

Morton Skull Collection

THOUGH NOT A SCIENTIFIC COLLECTION, THE PARIS CATACOMBS HOLD AS MANY AS SIX MILLION SKULLS GATHERED FROM LOCAL CEMETERIES.

Most people would prefer not to contemplate a human skull. As a memento mori, it's a little too close for comfort. But physical anthropologists love nothing so much as a well-preserved skull, with its hints as to the brain size, health, and diet of the owner. Particularly in the 19th century, natural scientists were eager to test out their theories about the human family by comparing skulls. One of the most ambitious of these researchers was American anatomist Samuel George Morton, who assembled one of the world's best, and ultimately most controversial, assemblages of human skulls in Philadelphia. The collection resides in the city at the University of Pennsylvania Museum of Archaeology and Anthropology.

Morton collected samples from all over the world in the mid-1800s. Other scientists, army surgeons, and missionaries sent him skulls (mostly crania, missing the jaws) from every continent. Some specimens were taken from graves or lifted from battlefields. Morton measured the shapes and capacities of each cranium in order to categorize what he believed were the five unequal races of humanity. His racial theories have been thoroughly debunked, but Morton's scrupulous measurements and preservation of the skulls, each one carefully varnished and labeled, left behind a valuable scientific collection. With additions to the inventory from Morton's protégé James Aitken Meigs, the museum holds about 2,000 crania, illustrating not only the shortness of human life but also the follies of human prejudice.

Shells

COMPOSER JERRY GOLDSMITH USED A CONCH SHELL TO CREATE A HOLLOW, EERIE SOUND IN THE SOUNDTRACK TO THE MOVIE CLASSIC *ALIEN*.

An underappreciated phylum of the animal kingdom, mollusks and their shells have contributed to art, medicine, and architecture. Smaller shells, including the money cowrie, have been used as currency throughout the world. Musicians have employed conch shells as trumpets from prehistoric times to today.

Several museums have extensive malacology (mollusk) collections, including the Bailey-Matthews National Shell Museum in Sanibel, Florida. More than thirty exhibits showcase living mollusks, their ancestors, and their coiling shells. On display are micro-mollusks the size of a grain of sand and the world-record horse conch shell, a whopping 24 inches. Visitors can step outside and find their own mollusk shells on Sanibel's beaches.

PEOPLE WHO CHANGED HISTORY

Elias Ashmole (1617–1692)

Elias Ashmole, English antiquarian and astrologer, parlayed a lifelong interest in natural history and the occult into a collection that became the foundation of the University of Oxford's Ashmolean Museum. Ashmole was born to a well-connected family and studied law, philosophy, and astrology in the 1640s. Marriage to a wealthy widow several years his senior and a lucrative position with the London Excise gave him the means to pursue his true interests: astrology, botany, and mystical manuscripts. In 1662 Ashmole inherited the extensive natural history collection of his friend John Tradescant the Younger. He offered this collection and his own store of manuscripts and curiosities to Oxford, which built a home for them and opened it in 1683 as Britain's first public museum.

Elias Ashmole, illustrated in the 1800s

Botanical Gardens

KEW GARDENS IS KNOWN FOR ITS SPECTACULAR GLASSHOUSES, WHICH INCLUDE THE LARGEST SUCH STRUCTURES BUILT IN VICTORIAN TIMES.

Although the very phrase *botanical garden* seems redundant, these specialized plant collections are a far cry from the backyard peony patch. Intended to be permanent installations for research, conservation, and education, botanical gardens trace their roots to ancient Egypt and Mesopotamia. By the 17th century some gardens had taken on a grander mission. The University of Oxford Botanic Garden, for instance, claimed, "As the species of all creatures were gathered together

into the Arke, comprehended as in an Epitome, so you have the plants of most parts of the world, contained in this garden."

In 1840 the world's largest botanical garden was inaugurated in Kew, in southwest London. Spread across 326 acres, Kew Gardens contain more than 30,000 different species of plants, including trees, herbs, roses, orchids, and carnivorous plants. Perhaps more valuable than its flora, however, is the effort it puts into plant conservation in a changing climate. Its Millennium Seed Bank, says Kew, "holds more living plant diversity per square meter than anywhere on earth."

Hair

IN 1855 THE PARIS EXPOSITION FEATURED A LIFE-SIZE PORTRAIT OF ENGLAND'S QUEEN VICTORIA CREATED ENTIRELY FROM HUMAN HAIR.

Hair is a uniquely personal keepsake. Made of keratin, a tough protein, it's very slow to break down and keeps its color when cut. That's why lovers in traditional romances exchange locks of hair, or mothers hold on to the curls from a baby's first haircut. Often hair has been kept in remembrance of the dead. The Victorians wove hair from the deceased into black mourning jewelry or into picture frames around the image of a willow tree.

Several collections around the world are devoted to hair. They include the curious Chez Galip Hair Museum in Avanos, Turkey. The museum features a long, cavelike room whose walls and ceiling are festooned with some 200,000 dangling locks of hair. According to local history, the collection began to take root in the 1970s when a local potter asked a female friend to leave him a lock of her hair. After he attached it to the wall, other visiting women would not be outdone and began to leave their own hair as well. Each sample is labeled with the name and address of its donor.

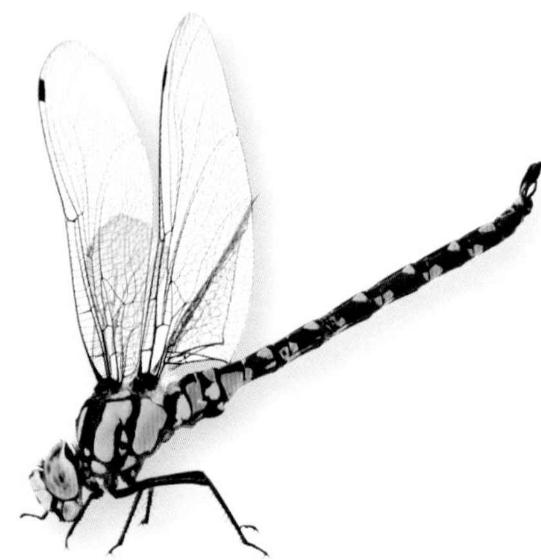

Insects

THE SMALLEST INSECT IN LONDON'S ENTOMOLOGY COLLECTION IS THE FAIRYFLY, ALMOST INVISIBLE WITH A WINGSPAN OF 0.008 INCH.

To be a collector of insects is both a curse and a blessing. Some 10 quintillion individual insects representing about 30 million species fill the world; many species have yet to be described by science.

WHAT'S INSIDE?

Formalin

When the national Museum of New Zealand, on the waterfront in Wellington, acquired a rare colossal squid in 2008, the curators knew that they had to work quickly to preserve the mollusk's 18-foot-long body. So they injected formalin into the animal's arms and carcass to "fix" it and prevent it from decomposing. Formalin is a biologist's all-purpose preservative, used in museums and classrooms the world over to kill bacteria and stiffen proteins in tissue samples. The colorless liquid is a solution of formaldehyde gas in water, stabilized with a little methanol. Off-gassing of the formaldehyde gives the solution its unmistakable, pungent odor. On its own, formaldehyde gas is highly toxic, so biologists learn to use formalin with care. It's great for the dead, but not so good for the living.

No entomologist can do more than scratch the surface of his or her specialty—but by the same token, there is no end to discovery.

Insects and their place in the animal kingdom have been a central part of zoology for centuries. Charles Darwin and Alfred Russel Wallace, for instance, collected and studied insects on their journeys as they developed the theory of evolution. Their finds are preserved at London's Natural History Museum, which has one of the richest entomology collections in the world. Dating to the 1600s the 30-million-plus specimens are housed in the museum's cocoon-shaped Darwin Centre. The Smithsonian National Museum of Natural History in Washington, D.C., vies with London for the largest collection, with some 35 million insects in more than 134,000 drawers and 33,000 jars. Visitors to either institution can see such splendid creatures as the white witch moth, with its 12-inch wingspan (London) and the 7-inch-long Hercules beetle (Washington)—not to mention the countless tiny mites, flies, and ants that make up in numbers what they may lack in splendor.

Rattlesnakes

BECAUSE SO MANY RATTLESNAKES ARE KILLED BY HUMANS AFTER THEIR RATTLING WARNING, SOME MAY BE EVOLVING TO BECOME RATTLE-LESS.

"She never begins an attack, nor, when once engaged, ever surrenders: She is therefore an emblem of magnanimity and true courage." So wrote Benjamin Franklin about the rattlesnake, which he considered the ultimate symbol of the American spirit.

The rattlesnake is a uniquely American reptile. Its 32 species live in diverse habitats from Canada to South America and feature prominently in American mythologies. Many people fear the rattlesnake, with reason. Although it strikes only in self-defense and warns of its attack by shaking the keratin rattles at its tail, it does account for most of the handful of fatal snakebites annually in the United States.

Zoos and private collections feature rattlesnakes, but for anybody interested in all things rattler, the American International Rattlesnake Museum in Albuquerque, New Mexico, features the world's largest collection of live rattlesnakes on exhibit in the world. It includes rare albino and melanistic (unusually dark colored) specimens, as well as rattlesnake memorabilia ranging from board games to beer. The museum is so pro-snake that visitors may come away agreeing with its assertion that "the only good snake is a live snake."

Real Recreations

Every sporting pastime builds a culture around it. It consists of legendary games and players, uniforms and equipment, rules and strictures, trophies and medals, and a host of superstitions and stories passed from one fan to another. In this section, we'll take a look at a few of the items, famous or otherwise, that are so representative of their various sports that they have been collected and studied in museums around the world—objects that range from the surprisingly ancient badminton shuttlecock to the more recent, and still evolving, skateboard.

Baseball Caps

A SO-CALLED RALLY CAP IS A BASEBALL CAP WORN INSIDE OUT OR BACKWARD TO INSPIRE A TEAM TO COME FROM BEHIND LATE IN A GAME.

Baseball caps, worn by truckers and astronauts, cops and duchesses, were originally designed for the demands of a summer sport. The earliest baseball teams wore an assortment of styles. The New York Knickerbockers, the first baseball team to use modern rules, started with straw hats in 1849 and later switched to the "Number 1" style—soft wool hats with a visor to keep the sun out of players' eyes. By the 1860s some baseball caps had acquired a rounded dome and visor, rather like a jockey's cap, though players could still wear flat-topped or bowler-style hats. Early in the 20th century, the rounded cap adopted the six-panel dome and stitched visor still seen today. From 1909 to 1914 the Philadelphia Athletics flirted with a tall pillbox style and attributed their multiple pennants in part to the good luck it brought. (The Pittsburgh Pirates reincarnated the unflattering cap in the 1970s and 1980s and won the World Series in 1979.) Otherwise, the six-panel domed hat has remained relatively unchanged for about a hundred years. Today it's made from a wicking polyester to keep players' scalps a little cooler.

The definitive repository of the national pastime's history, the National Baseball Hall of Fame in Cooperstown, New York, presents a wide collection of uniforms from days past, including about 750 caps. They include a plain blue cap worn by the Baraboo Baseball Club of Baraboo, Wisconsin, in 1866; a six-panel Yankees cap worn at the first game ever played at Boston's Fenway Park; and the classic blue cap that Jackie Robinson wore when the Brooklyn Dodgers beat the Yankees in the 1955 World Series.

Soccer Balls

AMERICA'S FIRST PROFESSIONAL SOCCER LEAGUE, THE USSA, RAN FROM 1919 TO 1921, AND PLAYERS EARNED 35 CENTS FOR EACH GOAL SCORED.

A tough ball game demands a tough ball, and the soccer ball has always been a durable object. Some form of soccer—"football" outside the United States—has existed since at least the Han dynasty (221–207 B.C.) in China; there, the game *tsu chu* required players to kick a leather ball filled with hair and feathers into a goal. The game flourished particularly in the British Isles, becoming a rough-and-tumble sport that might pit entire villages against each other with balls that consisted of leather strips sewn around an inflated or stuffed pig's bladder.

So disruptive was the game that many English monarchs attempted to snuff it out. In 1424 Scottish king James I went so far as to issue a proclamation "that na man play at the Fute-ball." The decree did little to suppress the sport, and James's direct descendant, Mary Queen of Scots, mentions playing soccer in her childhood journals. In the 1970s, in fact, what may be the world's oldest soccer ball was discovered behind the ceiling panels of Mary's old bedchamber in Scotland's Stirling Castle. The small object, made of stitched cow's leather around a pig's bladder, dates back at least to the 1540s and is in remarkably good shape. Historians don't know for sure that it belonged to the young Mary, but they note that it could have been a ball kicked into the rafters by a youngster and forgotten.

By the 19th century, football had become more organized. Rubber bladders replaced pig's bladders as the ball's inflatable core, but the balls continued to be covered with leather, tough on heads and feet, until the 1980s. Synthetic leather eventually replaced cowhide, and a new design of black and white patches allowed for an efficient use of materials that was highly visible on television—the classic soccer ball look recognized around the world.

PEOPLE WHO CHANGED HISTORY

Madame Tussaud (1761–1850)

Marie Tussaud, born Anna Maria Grosholtz in Strasbourg, France, grew up in the household of Dr. Philippe Curtius in Paris, where her mother was the housekeeper. Curtius was a physician with a talent for wax sculpture; Marie learned the skill from him and by her late teens was creating figures of such luminaries as Voltaire and Benjamin Franklin. When she was believed to harbor royalist sympathies, she was tasked with creating death masks from the heads of King Louis XVI and Marie Antoinette, which were severed with a guillotine. Marie married François Tussaud, traveled to England, and in 1835 established a collection on London's Baker Street. Today her wax museum is one of the most famous in the world, with branches in nearly two dozen cities, featuring hundreds of wax figures of famous people.

Wax figure of Madame Tussaud, 1794

Trophies

NO ONE COULD DRINK FROM TENNIS'S DAVIS CUP. WITH ITS MASSIVE BASE, THE TROPHY WEIGHS 231 POUNDS AND STANDS MORE THAN THREE FEET TALL.

The word "trophy" is derived from the Greek for a change or a defeat, and the first trophies were spoils of war, tokens of victory in battle. From this meaning it was an easy step to signifying an award for a victory in sports. Sacred olive wreaths were the trophies awarded to winners in the ancient Olympics, though medals have since replaced them. The 19th century gave birth to most of the famous sporting trophies known today. Sailing's America's Cup, an ornate silver ewer, was first awarded to the yacht *America* in 1851. Somewhat more modest, the silver Claret Jug has been given to the winner of the British Open golf championship since 1873. Hockey teams still drink champagne from 1893's hefty Stanley Cup, a yard tall and weighing 35 pounds.

Possibly the most beloved sports trophy is cricket's modest Ashes urn. In 1882 Australia defeated (and humiliated) England in a match in London. Afterward, the *Sporting Times* newspaper wrote a mock obituary for English cricket, claiming that "the body will be cremated and the ashes taken to Australia." English team captain Ivo Bligh vowed that he would bring those ashes back. After Bligh won some friendly matches in Australia the next year, a group of Melbourne women awarded him a bottle full of ashes—supposedly those of a cricket ball. Bligh triumphantly brought the urn home, where it has a place of honor at the Marylebone Cricket Club Museum at Lord's.

UNCOMMONLY KNOWN ...

BANKSY Not even the British Museum is immune to the British graffiti master and prankster. In 2005, Banksy sneaked a piece of "cave art" in that depicted a man pushing a shopping cart. The label read: "Early man venturing towards the out-of-town hunting grounds. This finely preserved example of primitive art dates from the Post-Catatonic era." It stood for three days before curators noticed it.

Goalie Masks

BEFORE CANADIAN JACQUES PLANTE STARTED WEARING A GOALIE MASK, HE HAD SUFFERED BROKEN CHEEKBONES, NOSE, JAW—AND SKULL.

Hockey goalies routinely take hits to the face from flying pucks and hockey sticks. It makes sense to protect that face with a mask, but in fact it took decades for hockey masks to be accepted in the big leagues. The tough players were worried about looking not so tough.

UNCOMMONLY KNOWN ...

FRICK BOWLING ALLEY Possibly New York City's most beautiful museum, the Frick Collection contains works by Rembrandt, El Greco, Vermeer, and more in a Fifth Avenue mansion built by wealthy industrialist Henry Clay Frick in 1914. Not on the usual tour, however, is a hidden masterpiece: Frick's bowling alley. The two-lane basement alley is as elegant as the building above it. White oak-paneled walls and pine and maple beds gleam with polish, and the bowling balls are the finest quality. The lanes remain pristine: Frick died soon after they were completed, and the alley is not open to the general public.

First on record to wear a protective mask was Queens University goaltender Elizabeth Graham. Having already had dental surgery, the Canadian woman didn't want to endanger her teeth further, so in 1927, she donned a fencing mask on the ice. Slowly the idea caught on. After a bad hit, Clint Benedict of the Montreal Maroons wore a leather mask for five games in the 1930s but discarded it because it obscured his vision. Other goalies experimented with cagelike or clear plastic masks in practice, but the first to wear a mask regularly in professional play was Jacques Plante of the Montreal Canadiens. In 1959, after taking a puck to the face, he returned to the ice with the fiberglass mask he wore in practice. Although the coach had forbidden it, Plante refused to play without it. Since he was the team's only goalie, he got his way, though not without criticism by fans.

By the 1970s goalies throughout the National Hockey League had stopped worrying about the wimp label and began sporting a variety of custom-made masks. The gear evolved into intimidating works of art, painted with stitches, bones, cobras, and lions. A colorful panoply of masks, from Plante's fiberglass model to modern versions, can be seen at Toronto's Hockey Hall of Fame.

Skateboards

IN 1964 JAN AND DEAN SANG THEIR HIT "SIDEWALK SURFIN' " ON *AMERICAN BANDSTAND* WHILE ATTEMPTING TO SKATE ACROSS THE STAGE.

If one individual invented the skateboard, his or her name is lost in the sands of 1960s California. Sometime in the course of those years, surfers looking for fun on calm days began attaching metal roller skate wheels to surfboard-shaped wooden boards, and the sport took off. Manufacturers began producing skateboards as early as 1959, but any kid with a plank and a set of wheels could make a board—and many did. In the 1960s skateboarding saw its first wave of popularity. However, metal or clay wheels made for an unstable ride, and so many people were getting injured that the pastime faded for a while.

In 1973 urethane wheels made skateboarding smoother and safer, and the sport revived. Skateboard designer Larry Stevenson helped with the invention of the kicktail, a curved end that allowed the skateboarder to launch himself into the air. Decks began to be made from fiberglass and aluminum as well as wood. As fads came and went—skating in empty pools, in skateboard parks, then back to the streets along handrails—the boards varied greatly in size. This up-and-down history can be seen at the Skateboarding Hall of Fame and Museum in Simi Valley, California. The museum features 5,000 vintage skateboards, from roller skate models to

a "banana peel blind spoof deck" from the 1990s. For a truly immersive experience, visitors can try their skill at the adjoining indoor skate park.

Olympic Torches

OLYMPIC TORCHES HAVE BEEN CARRIED TO THE NORTH POLE, UNDERWATER AT THE GREAT BARRIER REEF, AND INTO ORBIT ON A SPACE WALK.

The Olympic flame is an ancient tradition, but the Olympic torch is a relatively recent invention, with troubled origins. The idea of a torch relay from Olympia, Greece, to the location of the current games began with the Olympic organizing committee for the 1936 Berlin games.

WHAT'S INSIDE?

Olympic Gold Medals

Olympic athletes certainly don't value gold medals for the amount of gold they contain. That's a good thing, because the medals are not solid gold. The 1896 games began the medal tradition by offering silver and bronze medals to the first-place winner and runners-up. From 1904 to 1908, the victors did indeed get solid gold medals. But since then, "gold" medals have really been gold-plated. Today the Olympic Committee dictates that silver medals should contain at least 92.5 percent silver, and gold medals should be gilded with at least six grams of gold.

Lit by the sacred flame in Olympia, that year's polished stainless steel torch became the symbol of the Nazi Olympics. However, the tradition outlived the Third Reich, and each host country usually designs its own torch, or sometimes two—one for the relay and another for the final leg to light the cauldron. Most are metal and burn gas fuel (a 1956 torch using brilliant metallic fuel burned the runner as well). Older designs typically feature a handle and bowl, but more recent torches are streamlined and curvy, such as the five-foot-long version that accompanied a ski jumper in 1994. Celebrity designers include one of Walt Disney's Imagineers and French innovator Philippe Starck. Versions of the torches can be seen in many of the host countries, but the official Olympic Museum in Lausanne, Switzerland, maintains a sweeping display of the evolution of the torch.

Tennis Rackets

THE HEADS OF OLDER TENNIS RACKETS MEASURE ABOUT 65 SQUARE INCHES. TODAY'S TOP PLAYERS USE RACKETS WITH ABOUT 100-SQUARE-INCH HEADS.

Tennis has a history that dates back to medieval Europe. Tennis rackets have evolved with the game, and fans of the sport can peruse historical rackets at such institutions as the Wimbledon Lawn Tennis Museum in London and the International Tennis Hall of Fame & Museum in Newport,

PEOPLE WHO CHANGED HISTORY

James Smithson (1765-1829)

James Smithson, whose bequest founded the Smithsonian Institution, was an Englishman who never visited the United States. He was born James Lewis Macie, illegitimate son of Elizabeth Macie and Hugh Smithson, duke of Northumberland. (James didn't adopt the surname Smithson until his mother's death.) Educated at Oxford, Smithson became an adept scientist. When he died childless, he left his estate to his nephew with the stipulation that if the nephew died without heirs, it would go "to the United States of America, to found at Washington, under the name of the Smithsonian Institution, an establishment for the increase and diffusion of knowledge among men." And so it did, all $508,318, to the surprise of a grateful nation.

Statue of James Smithson at the Smithsonian Institution, Washington, D.C.

Rhode Island. There, they can see how rackets changed from heavy, laminated wood instruments with small heads, to the oversize aluminum specimens of the 1970s, to the current lightweight graphite models.

The Smithsonian's National Museum of American History has a smaller but significant set of rackets that illustrate the way tennis can reflect change in our society. They include Althea Gibson's wood racket she used to win Wimbledon in 1957—the first African- American player to do so. Arthur Ashe, a leader in both sports and in civil rights, is represented by the aluminum racket he wielded to win the tournament in 1975. And transgender pioneer Renée Richards donated the wooden racket that won her numerous titles in the 1960s as Richard Raskind.

Badminton Shuttlecocks

MODERN FEATHERED SHUTTLECOCKS CAN BE PROPELLED OFF THE RACKET'S STRINGS AT MORE THAN 200 MILES AN HOUR.

The game of badminton is, at its heart, the game of shuttlecocks. The small projectiles, traditionally made from overlapping feathers impaled in a cork base, form the core of the ancient game of battledore and shuttlecock, played in various incarnations since the days of ancient Greece and China. In early forms of the game, players simply kicked the shuttlecock back and forth or hit it with a wooden paddle. By the 1860s players in England and India added a net over which the shuttlecock had to fly. The pastime was apparently a favorite of the Duke of Beaufort; it bears the name of his country estate.

Shuttlecocks (also known as shuttles or birdies) were likely named for their motion—back and forth like a loom's shuttle—and for the feathers that give them their aerodynamic drag. Plastic shuttlecocks are more durable than the feathered variety, but professional players prefer the quick takeoff of the traditional models.

The National Badminton Centre is located in Milton Keynes, England. There, visitors can view the most comprehensive badminton artifacts, archives, and memorabilia in the world.

Everyday Relics

We know that people have been drinking wine for a long time—but seeing the actual wine jars from King Tut's tomb brings that fact home to us. We're aware that maps have been around for centuries. Discovering a Paleolithic hunting map more than 13,000 years old puts that knowledge into a new context. Throughout this section, we'll visit well-preserved everyday objects, from rubber balls to baby bottles, that remind us that our contemporary lives are not so very different from those of our ancestors hundreds or even thousands of years in the past.

Roman Bread

IN THE UPSCALE HOUSE OF THE STAGS IN HERCULANEUM, KITCHEN POTS WERE STILL SITTING ON THE CHARCOAL STOVE, LEFT BEHIND DURING THE ERUPTION.

Erupting catastrophically in A.D. 79, Mount Vesuvius was both a destroyer and a preserver. The volcano's pyroclastic surge killed the people of Pompeii and Herculaneum, and preserved intact their dwellings and household objects. Depending on the location, people were either vaporized to their skeletons or fossilized by a covering of ash. They lay unchanging where they fell, giving us an unparalleled picture of the last instants of life in these Roman Empire towns.

Among the objects discovered in the remains of Herculaneum, a small town just west of Vesuvius, is an ordinary loaf of bread. Now held by the Naples National Archaeological Museum, this blackened, rock-hard object (left) is surprisingly informative.

It was found in the elegant House of the Stags, which means that it was probably good-quality bread, made from the finest wheat flour, without the coarser admixtures found in cheaper bread. The baker ran a string around it to hold its shape; he also sliced eight grooves into the loaf. Most tellingly, he stamped it with his identification:

WHAT'S INSIDE?

Archival Board

Historical records and artwork on paper are delicate things, susceptible to damage from insects, moisture, mildew, and acid leaching out of their mats, frames, and wrappings. Most museums and good-quality framers mat and store their artwork in archival board. Refinements in the manufacturing process have been ongoing, especially in efforts to reduce the acid and mineral content of materials used in its production. The highest quality museum board is made from 100 percent cotton rag fibers. It's free of iron and acid, with a neutral pH of 7. In theory, museum boards will remain stable for at least 75 to 100 years.

"Celeris Q. Grani Veri Ser(vus)"—Property of Celer, the slave of Quintus Granius Verus. We don't know if Celer worked in a bakery owned by Quintus Granius Verus, or if he was a household slave who baked the bread in the kitchen of the House of the Stags. One thing we do know—he must have been quick, because the nickname "Celer" means "speedy."

Rubber Balls

A NUMBER OF COMMUNITIES ACROSS MEXICO STILL PLAY A VERSION OF THE ORIGINAL MESOAMERICAN BALL GAME NOW KNOWN AS *ULAMA*.

Mesoamerican cultures took their ball games very, very seriously. Beginning with Mexico's Olmec civilization around 1500 B.C., the game was picked up by later Maya and Aztec cultures and was still around when the first Spaniards arrived in the 16th century. In the game, two teams, each composed of one to four people, vied to propel a rubber ball across a court without using their hands. The balls were heavy, weighing up to eight or nine pounds, and despite wearing helmets and pads, players were often injured. In fact, some artwork suggests that the losing teams, possibly made up of prisoners of war, were executed.

Perhaps as remarkable as the bloodthirsty nature of the games is the fact that these cultures could produce rubber balls at all. Rubber is made from latex, the sap of a rubber tree, but untreated it becomes solid and brittle. In modern times, rubber didn't become practical until Charles Goodyear figured out how to vulcanize it using sulfur. Apparently Mesoamerican scientists had Goodyear beaten by some 3,400 years, having discovered a way to mix latex with juice from morning glory vines to produce stable, bouncy balls. Though almost all of these balls have been lost to time, the ancient Olmec site of El Manatí in Mexico has yielded a dozen rubber balls (left), hardened with time but preserved by the boggy environment of the sacred site.

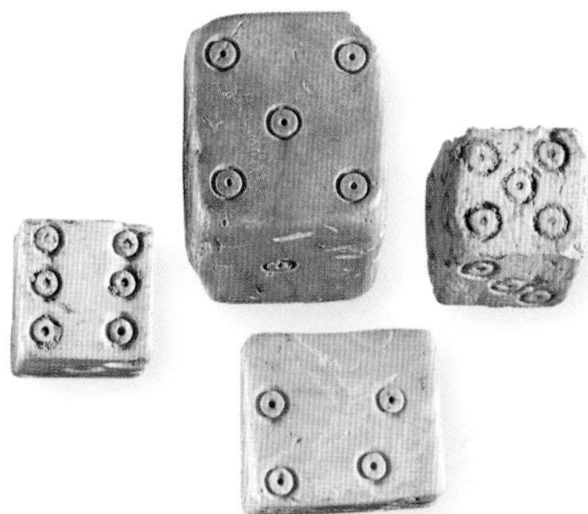

Dice

TWENTY-SIDED DICE, GEOMETRIC ICOSAHEDRONS, DATE BACK AT LEAST TWO MILLENNIA TO THE HELLENISTIC PERIOD IN EGYPTIAN HISTORY.

When Julius Caesar decided to cross the Rubicon in 49 B.C. and gamble on an invasion of Rome, he reportedly declared "*Alea iacta est*—The die is cast." Gambling with dice was tremendously popular among the ancient Romans—and among the ancient Greeks, ancient Egyptians, ancient east Indians, and in fact among the peoples

of almost every ancient civilization. By some accounts it is the oldest game in the world.

An early relative of dice were animal knucklebones, known as astragals, used in games and cast by diviners to predict the future. Gamers threw cubical and pyramidal dice in the Middle East at least 5,000 years ago; a well-preserved set of dice was found with a backgammon game in the rubble of Iran's Bronze Age "Burnt City." Dice have been discovered in ancient Sumerian digs and in King Tut's tomb. By Roman times the pastime was widespread, and standard dice (such as the ivory cubes above) turn up in a range of Roman archaeological sites.

Early dice were made of bone, wood, crystal, marble, amber, and other carvable materials. Many of today's dice are plastic. Those used in casinos are cut to a tolerance of 0.0001 inch in the eternal quest to create game pieces with perfectly random rolls.

PEOPLE WHO CHANGED HISTORY

Alexander the Great
(356–323 B.C.)

In his short life, Alexander of Macedon overthrew the Persian Empire and led armies from Greece to India. His most lasting legacy, however, was not so much martial as cultural. As the young general marched into Asia, he founded city after city in the Greek mode, some 20 of them named Alexandria. Alexandria, Egypt, grew to be a center of learning, with the jewel in its crown being the Museum of Alexandria and its famous library. For three centuries, the library held the classical world's greatest scholarship—until Roman emperor Aurelian burned it to the ground around A.D. 270.

Alexander in a second-century B.C. mosaic from Pompeii

Baby Bottles

INFANTS IN THE 16TH TO 18TH CENTURIES WERE OFTEN FED PAP, A MUSHY MIXTURE OF MEAL OR BREAD SOAKED IN WATER OR MILK.

How to feed a baby when the mother is unable to do so is a problem that's been around for as long as mothers have been having babies. One solution is the wet nurse. Hiring another woman to breast-feed an infant is an ancient tradition with professional codes and contracts. However, baby bottles or baby feeders represent an age-old practice as well. Clay bottles with traces of milk residue have been found dating back 4,000 years. Archaeologists in southern Italy uncovered a charming 2,400-year-old terra-cotta feeding bottle in the shape of a pig that also doubled as a rattle.

Over time, ingenious or desperate craftspeople made baby feeders from cow horns, ceramics, glass, pewter, and silver. Scraps of cloth or leather tied over their spouts served as nipples. By the Victorian era, glass jars (such as the one at left) that could be fitted with rubber tubes and teats were marketed with names such as "Mother's Darling." Unfortunately for mother's actual darlings, most of these contraptions were difficult to clean and therefore bred bacteria. By the 1900s, better sterilization and vulcanized rubber nipples that could withstand high heat made bottles less creative but much better for a baby's health.

King Tut's Vintage Wine

THE FERTILE NILE DELTA WAS WELL SUITED FOR PRODUCING WINE, WITH ITS IRRIGATED FIELDS, SUNNY DAYS, AND BRIEF RAINY SEASON.

On November 26, 1922, archaeologist Howard Carter opened a hole in the doorway to King Tutankhamun's tomb and saw a panoply of treasures within—"wonderful things," as he wrote later. Among the artifacts were 26 simple clay amphorae, two-handled jars that had once contained wine intended for the young pharaoh's journey to the afterlife.

Wine is an ancient beverage, dating back at least 8,000 years. By King Tut's time, around 1330 B.C., it was cultivated extensively in Egypt (pictograph above), and prosperous Egyptians typically placed wine in tombs to ensure that the deceased was provided for. Red wine was associated with the blood of Osiris, the god of resurrection, but chemical studies tell archaeologists that Tut's tomb contained both red and white varieties. Like today's wine bottles, Tut's amphorae had inscriptions testifying to the vineyard, the vintner, and the vintage. Amphora 6, for instance, was labeled "Year 4. Wine of the Estate-of-Aton, may he live, be prosperous and healthy, of the Western River. Chief vintner Men." Just a trace of residue remains in the jars, so oenophiles can only guess whether the wines were fruity, toasty, or complex. The amphorae now reside in Cairo's Egyptian Museum and the Metropolitan Museum of Art.

Native American Woven Bags

SO-CALLED SALLY BAGS ARE KNOWN AS *WAPAAS* OR *AQW'ALKT* IN THE WASCO AND WISHRAM LANGUAGES, NOW SPOKEN BY ONLY A FEW PEOPLE.

The Columbia River of the Pacific Northwest runs through a bountiful land. Before European cultures arrived, native peoples subsisted on the fish, game, and wild plants that flourished in the river and along its banks. To carry

roots, medicines, nuts, and seeds, women from Plateau-region tribes, particularly the Wasco and Wishram tribes, wove baskets and bags from plant fibers. Made from grasses, dogbane, and corn husks, the flexible bags could dangle from their belts as they worked. Weavers decorated the sacks in a distinctive Columbia River style: Broad-faced humans, elk, sturgeon, condors, and even water striders joined geometric patterns on the finely woven containers. Flat corn husk bags (previous page) had a different design on each side; cylindrical baskets known as "sally bags" featured animals, humans, or abstract designs around their circumference.

By the 20th century, collectors were searching for hard-to-find sally bags. The art survived, though it was practiced by only a few, who knew the full-turn twining techniques. Examples of corn husk bags (another type of handcrafted Native American bag) and sally bags are on exhibit in some museums, including the Museum of Natural and Cultural History at the University of Oregon.

Contemporary weavers now carry on the art using time-honored materials and sometimes incorporating modern yarns and beads. Traditional Native American images merge with modern motifs to link past and present on bags that are still practical as well as beautiful.

UNCOMMONLY KNOWN ...

THE V&A PITCHES IN German bombs threatened all of London's museums during World War II, and the Victoria and Albert Museum was no exception. Curators moved many of the valuable items to remote locations such as countryside mansions or deep quarries. But the museum not only stayed open; it served as an air-raid shelter, a school for children evacuated from Gibraltar, and a canteen for the Royal Air Force. Only in 1948 did it return to normal as a public museum.

Aquatic Fish Farms

FISH-FARMING HAS GROWN BY ABOUT 8 PERCENT A YEAR SINCE 1970. CHINA SUPPLIES MORE THAN HALF THE WORLD'S FARMED FISH.

Aquatic farms are a significant part of world agriculture. The nutrients provided by fish, shrimp, and mollusks account for about 17 percent of the animal protein taken in by the planet's growing population. Overfished wild species on the decline, and the ancient practices of sustainable aquaculture are reviving around the globe.

Fish farmers have been getting their feet wet since prehistoric times. Researchers have found evidence of eel ponds in Australia dating to 6000 B.C. Egyptians farmed tilapia in ponds along the Nile floodplain in 2500 B.C. and still do so today. But it was Asian fish farmers who brought aquaculture to a high art. Records of fish-farming in China go back 3,000 years. In 475 B.C., a scholarly fish farmer named Fan Li wrote the first treatise on the practice, complete with instructions on pond maintenance and brood-stock selection. Carp came to be the favored Chinese fish, but because the Chinese word for the common carp had the same pronunciation as the name of the

Tang dynasty imperial family, those rulers would not allow their citizens to eat it. The dictate actually benefited fish farmers, who branched out to cultivate other productive species.

In those years before artificial fertilizers and antibiotics, aquaculturists had no choice but to develop their own sustainable practices. Today Chinese fish farms (opposite) can be seen using similarly efficient and integrated methods as their ancient forebears. For instance, the uneaten food and wastes from farmed fish are reclaimed and used as fertilizer on land-bound farms. As living relics of an ancient system, modern fish farms owe a debt to Fan Li.

WHAT'S INSIDE?

Dehumidifiers

Museums are scrupulous about maintaining steady levels of humidity. Over time, paintings, textiles, furniture, and artifacts can be severely damaged by extreme variations in moisture: The works warp, crack, fade, or even grow mildew. Most museum curators prefer to keep a building's relative humidity hovering around 50 percent. That's why dehumidifiers are so important to galleries. Internal fans draw air into these machines, where it reacts with cooling coils. The air's moisture condenses into water on the coils and drips into a pan or a hose for collection. Then the dehumidifier releases reheated, drier air back into the room.

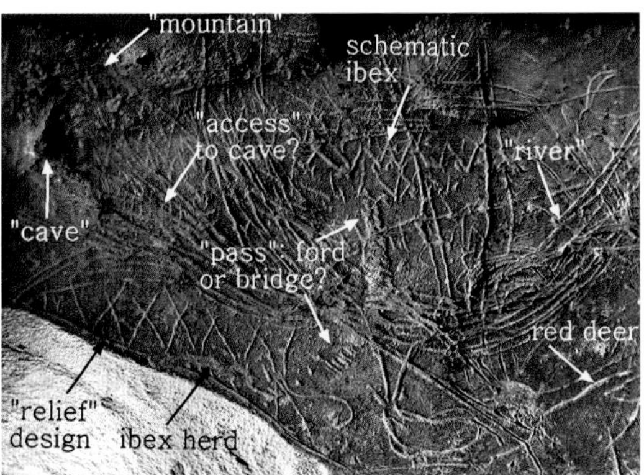

The World's First Maps

ABAUNTZ CAVE WAS PROBABLY A TEMPORARY SHELTER FOR HUNTERS. THE MAP MAY SIMPLY HAVE BEEN FORGOTTEN WHEN THE MEN MOVED ON.

Modern maps are symbolic representations of the world from high in the air. Icons represent features that aren't really there, such as country boundaries, and often ignore those that are, such as buildings. Large-scale, precise maps have their origins in the ancient cultures of Babylonia, Egypt, and Greece. The Greeks, particularly, combined the findings of their far-ranging explorers with the geometrical skills of their geographers to create sophisticated maps. By about A.D. 150, Greco-Egyptian mathematician Ptolemy had produced a geographic description of the known world, complete with lines of longitude and latitude.

But many millennia before Ptolemy finished his atlas, early artists had produced the kinds of maps that were most useful to them: small-scale depictions of local dwellings, rivers, and game animals. Researchers differ on the meaning of some of these early carvings, but by many accounts, the earliest map known is an engraved 25,000-year-old mammoth tusk from Pavlov in the Czech Republic, showing what may be mountains and a river. A carved sandstone rock from Abauntz Cave in Navarra, Spain (left), about 13,660 years old, is clearly a map of the surroundings. It depicts local rivers, a mountain in front of a cave and flooded plains, as well as reindeer, ibex, and a stag. According to its discoverers, it could represent a hunting tale or a plan for future activities. The mountains and rivers can still be seen from the cave just as they were when the ancient hunt set forth.

Artistic Passions

Common household objects have always encompassed more than utilitarian items such as tools or furniture. Artistic expression is as old as human culture, and its artifacts—from paintings to musical instruments to sculpture—can be found in caves and households many thousands of years old. In this section, we'll visit the curious history of just a few objets d'art. Some, such as jewelry, adorned the body. Others, such as Christmas ornaments, decorated the household. At least one, the flute, has apparently soothed the savage breast since time immemorial.

Flutes

ANTHROPOLOGISTS SPECULATE THAT MAKING MUSIC MAY HAVE HELPED EARLY MODERN HUMANS COMMUNICATE AND FORM TIGHTER SOCIAL BONDS.

Life among Europe's cave dwellers was more complex than one might imagine. In some caves, archaeologists have unearthed flutes, the oldest musical instruments ever discovered. A Slovenian find consists of a fragment of a cave bear's femur, pierced with four holes. At more than 40,000 years old, it could have belonged to a tuneful Neanderthal. Discoverers of a 40,000-year-old vulture-bone flute in southern Germany dispute that identification and say that theirs is the first true flute. With a V-shaped mouthpiece and five finger holes, the slender instrument is still playable.

As flutes became common in ancient civilizations, they evolved in two principal forms: end blown such as recorders and transverse such as modern concert flutes. Built in sections, with keys that allow for a wide range of notes, today's flutes are far more versatile than their Stone Age prototypes.

PEOPLE WHO CHANGED HISTORY

Walter O. Evans (1944-)

Georgia native Walter Evans wasn't allowed into segregated local art museums. Only as a young sailor in Philadelphia did he visit his first museums. In 1977 the director of a Detroit gallery showed him "The Legend of John Brown," a series of prints by African American Jacob Lawrence. Evans, by then a surgeon, bought the prints and began to build a collection that included works by artists such as Lawrence and Romare Bearden. His traveling collections helped inspire a wave of interest in African-American art.

Walter Evans, Detroit, Michigan, 2006

Illustration

ARTIST J. C. LEYENDECKER POPULARIZED THE IMAGE OF A NEW YEAR'S BABY WITH HIS ILLUSTRATIONS FOR THE *SATURDAY EVENING POST.*

In the decades after the Civil War, commercial publishing began to flourish in America due to advances in printing technology and motorized vehicles. The public demanded newspapers, magazines, and books, and advertisers jumped to reach a growing readership. Starting in the 1880s, illustration entered a golden age that would last through the 1920s. With the development of the halftone printing process, illustrators could create fine art that would be reproduced in sharp detail and full color.

Traditionally trained artists took on the challenges of deadlines, assignments, and printing constraints to create images that sold a product and both reflected and created popular culture. In his covers for the *Saturday Evening Post,* Norman Rockwell portrayed a warmhearted American ideal (above). Charles Dana Gibson's "Gibson Girl" could start a fashion trend simply by sporting a ribbon in her hair. And James Montgomery Flagg used himself as a model to create an American icon: Uncle Sam from the 1917 "I Want You" poster.

Today, illustration is considered a fine art, which can be seen in places such as the national Museum of American Illustration in Newport, Rhode Island.

Jewelry

ACCORDING TO ANCIENT LORE, RUBY JEWELRY WILL ATTRACT GOOD FORTUNE AND PROTECT AGAINST BAD LUCK IF IT IS WORN ON THE LEFT HAND.

Of all the forms of art, jewelry may be the most durable. As such, it is an anthropologist's joy. For instance, perforated mollusk shells found in Israel's Skhul Cave date back about 100,000 years. Evidently meant for a necklace or bracelet, the shells are some of the earliest human adornments known. "When we wear items like this, we are sending a message," said one of the discoverers, in an interview with the BBC. "The message may be that we are powerful, or wealthy, or sexy, that we're part of a particular group, or to ward off evil."

The message has stayed the same throughout history. To convey social status or provide mystical protection, precious metals and precious stones have been combined to exquisite effect from the days of ancient Egypt and Mesopotamia up to the present. Museums around the globe acquire unique items of jewelry; one of the most comprehensive collections resides in London's

Victoria and Albert Museum. Its assortment of European bling contains diamonds worn by Catherine the Great and the emeralds Napoleon gave to his daughter.

Miniature Rooms

IN THE 1700S, "BABY HOUSES" WERE BUILT TO ORDER FOR WEALTHY BRITISH PATRONS AND COULD SOMETIMES COST AS MUCH AS AN ACTUAL HOUSE.

Dollhouses and miniature rooms are known as children's toys, but historically adults have treasured them. The fascination lies not so much in the houses' architecture as in their painstakingly detailed interiors. Dollhouses began as collections of handcrafted individual rooms known as "baby houses" in 17th-century Europe. Children's dollhouses began to be mass-produced in the 19th century, but top craftsmen continued to make intricate miniature rooms for adult patrons. Among the most spectacular of these are the Thorne Miniature Rooms of the Art Institute of Chicago, designed by artist Narcissa Niblack Thorne in the 1930s and completed by skilled artisans. The 68 tiny rooms depict different eras and furnishings ranging from a medieval Gothic church interior to a 1940 California living room.

Possibly the most haunting set of miniature rooms is the Nutshell Studies of Unexplained Death, which can be seen at the Office of the Chief Medical Examiner in Baltimore, Maryland. Created by wealthy criminologist Frances Glessner Lee, the 18 dioramas depict a range of death scenes—complete with corpses, overturned furniture, and bloody footprints.

Christmas Ornaments

DIME-STORE ENTREPRENEUR F. W. WOOLWORTH MADE A FORTUNE FROM THE SALE OF IMPORTED GERMAN ORNAMENTS BEGINNING IN THE 1880S.

Christmas tree ornaments, like the trees themselves, began in Germany. The first holiday trees were decorated with edibles such as apples, nuts, and sausages. By the 1800s,

UNCOMMONLY KNOWN ...

THE MET The Metropolitan Museum of Art in New York, opened in 1870, is one of the world's premier galleries. It is famed for its outstanding collections of Egyptian antiquities and European and American paintings, among other treasures. It also contains a 29-foot-long carpet, a 1-inch-long Akkadian seal, the world's oldest piano, a staircase from the Chicago Stock Exchange, and the Antioch Chalice—once believed to be the Holy Grail.

the master glassblowers of central Germany began creating one-of-a-kind glass ornaments called *kugels*. After the *Illustrated London News* showed Queen Victoria hanging German ornaments on her Christmas tree in 1848, the practice caught on and spread to the United States. Germany dominated the holiday bauble market until the 1920s, when mass-produced decorations overtook them. The history of Christmas embellishment can be enjoyed at the German Christmas Museum in Rothenburg ob der Tauber, Germany, which contains glass balls, nutcrackers, and even "happy and grim Santas."

WHAT'S INSIDE?

Lucite

The versatile thermoplastic acrylic sold commercially under such names as Lucite, Plexiglas, and Perspex, has been embraced not only by industry but by the art world as well. The transparent substance is a synthetic polymer, a long chain of organic molecules generically known as polymethyl methacrylate. It was developed by DuPont in the 1930s and found wide use in sheet form during World War II as aircraft windshields and submarine periscopes. The acrylic resin can be molded into glasslike plates, cubes, and tubes. Artists have taken advantage of its clarity and malleability to paint on it, shape it into furniture, and craft it into jewelry, among other uses.

Quilts

BLOCK PATTERNS FOR PATCHWORK QUILTS ARE KNOWN BY TRADITIONAL NAMES SUCH AS SHOO FLY, PRAIRIE QUEEN, AND CONTRARY WIFE.

Quilts in the form of colorful patchwork bedspreads with repeated block patterns are primarily an American folk art, although quilting itself goes back thousands of years. The word "quilt" comes from the Latin for "stuffed sack": Quilts are typically composed of a decorated top layer of cloth, a plain bottom layer, and a soft filler or batting in the middle. Stitching holds the three layers together. Quilted carpets have been found in 2,000-year-old Mongolian tombs. Medieval knights wore quilted shirts under their armor to keep it from chafing, and quilted covers adorned European beds as early as the 14th century. Most of these quilts were made from whole cloth, with the stitching creating decorative patterns in a monochrome fabric.

Some early settlers reused their fabrics by creating patchwork for top layers of quilts. Women (quilters were almost always women) might decorate the quilts with fancy appliques and embroidery, or simply piece together bits of fabric for more homely patchwork quilts. African-American slaves made pieced quilts as well from cloth scraps and textile bags. Amish immigrants, valuing quilting as a community activity, became masters of the art by the 1920s. As mass-produced fabrics became cheaper, quilting flourished in myriad styles. Quilters and their friends might inscribe signature quilts or craft them from cigar box cloth; in "odd feller" or "charm" quilts, no two blankets were the same.

The rage for quilting died down in the mid-20th century but has since revived, with some quilts reaching the status of fine art, and notable quilts are on display in museums around the country.

Monumental Monuments

There are structures that contain the stuff of history: museums, galleries, and the like. And then there are structures that are history embodied. This section tours a few of the world's most significant buildings, monuments that have become so well known that they are part of our common history. Some, like the Taj Mahal, are famed for their beauty. Others, such as the Berlin Wall, are notorious for the ugliness they represented. And some are known for both, such as the Tower of London—a glowing castle on the Thames, a museum, and, in the past, an execution yard.

Washington Monument

FUTURE U.S. PRESIDENTS LINCOLN, BUCHANAN, AND JOHNSON WERE ALL PRESENT WHEN THE MONUMENT'S CORNERSTONE WAS LAID IN 1848.

When the monument was completed in 1885 it was the world's tallest building at 555 feet, 5⅛ inches. A recent official measurement takes about 10 inches off that figure, but the calculation was made from a different base point. The Washington Monument remains the world's tallest freestanding stone structure. However, for 22 years it was only half-built—a national embarrassment that Mark Twain called a "hollow, oversized chimney."

The idea for a tribute to America's first president had been around since the 1780s. In the 1830s a group known as the Washington National Monument Society began raising funds for an edifice on the Washington, D.C., National Mall. In 1848 construction began on the marble tower, designed by Robert Mills in the style of Egyptian obelisks to convey a sense of timelessness. However, the society ran out of money in 1854, and the monument's rise was halted. The truncated tower stood at 156 feet through the Civil War and construction didn't

WHAT'S INSIDE?

Security Systems

Keeping museum collections secure is a vast and tricky job. Security chiefs need to guard not only against nighttime break-ins but also against theft and vandalism from daytime visitors and staff. The first line of defense is physical: solid doors, good locks, and good lighting. Access must be controlled so that visitors enter and leave through doors where their bags can be searched if necessary. Closed-circuit TVs often monitor exits and rooms. Infrared or microwave motion detectors trigger alarms at nighttime movement; vibration sensors behind paintings can catch any attempt to dislodge them. And a human presence—a guard force—provides 24-hour protection.

resume until Congress took over its management in 1876. The new builder, Lt. Col. Thomas Casey, finished the obelisk in 1884 with an 8.9-inch aluminum cap, engraved with the heartfelt words, *Laus Deo*—Praise Be to God.

The *Cutty Sark*

THE SHIP WAS NAMED AFTER A FAST-RUNNING WITCH IN A ROBERT BURNS POEM. THE NICKNAME, "CUTTY SARK," MEANT "LITTLE SHIRT."

The beautiful *Cutty Sark,* now in dry dock in Greenwich, London, was the fastest clipper ship to ply the southern oceans. The three-masted vessel of 963 gross tons was built in 1869 during the last great days of the tea trade between England and China. Although it was never quite the swiftest on that lucrative route, when steamships took over the tea runs, the *Cutty Sark* turned to the wool trade between England and Australia. Sailing through the oceans of the perilous "roaring forties," coping with gales and icebergs, the clipper posted the fastest passage times ever known on the route, even overtaking the steamship *Britannia* on one run at 17 knots. By 1895 steamships were dominating the wool trade as well, so the *Cutty Sark* was sold to a Portuguese company, renamed the *Ferreira,* and employed hauling various cargoes until it was damaged by bad weather.

In the 1920s British captain Wilfred Dowman bought the clipper for 3,750 pounds and, with his wife Catharine, restored it to its original state. After a stint as a naval training vessel, the ship was purchased by a society of admirers and eventually opened to the public at Greenwich's National Maritime Museum, a testament to the age of sail.

Sydney Opera House

SOME ACCOUNTS SAY THAT FINNISH-AMERICAN ARCHITECT EERO SAARINEN PICKED THE DESIGN OUT OF A PILE OF REJECTED APPLICATIONS.

The sail-like, nested shells of the Sydney Opera House have become a symbol of Australia itself, but their serene beauty belies a contentious history. In 1956 a little-known Danish architect, Jørn Utzon, won the competition to design an opera house on a spit of land in Sydney Harbor. Utzon's soaring shapes were inspired by his background as a sailor and the son of a naval engineer. When the challenging project ran over budget, the new minister of works, critical of the design, stopped paying the architect. Utzon resigned and, despite marches in the streets of Sydney demanding his

reinstatement, left the country. Construction eventually resumed, and the building opened in 1973 without Utzon's presence.

The Sydney Opera House has since been acclaimed a masterpiece and named a UNESCO World Heritage Center. In 1999 Utzon and the Opera House reconciled, but he died in 2008 without ever returning to Australia.

Tower of London

ACCORDING TO LEGEND, IF THE TOWER'S RESIDENT RAVENS EVER LEAVE, NOT ONLY THE TOWER BUT ALSO THE KINGDOM ITSELF WILL FALL.

The Tower of London has in its long history been a fortress, a royal residence, a prison, a place of execution, a zoo, the repository of the crown jewels, a national museum, and an immensely popular tourist attraction. Construction on the imposing stronghold on the banks of the River Thames began under William the Conqueror in 1066. Over the centuries, many English monarchs added on to the castle, constructing towers, curtain walls, and moats. Often they took refuge in it as well, as when Edward II was besieged by discontented barons in the early 14th century.

Kings and queens sent high-ranking prisoners to it. The young princes Edward and Richard were supposedly murdered in the "bloody tower" in 1483. In Tudor times, Sir Thomas More, Anne Boleyn, and Elizabeth I were imprisoned in the Tower, and Boleyn and fellow queens Lady Jane Grey and Catherine Howard were beheaded on the grounds. In fact, the Tower continued to host executions through World War II.

Aside from the grim businesses of war, imprisonment, and execution, the Tower has also served as a zoo. Until 1835, royal menageries on the grounds included lions, bears, and elephants. Today the crown jewels are stored under guard in the Tower, and it remains the headquarters of the Royal Regiment of Fusiliers.

The Berlin Wall

EAST GERMANS MANAGED TO CROSS THE WALL IN SPECIALLY BUILT CARS, IN HOT-AIR BALLOONS, AND BY CRAWLING THROUGH THE TUNNELS.

In the years following World War II, the west half of Berlin, a nucleus of Western government in Communist East Germany, became an escape hatch for tens of thousands of East Germans fleeing to the West. Beginning on August 12, 1961, East German authorities put a stop to the emigration by abruptly putting up blockades and eventually a full wall around West Berlin. Eighty-seven miles long, the wall was reinforced with an interior fence and a so-called death strip between the two barriers, watched over by armed guards in 116 towers. During the course of the next 28 years, more than one million East Germans escaped from east to west across, under, and through checkpoints at the wall. About 140 others were killed in the attempt.

Communism faltered in Eastern Europe in 1989, and on November 9, crowds on both sides of the wall took hammers and picks to the structure. Within months, little of the wall remained. Stretches of the wall have been retained as a historical artifact, including the Berlin Wall Memorial on Bernauer Street, featuring a museum and eight city blocks of gray concrete barricade.

PEOPLE WHO CHANGED HISTORY

J. P. Morgan (1837–1913)

John Pierpont Morgan was a financier and industrialist who dominated U.S. business at the turn of the 20th century. While earning a fortune in banking, steel, and railroads, he also became an avid collector of art and rare books and manuscripts. Among his priceless possessions were three Gutenberg bibles, an autograph manuscript of Mozart's Haffner Symphony, and hundreds of Rembrandt etchings. Morgan kept his collection in the library he built for the purpose next to his mansion in New York City. The Italian Renaissance-style palazzo is open to the public as the J. P. Morgan Library & Museum.

J. P. Morgan with his children, 1902

Taj Mahal

DURING THE 1857 INDIAN REBELLION, THIEVING BRITISH SOLDIERS CHISELED PRECIOUS STONES OUT OF THE TAJ MAHAL'S INLAID WALLS.

In the Taj Mahal, elements of Indian, Persian, and Islamic architecture blend in perfect harmony. The palatial complex in Agra, India, is primarily a mausoleum. The Mughal emperor Shah Jahan ordered its construction as a tomb for his favorite wife, Mumtaz Mahal, who died in 1631 giving birth to their 14th child. Although the chief architect is not known with certainty, it was probably Persian architect Ustad Ahmad Lahori who directed the thousands of imported laborers. In 1648 the central domed mausoleum, built from white marble, was completed on its red sandstone base. Four freestanding minarets rose to flank the mausoleum, and on its east and west sides, two identical red sandstone buildings were added, a mosque on the west and an assembly hall on the east. The complex stands at the end of a long garden, not at the center, allowing visitors the famous view of the Taj Mahal's perfect symmetry.

In his old age, Shah Jahan was deposed and imprisoned by his son Aurangzeb. When Jahan died in 1666, he was entombed next to Mumtaz Mahal in the Taj.

Out of this nettle, danger,
we pluck this flower, safety.

–SHAKESPEARE, *HENRY IV* (CA 1597)

Danger Zone

One dictionary definition of "danger zone" is an area or scope of activity in which the probability of damage, injury, or loss is high. The Food and Drug Administration has its own definition: the range of temperatures at which bacteria can grow. In other words, a danger zone is a zone of peril. But this chapter doesn't actually describe danger. It describes both people and tools that combat danger in its many forms. In "Rescue Me," we look at the history of rescue equipment such as ambulances, avalanche beacons—even parachutes. You probably wouldn't be surprised to know that dogs have played an important part in rescues, but you'll also find out that dolphins for centuries have been coming to the aid of people stranded at sea. In the "Protective Coatings" section, you'll learn that the Kevlar in the bulletproof vests that have saved many lives, as well as the Gore-Tex that has protected hikers and skiers from the elements, were both accidental discoveries. "Defense Mechanisms" offers histories of a range of things that protect us from hazards, both natural and human. Did you know that the ingredient in pepper spray that stings eyes comes from chili peppers or that the first lighthouses burned wood or coal for beacons? "Articles of War" tells the story of important military equipment, such as mine detectors, night vision goggles, and two-way radios. We also learn the tale of the thousands of dogs that have served in wars from the American Revolution to Afghanistan. In "Rescue Vehicles" you'll find out that the first police "cars" had two wheels and the first ambulances were horse-drawn carts. You'll also discover that Edmond Halley is known for something more than discovering the comet that bears his name. Now it's time to enter the danger zone.

Rescue Me

Search and rescue is more than just the dedicated people who do the job. It's also the equipment that gets them where they need to go safely and aids them in saving lives. Avalanche beacons and sirens, for example, point the way to people in harm's way. Getting people out of danger takes familiar yet fascinating equipment such as life rings, airplane evacuation slides, and vehicle airbags. You'll also discover who invented the fire escape, meet a dog that helped stop an epidemic, and find out why a dolphin is a welcome sight if you're stranded at sea.

Parachute

NASA USED HUGE DRAG PARACHUTES TO SLOW THE SPACE SHUTTLE WHEN IT TOUCHED DOWN AND TO SLOW THE DESCENT OF ROVERS TO MARS.

Historians trace the parachute back to designs of Leonardo da Vinci in the 1470s. Still, the first jump didn't occur until 1783, when Louis-Sebastien Lenormand leaped from Montpellier Observatory in France, clinging to a 14-foot cloth parachute. His countryman André-Jacques Garnerin was the first person to jump safely from a high altitude. He was lifted 3,200 feet into the sky above Paris on October 22, 1797, by a hydrogen balloon, then cut the balloon's connections. The wind caught his 23-foot-wide canopy that unfurled and allowed Garnerin to drift safely to the ground.

The modern parachute was developed in the early 20th century. After Russia's Gleb Kotelnikov saw a good friend dic in an air show, lie became obsessed with inventing a workable escape chute for pilots. Kotelnikov's 1911 parachute could be strapped to its wearer and opened automatically or by pulling a cord.

The U.S. armed forces took increased interest in parachutes after World War I. While working for the military, James Floyd Smith developed a simple silk parachute in a soft pack, often called the first modern chute. Parachutes improved in the years between the world wars. The D-Day invasion of Normandy began with dropping paratroopers behind enemy lines.

Although today we often associate parachutes with the sport of skydiving, they're still used in rescues. Air Force pararescue teams drop into war zones to treat and rescue wounded soldiers. Parachutes also allow first responders to deliver urgent food and supplies to disaster zones after floods or earthquakes.

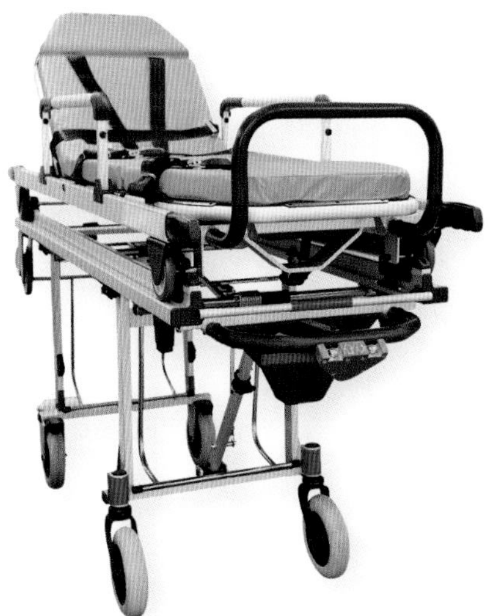

Stretcher

MORE THAN 50,000 STRETCHERS WERE USED TO TRANSPORT THE WOUNDED FROM BATTLEFIELDS DURING THE COURSE OF THE U.S. CIVIL WAR.

The earliest known stretchers were simple hammocks made of animal skins. By the 1700s and 1800s, wagons and carts carried wounded soldiers off the battlefield. Often litters were attached to horses or mules to transport the injured for medical care. The rides were rough from the inevitable jostling over uneven terrain and undoubtedly painful for the victims.

The mid- to late 1800s saw several innovations in stretchers. Proposals for the addition of fold-down legs to convert simple canvas stretchers to battlefield cots were welcomed during the Civil War. Overseas, stretchers that rolled on large carriage-like wheels and could be drawn by men or horses came into wide use. In the late 1800s in Europe and elsewhere, cacolets were in vogue—chairlike stretchers that clamped to the side of a horse or mule or camel and held the wounded in a seated position.

Plain canvas stretchers are still used today in many parts of the world, though in recent times modern versions have come on the scene. Scoop stretchers are made of rigid plastic and split down the middle so the two halves can be slid under a patient to raise the person from the ground with minimal movement. A Stokes basket, named for its American inventor, is a stretcher with raised sides that can be carried, wheeled, or hoisted into a helicopter. Emergency and hospital patients today are wheeled around on updated gurneys, collapsible stretchers that double as temporary beds.

CANINE WHO CHANGED HISTORY

Balto (1919–1933)

Dogs change history too. In early 1925 a diphtheria epidemic raged through remote Nome, Alaska. The only medication to combat it was in Anchorage, nearly 1,000 miles away. No conventional method could get it to iced-in Nome—not by road, boat, or plane. On January 28 Gunnar Kaasen left Anchorage, speeding north on a dogsled with a team led by a husky named Balto. The weather was horrific, with bitter winds and temperatures that dipped as low as 40°F below zero. Yet on February 2 the team emerged from the frozen wilderness, bringing Nome residents the lifesaving drugs. Balto became an instant celebrity. He and some of his sledmates traveled around the United States as heroes. The Nome mission is commemorated annually by the running of the Iditarod dogsled race between the two cities.

Balto with musher Kaasen, early 1920s

Jaws of Life

A STATE-OF-THE-ART JAWS OF LIFE SPREADER, DELIVERING UP TO 120,000 POUNDS OF FORCE, CAN PRY APART OBJECTS MADE OF STEEL.

Jaws of life is the name of a hydraulic tool that is used to extricate people trapped in vehicles after accidents or pinned under structures that have collapsed. People refer generally to all such tools as "jaws of life," though it is the trademarked name of one brand of these tools, manufactured by Hurst Performance.

Jaws of life are produced in several functioning varieties. Cutters slice through metal to free trapped people, spreaders force open crushed building frames or lift collapsed sections of vehicles and structures, and rams can push away heavy debris or pieces of a vehicle blocking access to pinned victims. Some of the tools combine multiple duties.

Inventor George Hurst was motivated to create the device after witnessing the death of a family pinned in a car wreck. Collaborating with engineer James F. Hobbins, Hurst introduced the tool in 1972. It was initially used exclusively at car racetracks, where high-speed collisions often left drivers wedged in their cars. Seeing the success of the Jaws of Life, emergency first responders gradually began to use them as well. The implement's name was chosen based on its ability to rescue people trapped in "the jaws of death."

WHAT'S INSIDE?

Life Buoy Foam

The interior of life buoys is usually a type of polyethylene plastic foam. The material is tailor-made for life rings because it's extremely lightweight and buoyant. In addition, it doesn't get waterlogged since it can't easily absorb water. Several variations of polyethylene are used in life rings, including standard high-density polyethylene and expanded polyethylene. To turn them into foam, gas is blown into a liquid form of the polyethylene, creating tiny cells when it solidifies. The cells are not connected, thus providing a structure that keeps life rings dry even when immersed in water.

Life Ring

JOHN WESLEY POWELL WORE A LIFE RING IN 1869 DURING HIS HISTORIC DESCENT OF THE COLORADO RIVER THROUGH THE GRAND CANYON.

Life rings are known by many names: life preservers, life buoys, life savers, kisby rings, perry buoys. They are distinct from life vests, which can keep a person's head above water for many hours. Life rings are especially useful as temporary rescue flotation. Hundreds of years ago, the first flotation devices were most likely objects such as sealed gourds or animal skins that helped people stay afloat fording a stream. Later, navies interested in life preservers for their sailors tried a number of materials. Seamen in Norway, for example, relied for a time on blocks of buoyant wood.

The first known patent for a life-preserving ring, made of cork, went to British physician John Wilkinson in 1765. Ninety years later, a British naval commander, J. R. Ward, developed a cork life belt. Still, flotation devices didn't become widespread until the latter part of the 1800s. Because of its lightness and buoyancy, cork remained the material of choice well into the 20th century.

After World War I, some preservers used balsa wood, but cork still dominated. However, by the mid-1900s, kapok had taken cork's place. Kapok is a tropical tree that has seedpods with air-filled fibers that are soft and buoyant. Life rings made of kapok were lighter and less bulky than cork. Eventually kapok itself gave way in the 1960s to new synthetic foams, which became the life-ring norm. Today the U.S. Coast Guard requires throwable life rings with attached lights on all boats in its fleet. Mandates for flotation devices on recreational boats vary by state.

UNCOMMONLY KNOWN ...

DOLPHINS RESCUE HUMANS Tales of dolphins saving people go back thousands of years. In ancient Greece, Plutarch wrote of a fisherman carried to shore by dolphins after his boat overturned. Through the centuries, there have been reports of dolphins forming a ring around people threatened by sharks. Other reports describe dolphins leading rescuers to a stranded swimmer or boater or guiding a person to shore. There are also stories of dolphins protecting other marine mammals under attack by predators.

Avalanche Beacon

RESCUE BEACONS ARE VITAL BECAUSE RESCUERS HAVE ABOUT 15 MINUTES TO FIND A PERSON BEFORE HE OR SHE SUFFOCATES UNDER SNOW.

People have always died in avalanches, and other people have always tried to rescue them. In the mid-1700s monks at the St. Bernard Hospice in Switzerland relied on dogs to locate victims in the snowy Alps. By the early 1900s some skiers and hikers wore avalanche cords—long, brightly colored ropes worn around the waist that would perhaps stick out of the snow if a person was buried.

Today's avalanche beacons are systems built around transceivers that send and receive radio signals. The Swiss developed the first such system, but its range was limited. The idea was perfected by the Cornell Aeronautical Laboratory, which developed an effective avalanche beacon in 1968.

As is true for the newest models, the first commercially available beacon transmitted a signal constantly while worn. If a person is lost under snow, rescuers set their transceiver to pick up the signal; the signal gets stronger and louder as rescuers approach the victim. Over time,

sensors have improved in range and accuracy. Digital versions debuted in the 1990s, and the latest can display the precise direction and distance to a beacon-wearing victim buried under the snow.

Evacuation Slide

OFFICIAL FEDERAL REGULATIONS STATE THAT IN AN EMERGENCY, A PASSENGER AIRCRAFT MUST BE EVACUATED IN FEWER THAN 90 SECONDS.

Evacuation slides are safety devices that allow passengers to exit an airplane quickly during an emergency. There are two types: the standard evacuation slide for emergencies on land and a slide raft for water landings. Slide rafts initially act as standard slides, allowing passengers to escape the aircraft. They then become rafts that keep everyone afloat until rescue boats arrive. Evacuation slides are generally stored inside the airplane door or under the doorsill.

James F. Boyle's company Air Cruisers invented the airplane evacuation slide. In the years before World War II, Boyle had already dreamed up an inflatable life jacket. He applied for a patent for the slide in 1954 and received it two years later. The slides were manufactured by his company, Air Cruisers, which still supplies about 65 percent of evacuation slides in use today. Modern slides are usually made of some type of plastic, but the first ones were made of canvas. They were awkward to use because of the difficulty of rigging them properly inside the aircraft panels where they were stored. Inflatable evacuation slides are crucial for complying with federal rules that require the ability to quickly evacuate large passenger aircraft.

Fire Siren

THE FIRST VOLUNTEER FIRE DEPARTMENT IN THE UNITED STATES WAS ESTABLISHED BY BENJAMIN FRANKLIN IN PHILADELPHIA IN 1736.

For firefighters, the time between the sounding of a fire alarm and their arrival at the scene of a fire is critical in saving both structures and lives. Fire engines must speed through the streets, requiring a loud warning to people and other vehicles to quickly get out of the way. Years ago, firefighters didn't have the powerful sirens available now. The noisemakers on some of the earliest fire trucks were bells and whistles. Trusty Dalmatians also acted as a type of siren in the days of fire wagons about a century ago. When an alarm went off, the dogs would sprint out of the firehouse, barking to warn people on the street to make way for the fire wagon. Then a pair of the dogs would run alongside the wagon or in front of it to clear the streets as the firemen came through, bells ringing and whistles blowing. To preserve the tradition, some firehouses still keep Dalmatians as pets—though not as sirens. The dogs ride inside the trucks instead of running in front of them. Today fire engines have electronic sirens capable of producing a range of ear-piercing sounds.

PEOPLE WHO CHANGED HISTORY

Anna Connelly

(birth and death dates unknown)

In 1887 American Anna Connelly patented an idea that would save countless lives: the metal fire escape. During the late 19th century, many fires in multistory buildings forced residents to jump to their deaths. Connelly designed a steel staircase that could be attached to the outside of a building. People could escape down it, and firefighters could go up it. Fire escapes changed the way buildings were constructed in the early 1900s as cities increasingly included the escapes in their building codes.

A metal fire escape in New York City

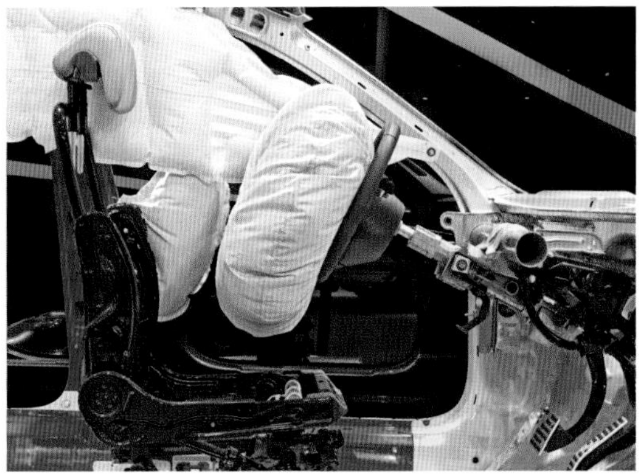

Air Bag

A VEHICLE DRIVER'S FRONT AIR BAG INFLATES IN 20 TO 30 MILLISECONDS IN AN ACCIDENT EQUALING AN IMPACT OF ABOUT 30 MILES AN HOUR.

Many historians credit John Hetrick with the invention of vehicle air bags. Hetrick was motivated by a near accident that almost threw his daughter through a car windshield. He was granted a patent in 1953 for his Safety Cushion for Automotive Vehicles. The auto industry soon realized the importance of air bags, and both General Motors and Ford experimented with them in the 1950s. But there were challenges in making air bags able to sense an accident and then inflate fast enough to protect passengers.

Engineer Alan Breed posted progress when he developed hardware that could sense crashes, and made the first electromechanical air bag system in 1968. Design issues remained, however, and carmakers continued to tinker with the technology through the 1970s. By the 1980s major problems were resolved, and on September 1, 1988, a law went into effect that mandated driver- and front-seat passenger air bags on all cars sold in the United States. Today there are "smart" air bags that inflate with a force based on the passenger's weight.

Protective Coatings

Staying safe from danger isn't just about rescue. It's also about safeguards to shield people from harm—whether from the natural environment or bullets or fire. This section explores things we wear that protect us. SPF clothing and Gore-Tex have short histories, while waxed fabrics date to the sailing ships of the 1800s. Kevlar, which has prevented countless deaths, was the result of a lab accident. Camouflage uniforms, however, resulted from years of study and design. Regardless of their origins, each piece of clothing here is literally a lifesaver.

Kevlar

KEVLAR NOT ONLY STOPS BULLETS; IT'S ALSO FIRE RESISTANT. TEMPERATURES NEED TO REACH ABOUT 850°F (450°C) BEFORE IT MELTS.

Kevlar is a rugged, lightweight material with five times the strength of steel, ounce for ounce. It was developed in the 1960s, largely thanks to the research of DuPont chemist Stephanie Kwolek. When she accidentally discovered the chemical formula in 1964, she was looking for a strong but light substitute for the steel in radial tires. The result of one of her experiments yielded a strange cloudy liquid.

Kwolek's colleagues urged her to dump the liquid and start again. But she wanted to find out what would happen if she put the solution through a machine that could process it into fibers. To everyone's surprise, the outcome was a fiber that seemed tough and was apparently unbreakable. Kwolek retested it several times, with the same finding. DuPont then assigned a research team to it. The material was eventually incorporated into multiple products as Kevlar. In 1975, police departments began to use Kevlar

WHAT'S INSIDE?

Steel-Toe Boots

Steel-toe boots are protective footwear designed to be worn where there is danger of injury from heavy or sharp objects falling on or rolling over feet. The first protective boots and shoes were made of wood or leather and worn by workers and farmers in Europe. Most steel-toe boots today still have a steel shield protecting the toes, though some shields are now plastic or a composite material. Steel-toe boots are often worn by firefighters and construction workers. Mandatory use of protective footwear in many workplaces is the result of the Occupational Safety and Health Act of 1970.

bulletproof vests. Since the 1990s, helmets worn by soldiers in combat are lined with lifesaving layers of Kevlar.

SPF Clothing

DARK OR VIVID COLORS ABSORB MORE ULTRAVIOLET RADIATION THAN LIGHT COLORS, COUNTERINTUITIVELY PROVIDING MORE SUN PROTECTION.

SPF (sun protection factor) is the rating for sunscreens based on the amount of protection they provide from the sun's ultraviolet radiation (UV). Exposure to UV is associated with conditions such as cataracts and skin cancers, including deadly melanoma. SPF clothing is now made from fabric embedded with chemical protection against UV. While SPF rates the protective level of sunscreen, UPF (ultraviolet protection factor) rates the protective level of clothing based on the percentage of UV that passes through it. So a UPF 20 means $^1/_{20}$ of the sun's UV can penetrate the fabric. The higher the UPF rating, the greater the protection. Consumers purchasing SPF protective clothing can look for the UPF rating on the tag.

Sun-protective wear was first sold in Australia in the 1980s in the wake of an epidemic of skin cancer. A range of clothing articles hit the market, including a neck-to-knee bathing suit. In 1992 the Australian government established the UPF standard for rating the protectiveness of clothing. Six years later, the Australian standard was adopted for use in the United States.

Gore-Tex

THE REVOLUTIONARY FABRIC HAS OVER NINE BILLION PORES IN EACH SQUARE INCH, PROVIDING THE MATERIAL ITS BREAKTHROUGH TRAITS.

Gore-Tex is a light, synthetic fabric used to make jackets, gloves, and shoes for active outdoor wear. Its discovery was a happy accident by Wilbert "Bill" Gore and his son, Bob. Their small Delaware firm started out in the 1950s producing cable for electronic equipment, but by the 1960s the Gores were diversifying. As part of that effort, they attempted to extrude PTFE (polytetrafluoroethylene) to produce a waterproof tape for pipe joints. Stretching it slowly was unsuccessful. But when pulled quickly, it stretched 800 percent into a light fabric with so many microscopic pores that it was 70 percent air.

The Gores applied for a patent in 1970, calling the new material Gore-Tex. It was lightweight and semipermeable, with pores too tiny for water molecules to pass through but large enough to allow air and water vapor in and out. As a result, Gore-Tex shoes and clothing are waterproof and windproof yet also breathable, letting heat and moisture from the body escape. Today the company has facilities worldwide and employs some 10,000 people.

Nonflammable Fabric

COTTON AND LINEN ARE TWO OF THE MOST FLAMMABLE NATURAL FABRICS, WHILE WOOL AND SILK REPRESENT TWO OF THE LEAST FLAMMABLE.

Nonflammable material is an old idea. In ancient Rome, a variety of substances were tried as fire retardants, but none of them was entirely successful. In England in the 1500s, a mix of alum, ammonium, and clay was rubbed on stage curtains to prevent fire, with promising results.

By the 1700s, alum and ammonium phosphate were commonplace fire retardants. Scientific experimentation on making nonflammable fabric started in earnest in the early 1800s. In 1820 French chemist Joseph Louis Gay-Lussac discovered that salts including borax caused fabric to resist burning. But there was a downside: They easily washed out.

The U.S. military's need for flame-retardant materials spurred research in the 20th century. Chemists identified ways to make fibers flame resistant both on the surface and internally, also a boon for firefighters.

The specialized clothing most firefighters wear today is made of fire-resistant or nonflammable synthetic fabric such as CarbonX or Nomex, sometimes blended with Kevlar to increase strength and durability.

Waxed Fabric

HISTORICALLY, PEOPLE WHO WANTED WATERPROOF CLOTHING SMEARED IT WITH MATERIALS SUCH AS GREASE, BEESWAX, SOAP, OR EVEN TAR.

Traditional waterproof clothing came from the desire of sailors to keep dry. There was little protection from the elements on sailing ships centuries ago. As early as the 1500s sailors spread grease and fish oil on their sailcloth to make the sails more efficient in the wind. They often cut capes for themselves out of any material left over. The "waterproof" capes protected them against rain, wind, and ocean spray.

In the early 19th century, sailors started using linseed oil for the same purpose. Clipper ships, developed in the 1800s with three tall masts crammed with canvas, were built for speed. As the ships were refined to be ever faster, lighter sails were needed. Cotton sails with linseed coating became the norm, and sailcloth remnants again were welcomed as a lighter weight, waterproof clothing option.

In the latter part of the 19th century, a waterproofing wax made largely of paraffin was developed for cotton cloth. The combination of the two created better protection and a more breathable fabric. By the early 20th century, waxed garments became popular, especially for people who spent a lot of time outdoors. Men's clothing ads of a century or so ago touted the clothes as "serviceable and water resistant. A real friend to the man in the open."

In the 1930s a method for infusing paraffin wax into fibers was developed. That process resulted in created a waterproof material that was lighter still as well as softer on the skin. Today synthetic waterproof materials have largely replaced waxed cotton and canvas. But hunters and others who spend time in the open often still wear the traditional protective fabrics.

UNCOMMONLY KNOWN ...

ARMORED TRAINS With thick steel protection, they include cars fitted with machine guns and other heavy weapons. Armored trains were first used in warfare about the time of the Civil War. Initially they were open cars with makeshift protective barriers. During the World Wars, they were outfitted with artillery. Armored trains carrying ballistic missiles rolled into the 21st century.

Camouflage

IN THE EARLY 1900S, FAMOUS ARTISTS SUCH AS GRANT WOOD TOOK PART IN THE DESIGN OF THE FIRST U.S. MILITARY CAMOUFLAGE UNIFORMS.

Camouflage military uniforms are a recent invention. In the past, uniforms were showy. During the Revolutionary War, British troops wore bright red coats. A century later in the Spanish-American War, U.S. soldiers wore blue jackets, which made them easy targets for snipers. By the early 1900s changes in warfare showed the usefulness of being hidden. The U.S. Army organized a unit of camoufleurs, largely artists and designers, to devise a camouflage uniform. By World War II the army had decided on a brown and green "frog" pattern, but it was used only sporadically.

In the 1960s the military chose an olive color for the jungles of Vietnam. Then in the 1970s, a pattern with irregular patches of brown, green, black, and tan was adopted, suitable for forests. In 1992 the Gulf War saw a change to a light tan, brown, and green desert motif. A computer-generated design of green, gray, and tan called the universal camouflage pattern was rolled out in 2004 to work in forests, deserts, and urban spaces. And camo style changes keep on coming, with a new look of light green, beige, and brown scheduled for 2015.

Defense Mechanisms

The subjects featured in this section are about guarding against injury—or worse. Some, such as hard hats and riot gear, are personal protection for people performing dangerous jobs. Other defense mechanisms focus on different kinds of protection. The tsunami warning systems in our oceans trigger lifesaving alarms for coastal dwellers. The humble sandbag protects waterfront communities from devastating storm-driven floods. And towering lighthouses have a storied history protecting mariners. Indeed, defense mechanisms come in all shapes and guises.

Hard Hat

SOME 20 MILLION AMERICAN WORKERS HAVE JOBS THAT REQUIRE THEM TO WEAR HARD HATS FOR PROTECTION.

The familiar hard hat so common now in construction had its origin in the military. During World War I, British and American soldiers wore the British Mk-I steel helmet, which protected the head and shoulders of soldiers from shrapnel. American Edward Bullard returned home after his service in the war with a steel helmet as a keepsake. The helmet inspired his "hard-boiled hat," which he produced by gluing together several layers of resin-hardened canvas and applying varnish to the outside. The headgear became available in 1919, just after the war. The U.S. Navy contracted with the Bullard Company to provide the hats to shipyards.

The first major uses of hard hats in civilian workplaces came during the 1930s—first at the Hoover Dam site and then at the Golden Gate Bridge. The bridge's chief engineer, Joseph Strauss, wanted the massive construction project to be as safe as possible and mandated the use of hard hats. Bullard designed a special hat for workers doing sandblasting: It shielded their faces but had a narrow window so they could see. As artificial materials were developed in the 1940s, hard hats of fiberglass and later plastic became standard. Inserts were added to strengthen head protection and provide a snugger fit.

UNCOMMONLY KNOWN ...

RECYCLING ELECTRONIC WASTE In today's increasingly electronic world, recycling potentially hazardous e-waste–computers, VCRs, scanners, printers, cell phones, batteries, and more–is essential. Recycling allows precious components such as copper and silver to be recovered. But e-waste also contains toxic substances such as nickel, lead, mercury, and arsenic. Proper disposal of those substances avoids endangering human health or the environment.

Tsunami Warning System

A 1958 EARTHQUAKE CAUSED A 1,720-FOOT-HIGH TSUNAMI THAT SWEPT THROUGH LITUYA BAY, ALASKA, THE HIGHEST WAVE EVER RECORDED.

A tsunami is a set of waves caused by undersea earthquakes or volcanoes. The waves travel rapidly across the ocean and reach mammoth heights when they slam into coastal areas. The creation of the tsunami warning system was the result of an Aleutian Island tsunami that sped across the Pacific and destroyed much of Hilo, Hawaii, in 1946. The first warning center was set up near Honolulu in 1949. The heart of the current system is a series of pressure and tide sensors three miles below the surface of the ocean. The sensors transmit data to buoys on the surface; the buoys send the data to satellites that beam it to warning center computers for analysis. An alert goes out when a tsunami pattern is identified.

The National Oceanic and Atmospheric Administration today operates two warning centers. The Pacific Tsunami Warning Center was established in 1968 at the same location as the 1949 center and monitors vast regions of the Pacific and Indian Oceans. A second center was established in the aftermath of a huge 1964 earthquake in Alaska when a tsunami killed more than 100 people. The Alaska Regional Tsunami Warning System came online in 1967 near Anchorage. Over the years, its responsibilities have expanded to include the entire West Coast and the Caribbean, and it's now named the National Tsunami Warning Center.

Sandbag

EMPTY BAGS ARE GENERALLY 26 INCHES LONG AND 14 INCHES WIDE. FILLED WITH SAND TO THE CORRECT CAPACITY, THEY WEIGH ABOUT 40 POUNDS.

Burlap sandbags have been around since the late 1700s and often became a defensive tool of war. During the American Revolution, soldiers used them to build temporary fortifications. Loyalist troops, for example, employed sandbags as part of their defense against the colonists in 1781 during the Siege of Ninety-Six in South Carolina. Sandbags came into more general use with French forces at the turn of the 19th century in the Napoleonic Wars; as part of their gear, all French soldiers carried empty sandbags, ready to construct makeshift fortifications. Armies have found uses for the versatile bags in every conflict since that time, from the U.S. Civil War through the recent wars in Iraq and Afghanistan.

The use of sandbags to protect vulnerable floodplain areas from inundation by rivers and streams goes back hundreds of years. Some things don't change: Images of people filling and

stacking sandbags are common in video news reports of floods today, though the bags are more likely to be made of plastic than burlap.

Lighthouse

THE FIRST LIGHTHOUSE, THE PHAROS OF ALEXANDRIA, ONE OF THE SEVEN WONDERS OF THE ANCIENT WORLD, STOOD PERHAPS 400 FEET TALL.

Rare early lighthouses sat at harbor entrances, and for centuries the light sources—open fires or candles—were vulnerable to wind and rain. Some improvements were incorporated over the centuries, such as enclosing the lantern with glass. But widespread construction of lighthouses did not begin until the age of discovery in the 1500s.

In the 1700s lights were fitted with mirror reflectors to boost their power, but the beacons were still not bright enough to prevent shipwrecks, which still occurred frequently. That changed in 1822 when Augustin Jean Fresnel designed a lens that gathered light from the lamp, focused it, and projected it in an extremely bright beam. His first lens, installed in a lighthouse in France, created a beacon that could be seen 20 miles away. The Fresnel lens became the standard, and almost every U.S. lighthouse had one by the early 1860s.

For most of their existence, lighthouses were important navigation aids. They warned ships of rocks or shoals, and their unique markings and timed flashes identified them and helped mariners pinpoint a ship's position. With the use of satellite navigation systems today, the role of lighthouses is fading.

Riot Shield

LIGHTWEIGHT LAW-ENFORCEMENT SHIELDS PROTECT AGAINST HURLED OBJECTS; THEY ARE OFTEN BULLET RESISTANT BUT NOT BULLETPROOF.

Shields have been important military equipment for more than 2,000 years. In ancient Greece they were often defensive weapons that, when held in close formation, formed a protective wall for a line of soldiers—a phalanx—advancing across a battlefield. Roman legions sometimes used shields as offensive weapons, charging opponents and knocking them down to be easily dispatched. Some early shields sported deadly spikes. Over time, shields fell out of favor with armies as weapons and styles of fighting changed. During the Renaissance years between the 14th and 17th centuries, the development of effective body armor reduced the necessity of shields.

Today a bulletproof vest is more likely to protect a soldier. But shields are still important civilian law enforcement tools. In the protest era of the late 1950s police began using so-called riot shields for crowd control and for protection of officers during events that could become violent. Shields are frequently employed in much the same way as in an ancient phalanx—police in a tight line, with their shields forming a barrier. The lengthy riot shields are generally composed of high-impact plastic.

PEOPLE WHO CHANGED HISTORY

Garrett Morgan (1877–1963)

In 1912 Garrett Morgan applied for a patent for his Morgan Safety Hood, which allowed wearers to breathe even in the midst of smoke or dangerous gases. The entrepreneurial Cleveland, Ohio, resident marketed the hood personally to firefighters around the country, demonstrating its ability to help keep them from harm. As an African-American inventor in the early 20th century, he frequently met resistance. But in 1914 the device garnered first prize at the International Exposition of Safety and Sanitation in New York City.

The hood gained national attention in 1916 when Morgan himself, with his brother, donned the invention and assisted in a rescue of construction workers trapped in a tunnel underneath Lake Erie following a deadly gas explosion. The Morgan Safety Hood became the prototype for the lifesaving gas masks that protected American soldiers during World War I.

Garrett Morgan, 1945

Pepper Spray

SCOVILLE HEAT UNITS (SHUS) MEASURE THE HEAT IN CHILI PEPPERS. A HABANERO MIGHT HAVE 350,000 SHUS. PEPPER SPRAY HAS TWO MILLION.

The use of chemical irritants for both offensive and defensive purposes has a long history. Soldiers in ancient China put ground cayenne peppers in rice paper and threw the packets in the faces of their opponents.

Through the centuries, armies around the world learned that certain chemicals could incapacitate enemies on the battlefield. In the late 1800s and early 1900s, potent agents such as tear gas and fearfully lethal mustard gas were introduced into warfare.

Pepper spray is another type of irritant, initially created for use by hunters as defense against bear attack, as well as for postal carriers to discourage aggressive dogs. It took until 1973 for scientists to develop a sprayable form of capsaicin. Derived from chili peppers, capsaicin is the chemical irritant in pepper spray that causes stinging eyes, burning skin, and respiratory distress.

In the 1980s an FBI study supported using pepper spray to control unruly crowds in the United States. In that capacity its use became widespread, with police finding it to be an effective, nonlethal tool. By the end of the decade, they were using it increasingly to control violent prisoners. Today many people carry pepper spray in handy small containers for their personal protection.

Articles of War

A wartime battlefield is the ultimate danger zone. Some of the entries in this section are products of modern technology—night vision goggles, cell phone jammers, aircraft ejection seats. Others have roots that trace back thousands of years. The first gas masks, for example, were crude 17th- and 18th-century devices that offered limited protection to miners and firemen from smoke and poisonous fumes. War dogs have been used in combat since early Egypt and Rome. Articles of war evolve but don't necessarily change. Their utmost goal remains the same.

Two-Way Radio

EARLY MILITARY WALKIE-TALKIES WERE HUGE, REQUIRING USERS TO CARRY BULKY BACKPACKS CONTAINING THE 35-POUND TRANSCEIVERS.

Home radios can only receive a signal, but a two-way radio or transceiver can both receive and transmit a signal. Sometimes called walkie-talkies, two-way radios were developed for military use during World War II. Several inventors were working simultaneously on the technology, and there are competing claims as to who was the first to succeed. The story goes that Canadian Donald Hings recognized the need for a two-way radio after he became stranded in the wilderness without a means to call for help. He developed his two-way radio in 1937. During World War II, walkie-talkies based on Hings's design were used by both Canadian and British troops.

Around the same time, the Chicago-based Galvin Manufacturing Company, which later became Motorola, developed its own version of the walkie-talkie. A team of engineers led by Dan Noble and Henryk Magnuski invented a two-way AM radio called the Handie-Talkie that was widely used by U.S. troops in the war. In 1943 Galvin introduced the first FM walkie-talkie, which had a range as great as 20 miles, but the device was cumbersome. In the years following World War II, advancements in radio technology made smaller components possible. When clunky vacuum tubes gave way to transistors by the late 1950s, walkie-talkies became compact enough to make sense in police cars. Although they continue to have military uses, walkie-talkies have come to be essential tools for first responders and other emergency services.

U.S. Battle Helmet

IN ADDITION TO PROTECTING HEADS, U.S. STEEL BATTLE HELMETS HAVE BEEN USED TO COOK, DIG, AND BAIL WATER FROM LANDING CRAFT.

The battle dress uniform (BDU) was used by U.S. soldiers in combat from 1981 through the mid-2000s. The BDU (as opposed to display dress, worn for parades and other functions) featured a camouflage pattern with irregular patches of brown, green, tan, and black. Variations for desert or jungle terrain became available as missions arose.

The BDU helmet descended from the M1 steel helmet, the main battle head protector that U.S. armed forces wore from World War II until the mid-1980s. The M1 was designed for fuller coverage against shrapnel, a decided improvement over the World War I–vintage helmet that protected only the top of the head. In 1985 the M1 was replaced by a bulletproof Kevlar helmet. All military helmets today contain inserts for added protection and better fit.

Standard battle dress uniform headgear included a cloth patrol cap along with the helmet. The looks of both have changed from time to time, corresponding to the changing color patterns of the uniform. Removable cloth covers on the helmets allowed soldiers to alter the pattern as needed. But the only constant is change, and the BDU has been phased out in favor of newer designs.

UNCOMMONLY KNOWN ...

HEDY LAMARR (1914-2000) She is best known as a glamorous movie actress, but Hedy Lamarr also starred as an inventor. In 1942 she and composer George Antheil patented a "Secret Communication System." The technological principle, spread spectrum communication, was important in the eventual development of cell phones and other wireless devices. During the Cuban missile crisis in 1962, it was used to create an antijamming mechanism for radio-controlled torpedoes.

Ejection Seat

NASA GEMINI SPACE CAPSULES HAD EJECTION SEATS FOR THE ASTRONAUTS IN CASE THE ROCKET UNDER THEM EXPLODED ON THE LAUNCHPAD.

In the early 1900s steady improvements in technology created airplanes that flew faster and higher, and there was increasing concern about emergency escape for pilots. The German and Swedish air forces tested ejection seats in the 1930s, but the identity of the first person to invent a reliable version is in dispute. German technology had clearly advanced by World War II. The first use of an

ejection seat during an emergency took place in January 1942, from a German aircraft and incorporated an explosive charge under the seat. Sixty other German pilots are known to have ejected safely from their planes. At the height of the war in 1944, British aircraft manufacturer James Martin developed a system similar to Germany's, and the seat was ready for production not long after. The United States lagged behind the Europeans. Information captured about the German system was the foundation of advanced American research after the war. The first ejection by a U.S. pilot occurred in 1946 from a Navy aircraft. Today all military planes have ejection seats.

WHAT'S INSIDE?

Bulletproof Glass

Bulletproof glass is generally a piece of polycarbonate—a tough, strong transparent plastic—sandwiched between layers of glass. The thickness and the number of layers largely determine how effective the product is. Bullets can penetrate the first layer, but the polycarbonate layer absorbs the energy of the bullet without letting it through. A better term for bulletproof glass is bullet-resistant glass, because even so-called bulletproof glass can withstand only a certain number of high-powered hits. How well it works depends not only on its construction but also on the type of weapon and ammunition used. Bulletproof glass is found in armored cars and police cruisers—even in the Popemobile. The windows of military aircraft and vehicles such as tanks and Humvees resist gunfire and shrapnel.

Gas Mask

IN WORLD WAR I, WHEN HORSES STILL HAD A ROLE IN THE U.S. MILITARY, GAS MASKS WERE MADE TO PROTECT THEM FROM CHEMICAL ATTACK.

Perhaps the oldest example of a gas mask is a simple sponge in ancient Greece that was held over the face. In the Middle Ages, doctors wore masks to keep out "bad air" exhaled by plague patients. An early gas mask for firemen was invented by British brothers John and Charles Deane in 1823—a copper helmet with an attached air hose.

Concern about smoke from fires and poisonous gases in mines was compounded in the 1900s by worry about gases released on the battlefield. In 1915 Britain created a respirator to protect against carbon monoxide from unexploded shells. Chlorine and mustard gas were used against troops in several World War I battles, including the infamous German chlorine attack at Ypres, Belgium, in 1915. The first device to protect against a chlorine weapon—a fabric helmet containing substances to collect and neutralize the chemical—was designed by Canadian Cluny Macpherson. During World War II, the fear of Nazi gas attacks in North America, and especially in Europe, created a demand for civilian masks. A Mickey Mouse gas mask was even produced for children.

Today's masks protect against a wide variety of substances from dust to nerve gas. Gas masks are standard issue for soldiers vulnerable to attack by chemical or biological weapons.

Phone Jammer

CELL PHONE JAMMERS DON'T JUST BLOCK CELL PHONES. THEY ALSO DISRUPT WI-FI NETWORKS, GPS UNITS, 911 CALLS, AND TEXT MESSAGING.

Cell phones are basically two-way radios that send and receive signals via cell phone towers. A jamming device transmits on the same frequency as the cell phone, blocking communication with nearby towers. The call will be dropped, leaving the phone user to think the call was lost due to low signal strength.

Cell phone jamming equipment was originally developed for the military and law enforcement to disrupt the communications and activities of criminals and terrorists. Jammers can be important tools in antiterrorism efforts, because cell phones are known to have been used to trigger explosions in attacks. It was a cell phone signal that detonated the bombs that blew up trains in Spain in March 2004, set off bombs in Indonesia that killed 202 people in Bali in 2002, and devastated the Marriott hotel in Jakarta in 2003. In Iraq and Afghanistan, improvised explosive devices (IEDs) have frequently been triggered by cell phones.

Civilian use of jamming equipment, though illegal in the United States, has grown along with the proliferation of cell phones—and the irritation many people feel when forced to listen to personal conversations on public transportation, movie theaters, and restaurants.

UNCOMMONLY KNOWN ...

NAUTICAL FLAGS For 150 years the International Maritime Flag System has been used to communicate between ships and from ship to shore. They are colored flags, a square flag for each letter of the alphabet and ten pennants for numbers 0 to 9. Flags are displayed in certain combinations to send messages. The code was introduced in 1857 by the British Board of Trade as the International Code of Signals and was expanded in 1932 and 1969 to add languages.

Night Vision Goggles

ROMAN ARMIES DIDN'T HAVE NIGHT VISION TECHNOLOGY. WHAT THEY HAD WERE GEESE THAT CACKLED AT NIGHT WHEN ENEMIES APPROACHED.

Night vision technology got its start before World War II, when American engineer William E. Spicer invented a device that could detect and compare the radiation levels of objects. He made his device in goggle form, which soldiers could slip on and scan the dark. Special operation forces tested the goggles but found them ineffective for covert use because an additional infrared

(IR) energy source was required, making them visible to other such devices.

As late as the 1960s, the usefulness of night vision goggles was still limited by the need for an external IR source. New designs in the 1970s resolved that problem, but the image wasn't sharp enough. Further refinements in the 1980s made night vision goggles lighter and created a better image. Designs are now on the drawing board for goggles that use cutting-edge technology. These so-called fourth-generation goggles would combine current night vision capabilities with enhanced thermal scanning, allowing much sharper images in virtually total darkness.

PEOPLE WHO CHANGED HISTORY

Ghost Soldier Rescue

In January 1945, after more than two years, several hundred American, British, and Canadian prisoners were still being held under harsh conditions in a Japanese prisoner-of-war camp in the Philippines, the last survivors of the brutal Bataan Death March. U.S. Army Rangers and Filipino guerrillas penetrated 30 miles behind enemy lines, entered the heavily guarded camp, and freed the prisoners. The men, who had been mistreated and starved, called themselves "ghost soldiers" because they thought America had forgotten them. The rescue of the ghost soldiers came on the heels of the brutal slaughter of American prisoners at a camp on the Philippine island of Palawan the previous month. Concerned that the Japanese planned a similar massacre for Bataan survivors in central Luzon, Gen. Walter Krueger ordered the daring rescue. Credit for the raid's success is also due to hundreds of Filipino farmer-soldiers who held off Japanese troops while Rangers freed prisoners in the camp.

The soldiers' rescuers return from the POW camp, 1945.

War Dogs

ABOUT 2,300 DOGS ARE DEPLOYED WITH U.S. COMBAT FORCES. THE PREFERRED BREEDS ARE GERMAN AND DUTCH SHEPHERDS AND BELGIAN MALINOIS.

Dogs have been used as instruments of war for thousands of years. Ancient Egyptian murals depict war dogs on the attack, and the Greek writer Strabo describes war dogs wearing armor. Roman soldiers unleashed starved, vicious dogs on their enemies. In the 1500s, Spanish conquistadors arrived in the New World with packs of dogs. Centuries later, Napoleon's memoirs describe a valiant dog that died on the battlefield. During World War I, Germany employed about 30,000 dogs that carried water and food to the wounded on the battlefield and were trained for search and rescue.

The U.S. military has used war dogs since the 1700s. They were harnessed as pack animals during the Revolutionary War and killed rats in the trenches of World War I. During World War II, more than 10,000 war dogs became sentries, messengers, and mine detectors. Dogs stood guard in Vietnam and worked as scouts and trackers. Today dogs are widely deployed with U.S. troops. In Afghanistan they're used for security and to detect bombs and other explosives.

Mine Detector

IT'S ESTIMATED THAT 110 MILLION LIVE LAND MINES ARE NOW DEPLOYED AROUND THE WORLD, AND ANOTHER 100 MILLION ARE STOCKPILED.

One of the earliest examples of a pressure-triggered land mine comes from Germany in the early 18th century. The *fladdermine* ("flying mine") was a ceramic container containing gunpowder and metal fragments that triggered on touch. But land mines did not become a common weapon of war until the mid-20th century. By World War II, mines were the method of choice to stop assault tanks. Needing a way for its own tanks to avoid mines, the British War Office commissioned development of a detector in the early 1940s. Metal-detection devices existed previously, but none were specifically adapted for mines.

Bernard Montgomery, the British general, used the new detectors to clear mines before the battle of El Alamein in North Africa, allowing his tanks and troops to move through the sandy landscape much more quickly and safely. U.S. soldiers deployed to the Persian Gulf in the 1990s were still using detectors of the same basic design.

Today, sensitive detectors locate two types of mines. Antitank or antivehicle mines are set along roadways; the weight of a person is usually not enough to trigger them. In contrast, antipersonnel mines are triggered by movement of people and designed to maim or kill. Ground-penetrating radar can detect mines that are not encased in metal. Mine-sniffing dogs are often deployed along with detection equipment. Once located, mines can be defused or safely detonated. Future detectors may employ thermal imagery, ultrasound, and robots.

UNCOMMONLY KNOWN ...

BODY ARMOR Soldiers of the past protected themselves with everything from animal hides to suits of metal armor. As weapons evolved, armor did too. In recent years police and military have favored Kevlar vests. But in combat, the vests don't fare well against rifle fire. The latest vests incorporate plates called SAPIs (small arms protective inserts). SAPIs have a super-hard boron carbide outer layer backed by a tactical fabric that's stronger than Kevlar.

Rescue Vehicles

For most of us, a rescue vehicle is an ambulance with lights and siren blazing, or maybe a medical helicopter airlifting badly injured patients to hospital trauma centers. This section also describes the history of sea rescue vehicles and four-legged first responders to frozen backcountry areas where airplanes and motor vehicles can't go. You'll read about the first fire engines, which were water pumps that firemen pushed or dragged to fires on foot. You'll also learn that the first police cars raced to the scene of a crime at 16 miles per hour.

Snowmobile

IN 2014 157,106 SNOWMOBILES WERE SOLD WORLDWIDE. MORE THAN 100,000 OF THEM WERE PURCHASED IN THE UNITED STATES AND CANADA.

The 1920s saw the first snowmobile, essentially a sled on skis with an airplane motor mounted to propel it across the snow. A Wisconsin man, Carl J. Eliason, received a patent for a prototype "snow machine" in 1927. It looked a lot like later versions, propelled by an endless track, but it was larger: Early engines were extremely heavy, and their weight needed to be distributed.

By the 1950s motors had become smaller and lighter, paving the way for sleeker snowmobiles. The first modern snowmobile was designed in 1958 by Joseph-Armand Bombardier, who successfully marketed his machine in 1959 under the Ski-Doo brand. Canada granted Bombardier a patent for the snowmobile in 1960, and the United States followed suit in 1962.

Snowmobiles are thought of as recreational vehicles, but they are also winter workhorses used in maintaining forest areas and repairing power lines. Snowmobiles are often involved in rescues on ski slopes and wilderness areas.

WHAT'S INSIDE?

Liquid Bandage

The bandage of the future might come out of a bottle. Soldiers in the field don't always have a full kit of bandages, dressings, and adhesive tape to treat wounds. The solution: a dual syringe filled with two liquid polymers that blend as they are applied to the skin. They form a gel-like dressing that adheres to and follows the contours of the skin surface, covering and protecting a wound without sticking to it. The dressing can be sprayed on to create a thin layer of waterproof plastic over the affected area. Though the liquid bandage was invented for military use, it's equally useful for civilian emergency rescue units dealing with traumatic burns or other injuries. The bandages form a tight, sterile seal over any type of wound.

Floating Hospital

THE LARGEST HOSPITAL SHIPS WOULD FIT THREE FOOTBALL FIELDS STRETCHED END TO END FROM BOW TO STERN.

Historians believe there were ships in ancient Greece and Rome used for transporting wounded soldiers, but hospital ships didn't officially appear until the 1600s. Britain's H.M.S. *Goodwill,* commissioned in 1608, was the first hospital ship. Modern floating hospitals made their debut in the 1850s during the Crimean War. A decade later in the United States, both sides in the Civil War used them. *Red Rover,* a Confederate steamer that was captured by Union troops, became the U.S. Navy's first hospital ship in December 1862. Prior to the war, U.S. ships had no dedicated areas for the sick or injured; the cots of injured men had to be moved around if a ship went into battle.

By World War I, Britain boasted 77 hospital ships, and the United States was getting started. A 1927 issue of a popular magazine featured a story on the nation's first ship specifically designed as a hospital, the U.S.S. *Relief.* It had 500 beds, an operating room, and an x-ray room. Today the largest floating hospital ships rival aircraft carriers in size. The world's biggest, the U.S.N.S. *Comfort* and *Mercy,* in service since the 1980s, provide care to U.S. military personnel as well as rendering disaster relief. Each has 12 operating rooms and 1,000 beds. Hospital ships display a prominent red cross or red crescent and are protected by the Geneva Convention. Firing on them is a war crime.

UNCOMMONLY KNOWN ...

EARLIEST MEDICAL FACE MASKS Doctors who treated victims of bubonic plague—the Black Death—in London during the 1600s wore protection: a long coat, gloves, boots, a hat—and a mask that featured a birdlike beak. Herbs and perfumes were placed in the beak to block the foul odors and cleanse the air.

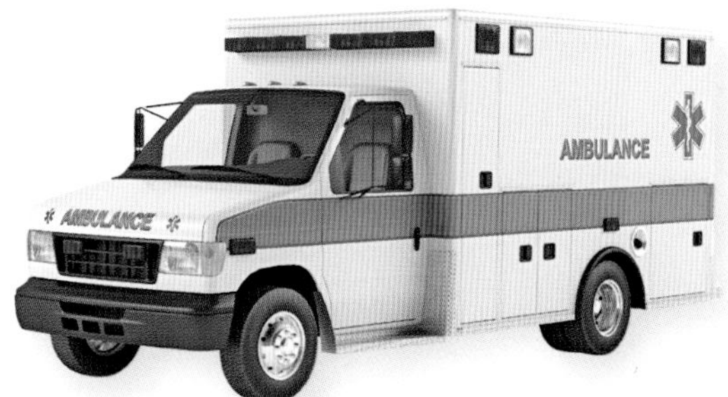

Ambulance

COMMERCIAL HOSPITAL IN CINCINNATI (NOW CINCINNATI GENERAL) INAUGURATED THE NATION'S FIRST PUBLIC AMBULANCE SERVICE IN 1865.

Chariots doubled as ambulances in ancient Greece and Rome. By the 1400s armies used various makeshift carts and stretchers to move wounded soldiers for treatment, but it was not uncommon for the wounded to remain on the battlefield until the fighting stopped. Napoleon's campaigns in the late 1700s and early 1800s employed an ambulance volante, a nimble two-wheeled horse-drawn cart that carried the injured to a hospital tent.

The Ambulance Corps Act of 1864 established

an ambulance system in the U.S. Army. By the late 1800s many military and civilian ambulance services were up and running; hospitals commonly organized their own ambulance corps. Motorized ambulances started to appear around the turn of the 20th century. The first went into service in 1899 at Michael Reese Hospital in Chicago. Horse power still predominated, but its end was in sight. During World War I, the Red Cross began widespread use of motor vehicles to remove the wounded from battlefields. When the United States entered the war in 1917, Americans brought over Ford Model T's with extended frames that became ambulances.

By the 1950s and 1960s, the importance of emergency treatment during transport was understood. Today ambulance crews provide lifesaving care before patients reach the hospital.

Lifeboat

ABOUT TWO-THIRDS OF THOSE ABOARD THE *TITANIC* DIED, IN PART BECAUSE THE SHIP DID NOT HAVE ENOUGH LIFEBOATS FOR EVERYONE.

Offshore tragedies have occurred for as long as men and women have gone to sea, but it took until the latter part of the 18th century before a concerted effort was made to design dedicated lifesaving craft. After a particularly deadly wreck off the English coast in 1789, a prize was offered for the best lifeboat design. The creativity of two British builders, Henry Greathead and William Wouldhave, was instrumental in the design of early boats.

In the United States, small coastal rescue stations began to sprout around the turn of the 19th century, but near-shore wrecks continued

PEOPLE WHO CHANGED HISTORY

Edmond Halley (1656-1742)

Most people know Edmond Halley as the astronomer who calculated that the comet now bearing his name returns every 76 years. But Halley was also the inventor of an early diving apparatus that aided wreck salvage. Air for a diving bell, which was tethered to a ship, was replenished by weighted barrels lowered from the surface. A diver could venture out from the bell wearing what Halley termed a "cap of maintenance," resembling an upside-down bowl, connected to the bell by a leather air hose. Halley himself dove 60 feet to the bottom of the River Thames.

Portrait of Edmond Halley, early 1700s

to claim many victims along unprotected sections of coastline. A more systematic approach came with the creation of the U.S. Life-Saving Service in 1878. The service was folded into the newly created U.S. Coast Guard in 1915. In recent decades the Coast Guard's main rescue vessel has been the motorized lifeboat (MLB). The 47-foot MLBs are designed to cut through heavy seas and right themselves if they capsize. Large ships carry self-contained evacuation lifeboats to be launched when the vessel is in danger of sinking. Ocean liners have long been required to provide enough lifeboat capacity for all passengers and crew.

UNCOMMONLY KNOWN ...

FIRST SOS The Marconi Company established the first international distress signal for ships at sea in 1904: CQD, which meant "all stations, distress." Its replacement by SOS came two years later at the Berlin Radiotelegraphic Conference. The first use of SOS during an emergency occurred on June 10, 1909, when the ocean liner *Slavonia* ran aground on rocks off the Azores. Two ships received the call and steamed to the rescue with no loss of life.

Police Car

IN 1921 DETROIT'S POLICE DEPARTMENT INSTALLED A RECEIVER IN A FORD MODEL T AND BECAME THE FIRST TO INTRODUCE RADIO CARS.

Police departments didn't begin to use motorized vehicles until around the turn of the 20th century. Before then, police rode horses or bicycles or walked the beat. Some departments, including Houston's and Pittsburgh's, employed motorcycles as early as 1909. But the majority of early police vehicles were essentially motorized wagons. According to some sources, the first to hit U.S. streets was in Akron, Ohio, in 1899. It was propelled by an electric motor, with a blazing top speed of about 16 miles an hour. By the 1920s and 1930s departments across the country had fleets of cars and motorcycles, allowing police to cover vastly more territory than before. The vehicles were basically civilian models fitted with extra lights, a siren, and insignia by the departments themselves. Car radios were a gradual addition; during the 1920s local broadcasts were interrupted to communicate police matters.

In the 1930s police cars became faster and more powerful to compete with bootleggers and other criminals. The standard four-cylinder motors were abandoned in favor of V8s. The Ford Flathead became the engine of choice, and Ford maintained its dominance in the police car market until the 1960s. Automobile companies after World War II began manufacturing cars with the "police package"—modifications developed to fit the needs of law enforcement. Standard equipment in most police vehicles today includes heavy-duty suspension, a two-way radio, emergency lights, electronic sirens, video cameras, and sophisticated speed-measuring devices.

Favored police car models have come and gone over the years. In the 1970s the preferred cars were General Motors' Chevrolet Caprice and Ford's LTD and 1983 debuted the Crown Victoria. In the past decade, Chrysler stepped in with its Dodge Charger. But many police cars aren't sedans: Vans, SUVs, and even quasi-military vehicles are now common in many police fleets.

Dogsled

A LIGHTLY LOADED SLED MUSHING THROUGH THE SNOW WITH A DRIVER AND FULL TEAM OF DOGS CAN TRAVEL AS FAST AS 20 MILES AN HOUR.

Dogsleds were the major mode of transportation in the Arctic for thousands of years. In North America the Inuit used dogs because the animals could withstand the cold and had great endurance on long hunting expeditions and pulling heavy loads. Breeds include the Canadian Inuit dog, Alaskan huskies and malamutes, the chinook, the Samoyed, and others. In the 19th century white settlers in the far north of Alaska and Canada adopted dogsleds for delivering mail and supplies. By 1870, the Royal Canadian Mounted Police were patrolling Canada's northern territories by dogsled.

Dog-powered sleds were often the only means of aid for communities unreachable by road or air. Rescues frequently made headlines in the first half of the 20th century. The world-famous Iditarod dogsled race commemorates an epic run from Anchorage to Nome bringing lifesaving diphtheria vaccine in 1925. The next year, rescuers on dogsleds saved hunters from starvation at a remote outpost on Hudson's Bay. In 1928 a dogsled team carrying food and supplies reached a village in northern Michigan isolated for 16 days by blizzards. During World War II hundreds of wounded soldiers were transported off northern battlefields. In Maine in 1951, a dogsled helped rescue a teenage boy seriously injured after falling a thousand feet down the slopes of Mount Katahdin.

Dogs pulling sleds are still occasionally involved in rescues in remote areas, but the proliferation of reliable snowmobiles—"iron dogs"—has greatly lessened their importance.

UNCOMMONLY KNOWN ...

ROBOTIC RESCUE DEVICE A remote-controlled "snake" currently under development could aid search-and-rescue efforts in collapsed buildings or help extinguish fires in underground tunnels. The robotic device has a steel casing, hydraulic motors for power, and hydraulic joints that let it move in snake-like fashion. The robot can squeeze into places where even rescue dogs can't go and perform tasks too dangerous to be carried out by people.

Fire Engine

TODAY'S PUMPER TRUCKS CAN CARRY HUNDREDS OF GALLONS OF WATER; TELESCOPING LADDERS ON BIG LADDER TRUCKS EXTEND 100 FEET.

A common fire engine in the 18th century was a hand-operated water pump and tank on wheels that firefighters pulled to a fire. The hose was short and water pressure was limited, so the pump had

WHAT'S INSIDE?

Water Purification Device

After natural disasters such as floods, hurricanes, and tornados, drinking water supplies can sometimes be compromised. Home water filtration devices are useful for removing pathogens and other toxic substances. Filters that protect against microorganisms contain a membrane that blocks certain bacteria and protozoa, as well as the eggs and larvae of parasites. Filters containing activated carbon are used to remove pollutants. Activated carbon is charcoal treated with oxygen to create countless tiny spaces between the carbon atoms. Organic chemicals and other pollutants in the water bond to the spaces, thus purifying the water.

to get close, which was often dangerous. When more water was needed, bucket brigades—long lines of people passing pails of water from hand to hand—supplied the pump.

By the mid-1800s firefighting was undergoing a transformation. Paid firemen were the norm in many places. Their efforts still relied on hand pumps, but the pumps were bigger and were pulled by horses. Running boards were installed on the sides of pump wagons so firefighters could ride to the fire.

As apparatus got heavier, it became harder for horses to pull quickly. In 1841 the first fire truck powered by a steam engine was rolled out. By 1910 motorized fire vehicles were becoming more common. With the increasing height of buildings in urban areas, the 1930s saw the introduction of fire trucks fitted with tall ladders. Following World War II, "cherry picker" buckets attached to long, hinged booms were put to use to get firefighters and equipment to higher stories and rescue trapped people.

Alongside basic pumper and ladder trucks, specialized fire apparatus includes big tiller trucks with steering wheels at both ends, off-road four-wheel-drive trucks, and crash tenders loaded with chemicals to fight aircraft fires.

Rescue Chopper

TRAUMA PATIENTS TAKEN TO HOSPITALS BY HELICOPTER HAVE A 16 PERCENT HIGHER RATE OF SURVIVAL THAN THOSE WHO GO BY AMBULANCE.

In World War II, helicopters were just beginning to come into their own, but there were several instances of the vertical-takeoff-and-landing craft rescuing downed pilots. The technology skyrocketed in the ensuing years, and during the Korean conflict, choppers were routinely used for reconnaissance and supply. Importantly, their search-and-rescue mission expanded, ferrying wounded soldiers to a hospital ship or MASH (mobile army surgical hospital) unit.

Larger, more powerful helicopters were built the 1960s and became important workhorses during the Vietnam War. By the 1980s search-and-rescue choppers were outfitted with night vision and thermal-imaging equipment to be able to locate victims in the dark. Since the 1990s they've also incorporated GPS technology.

Helicopters continue to play a vital role in search-and-rescue work. The U.S. military employs state-of-the-art choppers to fly behind enemy lines to rescue military personnel in overseas conflicts. And across the nation, emergency medical helicopters transport critically injured patients to trauma centers.

Necessity is the mother of invention.

—ATTRIBUTED TO PLATO (428–347 B.C.)

Tried and True

The expression "tried and true" was coined in the late 18th century, but never has it seemed more applicable than in this chapter, where it describes the collective histories of dozens of innovations that have helped change the course of our human experience. When an idea transforms how we think, how we live, and the ways in which we interact with our fellow human beings and with the world at large, then it can truly be said to be tried and true. Gathered in this chapter is an assortment of some of humanity's boldest concepts, from basic tools—early forms of which our distant forebears used to dig holes and build shelters—to contemporary farm equipment, complex tools that today help feed our crowded planet; and from exotic and intricate forms of clothing for our bodies, to intellectual pursuits for our minds through books or the lens of visual artistry.

Human progress has marked ever greater gains by implementing a vast range of inventions. When you peer inside these affectionately termed "common things," you will appreciate their uncommon history. Every item featured has its own story to tell, yet together they paint a larger portrait of us—who we are and where we come from. From time immemorial, each generation has stood on the shoulders of the one before, inspired by and adapting its styles, designs, and gadgets. For our modern advances, we've incorporated more ideas and tools in new and inventive ways. Sometimes they're breakthroughs sparked by brilliant flashes of inspiration; other times they're simple tweaks, guided by the tried-and-true adage—if it ain't broke, don't fix it. What follows, then, are testaments to the human imagination and the spirit of creativity that drives it. They are fascinating bits and pieces of our shared human narrative.

Perfect Tools

From the invention of movable type centuries before the Gutenberg Bible to the creation of scissors more than 3,500 years ago, history reminds us that people have always been resourceful. Some tools are more than simply popular: They achieve their lasting legacies by being perfect in form and function. They help us see the universe more effectively through the language of mathematics and measurement, they allow us to build our homes, and they give us outlets to express our dreams and our creativity. These tools have all truly stood the test of time.

Book

IN 1907 AN EXPLORER FOUND THOUSANDS OF BOOKS IN A CAVE IN CHINA, INCLUDING THE OLDEST EVER BEARING A DATE: MAY 11, A.D. 868.

Ancient Sumerians developed a form of writing known as cuneiform around 3000 B.C., using symbols and pictographs impressed on clay tablets. They even created the oldest known written story, the *Epic of Gilgamesh*, dated to the same period. But historians generally cite woodcuts as the first form of the modern book. Ancient scribes carved letters and other symbols into flat blocks of wood and inked them. Pressed onto paper or other material, the symbols were transferred. Historians have found examples of woodcuts dating to the fifth century A.D., but the technology of creating books as we know them begins with movable type. Germany's Johannes Gutenberg is often credited, but the father of movable type was in fact a Chinese man named Bi Sheng, who shaped individual characters from porcelain somewhere between A.D. 1041 and 1058. He carved thousands of characters to be placed on

WHAT'S INSIDE?

Halogen Lightbulb

Much like familiar incandescent lightbulbs, halogen bulbs contain a tungsten filament at their centers. But the filament is enveloped in a tough fused-quartz capsule that can withstand higher heat than the thin glass used in standard incandescent bulbs. Inside the quartz envelope is a halogen gas, usually bromine. The gas combines with released tungsten particles and is reabsorbed by the filament, creating what is known as the tungsten-halogen cycle, which maintains a steady bright light over the life of the bulb. Halogen lights last longer than standard bulbs and require less energy to operate.

two large iron boards. When they were arranged in the proper order, a "page" was created. As one board was being used for printing, the other could be prepped. Later Chinese scribes made improvements to the process, and beginning in the late 1300s, Korea developed similar methods. Famously, Gutenberg invented his wood printing press and produced the first printed Bible in 1455.

PEOPLE WHO CHANGED HISTORY

Ammar ibn Ali Al-Mawsili
(d. circa 1010)

A tenth-century eye doctor is responsible for the invention of the hypodermic syringe. Long before sophisticated ophthalmological techniques, Ammar ibn Ali Al-Mawsili developed a method for removing cataracts, a leading cause of blindness. In those days, people who went blind often died shortly after. The groundbreaking syringe was a glass tube that used suction to perform the task. Al-Mawsili was born in what is now Iraq but moved to Egypt as a young man. The technique he developed roughly 1,000 years ago still influences how cataracts are removed today.

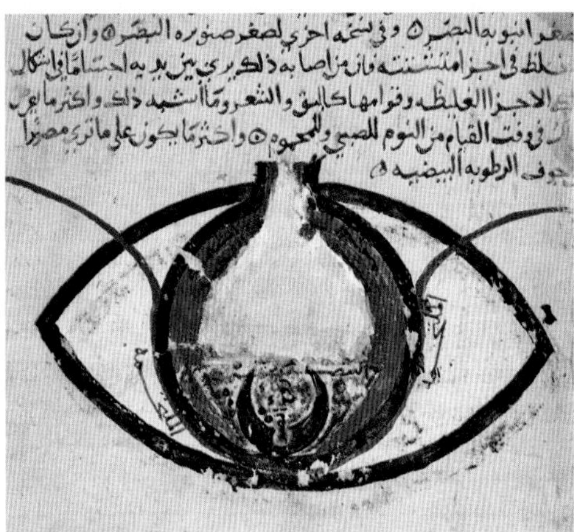

Twelfth-century Egyptian book on eye diseases

Hammer

THESE TOOLS WERE THE FIRST EVER USED BY HUMANS. THE OLDEST HAMMERS TO SURVIVE, MADE OF STONE, DATE BACK 2.6 MILLION YEARS.

The instinct to use rocks, wood, and other hard objects as hammers seems ingrained in many primates, and early humans bore that out. Stone tools dating back about two million years have been found at archaeological sites in Ethiopia. Further evidence unearthed in South Africa shows that humans first began hafting—adapting handles for weapons and tools—500,000 years ago. Around 30,000 B.C., Stone Age peoples hammered with rocks. By the Bronze Age, humans were inventing metal tools, including metal hammers. While tools used for pounding have been around nearly as long as humanity itself, nails entered the picture far later, as recently as 5,000 years ago. Bronze nails were used at that time to help construct homes and other structures. Iron hammers dating to 200 B.C. have been found in Rome, evidencing refinement of not only the haft but also the basic form of the hammer itself. Romans also developed the claw hammer (left), which is fitting since they needed an efficient method of pulling out the iron nails they invented. Hammers have continued to evolve over the centuries, with various types designed for different purposes, including ball-peen or machinist's hammers for metalworking and sledgehammers for heavy construction.

Paintbrush

AUSTRALIA'S HOUSING BOOM AFTER WWII LED TO A SHORTAGE OF PAINTBRUSH BRISTLES. THE MILITARY IMPORTED 28 TONS OF THEM FROM CHINA.

Human cultures began painting as far back as the Paleolithic era, as seen in Africa and the famous caves of Spain and France. Ancient Egyptians used reed or other plant fibers for painting. Many cultures made brushes from animal hair, such as hog bristles. In 2008 archaeologists excavating a cave in South Africa uncovered what may be the longest-surviving examples of paintbrushes. Known as Blombos Cave and lying outside Cape Town, the site contained rocks marked with ocher, one of the earliest types of clay-based pigments, and a 100,000-year-old tool kit of bones thought to have been used to mix paint.

Modern brushes are usually made using a range of animal hair, from horses and oxen to badgers and even squirrels. Canadian Norman Breakey invented the first roller paintbrush in 1940, but he was never able to produce enough to meet demand (he was working out of his basement), and he couldn't protect the patent. Credit for the invention of the device now often goes to an American, Richard Croxton Adams. Adams, a descendant of Presidents John Adams and John Quincy Adams, developed his roller in 1940 while an employee of the Sherwin-Williams Paint Company.

Scissors

THE WORLD'S LARGEST FUNCTIONAL SCISSORS, DESIGNED FOR A RIBBON-CUTTING CEREMONY IN INDIA, MEASURE NEARLY EIGHT FEET LONG.

Leonardo da Vinci is often credited—for once, incorrectly—with inventing scissors. The real inventors were the ancient Egyptians, sometime around 1500 B.C. The earliest known scissors were bronze spring cutting devices—a C-shaped handle with two blades on either end. When the ends were squeezed together, the blades cut whatever was placed

UNCOMMONLY KNOWN ...

BARBECUE GRILL Many cultures lay claim to the invention of roasting different types of meat and vegetables on sharp sticks over a heat source. However, the oldest example of sophisticated grilling cookware found so far is a Mycenaean souvlaki tray that dates back to around 1200 B.C. Archaeologists theorize that the ancient Greek civilization's chefs placed charcoal inside it and other such trays, then positioned skewers in notches on the trays' sides, creating what might be considered the world's first barbecue. Rendering the grills even more effective was their portability, indicating they might have been used to prepare food for ancient picnics.

between them. That design spread through other areas of the world, including Europe and Asia, and remained the most popular form of scissors design until the Middle Ages—despite the fact that pivot-point scissors, in which two blades with handles are joined by a rivet, were invented in Rome in the first century A.D.

It took many more centuries before scissors of either type were mass-produced. England's William Whiteley & Sons began manufacturing spring scissors in 1760. A year later another Englishman, Robert Hinchliffe of Sheffield, is credited with popularizing the pivot-point style, mass-producing hand-forged steel scissors, often with ornate handles. He proudly proclaimed himself a scissors maker by mounting a sign on his shop. In 1840 Queen Victoria awarded Thomas Wilkinson & Son the prestigious title of "Manufacturers of Scissors in Ordinary," and their products were installed at Windsor Castle for the use of the queen and her husband, Prince Albert, whom she married that year.

Scissors, now common household tools, have made some unusual long-distance journeys. Beginning in the 1960s, each U.S. astronaut was given a personal pair to open food packets in space.

Spatula

A CT SCAN OF A 2,600-YEAR-OLD EGYPTIAN MUMMY REVEALED A SPATULA IN HIS SKULL, LEFT BEHIND WHEN HE WAS PREPARED FOR BURIAL.

Spatulas were created far from the kitchen. Originally they were medical devices, developed around the first century A.D. (The word, in English use since the 1500s, is from the Latin *spatha,* or "broadsword.") Made out of bronze, the early tools served a dual purpose. On one side, the rounded end of the handle was perfect for stirring medicinal concoctions; the other side featured a flat-headed blade that could spread the medicine where it needed to be applied. The versatile device was quickly employed for other medical tasks, including tongue depressor. Physicians also found that spatulas could be heated and used to cauterize wounds (unfortunately for patients, anesthesia was as yet undiscovered). According to sources, spatulas were so popular in ancient medical circles that every surviving instance of medical writing from Greece and Rome contains at least one reference to them.

Over the centuries the spatula has taken on multiple identities, and the word has come to be applied to distinctly different devices. Painters began adopting spatulas to mix their paints as well as to spread them on certain surfaces. Small dental spatulas have been used for mixing bonding cements since the 19th century. Most familiar, of course, cooks employ spatulas for leveling dry ingredients, flipping foods, spreading frosting, mixing batter, and a host of other jobs. Indeed, the spatula is a timeless workhorse in kitchens around the world.

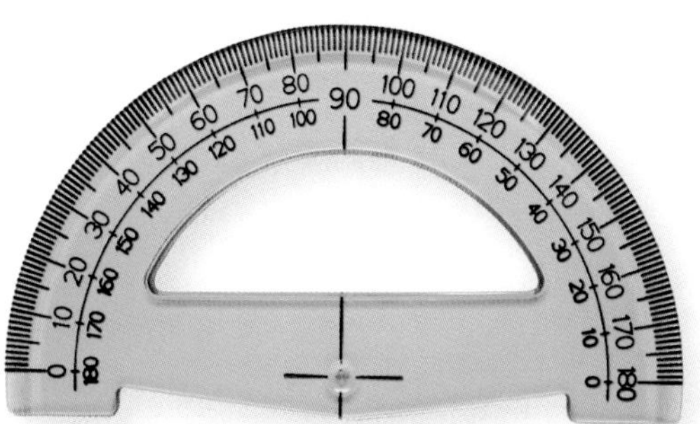

Protractor

ALTHOUGH METHODS FOR MEASURING ANGLES EXISTED PRIOR TO 1611, THE FIRST USE OF THE WORD "PROTRACTOR" OCCURRED IN THAT YEAR.

The birth of geometry (literally "land measurement") can be traced to ancient Babylon and Egypt around 3000 B.C., as well as other cultures around the globe. But what we think of as geometry today, Euclidian geometry, began around 300 B.C. when Greek mathematician Euclid began accumulating theorems and formulating his own. Euclid and his colleagues worked without the benefit of protractors. Simple forms of the device, which uses a semicircular disk to measure from 0° to 180°, were invented as early as the 13th century. But the official first citation of the tool being used as a "Mariner's Flie"—helping read a ship's course—came in writer Thomas Blundeville's 1589 book, *Briefe Description of Universal Mappes & Cardes.* Blundeville's work also catalogues how the protractor aided mapmaking, which led some historians to name him as the device's inventor. However, when evidence came to light of similar tools preceding the protractor, that notion was discredited. The name of the actual inventor remains shrouded in history. After protractors became more common in the 1600s, they were regularly used by sailors and land surveyors alike. The devices began working their way into classrooms in the United States in the 18th century, providing all the angles for generations of geometry students.

Shovel

U.S. INDUSTRIAL ENGINEER FREDERICK WINSLOW TAYLOR PERFORMED SHOVELING STUDIES ON WORKERS TO QUANTIFY THEIR "HORSEPOWER."

The history of the shovel, broad and concave, is closely linked to that of the spade, which is sharper and flatter. Both implements have been essential for farming, mining, and moving debris—not to mention digging graves—for much of human

WHAT'S INSIDE?

Plastic Injection Molding

Depending on the type of plastic, the material melts at between 200°F and 600°F. To create plastic shapes, manufacturers use durable steel or aluminum molds and inject them with molten plastic. It hardens in the cooling—or "dwelling"—phase. The process was inspired by the first injection-molding machine, patented by John and Isaiah Hyatt in 1872 to make celluloid billiard balls. Today plastic injection molding is employed in a vast range of products, including vehicle parts, furniture, electronics, medical devices, toys, and innumerable varieties of containers.

history. Although the tools' exact beginnings are hard to pinpoint, sometime between 3000 and 2000 B.C. excavation began at a flint deposit in Norfolk in present-day England. Neolithic people of the time relied on flint to make blades, axes, and spearheads. The miners used deer antlers as picks and probably wooden shovels to excavate material from the site, which was in operation for some 600 years. Many Neolithic and Bronze Age shovels unearthed around the world employ shoulder blades of oxen and other animals. The so-called Tollund man, discovered in Denmark in 1950, was the perfectly preserved mummy of a man from the fourth century B.C. He was found with a peat spade close by. Eventually people learned how to make metal tools for lifting and digging; by the first century A.D., farmers were turning over the soil with cast-iron shovels.

When America was newly settled, colonists were reliant on imported British shovels for farming and other tasks. John Ames of Bridgewater, Massachusetts, became the first American shovel maker in 1774 and in time handed down the business to his sons. From the Civil War to the Korean War, the U.S. Army chose Ames shovels for its soldiers.

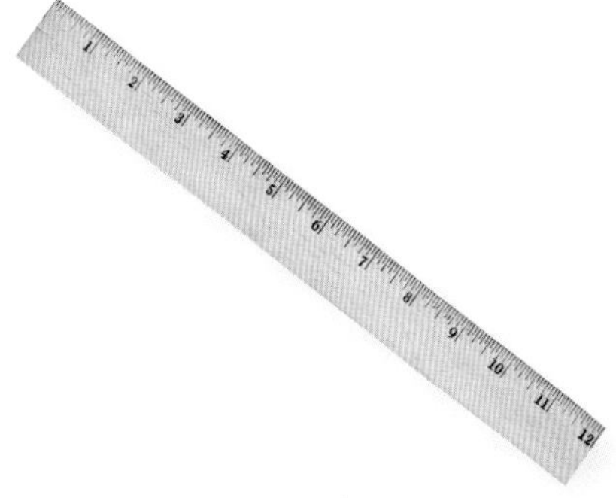

Ruler

AT THE END OF WORLD WAR I, BRITISH AND FRENCH OFFICIALS USED A RULER TO DRAW UP NEW BORDERS IN THE FORMER OTTOMAN EMPIRE.

Ancient units of measure were usually based on body parts. A cubit was the distance from a man's elbow to the tip of his middle finger, and a foot was, well, the length of his foot. Even the word "mile" is based on the human body. It's derived from the Latin *mille passus,* meaning "a thousand paces." Depending on the monarch in power, the basis for measurement varied as wildly as the measurements themselves. King Henry I is said to have decreed that a yard was the distance from the tip of his nose to his outstretched thumb. In the 13th century, King Edward I had the "Iron Ulna" forged as the official yardstick of the British Empire. He decreed it would be "three feet and no more; and the foot must contain twelve inches."

In 1791 the French Academy of Sciences set a new standard for measurement. They settled on the meter—one ten-millionth of the distance from the equator to the North Pole, assuming the line ran directly through Paris. By 1799 the meter was the compulsory standard of measurement in France. In 1983 the measure of a meter was redefined as the distance that light travels in 1/299,792,458 of a second.

Design Classics

When form and function meld seamlessly, the results are magical—like the jovial helpfulness of the jolly Ampelmänn, or the take-out containers that transform into plates. Other designs change how we interact with our food and beverages. The ubiquitous milk carton and juice box are staples for children and adults. Then there are designs that contribute to our safety, such as police whistles; those that help us read and understand the events of the day more clearly with a type font that's easy on the eyes; and those that keep food fresher longer, like classic Tupperware.

Jolly Ampelmänn

A DESIGN FROM THE COLD WAR ERA, AMPELMÄNN LEADS THE WAY FOR PEDESTRIANS ACROSS BUSY INTERSECTIONS OF A UNITED GERMANY.

Psychologist Karl Peglau was worried about public safety. Between 1955 and 1960, East Germany had seen 10,000 pedestrian deaths, many of them children, as a result of traffic accidents. When crossing streets, walkers were forced to rely on the same traffic lights that drivers followed, snarling traffic and endangering lives.

Peglau wanted something that would help every citizen, whether young, old, or even color-blind, cross the street safely. His solution, proposed to the East German traffic commission in 1961, was to use lighted figures, to be known as Ampelmännchen ("little traffic light men"), at intersections.

The green—or "walk"—version showed the jaunty character's profile mid-stride; the red—"don't walk"—version was a straight-on shot of the man with his arms outstretched. Peglau wanted the figure to be large, so that those with poor vision could easily spot him. The designer also gave him a hat, though he worried that it might be rejected for being too "bourgeois." That wasn't the case—but the traffic board did force Peglau to change the walking design so the figure faced left, not right.

The first Ampelmänn was installed in 1969, when he hit his stride at a major crosswalk in East Berlin. The safety lights quickly caught on and appeared on more corners as well as in a children's television program, *The Sandman;* animated traffic-safety videos; coloring books; toys; and apparel. In 1994 a now united Germany at first considered doing away with the figure, but concerned citizens launched a "Rescue the Ampelmännchen!" campaign and managed to preserve this cultural icon of a once divided nation.

Times(New)Roman

IN 1932 THE *TIMES* OF LONDON DECLARED THAT THIS FONT WOULD MAKE THE PAPER "THE MOST COMFORTABLY READABLE JOURNAL IN THE WORLD."

British typographer Stanley Morison issued a challenge to one of London's leading newspapers, the *Times,* in 1929. He wanted it to change its clunky old type to a more readable version. The newspaper issued him a challenge in response: Design it, and we'll use it. So Morison went to work. His aim was readability but also economy of space, so that more words could fit on each line. He based his effort in part on guidelines issued by the British Medical Research Council in its 1926 *Report on the Legibility of Print.* He even submitted his new font for ophthalmologic review. For its part, the *Times* assembled a team to test the font under both natural and artificial light. It passed. Three years after Morison's challenge, his font was ready to appear in the newspaper—and one of the most successful typefaces in history was born. Two companies manufactured typesetting machines for the font: Monotype Corporation named its version Times New Roman, and the Linotype Company called its Times Roman. Decades later, Microsoft would license Monotype's fonts, and Apple would do the same for Linotype's. Thus the slight distinction in the naming of the classic font survived into the digital era.

PEOPLE WHO CHANGED HISTORY

Buckminster Fuller (1895–1983)

R. Buckminster Fuller, born in Massachusetts in 1895, was an indefatigable visionary. He designed the three-wheeled Dymaxion vehicle and thought up dozens of other inventions. The strong, lightweight geodesic dome he designed for the U.S. Pavilion at the 1967 Montreal Expo stands as an environmental museum and tourist attraction. According to Fuller, his life was one long experiment to see how he could benefit humanity. Famed for his geodesic breakthrough, much of his impact came from thinking outside the dome.

Buckminster Fuller at New City Hall, Toronto, 1978

Metropolitan Police Whistle

THE ORIGINAL POLICE WHISTLE COULD BE HEARD A MILE AWAY, SO A LONDON BOBBY KNEW THAT HELP WOULD BE ARRIVING.

In 1883 England's Scotland Yard was looking to replace the police rattle that patrolmen used to sound an alarm in an emergency. Because his hands might be otherwise occupied, the rattle was inefficient at best. Birmingham toolmaker Joseph Hudson answered the call with a better idea: a nickel-plated brass pipe whose sharp sound could travel over a great distance. Hudson reportedly based his whistle's sound on the screech he heard when he dropped his violin. After a successful test in Clapham Common, Hudson was awarded a contract for 7,000 whistles. Thereafter, he devoted much of his business to whistle making, and not just police whistles. In 1884 he created the Acme Thunderer, which had a small piece of wood or cork inside to produce a trilling noise. Referees around the world still use variations of that whistle.

Eames Lounge Chair

CHARLES AND RAY EAMES DESIGNED THEIR HOME IN CALIFORNIA. MADE FROM INDUSTRIAL MATERIALS, IT IS AN ICON OF MODERN ARCHITECTURE.

The husband-and-wife team of Charles and Ray Eames transformed the inside of the American home with their bold ideas, using plywood to craft chairs, sofas, and dining sets. The furniture's hallmark was that its shape conformed to the contours of the human body better than any that had come before. The Eameses' contributions weren't limited to the home: They also made seating for stadiums, schools, and airports.

The couple met in art school in Michigan in 1940 before moving to Los Angeles to design furniture. In 1946 they formed a partnership with Herman Miller's Plyformed Wood Company to manufacture and sell their work. Chairs they produced in 1946 crafted from two pieces of molded plywood, one for the seat and one for the back, were hailed for their innovation. But it would take another decade before the Eames lounge chair and ottoman truly rocked the design world. The lounger was partly inspired by famed Hollywood director Billy Wilder, a close friend of the Eameses'. Wilder took naps in his office in the afternoon, and he wanted something comfortable. But, Wilder cautioned, it should not look like a casting couch. "It's too obvious a symbol of lechery," he noted. The chair and ottoman, made from molded rosewood plywood and upholstered in soft leather, were upscale pieces at the time. The chair cost $404 and the ottoman $174. Likely fewer than 500 sets were sold the first year, but eventually they became so popular that they've never stopped being produced. An original lounge set is on permanent display at the Museum of Modern Art in New York City.

UNCOMMONLY KNOWN ...

PEACE SYMBOL British designer Gerald Holtom's inspiration in 1958 was a self-portrait. He depicted himself with his palms out and hands down, a sign of resignation. That evolved into using the semaphore alphabet, the arrow shape representing N and the vertical line D—standing for nuclear disarmament. The design was later adopted as a general emblem of peace.

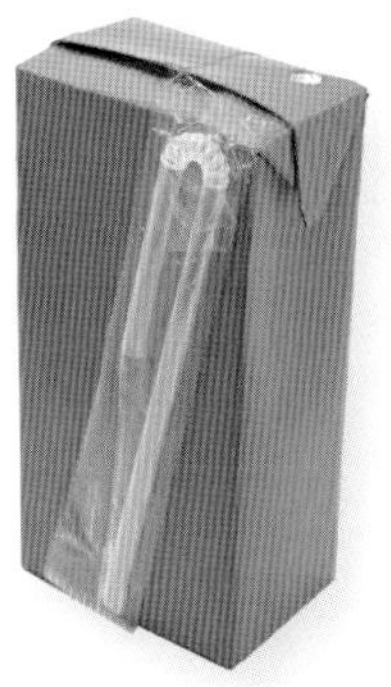

Juice Box

OCEAN SPRAY INTRODUCED THESE BOXES TO U.S. CONSUMERS IN 1982. PRIOR TO THAT, THEY'D BEEN USED FOR DAIRY PRODUCTS OVERSEAS.

Juice boxes combine three separate components to protect their contents. The paper provides the basic shape and structure, polyethylene plastic keeps the liquid from saturating the paper, and aluminum protects the contents from the effects of sunlight, heat, and other factors. Swedish entrepreneur Ruben Rausing founded the Tetra Pak company based on an idea by engineer Erik Wallenberg for a tetrahedron-shaped container. Beginning in the 1950s, the company packaged cream and milk in the plastic-lined cartons. The packaging was popular in Sweden and later expanded to Germany and then around the globe. Tetra Pak is now the world's largest food packager.

The Tetra Brik, the rectangular shape that would became synonymous with juice boxes, was introduced in 1963. It was followed by myriad variations, including wedge-shaped, rounded, and pouch-shaped versions. The technology works because the cartons and the contents are sterilized before the liquid is inserted. Because no bacteria are present, the contents cannot spoil for at least six months, and the product can therefore be stored at room temperature. The containers themselves last far longer than the drinks—for better or worse. With their plastic interiors, containers take hundreds of years to break down.

Chinese Food Containers

THE DESIGN OF TAKE-OUT FOOD CONTAINERS AT CHINESE RESTAURANTS WAS INFLUENCED BY 19TH-CENTURY WOODEN OYSTER PAILS.

Much like fortune cookies, the well-known containers associated with Chinese food are an American invention—and you aren't likely to see many of them in China. Chicago inventor Frederick Weeks Wilcox patented his paper container in 1894. The production of the boxes coincided with the burgeoning availability of Chinese food in this country in the early 1900s. For Chinese immigrants, frequently discriminated against, good-paying jobs were scarce at the turn of the century, so they often opened restaurants. The boxes they used for takeout were manufactured by Bloomer Brothers, which were putting Wilcox's invention to good use. Bloomer Brothers has since been renamed the Fold-Pak Corporation and today is the largest manufacturer of Chinese take-out cartons in the world. Since the boxes were not only inexpensive but also trapped heat remarkably efficiently, they were well suited for the task. They were popular with consumers too, who found them convenient to use. In the 1970s a designer for Fold-Pak placed a red pagoda (red is associated with good luck in China) and the words "Thank you" on each box. In the United States, the containers have become virtually synonymous with Chinese food.

Milk Carton

EARLY WAXED PAPER CARTONS COST ABOUT A PENNY TO MAKE, COMPARED WITH FIVE CENTS FOR A BOTTLE, BUT CONSUMERS WERE WARY OF THEM AT FIRST.

Before the invention of refrigerators, milk was delivered to homes almost daily in glass bottles, and before that, it was purchased directly from farmers and carried home in pails. With the spread of affordable refrigeration in the early 20th century, milk could be stored longer, but bottles were heavy, breakable, and relatively expensive. The race was on to create a milk carton. In Philadelphia James Kimsey patented a model in 1904 that was coated with protective wax. By 1906 San Francisco inventor G. W. Maxwell had created his own version and a machine to produce it. But his cartons needed to be fully assembled and glued before they were shipped out, which meant they took up a lot of precious storage space on dairy farms before being filled with milk. In 1915 Toledo, Ohio, toymaker and inventor John Van Wormer patented a new idea, the Pure-Pak, also known as the gable top, which could be assembled and glued right at the dairy. A century later, the design is still being used—for milk, juice, and many other products.

Tupperware

EARL TUPPER PATENTED HIS AIRTIGHT SEAL IN 1949. PROPERLY CLOSED, THE LID CREATES A VACUUM FOR THE FAMOUS "TUPPERWARE BURP."

Tupperware changed far more than just how leftovers were stored: It gave American women a chance to earn income when it was difficult for them to get ahead in the workforce. By World War II, American chemist Earl Tupper had been dabbling in plastics for years. After the war, when many manufacturers had leftover inventory, Tupper bought up surplus raw materials and tried to give them new life. One of his finds was polyethylene, which Tupper figured out how to turn into lightweight plastic containers.

He didn't manage to move much of his product until a saleswoman named Brownie Wise began hosting Tupperware home parties. Wise until then had been selling cleaning supplies, but she recognized the potential of Tupperware and is said to have sold $150,000 worth in 1949 alone. Wise became an executive, convincing Tupper to forgo marketing to department stores and focus exclusively on direct sales. The rest, of course, is history. Tupperware's profits shot into the millions, and in 1954 Wise became the first woman to appear on the cover of *Business Week.* The company has changed hands over the decades, but Tupperware parties continue around the world—and leftovers stay fresh.

PEOPLE WHO CHANGED HISTORY

Michael Thonet (1796-1871)

Making a name for himself building cabinets and furniture in the utilitarian Biedermeier style, German-born Michael Thonet pioneered a wood-bending technique that preserves the wood's strength. It caught the attention of Austrian prince Richard Klemens von Metternich in 1842, who invited Thonet to move to Vienna. There, Thonet helped restore the Palais Liechtenstein and developed a method for bending laminated veneer. Along with his sons, he built up a business that produced chairs, tables, and couches that won wide acclaim. In 1859 Thonet unveiled his signature work: the No. 14 Chair, an innovative piece of affordable furniture that appealed to both rich and poor with its comfort and simple elegance. Thonet's techniques inspired a booming bentwood industry in furniture making. Today the No. 14 Chair is still being produced; it has reportedly seated more people than any other chair in history.

Michael Thonet's bentwood chair design

Anglepoise Lamp

THE FIRST NAME FOR THE ANGLEPOISE SPRING—"EQUIPOISE"—WAS REJECTED BECAUSE A PRODUCT WITH THE SAME NAME WAS ALREADY PATENTED.

The anglepoise lamp was a joint venture in more ways than one. Its key design feature, the anglepoise spring, was created in 1931 by English automotive engineer George Carwardine. He wanted to mimic the constant tension that limbs of the human body possess even when they move. Sensing that the screw could be used to hold a light source in place at multiple angles, Carwardine tinkered with several designs. The first lamp, manufactured by Herbert Terry & Sons, appeared at the British Industries Fair in 1934. It had four springs and was intended solely for industrial use. Carwardine feared so many springs posed a risk at home—for example, hair could get entangled. To help build a household version, Carwardine enlisted the aid of Terry's designers. The partnership worked to great advantage because they figured out how to modify the lamp with just three springs. The result was safer for home use and provided the classic design now associated with the anglepoise. The lamp debuted in 1935 and has been a domestic—and dorm room—favorite ever since.

Dream Machines

To the ends of the Earth—and even to the moon—the machines featured in this section have made history. Whether they're recording some of the most remarkable images ever captured on film or helping farmers plant crops to feed the planet, these inventions have been working overtime. Today they set the standard for excellence, elegance, and functionality, making a large world seem a little smaller and more maneuverable. Dream machines allow us to travel to remote destinations and turn home cooks into top chefs. And they do it all with remarkable style.

Hasselblad

A DOZEN HASSELBLAD CAMERAS RESIDE ON THE LUNAR SURFACE, PURPOSELY LEFT THERE BY ASTRONAUTS TO MAKE ROOM FOR MOON ROCKS.

One of the most historic pictures made in human history, capturing Buzz Aldrin and the American flag on the moon, was taken by Neil Armstrong using a Hasselblad camera. The Hasselblad family has a long history as a trading company in Sweden, beginning with the formation of F. W. Hasselblad & Co. as an import-export firm in 1841. The company established a photographic division in 1885 and formed a business partnership with Eastman Kodak in 1908. It was Victor Hasselblad, great-grandson of the company's founder, who revolutionized the camera. During World War II the Swedish government asked him to analyze a high-tech German camera and build a better one. He did exactly that. After the war he turned his attention to creating a camera for civilians; the Hasselblad 1600F debuted in 1948 followed by the even more successful 1000F. That model earned Hasselblad cameras a reputation for quality and durability, but it was the 500C model, the first of the company's V System introduced in 1957, that truly put Hasselblad on the map—and into space. Astronaut Wally Schirra picked up a 500C at a Houston camera shop and liked it so much that he wanted to bring it with him on his Mercury Sigma 7 mission in 1962. After being modified to better suit NASA's needs, Hasselblad cameras were taken on flights from the early 1960s through the 1970s. The cameras were aboard all the lunar missions, including the six that landed on the moon's surface. The exposed film was always brought back to Earth, but many of the cameras themselves were left behind to reduce weight on the spacecraft.

Pencil Sharpener

IN 1795 ONE OF NAPOLEON'S SOLDIERS PATENTED AN IDEA FOR A PENCIL THAT COMBINED GRAPHITE AND CLAY AND IS STILL IN USE TODAY.

Prior to 1828 the only way to sharpen a pencil was to hone its point with a knife. That was the year a Frenchman named Bernard Lassimone invented the pencil sharpener. It held two metal files arranged in a 90-degree angle; together, they ground the pencil to create a usable point. Though a step in the right direction, the process was still laborious and proved less popular than simply using a knife. In 1847 another French inventor, Therry des Estwaux, improved the design substantially, creating what is now known as the prism pencil sharpener. In des Estwaux's version, the pencil was placed in a cone-shaped compartment so two files could grind the tip. Across the Atlantic, Walter K. Foster refined the prism sharpener and patented his own model in 1851. More improvements followed over the years, coinciding with increased pencil sales and production.

The most essential component of what we now consider a truly useful pencil sharpener didn't come until 1896 in Chicago, when the A. B. Dick office supply company introduced its Planetary Pencil Pointer. That was the innovation that pencil users were waiting for, because it held the pencil tightly. Previous designs required a user either to hold the pencil in place or hold the sharpener firmly. No longer. The planetary sharpener attached to a surface; a crank turned two mills that rotated around the pencil's tip. A year later American John Lee Love patented his small, portable Love Sharpener, which held pencil shavings inside its cylindrical compartment; today, it's still making the point.

WHAT'S INSIDE?

Computer Keyboard

Under every character on your keyboard is a broken circuit. Pressing the key completes the circuit, delivering current to a small processor containing a memory "map" that correlates to the keys being pushed. That's how it tells the difference between A and shift + A. The keyboard also holds three plastic contact layers for the circuits and a power cable connected to the mainframe.

John Deere Tractor

THE COMPANY COLORS ARE GREEN AND YELLOW, BUT THAT WASN'T ALWAYS TRUE. THEY LIKELY BECAME LINKED WITH THE BRAND IN THE EARLY 1900S.

Although the company name has long been synonymous with tractors, John Deere didn't invent the farm machine. Gasoline-powered tractors evolved from steam-powered versions in the 1890s, but Deere didn't get into the business until the end of World War I, nearly 80 years after the company was founded. The business had focused on plows, cultivators, planters, and other farming equipment. But in 1918, with the growing tractor market becoming essential to agriculture, the John Deere Company acquired Waterloo Gasoline Engine Company, maker of the Waterloo Boy tractor. Despite the fact that other manufacturers were far ahead of Waterloo Boy in sales and influence (Ford Motor Company sold 34,000 tractors in 1918 compared to Waterloo's 5,600), the investment proved to be a remarkably good one. When Deere bought the company for $2.3 million, it acquired the 20 Waterloo employees along with its 5,000-square-foot facility; by 1919, the company had 1,000 employees and its plants occupied 50 acres. The two-cylinder Waterloo Boy tractor at $750 was less expensive than most of its four-cylinder competitors, but in 1923 John Deere decided to replace it with the Deere-branded Model D, which sold for a hefty $1,000 (by comparison, a Model T car cost around $300).

WHAT'S INSIDE?

Running Shoe Sole

Running shoes require a special kind of sole because they must be soft enough for comfort yet tough enough to withstand countless impacts. Soles generally have three layers: an insole (where the foot touches the shoe), outsole (the part that touches the pavement), and midsole (which lies between the other two and is most responsible for the comfort the wearer feels). The insole, made from either hard or cushiony foam, may also have a sock liner that helps absorb moisture from the foot. The most common materials for the midsole are polyurethane plastic and ethyl vinyl acetate, and they usually surround gel or liquid silicone, or sometimes just air or a type of gas—all of which provide cushioning. The outsole is frequently made of tough carbon rubber to withstand the pounding that the shoe takes during rigorous runs.

The Model D was produced for the next 30 years, longer than any other tractor in the company's history. The Model C was introduced in 1927, followed by Models A and B in 1934 and 1935. Today the company is valued at over $3 billion—a far cry from the blacksmith shop of 1837, whose owner, John Deere, dreamed of making a better plow.

Electric Coffeemaker

AROUND THE WORLD, MORE THAN 75 MILLION PEOPLE REPORTEDLY DEPEND ON COFFEE PRODUCTION FOR ALL OR MUCH OF THEIR LIVELIHOOD.

Legend has it that an Ethiopian goatherd named Kaldi stumbled across coffee around A.D. 800, when he noticed how energetically his flock reacted after eating the berries from a particular tree. Kaldi picked some himself and brought the berries to the local monastery. An abbot made a beverage by soaking them in water, and discovered a stimulating and satisfying drink that kept him alert through evening prayers.

While the discovery of coffee may have been

UNCOMMONLY KNOWN ...

WAFFLE IRONS They've been serving up breakfast (and dessert) since the 1300s, but in 1869 an American, Cornelius Swarthout of New York, developed a better waffle iron, with handles and a clasp. His innovation meant the utensil could be easily flipped, helping the waffle cook evenly. The date Swarthout received his patent, August 24, is now celebrated as National Waffle Day.

monumental, the best way to brew it has been debated for centuries. In the modern era, coffee making went electric twice: initially in the 1920s with the electric percolator (that continuously bubbled the brew through the grounds) and then with electric drip machines. The first of those, the Wigomat, was patented in Germany in 1954. The device was mildly successful, but other brewing methods remained more popular until 1972 and the introduction of Mr. Coffee.

Mr. Coffee was the brainchild of the owners of a Cleveland coffee delivery company, Samuel Glazer and Vincent Marotta, inspired by the large Bunn-O-Matic brewers found in restaurants and delivery trucks. The men hired two former Westinghouse engineers to design a coffeemaker for home use based on the big machines. One challenge they faced was to avoid overheating the coffee grounds, which can become too bitter at 200°F and higher. The final design allowed controlled heating of the water before it dripped over the grounds; the infused liquid then ran through a paper filter and into a carafe that sat on a warming element. To pitch their coffeemaker on TV, Glazer and Marotta hit a home run: Baseball legend Joe DiMaggio became the Mr. Coffee spokesman, and more than a million machines were sold in a year. Soon electric drip machines represented half of all coffeemaker sales in the United States, signaling the death of the electric percolator and helping jump-start the coffeehouse boom.

Mini Cooper

AS PART OF HIS FEE FOR DESIGNING THE VEHICLE, JOHN COOPER NEGOTIATED A DEAL TO EARN TWO BRITISH POUNDS FOR EVERY CAR SOLD.

The first Minis were a response to German engineering. The British Motor Corporation (BMC) asked engineer Alec Issigonis to create a fuel-efficient car that could compete with popular small German models. Issigonis unveiled his design in 1959. With its engine mounted sideways and front wheels pushed forward, the Mini, as it would become known, was an engineering marvel. It measured only ten feet long but could seat four adults and had ample trunk space, all for about $800. In 1961 engineer and racer John Cooper saw something he liked in the Mini and joined forces with Issigonis. After a few design modifications—including a souped-up engine and improvements to the transmission and braking—the Mini Cooper was born. In 1963 a new edition, the Mini Cooper S, took third place in the Monte Carlo Rally. For the next two years, it won the race. The car became popular with rock stars, including members of the Beatles, as well as British royalty and other celebrities. It had a starring role as the getaway car in the 1969 film *The Italian Job*. Ironically, the brand was eventually acquired by German BMW, which reintroduced the Mini Cooper in 2002.

TGV

FRANCE'S HIGH-SPEED *TRAIN À GRANDE VITESSE*, OR TGV, HAS CARRIED TWO BILLION PASSENGERS SINCE IT BEGAN SERVICE IN 1981.

Japan initiated the age of high-speed rail travel in 1964 with the launch of its Shinkansen bullet trains. France got aboard the technology in 1981 with the TGV, radiating out from Paris to a host of destinations across the country and beyond. Some of the major cities served by TGV are Bordeaux, Marseille, Cannes, Brussels, Milan, Frankfurt, Amsterdam, and London. All told, the TGV system covers nearly 1,200 miles, with trains typically traveling at speeds around 200 miles an hour. (Under ideal conditions, TGV trains have clocked over 350 miles an hour.)

The idea for the TGV was born with France's national railways commission, the SNCF, and its desire to match Japan's trains. In 1967 an exploratory project between SNCF and industry partners, translated as "Rail Possibilities on New Infrastructures," got underway. Test models for the high-speed conveyances were put through their paces beginning in 1971, with the gas-turbine-powered TGV 001 prototype rolling out in 1972. Oil shortages in the 1970s caused the development team to move away from turbo toward electric power, but the changeover didn't delay the September 27, 1981, maiden run from Paris to Lyon. In 2008 France debuted an updated service, the AGV—*automotrice à grande vitesse*. It uses less energy yet travels faster, some 225 miles an hour.

Food Processor

THIS KITCHEN WORKHORSE CAN DO MANY THINGS, BUT EXPERTS ADVISE AGAINST USING IT TO MASH POTATOES, GRIND COFFEE, AND CRUSH ICE.

Pierre Verdon was a salesman for a French catering company when he invented a better way to prep food. He intended his appliance for restaurants, so he designed it to knead, cut, slice, and chop large quantities. Carl Sontheimer, a quirky American inventor, physicist, and engineer holding more than 40 patents, saw Verdon's machine, named Le Magi-Mix, demonstrated at a French housewares show in 1971. Sontheimer reasoned that if modified for home use, it would be a hit with cooks. He signed a distribution deal with Verdon's company to create a version for sale in the United States and then spent the next year and a half designing it. He made it smaller and safer, modifying the blades, and gave it a new name: Cuisinart. Sales at first were sluggish, in part because of the steep price ($175). But after a 1975 rave from *Gourmet* magazine, as well as praise from chefs such as Julia Child and James Beard, the Cuisinart was a fait accompli.

PEOPLE WHO CHANGED HISTORY

Margaret Knight (1838–1914)

Knight was born in Maine in 1838, had scant schooling, and never traveled far from home. Yet she became one of our nation's most prolific inventors. Before electricity, mills making textiles, shoes, and other products were powered by waterwheels turned by rivers—plentiful in New England. Like many other young women, Knight became a factory girl.

Reportedly, she began inventing at the age of 12 after witnessing an accident at her textile mill. The device she created stopped machines if objects were caught in them. Her invention gained wide acceptance, but she didn't receive a patent. Years later, working at a paper-bag factory, she invented the first machine to make flat-bottomed bags—the kind we still use today. When a fellow machinist tried to patent it himself, she took him to court—and won. Knight earned dozens more patents during her lifetime, including a machine to cut leather soles, a sewing-machine reel, and a rotary engine.

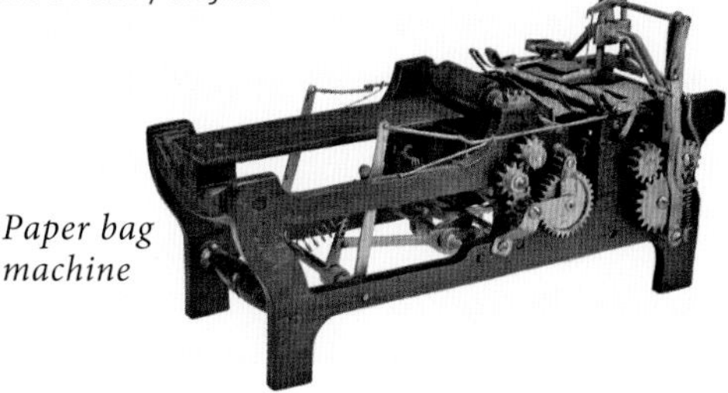

Paper bag machine

Motorcycle

THE LONGEST MOTORCYCLE IN THE WORLD, ASSEMBLED IN RUSSIA IN 2005, STRETCHES 31 FEET AND SEATS AS MANY AS 16 RIDERS.

Before motorcycles roared, they hissed. As early as 1868, Frenchman Louis Guillaume Perreaux attached a small steam engine to a regular bicycle, creating the *vélocipède,* or "fast foot." American inventor Sylvester Roper had built a steam-powered automobile during the Civil War. Shortly he too built a motorcycle by fitting a bicycle with a two-cylinder steam engine. He went on to create updated versions that could reach speeds of 40 miles an hour. The first successful two-wheel, internal combustion motorcycle was produced by Germany's Gottlieb Daimler and Wilhelm Maybach in 1885. They added a motor to an existing bicycle and invented a carburetor that used gasoline as fuel. Creating motorcycles by attaching engines to bicycles continued into the early 1900s, inspiring enthusiasts like William Harley and Arthur Davidson. In 1907 a series of motorcycle races began on the Isle of Man that tested the machines' speed, endurance, and performance. The races were pivotal in the development of the modern motorcycle, motivating manufacturers to push harder for stronger, more resilient designs.

Multipurpose Inventions

Not content to perform only a single task, the inventions in this section take on multiple jobs and solve a host of problems, whether serving as storage while holding up our feet, or keeping missiles from rusting while stopping a hinge from squeaking. Some will even help you get into your car when you've locked your keys inside, or perhaps remove unpleasant odors from your refrigerator. With these handy items, two uses are better than one—but some don't stop there. Large and small, the innovations here make many other discoveries look like underachievers.

Ottoman

ALLUDING TO THE EMPIRE OF THE SAME NAME, THE OTTOMAN RECALLS THE EUROPEAN FASCINATION WITH EASTERN WAYS IN THE 18TH CENTURY.

Ottomans have gone through many forms and functions in their centuries-long history. Originally the name referred to any of several types of squared-off upholstered furniture used for seats or as tables in Turkish homes. In the days of the Ottoman Empire, a large upholstered piece was often piled with pillows and served as the principal seating in a home. In the 1700s, when furniture design began migrating first to Europe and then to America (Thomas Jefferson referenced ottomans in a 1789 work), pieces with back cushions were sometimes aligned against three of the four walls in the main room of a house, providing seats for a family. Europeans over time changed the shape of the furniture—which was now commonly called an ottoman—from square to circular or octagonal. Ottomans frequently found their way into clubs, salons, and hotels. European designers early on gave them armrests, which later fell out of fashion. By the 19th century ottomans were beginning to transform into the footrests we mostly think of them as today, covered in a variety of fabrics but especially leather.

WHAT'S INSIDE?

CorningWare

Donald Stookey was a Corning Glass Works scientist testing the limits of photosensitive glass when he placed a piece in an oven. The heat accidently soared above 1,600°F. To Stookey's surprise, the glass didn't melt but turned milky white. When he dropped it, the glass bounced instead of shattering. Besides being durable and heat resistant, the new ceramic glass was invisible to radar, making it perfect for guided missiles. But the most enduring use of CorningWare is in kitchens, where it can safely be transferred from burner to oven to table to refrigerator or freezer.

WD-40

IT TOOK 40 ATTEMPTS FOR SAN DIEGO TECHNICIANS TO PERFECT THEIR WATER-DISPLACEMENT FORMULA–HENCE, THE APTLY NAMED "WD-40."

The Rocket Chemical Company—just three people, including founder Norm Larsen, when it got its start in 1953—is responsible for developing this multipurpose spray. It was immediately put to use by the aerospace company Convair to prevent corrosion on the Atlas missile. It worked so well that Rocket employees reasoned it would be good for home use as well, and they began sneaking cans out of the California plant. WD-40 made its way to San Diego stores in 1958 and then to stores around the country, but it wasn't an instant hit because people weren't sure what to use it for. Sales increased after Hurricane Carla struck the Gulf Coast in 1961 and WD-40 was used to treat flood-damaged vehicles. When John S. Barry took over as president of Rocket in 1969, he immediately changed its name to the WD-40 Company and began intensive marketing.

Today WD-40 is found in about 80 percent of American homes. A few of its claimed 2,000 uses include lubricating, degreasing, preventing rust, removing crayon stains, unsticking gum, protecting silver from tarnishing, keeping pigeons away, cleaning scuff marks from floors, and eliminating squeaks. The company has never patented WD-40 because that would require disclosing its secret formula.

Duct Tape

WHEN AN OXYGEN TANK IN THE APOLLO 13 SERVICE MODULE EXPLODED, DUCT TAPE HELPED SAVE THE LIVES OF THE THREE ASTRONAUTS.

The first roll of duct tape was military green, not gray. A division of Johnson & Johnson created the tape in the early 1940s from polyethylene, mesh fabric, and a rubber adhesive. It was water resistant, but it didn't make a splash until Vesta Stoudt, a mother of two sons serving in the Navy, started working at an Illinois munitions plant. She was responsible for packaging rifle grenade cartridges and ensuring they were sealed to keep them dry for shipping to soldiers overseas. The tape Stoudt's plant used was hard for soldiers to tear open—they needed a knife or sharp object—so Stoudt wanted to use tearable duct tape. Rebuffed by her employer, she wrote a letter to President Roosevelt: "We can't let [the troops] down by giving them a box of cartridges that takes a minute or two to open, enabling the enemy to take lives that might be saved had the box been taped with strong tape that can be opened in a split second." Stoudt received a reply from the Office of the Chief of Ordnance, stating, "It is cooperation of this type that will win the war." Her suggestion was implemented a few weeks later.

PEOPLE WHO CHANGED HISTORY

Ole Kirk Christiansen (1891–1958)

Danish carpenter Ole Kirk Christiansen, the youngest of ten children, was born in 1891. By 1932, with the Depression in full swing in Denmark, he was a widowed father of four and the owner of a small woodworking shop that made ladders, stools—and toys. His small painted birch-wood bricks were his most popular offerings and inspired Christiansen to focus on making more. He renamed the company LEGO, after the Danish words *leg* and *godt*, literally "play well." LEGO blocks with their patented interlocking tubes were introduced in 1958, the same year Christiansen died. The LEGO company is still run by the Christiansen family.

The original LEGO workshop in Denmark, 1932.

Boxed Baking Soda

ANCIENT EGYPTIANS USED A SUBSTANCE CALLED NATRON, WHICH IS PARTLY MADE OF BAKING SODA, IN THEIR MUMMIFICATION PROCESSES.

Baking soda has been used for so long by so many cultures that its history is somewhat shrouded. Ancient civilizations knew to use it along with yeast in baking for leavening (which we know to react with heat and acid to produce gas). In the 19th century baking soda became popular with American and European bakers as a primary ingredient for quick breads—cookies, cakes, and other baked goods that do not require yeast to rise.

New England brothers-in-law John Dwight and Dr. Austin Church formed John Dwight & Co. and began selling boxed sodium bicarbonate, labeled simply "soda," in 1846. Church was the principal developer of the product, and Dwight was the marketer. In 1867 Church's sons inherited the baking-soda company, renamed Church & Co., and unveiled their logo—the arm of the Roman fire god Vulcan holding a hammer. The companies merged in 1896 and eventually became Arm & Hammer. Along with its original use, baking soda aids in sunburn relief, teeth whitening, jewelry polishing, fire extinguishing, odor absorption, and dozens more.

WHAT'S INSIDE?

Sofa Stuffing

Modern sofas are commonly stuffed with synthetic upholstery foam, batting, feathers, or a mixture of all of those. The batting keeps the foam, which is usually made from polyurethane, from slipping and may be made from cotton, wool, polyester, or a blend. Many furniture buyers want the comfort of down feathers, but since down loses its shape easily and needs frequent refluffing, most manufacturers use it to surround a foam core. Hair from horses' tails and manes was often used in place of feathers in antique furniture.

Listerine

A 1925 ADVERTISEMENT FOR THE MOUTHWASH IS CREDITED WITH POPULARIZING THE PHRASE "ALWAYS A BRIDESMAID, NEVER A BRIDE."

Joseph Lister, a British physician practicing in Glasgow, didn't invent Listerine, but he did lend it his name. Inspired by Louis Pasteur's research into germs, in the 1860s Lister began implementing antiseptic procedures such as hand washing before performing surgery, and he soaked dressings in carbolic acid before applying them to wounds. His work inspired an American chemist, Joseph Lawrence of Missouri, to develop a surgical antiseptic. Lawrence named the liquid he invented in 1879 "Listerine" as a tribute to Lister. Then he began selling it to other doctors, marketing it for many uses including treating colds, eliminating dandruff, and even preventing sweaty feet.

Listerine was moderately successful from the start, but its usefulness as a mouthwash went undiscovered for years. In 1881 Lawrence sold the rights to the product to a St. Louis pharmacist, Jordan Wheat Lambert. An 1895 study showing Listerine was effective at killing germs in the mouth gave the product a new and defining purpose: fighting bad breath. The word "halitosis" soon entered the vernacular, a sign of the product's influence on the culture at large. In 1914 Listerine became the first prescription medication to be sold over the counter in the United States.

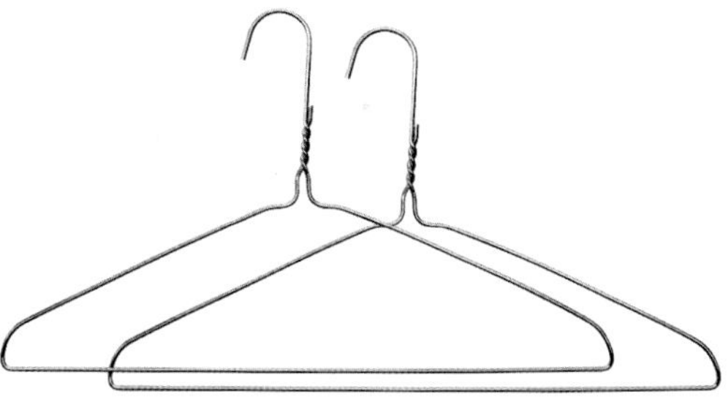

Wire Coat Hanger

RUMOR HAS IT THAT WOODEN COAT HANGERS WERE INVENTED BY THOMAS JEFFERSON, BUT WIRE VERSIONS HAD TO WAIT ANOTHER CENTURY.

It's only fitting that wire coat hangers were invented in a wire factory. Albert J. Parkhouse, an employee at the Timberlake Wire and Novelty Company in Jackson, Michigan, is responsible for the wire coat hangers now found in closets around the world. On a cold day in 1903, several employees complained to Parkhouse that there weren't enough places to hang their coats. Improvising a quick solution, Parkhouse took a piece of wire and bent it into a hanger shape then fashioned a hook from another.

The simple idea solved the problem and caught the eye of Parkhouse's employer, who filed for a patent in 1904. Parkhouse's design has stood the test of time, but people all over the world had ideas too: Between the years 1900 and 1906, nearly 200 patents were granted on various versions of clothes hangers.

Parkhouse's hanger was revolutionary in its simplicity, though even simpler solutions were in place. Basic clothes hooks had been around since 1869, patented by a Connecticut man named O. A. North. Meyer May, a clothier in Grand Rapids, Michigan, became the first to display his wares on wooden hangers in 1906.

It took a while for the newfangled hangers to catch on. In 1932 Schuyler C. Hulett invented a way to prevent hangers from causing wrinkles by adding cardboard tubes. Elmer D. Rogers made his own contribution: He put cardboard around the bottom of the hanger to allow pants to be hung without creasing. The design of the humble hanger has changed very little in the decades since.

UNCOMMONLY KNOWN ...

CORKSCREW The first spiraled bottle openers were most likely variations on screw-shaped musket-cleaning devices known as gun worms. Prior to that time, a bit of corking material used to cap wine was left above the bottle's rim to make it easier to remove. The "steel worm" developed in the 1680s changed that, but it wasn't until 1795 that the first true corkscrew came along. It was patented by a man of the cloth, Rev. Samuel Henshall of Oxford, England.

Extendable Tables

IT'S A MYTH THAT THE MODESTY OF THE VICTORIAN AGE—WHEN EXPOSED LEGS WERE CONSIDERED INDECENT—EXTENDED TO THE LEGS OF TABLES.

Throughout recorded history, families, friends, and communities have gathered around tables for meals, celebrations, and entertainments. And when there were more people than there were places to put them, the tables needed to get bigger.

The challenge historically was that many living spaces were too small to hold permanent large tables; only the wealthiest families could afford banquet dining halls. Drop leaf tables, in which a hinge or a lever allows the end section or sections of a table to be folded up or down as needed, were the initial solution to the problem.

Exactly where and when the drop leaf innovation first appeared is uncertain, but the evolution of "leaf" offers a clue. The word's original Old English use applied to plants or pages of a book (inspiring such phrases as "turn over a new leaf" and "take a leaf from someone's book"), but in the 1550s it gained an additional meaning, describing hinged items such as doors and flaps. That suggests the drop leaf design was introduced in England as early as the 16th century. Unfortunately, no examples of drop leaf tables are known to have survived the 1500s;

the earliest hard evidence dates from the following century.

By the 1800s, furniture makers were becoming more creative with extendable tables and the arrangement of the leaves. The tabletops themselves were composed of separate pieces that could be pulled open so that one or more spare leaves, stored separately, could be secured on built-in telescoping wood or metal supports. Gaming tables also gained popularity in the 19th century and adopted similar designs, allowing leaves to be inserted to extend the fun and games to more players.

Trundle Bed

IN COLONIAL TIMES THE LARGE BED THAT THE TRUNDLE TUCKED BENEATH—CALLED A JACK BED—WAS OFTEN SO TALL A LADDER WAS NEEDED TO CLIMB INTO BED.

The term "trundle bed" derives from the word for the casters on its feet. Resting on wheels or rollers, a trundle bed was easily moved under a larger master bed. The space-saving idea for the trundle bed came about in the 16th century as a convenient way for the lord and lady of the house to keep their servants nearby to protect them should danger arise in the night. In England they were originally known as truckle beds, and the phrase endures in an obscure expression "to truckle under," meaning to submit to superior power or to be servile. They were commonly constructed of local oak. Instead of cross-wise slats to hold a mattress and sleeper, ropes or straps of canvas or leather were suspended from the frame.

The original American colonists brought the beds with them across the Atlantic and called them trundle beds. In the New World, the beds also took on a new use: Cribs had not been invented, and trundle beds became sleeping quarters for children and infants. Nursing mothers found it convenient to have their newborns close by at night. Early colonial houses were small, and trundle beds saved a considerable amount of space. Since most homes did not have many rooms, the main hall or central room transformed into the bedroom at night, and the trundle bed was pulled out from under the parents' bed to make space for a child. Often several children shared a single mattress. As true of most beds of the era, trundle bed mattresses were made from straw stuffed inside wool or linen liners. Old straw was exchanged for new during the summer months, when the straw was fresh.

WHAT'S INSIDE?

Tatami Mats

These mats have been fixtures in Japanese homes for hundreds of years, dating to the eighth century. Traditionally nobility used the mats to cover wood or dirt floors and sometimes even for sleeping. *Tatami* comes from a word meaning "to fold"; when not in use, they can be easily stored. The mats have two layers: an inner core woven of rice straw or sometimes made of wood chips (or these days polystyrene foam) and an outer layer composed of durable rush grass. Tatami mats are prized for their softness as well as their feel and smell of fresh grass.

Styles That Stick

Good taste never goes out of style, and neither do these modern favorites. Some of the items featured in this section, such as watches and outerwear, are updated versions of history's originals. Others, such as plaid scarves and flowing sarongs, would look familiar to countless bygone generations. High-top sneakers and aviator shades will assuredly be classics for generations to come. The styles here speak to the diversity of our heritage yet can evoke feelings we hold in common, whether we're wearing the designs ourselves or watching them go by.

Plaid

ALAN BEAN, AN AMERICAN ASTRONAUT OF SCOTTISH DESCENT, TOOK HIS TARTAN WITH HIM TO THE MOON. RUMORS PERSIST THAT IT'S STILL THERE.

The story of the tartan is complex, dating all the way back to the ancestors of the Scottish Celts, who had settled in continental Europe by 400 B.C. Ancient tartans were discovered there in 2004, changing the views of some historians about the invention of the fabrics. Tartans—in which cloths of different colors but equal warp and weft are woven into crisscross patterns—were traditionally made from wool.

Tartan and plaid are not the same thing, though the terms are often used interchangeably outside Scotland. Historically, a plaid was a tartan worn around the waist or thrown over the shoulder. (The word "plaid" derives from the Gaelic for "blanket.") Plaids likely evolved out of tartan patterns in the early 16th century and were predecessors of the kilt. After the 1745 Jacobite Rising, British Parliament passed the Dress Act, which forbade the wearing of plaid by any Scottish male. Punishment for a first offense was six months in prison. A second conviction

UNCOMMONLY KNOWN ...

SHAKER CHAIR RAILS Furniture designed by the 18th-century religious sect was noted for its unadorned simplicity, and Shaker chairs were particularly admired. The Shakers didn't invent chair rails, which had a decorative and practical history of minimizing damage to walls from chairs being pushed against them. But it is said that they introduced evenly spaced wooden pegs to hold the chairs aloft while the room was being swept.

brought seven years on one of the king's foreign plantations. The act was finally repealed in 1782. Plaid came to the United States in the mid-19th century. It's been in and out of fashion ever since but probably never more popular than in the heyday of grunge music in the 1990s.

Sarong

SARONGS ARE DEPICTED IN 1,300-YEAR-OLD BAS-RELIEF SCULPTURES AT THE BUDDHIST BOROBUDUR TEMPLE IN MAGELANG, IN CENTRAL JAVA.

The flowing garment tied at the waist for men or just below the arms for women is closely associated with the South Pacific islands. The exact date of its creation is uncertain, but for centuries, the garb has been worn as an ideal choice in hot-weather climates. Sarongs are common across Asia, and it's believed that sarong fashion was exported from Indonesia in the course of its extensive spice trade with Asian and European countries. The garments are renowned for their colorful designs, usually applied through methods known as batik or ikat. In batik, melted wax is dripped on cloth and allowed to dry before the fabric is dyed; the wax prevents color from seeping in. Examples of batik have been discovered in Egyptian tombs dating back to the fifth century A.D. The technique was truly mastered and popularized in Java in the early 19th century, when it acquired its name based on the Javanese word meaning "to dot." Ikat (derived from the Malaysian word "to tie") is a form of tie-dying in which the thread is dyed before it's woven into fabric. Though the technique has been in use since the Dark Ages, the word ikat didn't appear in English print until 1927.

PEOPLE WHO CHANGED HISTORY

Michael Graves (1934-2015)

Michael Graves was an American architect and designer whose simple yet elegant treatments of everyday articles became staples in households around the world. His takes on the teakettle and pepper mill were two of his most recognized works. In all, he designed about 2,000 common objects–including spatulas, toasters, dustpans, and colanders–for retailers such as Target and JC Penney, among others. An inveterate innovator, Graves was a member of the New York Five, a group of architects who pledged to advance modernism in their works. After a spinal cord infection in 2003 left him paralyzed, Graves's career took a new direction: designing for the disabled. He reimagined canes, wheelchairs, and hospital layouts before his death in 2015 at age 80.

Michael Graves with his architectural models, 1970s

Chuck Taylors

IN 1936, THE FIRST YEAR BASKETBALL WAS PLAYED AT THE OLYMPICS, THE U.S. TEAM RAN THE COURT IN CHUCK TAYLORS AND WON GOLD.

Converse has been producing its All-Star shoes since 1917. They were originally intended for tennis and netball, a game similar to basketball. But a high school basketball player named Charles Hollis "Chuck" Taylor took an immediate liking to the shoes, wearing them as he played in his native Indiana and later for semiprofessional leagues in Ohio. He was so impressed that he applied for a job at the company's Chicago sales office in 1921, at the age of 20, and was hired on the spot. From the start, Taylor offered design ideas, and he spent years on the road championing the shoes. The gregarious promoter met countless basketball players and coaches, who started calling Converse to ask for "Chuck Taylor's shoe." The company realized Taylor's name itself was a powerful sales tool—so much so that they added his signature to the shoe in 1932, where it's remained ever since.

Through Taylor's efforts, the shoe became "cool" with kids around the country. He ran basketball clinics in multiple cities and even coached the company team, the Converse All-Stars. He also produced a popular basketball yearbook for Converse, adding to the shoe's cool factor. All-Stars were the official Olympic shoe from 1936 to 1968. The last major design update came in 1949, introducing the original high-top and classic black-and-white color scheme. Taylor died in 1969, just months after his enshrinement in the Basketball Hall of Fame. But his legacy lives on: At some time in their lives, roughly 60 percent of all Americans have worn Chuck Taylor All-Stars.

Salwar Kameez

IN COUNTRIES WHERE THE *SALWAR KAMEEZ* IS PREVALENT, BRIDES PREFER PINK, GOLD, ORANGE, OR RED VERSIONS, RATHER THAN WHITE, FOR THEIR WEDDING.

The ubiquitous Indian fashion known as the salwar kameez is thought to have been introduced to the country following the 16th-century Timurid invasion led by Prince Babur. He was the founder of the Mughal Empire, which ruled over what's now Central Asia, Iran, and Afghanistan, then moved into India.

Under the Mughals, regional cultures began to merge in various aspects, including clothing. The salwar kameez became popular across Central Asia as it was designed to minimize the impact of extreme heat and sandstorms. It combines two articles: the salwar, or pajama-style pants, and the kameez, a tunic or long, flowing shirt. Worn together, the loose-fitting outfit protects the wearer's modesty while providing good freedom of movement.

Although the garment can be worn by either gender, it has traditionally been more popular with women, who over the centuries have modified its styles, collar designs, hemlines, and more. Fabrics used to create the versatile clothing range from traditional cotton to synthetics to heavily embellished silks and chiffons, with accessories to match.

Widespread popularity of the salwar kameez diminished somewhat under British rule, during which it was favored mostly by Muslim women. After Indian independence in 1947, the growing film industry began creating celebrity actresses, who brought the style back into vogue. In the decades since, the salwar kameez has become synonymous with Indian fashion and remains popular across the region.

UNCOMMONLY KNOWN ...

CLUE BOARD GAME Clue originated with a factory worker in England named Anthony Pratt. During World War II, Pratt worked as a fire warden and realized that impromptu gatherings in bomb shelters resulting from air-raid warnings were affecting how people socialized. Pratt's original idea for a mystery game he called Murder! featured ten suspects rather than six and nine weapons instead of six, including a syringe and a bomb. When Pratt sold the game to a manufacturer, Waddingtons, only the original mansion playing board stayed unchanged. Pratt received just 5,000 British pounds for what became one of the most popular board games in history.

Trench Coat

THE "MAC," A NICKNAME FOR A TRENCH COAT, LIKELY DERIVES FROM CHARLES MACINTOSH, A SCOT WHO INVENTED A WATERPROOF FABRIC IN 1823.

Long a fashion staple for men and women, the trench coat came of age in the mud and blood of trench warfare. In 1853 the British company Aquascutum patented waterproof wool that was used to produce coats for soldiers in the Crimean War. Decades later in 1895, Thomas Burberry used his patented gabardine—waterproof and breathable—to clothe British military in the Boer War. Both companies to this day take credit for creating the trench coat.

In World War I the coats were essential—every feature served a function. Epaulettes denoted soldiers' rank; double-breasted design protected from cold and moisture; belts at the waist, cuffs, and collar could be cinched for increased protection; a removable wool liner added a layer of warmth; hoods were sewn in to protect from gas attacks; shoulder holsters and D-rings held weapons and supplies; deep pockets provided extra storage. The coats were khaki colored to blend in with the earthen trenches. After the war, they were quickly adopted by the general public and became available in many colors.

Sunglasses

A PHOTO OF GEN. DOUGLAS MACARTHUR WEARING AVIATOR SUNGLASSES WHEN HE LANDED IN THE PHILIPPINES CLINCHED THEIR POPULARITY.

In their first 400 years of existence, dark glasses didn't do much to protect wearers' eyes from the sun, nor did they really help anyone's vision. Made from smoky quartz and introduced in China around 1300, they were intended to shield the facial expressions of judges in court. Because they did reduce glare somewhat, they also found their way to the street.

It wasn't until English optician James Ayscough began experimenting with tinted lenses in the mid-1700s that dedicated sunglasses took shape. Ayscough thought the glare of traditional clear lenses impeded vision, so he started making green- and blue-hued versions. In the United States in 1929, an entrepreneur named Sam Foster sold his sunglasses, called Foster Grants, on the Atlantic City boardwalk. Around the same time, Hollywood stars began hiding behind sunglasses in the glare of Tinseltown, and the eyewear's popularity soared.

When Edwin H. Land patented a polarized filter in 1936, sunglasses were truly ready to step into the spotlight. (His company, the Polaroid Corporation, became far more famous for its cameras.) In 1937 the U.S. military started issuing aviator-style glasses to protect pilots' eyes, and sunglasses took on a whole new level of cool.

Anorak

ARCTIC EXPLORERS, INCLUDING ROBERT E. PEARY, WHO REACHED THE NORTH POLE IN 1909, RELIED ON INUIT-STYLE ANORAKS AND BOOTS.

Far-northern cultures created anoraks out of animal fur and hide to shield themselves from the harsh Arctic elements. The word "anorak" derives from a Greenlandic dialect; anorak and parka (from Aleutian and Russian languages) are often used

UNCOMMONLY KNOWN ...

WHY BRITISH LAWYERS WEAR WIGS A holdover from the 17th century, when King Charles II made wigs a sign of distinction, judicial wigs are no longer officially required in all British courts. The gray headgear, often made from horsehair, was retained by the judiciary to convey decorum and to be an equalizer for barristers. In the 21st century, they remain in use in higher courts and for criminal cases. Wigs can range in cost anywhere from hundreds to thousands of dollars. The large, elaborately stylized wigs worn by high court justices are said to have inspired the term "bigwig." Around the world, many former colonies currently require lawyers and judges to don wigs.

interchangeably, but the anorak is typically shorter while parkas are knee length. Both styles sport full hoods. Dates for development of the outerwear are hard to pin down, but versions have no doubt existed for at least 1,000 years.

To create the garments, Inuit collected animal pelts of varying warmth and weight to accommodate seasonal needs. In summer, when animals were better fed, their fur was thicker and would make heavy-duty anoraks for winter wear. In spring, animals were leaner from the challenges they had faced in winter, which for the Inuit meant the hides would create thinner garments for use in warmer months.

Caribou and seal were the preferred skins, but other animals, including birds and whales, were also used. For a hunting culture, an added benefit of wearing animal hide and fur was that they provided natural camouflage when stalking game. Inuit women created a version of an anorak called an *amauti,* featuring a pouch on the back for carrying a baby and for that reason traditionally had the fur facing inward for the child's added protection.

During World War II the U.S. Army began providing hooded parkas for cold-weather duty. Today they're a coat staple around the world.

Swatch Watch

THE SWATCH GROUP HAS BEEN THE OFFICIAL TIMEKEEPER OF SEVERAL OLYMPICS SINCE 1932 AND INTRODUCED GPS TO THE GAMES THAT YEAR.

For centuries watches were costly, minutely crafted jewelry. The 1970s brought change: Asian manufacturers were producing less expensive quartz watches and taking a bite out of the traditional Swiss market. The two largest Swiss watchmakers faced bankruptcy. A Swiss consortium asked entrepreneur Nicolas G. Hayek to formulate a plan to save the industry. His solution was the Swatch—the "second watch." The concept of owning more than one watch was radical at the time. Hayek's big idea was to make watches out of colored plastic with far fewer working parts and sell them for $35 or less.

When the Swatch debuted in 1983, it was an instant hit. Watches in a rainbow of colors could now be paired with clothing, shoes, or purses, and were sometimes worn two or three at a time. In the first year in the United States alone, 3.5 million Swatches were sold. Hayek advised high-end Swiss watchmakers to label their products "Swiss-made," creating greater perceived value. His strategic one-two punch rescued the Swiss watchmaking industry.

Further Reading

Bergan, Ronald. *The Film Book: A Complete Guide to the World of Cinema*. DK, 2011.

The Big Idea: How Breakthroughs of the Past Shape the Future. National Geographic, 2011.

Carlisle, Rodney. *Scientific American Inventions and Discoveries: All the Milestones in Ingenuity from the Discovery of Fire to the Invention of the Microwave Oven.* Wiley, 2004.

Ceruzzi, Paul. *Computing: A Concise History.* MIT Press, 2012.

Gray, Theodore. *The Elements: A Visual Exploration of Every Atom in the Universe.* Black Dog & Leventhal, 2012.

Isaacson, Walter. *The Innovators: How a Group of Hackers, Geniuses, and Geeks Created the Digital Revolution.* Simon & Schuster, 2014.

Levy, Joel. *Really Useful: The Origins of Everyday Things.* Firefly, 2002.

Macaulay, David. *The New Way Things Work.* Houghton Mifflin, 1998.

National Geographic Answer Book: 10,001 Fast Facts About Our World. National Geographic, 2015.

National Geographic Concise History of Science and Invention: An Illustrated Time Line. National Geographic, 2009.

National Geographic Illustrated Guide to Nature: From Your Back Door to the Great Outdoors. National Geographic, 2013.

National Geographic Science of Everything: How Things Work in Our World. National Geographic, 2013.

The New York Times Guide to Essential Knowledge: A Desk Reference for the Curious Mind. St. Martin's Press, 2011.

Panati, Charles. *Panati's Extraordinary Origins of Everyday Things.* Harper & Row, 1987.

Petroski, Henry. *The Evolution of Useful Things.* Knopf, 1993.

Schott, Ben. *Schott's Original Miscellany.* Bloomsbury, 2003.

Smith, Andrew. *The Oxford Encyclopedia of Food and Drink in America.* 3 vols. Oxford University Press, 2012.

Standage, Tom. *An Edible History of Humanity.* Walker, 2010.

Zirin, Dave. *People's History of Sports in the United States: 250 Years of Politics, Protest, People, and Play.* New Press, 2009.

Contributors

Kate J. Armstrong writes about many of the things she loves most: nature, travel, history, and adventure, to name a few. She put her passion for mountain climbing and hiking to good use in editing National Geographic's *Everest: Mountain Without Mercy* and writing National Geographic's *Greatest Parks of the World*. She also teaches classic novels and writing to high school students. Armstrong splits her time between Washington, D.C., and Brisbane, Australia. You can find her at www.katejarmstrong.com. (Chapters 1 and 6)

Patricia Daniels is a writer and editor with a particular interest in history and science. Among her other books for National Geographic are *The Body: A Complete User's Guide, The New Solar System, Great Empires,* and *The National Geographic Almanac of World History.* She is also a member of the board of editors for Macmillan's Discoveries in Modern Science. Daniels has been a managing editor for Time-Life Books and a senior writer for *National Wildlife* magazine. She lives in State College, Pennsylvania, with her husband. (Chapters 2 and 7)

Olivia Garnett is a former staff editor for National Geographic Books and has contributed as an author or editor to more than 30 National Geographic titles, including several guides to the national parks. Garnett is also trained as a landscape architect and has worked on design projects for museums, estates, and parks in the United States and Great Britain. She is originally from Gettysburg, Pennsylvania. (Chapter 4)

John Hogan is a freelance writer and editor whose previous positions include editor-in-chief of *Pages* magazine and editorial director of GraphicNovelReporter.com. He has contributed articles to various entertainment and general interest publications, including *TV Guide* magazine and *Mental Floss,* and wrote for the popular Uncle John's Bathroom Reader series. Hogan is also a travel writer and nonfiction ghostwriter. He resides in New York City and is at work on a novel. (Chapters 5 and 9)

Henry Petroski is a professor of engineering and of history at Duke University. He has written a number of books on the history of everyday objects, among them *The Pencil, The Evolution of Useful Things, The Book on the Bookshelf, The Toothpick,* and *The House With Sixteen Handmade Doors.* He is working on a book about America's infrastructure, including discussions of its often-overlooked smaller components, such as curbs, lane markings, and stop signs. His books have been translated into more than a dozen languages, and he lectures nationally and internationally on topics small and large. (Foreword)

Renee Skelton has written frequently on the history of common and uncommon things. The former editor at Sesame Workshop is author of several children's books on U.S. history and the natural environment. As a researcher and writer for a major environmental advocacy organization, she wrote on the history of the environmental movement. Her book *Forecast Earth* is a biography of former NASA scientist Inez Fung, a pioneer in research on climate change. Her writing has also appeared in *The Amicus Journal* (now *OnEarth*) and the *Washington Post*. Renee lives and writes in New Jersey. (Chapters 3 and 8)

Acknowledgments

National Geographic thanks Robert L. Booth and Bethanne Patrick for their vision and dedication to excellence. Our gratitude also goes to Dr. Henry Petroski, who graciously contributed the Foreword to this book and to the first book in the Uncommon series.

Illustrations Credits

Front cover: (Car) Blade_kostas/iStockphoto; (Popcorn) Richard Peterson/Shutterstock; (Paintbrush) Valentina Proskurina/Shutterstock; (Diamond) everything possible/Shutterstock; (Drink) combomambo/iStockphoto; (Lighthouse) shaunl/iStockphoto. Back cover: (Flower) Elena Danileiko/iStockphoto; (Nickel) Jjustas/Shutterstock; (Lamp) dencg/Shutterstock; (Purse) AddyTsl/Shutterstock; (Snail) Kletr/Shutterstock; (Skateboard) Sergiy1975/Shutterstock; (Ice Bucket) stockphoto-graf/Shutterstock; (Brooch) sachek/Shutterstock.

1, Andrey Kuzmin/Shutterstock; 4, Vladimir Badaev/Shutterstock; 6, Thomas Bethge/Shutterstock; 12, Syldavia/iStockphoto; 14, Vladislav S/Shutterstock; 15 (LE), Keng Po Leung/123RF; 15 (RT), Jiang Hongyan/Shutterstock; 16 (LE), Chris Lenfert/Shutterstock; 16 (RT), trekandshoot/Dreamstime.com; 17, Stefan Ataman/Dreamstime.com; 18, Valentyn Volkov/Shutterstock; 19 (LE), ryby/Shutterstock; 19 (RT), vitcom/iStockphoto; 20 (LE), Carrie Merrell/iStockphoto; 20 (RT), Yastremska/BigStock.com; 21 (UP), Taigi/Shutterstock; 21 (LO), Underwood & Underwood/CORBIS; 22, yasinguneysu/iStockphoto; 23 (UP), Andrew Johnson/iStockphoto; 23 (LO), Richard Cummins/Getty Images; 24 (UP), spline_x/iStockphoto; 24 (LO), serezniy/123RF; 25, kzww/Shutterstock; 26 (UP), Artem Samokhvalov/Shutterstock; 26 (LO), Creativeye99/iStockphoto; 27 (LE), Andrew Lichtenstein/Sygma/CORBIS; 27 (RT), Li Jingwang/iStockphoto; 28, Uros Petrovic/Dreamstime.com; 29 (UP), SPL/Science Source; 29 (LO), Daniel Boone escorting settlers through the Cumberland Gap, 1851-52 (oil on canvas), Bingham, George Caleb (1811-1879)/Washington University, St. Louis, USA/Bridgeman Images; 30 (UP), NoDerog/iStockphoto; 30 (LO), Tom Grundy/Shutterstock; 31, Timothy Geiss/Shutterstock; 32 (UP), Materio/iStockphoto; 32 (LO), vlabo/Shutterstock; 33, inkit/iStockphoto; 34, mehmettorlak/iStockphoto; 35 (UP), pepifoto/iStockphoto; 35 (LO), 1Photodiva/iStockphoto; 36 (UP), juniorbeep/iStockphoto; 36 (LO), National Geographic Television; 37 (UP), Difydave/iStockphoto; 37 (LO), Darlyne A. MurawskiNational Geographic Creative; 38, Piotr Malczyk/iStockphoto; 39, Moolkum/Shutterstock; 40, rimglow/iStockphoto; 41 (UP), antpkr/iStockphoto; 41 (LO), Library of Congress Prints and Photographs Division, #3b0011; 42 (UP), Dustin Dennis/Fotolia; 42 (LO), andreynik/iStockphoto; 43, Olga Kovalenko/Shutterstock; 44 (UP), Vladimir Prusakov/Shutterstock; 44 (LO), Hugo Van Lawick/NGS Archives; 45, Alison Wright/CORBIS; 46, Mark Thiessen/National Geographic Creative; 48, narvikk/iStockphoto; 49 (LE), tolisma/iStockphoto; 49 (RT), Elenathewise/iStockphoto; 50 (LE), Devonyu/iStockphoto; 50 (RT), nenetus/Shutterstock; 51 (UP), Akhilesh Sharma/Dreamstime,com; 51 (LO), Bain Collection, Library of Congress Prints and Photographs Division, #22078; 52, Dmitry Lobanov/Shutterstock; 53, Mr. Prasong/Shutterstock; 54 (UP), Dmitry Vereshchagin/Shutterstock; 54 (LO), Dr. Torsten Wittmann/Science Source; 55 (UP), RidvanArda/Shutterstock; 55 (LO), SASIMOTO/Shutterstock; 56 (UP), Matthias Kulka/CORBIS; 56 (LO), Steven Wolf/iStockphoto; 57, Malota/Shutterstock; 58, Africa Studio/Shutterstock; 59 (UP), bentaboe/iStockphoto; 59 (LO), Mark Thiessen/National Geographic Creative; 60 (UP), Val Lawless/Shutterstock; 60 (LO), Atelier_A/

Shutterstock; 61, jfmdesign/iStockphoto; 62 (LE), Karin Hildebrand Lau/Dreamstime.com; 62 (RT), mubus7/Shutterstock; 63, George Wiltshier/Shutterstock; 64, ODM/Shutterstock; 65 (UP), Sam DCruz/Shutterstock; 65 (LO), Chiyacat/Shutterstock; 66 (LE), Shawn Hempel/Shutterstock; 66 (RT), William Coupon/CORBIS; 67, after6pm/Shutterstock; 68 (UP), Taigi/Shutterstock; 68 (LO), Africa Studio/Shutterstock; 69, Yuliia Davydenko/Shutterstock; 70 (UP), Martin Hejzlar/Shutterstock; 70 (LO), Joseph Priestley, engraved by Thomas Holloway, 1795 (engraving) (b/w photo), Artaud, William (1763-1823) (after)/Private Collection/Bridgeman Images; 71 (LE), Keith Szafranski/iStockphoto; 71 (RT), Brandon Cole/Offset; 72, Ilya Akinshin/Shutterstock; 73 (UP), GlobalP/iStockphoto; 73 (LO), GlobalP/iStockphoto; 74, Frank Leung/iStockphoto; 75 (UP), Donhype/iStockphoto; 75 (LO), Thomas J. Abercrombie/National Geographic Creative; 76, Brent Hofacker/Shutterstock; 78, O. Bellini/Shutterstock; 79 (UP), T-Design/Shutterstock; 79 (LO), Estate Of Evelyn Hofer/Getty Images; 80 (UP), graja/Shutterstock; 80 (LO), Guzel Studio/Shutterstock; 81, Paul Orr/Shutterstock; 82 (LE), Karen Mower/iStockphoto; 82 (RT), AlenKadr/Shutterstock; 83 (UP), Africa Studio/Shutterstock; 83 (LO), Bettmann/CORBIS; 84, Brandon Blinkenberg/Shutterstock; 85 (UP), bhofack2/Shutterstock; 85 (LO), Joe_Potato/iStockphoto; 86 (LE), baibaz/Shutterstock; 86 (RT), robynmac/Shutterstock; 87, Andrey Starostin/Shutterstock; 88, milanfoto/Shutterstock; 89 (UP), Madlen/Shutterstock; 89 (LO), UniversalImagesGroup/Getty Images; 90 (UP), Herbert Lehmann/the food passionates/CORBIS; 90 (LO), milanfoto/iStockphoto; 91, Fanfo/Shutterstock; 92 (UP), Viktor1/Shutterstock; 92 (LO), photohomepage/iStockphoto; 93 (LE), Lafcadio Hearn (1850-1904) c.1930 (engraving) (b&w photo), Kuwahara, Robert (20th century)/Private Collection/Bridgeman Images; 93 (RT), ermingut/iStockphoto; 94, Elenathewise/iStockphoto; 95 (UP), Anawat Sudchanham/Shutterstock; 95 (LO), Kais Tolmats/iStockphoto; 96 (LE), Andrea Skjold/iStockphoto; 96 (RT), PicturePartners/iStockphoto; 97, Fanfo/Shutterstock; 98, Andrey Starostin/Shutterstock; 99 (UP), Kativ/Shutterstock; 99 (LO), eddieberman/iStockphoto; 100 (LE), deepblue-photographer/Shutterstock; 100 (RT), Handmade Pictures/Shutterstock; 101 (UP), alisafarov/Shutterstock; 101 (LO), Pasteur discovering fermentation, advertising card for the Chocolaterie d'Aiguebelle (chromolitho), French School, (20th century)/Private Collection/Archives Charmet/Bridgeman Images; 102 (UP), egal/iStockphoto; 102 (LO), The cleaning of grain, detail of frieze depicting stages of baking bread, from tomb of baker, Marcus Virgilius Eurisace, Roman Civilisation, 1st Century BC/De Agostini Picture Library/A. Dagli Orti/Bridgeman Images; 103 (UP), Marco Mayer/Shutterstock; 103 (LO), Coprid/iStockphoto; 104 (UP), Suzifoo/iStockphoto; 104 (LO), lutavia/iStockphoto; 105, Mariusz Blach/iStockphoto; 106, romakoma/Shutterstock; 108, Pete Ryan/National Geographic Creative; 109 (UP), Fotoksa/Shutterstock; 109 (LO), Michael Stuparyk/Getty Images; 110 (UP), glenda/Shutterstock; 110 (LO), Albert Nowicki/Shutterstock; 111, Wolfgang Zwanzger/Shutterstock; 112 (UP), ArTono/Shutterstock; 112 (LO), Menzl Guenter/Shutterstock; 113 (LE), AP Photo/File; 113 (RT), FloridaStock/Shutterstock; 114, Javen/Shutterstock; 115, kropic1/Shutterstock; 116 (UP), Yongyuan Dai/iStockphoto; 116 (LO), Alberto Masnovo/Shutterstock; 117 (LE), Viacheslav Lopatin/Shutterstock; 117 (RT), Mohamed Alwerdany/Shutterstock; 118, f11photo/Shutterstock; 119, JESSICA RINALDI/Reuters/CORBIS; 120, Reuters/CORBIS; 121 (LE), melowilo/Shutterstock; 121 (RT), think4photop/Shutterstock; 122 (LE), Luis Javier Sandoval Alvarado/SuperStock/CORBIS; 122 (RT), Frans Lemmens//CORBIS; 123, rjycnfynby/iStockphoto; 124, KPG Payless2/Shutterstock; 125 (LE), Courtesy Hurricane Fabric, LLC; 125 (RT), Courtesy Concrete Canvas Ltd.; 126 (LE), FooTToo/Shutterstock; 126 (RT), Ágúst G. Atlason - Gusti.is; 127, Africa Studio/Shutterstock; 128, Ratikova/iStockphoto; 129 (LE), filipw/Shutterstock; 129 (RT), fotoknips/Shutterstock; 130 (UP), allou/iStockphoto; 130 (LO), Fotosearch/Stringer/Getty Images; 131, Barna Tanko/Shutterstock; 132, art2002/iStockphoto; 133 (LE), Rudy Sulgan/CORBIS; 133 (RT), Robert Churchill/iStockphoto; 134 (LE), olaser/iStockphoto; 134 (RT), sstop/iStockphoto; 135 (UP), CRAIG LASSIG/epa/CORBIS; 135 (LO), Bernard Bisson/Sygma/CORBIS; 136, Intrepix/Shutterstock; 138 (UP), Evan Fariston/Shutterstock; 138 (LO), AP Photo/Jae C. Hong; 139 (LE), pagadesign/iStockphoto; 139 (RT), YAY Media AS/Alamy; 140, Myst is the sole property of Cyan Worlds, Inc. Copyright 2003 Cyan World, Inc. All rights reserved. Used with permission; 141 (LE), Annette Shaff/Shutterstock; 141 (RT), panchof/iStockphoto; 142, trekandshoot/ Shutterstock; 143 (UP), Lawrence Manning/CORBIS; 143 (LO), focal point/Shutterstock; 144 (LE), Zoltan Kiraly/Shutterstock; 144 (RT), pagadesign/iStockphoto; 145 (LE), Bloomberg/Getty Images; 145 (RT), Skovoroda/Shutterstock; 146 (UP), The Hole Book by Peter Newell, Harper & Brothers, 1908; 146 (LO), T.J. Kirkpatrick/Bloomberg via Getty Images; 147 (LE), Africa Studio/Shutterstock; 147 (RT), pictafolio/ iStockphoto; 148 (LE), portishead1/iStockphoto; 148 (RT), Susie Slatter/Alamy; 149, Hulton Archive/ Getty Images; 150, AlinaMD/Shutterstock; 151, Johan Lundberg/Corbis; 152 (UP), Julius Kielaitis/ Shutterstock; 152 (LO), Evening Standard/Stringer/Getty Images; 153, John Verner/iStockphoto; 154 (UP), IMAX.com; 154 (LO), Colin McConnell/Getty Images; 155 (LE), Time Life Pictures/Getty Images; 155 (RT), Louie Psihoyos/CORBIS; 156, Maksim Mazur/iStockphoto; 157 (LE), John Korduner/Icon SMI/ CORBIS; 157 (RT), Pamela Uyttendaele/Shutterstock; 158 (LE), Rick Friedman/CORBIS; 158 (RT), chictype/iStockphoto; 159 (UP), Ivica Drusany/Shutterstock; 159 (LO), Heritage Images/Getty Images; 160, Eileen Darby/Getty Images; 161 (UP), Vitalliy/iStockphoto; 161 (LO), Earl Theisen Collection/Getty Images; 162 (UP), cinoby/iStockphoto; 162 (LO), Lucy Liu/Shutterstock; 163, Peter Bischoff/Stringer/ Getty Images; 164 (LE), VP Photo Studio/Shutterstock; 164 (RT), ISSEI KATO/Reuters/CORBIS; 165, IS_ ImageSource/iStockphoto; 166, anaken2012/Shutterstock; 168, abhbah05/BigStock.com; 169 (UP), toktak_ kondesign/iStockphoto; 169 (LO), Thurston Hopkins/Picture Post/Hulton Archive/Getty Images; 170 (UP), lucentius/iStockphoto; 170 (LO), Science Photo Library; 171, s-st/Shutterstock; 172 (UP), airobody/ Shutterstock; 172 (LO), mj_23/BigStock.com; 173 (UP), Spectral-design/Dreamstime.com; 173 (LO), Galen Rowell/Corbis; 174, Bet_Noire/iStockphoto; 175 (UP), Cienpies Design/Shutterstock; 175 (LO), George Dolgikh/Shutterstock; 176, Kisan/Shutterstock; 177 (UP), dcdp/iStockphoto; 177 (LO), Jodie Coston/iStockphoto; 178, Scorpp/Shutterstock; 179 (UP), Dmitriy Titov/Shutterstock; 179 (LO), Copernicus observing in Rome an eclipse of the moon, Presno, J. (19th century)/Private Collection/© Look and Learn/Bridgeman Images; 180, Lighthaunter/iStockphoto; 181 (UP), zstockphotos/Bigstock. com; 181 (LO), Paul Popper/Popperfoto/Getty Images; 182 (UP), Capifrutta/Shutterstock; 182 (LO), beerkoff/iStockphoto; 183, hidesy/iStockphoto; 184 (UP), simpson33/iStockphoto; 184 (LO), Marcos Martinez Romero/iStockphoto; 185 (UP), 26ISO/iStockphoto; 185 (LO), CORBIS; 186, nullplus/ iStockphoto; 187 (UP), Devonyu/iStockphoto; 187 (LO), Rocketclips, Inc./Shutterstock; 188, FotografiaBasica/iStockphoto; 189, demidoff/Shutterstock; 190 (UP), Nordling/Shutterstock; 190 (LO), D3Damon/iStockphoto; 191 (UP), Ingvar Bjork/Shutterstock; 191 (LO), Roger Ressmeyer/CORBIS; 192, Raymond Kasprzak/Shutterstock; 193, Be Good/Shutterstock; 194 (UP), Value ho/Shutterstock; 194 (LO), Werner Fellner/Fotolia; 195 (UP), ladyminnie/iStockphoto; 195 (LO), Phil Bath /Sports Illustrated/Getty Images); 196 (UP), penguenstok/iStockphoto; 196 (LO), Courtesy Endless Pools; 197, Mikkaphoto/ iStockphoto; 198, Tomas Sereda/iStockphoto; 200, NoDerog/iStockphoto; 201 (UP), ma-k/iStockphoto; 201 (LO), Claudiad/iStockphoto; 202 (LE), frentusha/iStockphoto; 202 (RT), Gao Jing/Xinhua Press/ CORBIS; 203, Peter Titmuss/BigStock.com; 204, Baimieng/Shutterstock; 205 (UP), Antagain/iStockphoto; 205 (CTR), Kamira/Shutterstock; 205 (LO), Universal History Archive/Getty Images; 206 (LE), Anna Subbotina/Shutterstock; 206 (RT), Antagain/iStockphoto; 207, amwu/iStockphoto; 208, Jason Lugo/ iStockphoto; 209 (UP), irin-k/Shutterstock; 209 (LO), Michael Nicholson/CORBIS; 210 (UP), Chones/ Shutterstock; 210 (LO), gvictoria/Bigstock.com; 211, Heike Brauer/Shutterstock; 212 (UP), ALBERTO PIZZOLI/AFP/Getty Images; 212 (LO), C-You/iStockphoto; 213 (LE), PictureNet/CORBIS; 213 (RT), DeZet/Shutterstock; 214, DeAgostini/Getty Images; 215 (UP), Kenneth Garrett/National Geographic Creative; 215 (LO), DEA/G. DAGLI ORTI/De Agostini/Getty Images; 216 (RT), Araldo de Luca/Corbis; 216 (LE), Science Photo Library; 217 (UP), Erich Lessing/Art Resource, NY; 217 (LO), Courtesy National Park Service Museum Management Program and Nez Perce National Historical Park, NEPE 1955; 218, Atthawut Nitaphai/Shutterstock; 219, European Pressphoto Agency; 220 (UP), Stokkete/Shutterstock; 220

(LO), Monica Morgan/WireImage/Getty Images; 221 (LE), Two Children Looking for Santa Claus Near Fireplace, Illustration by Norman Rockwell, Life Magazine Cover, December 16, 1920, Rockwell, Norman (1894-1978)/Private Collection/J. T. Vintage/Bridgeman Images; 221 (RT), ZoneFatal/Shutterstock; 222 (UP), John Zweifel/Barcroft USA/Getty Images; 222 (LO), Roman Samokhin/Shutterstock; 223, Hurst Photo/Shutterstock; 224, Robert Dodge/iStockphoto; 225 (LE), Tamara Kulikova/BigStock.com; 225 (RT), Dan Breckwoldt/Shutterstock.com; 226 (LE), aslysun/Shutterstock; 226 (RT), Noppasin/Shutterstock; 227 (UP), Ruth Choi/Shutterstock; 227 (LO), NY Daily News via Getty Images; 228, potowizard/Shutterstock; 230, zwo5de/iStockphoto; 231 (UP), uatp1/BigStock.com; 231 (LO), AP PHoto, FIle; 232 (UP), modustollens/Bigstock.com; 232 (LO), new_lady/iStockphoto; 233, AP Photo/Rick Bowmer; 234 (LE), Hannibal Hanschke/dpa/Corbis; 234 (RT), AlexRoz/Shutterstock; 235 (UP), testing/Shutterstock; 235 (LO), Pete Spiro/Shutterstock; 236, fotokostic/iStockphoto; 237 (LE), Gary Alvis/iStockphoto; 237 (RT), Engin Sezer/Shutterstock; 238 (LE), DigtialStorm/iStockphoto; 238 (RT), Miguel Garcia Saavedra/Shutterstock; 239, MivPiv/iStockphoto; 240, Vladis Chern/iStockphoto; 241 (LE), Dadang Tri/Reuters/Corbis; 241 (RT), junak/iStockphoto; 242 (LE), scanrail/iStockphoto; 242 (RT), Arindam Banerjee/Shutterstock.com; 243 (UP), cristi180884/Shutterstock; 243 (LO), AP Photo; 244, Oliver Jenkins/Shutterstock; 245 (UP), Jovan Mandic/Shutterstock; 245 (LO), MANOCH LUADSONGKRAM/Shutterstock; 246, Siverscreen/Shutterstock; 247 (UP), aycatcher/Shutterstock; 247 (LO), CreativeHQ/Shutterstock; 248 (UP), Jagodka/Shutterstock; 248 (LO), Carl Mydans/The LIFE Picture Collection/Getty Images; 249, Oleg Zabielin/Shutterstock; 250, bikeriderlondon/Shutterstock; 251 (UP), U.S. Navy Handout/Getty Images; 251 (LO), Denys Kurylow/Shutterstock; 252 (LE), Hellen Sergeyeva/Shutterstock; 252 (RT), Portrait of Edmond Halley (1656-1742), Kneller, Sir Godfrey (1646-1723) (circle of)/Private Collection/Photo © Philip Mould Ltd, London/Bridgeman Images; 253, Travis Manley/Shutterstock; 254 (UP), Benoit Rousseau/iStockphoto; 254 (LO), Le Do/Shutterstock; 255, Mikadun/Shutterstock; 256, victoriaKh/Shutterstock; 258, studioVin/Shutterstock; 259 (LE), PhotoBalance/Shutterstock; 259 (RT), Anatomy of the Eye, from a book on eye diseases (vellum), Al-Mutadibi (fl.1170-99)/Egyptian National Library, Cairo, Egypt/Bridgeman Images; 260 (LE), Seregam/Shutterstock; 260 (RT), Yganko/Shutterstock; 261, Marek Mnich/iStockphoto; 262 (LE), Laborer/iStockphoto; 262 (RT), Lezh/iStockphoto; 263, kermitgrn/iStockphoto; 264, Delpixel/Shutterstock; 265 (LE), Frank Lennon/Toronto Star via Getty Images; 265 (RT), Iridium Photographics/iStockphoto; 266, Pablo Scapinachis/Dreamstime.com; 267 (LE), kbwills/iStockphoto; 267 (RT), Hurst Photo/Shutterstock; 268 (LE), diane39/iStockphoto; 268 (RT), absolutimages/Shutterstock; 269 (UP), dencg/Shutterstock; 269 (LO), Thonet Bentwood Chair (modern example) (wood), Thonet, Michael (1796-1871)/University of East Anglia, Norfolk, UK/UEA Collection of Abstract and Constructivist Art/Bridgeman Images; 270, muratkoc/iStockphoto; 271 (UP), Srdic Photo/iStockphoto; 271 (LO), AWSeebaran/iStockphoto; 272, J. Y. Loke/Shutterstock; 273, ProjectB/iStockphoto; 274 (UP), ollo/iStockphoto; 274 (LO), B Calkins/Shutterstock; 275 (UP), fckncg/BigStock.com; 275 (LO), Graphic Arts Collection, National Museum of American History, Smithsonian Institution; 276, Ljupco/iStockphoto; 277 (LE), RioPatuca/Shutterstock; 277 (RT), Ratth/iStockphoto; 278 (UP), Gts/Shutterstock; 278 (LO), Lego/Handout/Corbis; 279 (LE), colematt/iStockphoto; 279 (RT), Spiderstock/iStockphoto; 280, DeAgostini/Getty Images; 281, Walmart.com; 282, subjug/iStockphoto; 283 (LE), Jon Arnold/JAI/Corbis; 283 (RT), Bernard Gotfryd/Getty Images; 284 (UP), Marek Mnich/iStockphoto; 284 (LO), Vikram Raghuvanshi/Getty Images; 285, Tarzhanova/Shutterstock; 286 (UP), Waynerd/iStockphoto; 286 (LO), Stian Johansen, courtesy Bergans of Norway; 287, Valentin Flauraud/Bloomberg via Getty Images.

Index